Metric Pattern Cutting for Menswear

Fifth edition

Winifred Aldrich

**WILEY**

A John Wiley & Sons, Ltd, Publication

This edition first published 2011
© 1980, 1990, 1997, 2006 and 2011, Winifred Aldrich

Reprinted March 2013

Registered office
John Wiley & Sons Ltd, The Atrium, Southern Gate, Chichester, West Sussex, PO19 8SQ, United Kingdom

Editorial office
John Wiley & Sons Ltd, The Atrium, Southern Gate, Chichester, West Sussex, PO19 8SQ, United Kingdom

For details of our global editorial offices, for customer services and for information about how to apply for permission to reuse the copyright material in this book please see our website at www.wiley.com.

ISBN 9781405182935

A catalogue record for this book is available from the British Library.

Set in 9/10 pt Palatino by Toppan Best-set Premedia Limited
Printed in Italy by Printer Trento srl

Contents

Acknowledgements

I would like to thank Alec Aldrich, Ann Rodgers and Dawn Stubbs for their help with the earlier editions of this book; James Aldrich for his technical support; Stephen Chalkley for the provision of my CAD system.

I would also like to thank the following companies who have supplied information and photographs for the chapter on computer aided design:
assyst bullmer Ltd, UK.
Browzwear International Ltd, Israel.
Dassault Systemes, France.
Fast React Systems Ltd, UK.
Gerber Technology, UK.
GRAPHIS-software, Germany.
Human Solutions, Germany.
Lectra, France.
Visualretailing, The Netherlands.

Finally, I would like to thank Nicole Burnett and Andrew Kennerley of *John Wiley & Sons* who have been responsible for the technical production of this book.

To see other available titles please visit www.wiley.com.

Introduction

The fifth edition

Alterations and additions in this edition have been made in order to ally it to the recent changes in the new editions of my books on women's wear and children's wear. This has meant the re-organisation of the different sections of the book. The popularity of easy fitting styles and knitted fabrics has meant that basic *'flat' pattern cutting* is used by a large sector of the retail mass-market. Manufacturers of this type of clothing are quite different from those who specialise in formal clothing such as suits. This latter type of manufacture involves *'form' pattern cutting,* in which the body shape or the particular traditional style of the garment, dictates the cut.

The introduction of colour in this book has improved the expanded CAD section, and the colour coded sections have made it easier to identify specific processes in the book. After Chapter One, 'The basic principles – sizing – using the blocks', the book is divided into five parts.

Part One   covers 'flat' blocks and pattern adaptation for a wide range of garments for leisurewear, workwear and nightwear.

Part Two   covers the pattern cutting of the basic sleeves and collars. These are standard processes that are used in almost all types of pattern cutting adaptations.

Part Three   demonstrates *'form' pattern cutting,* this method requires blocks that conform more closely to the body form and often involves complex methods of cut and construction. This section includes basic blocks for classic formal garments; suits, shirts and coats. It also demonstrates the cutting of the types of leisurewear which some manufacturers like to cut to the male body shape.

Part Four   includes a chapter on simple grading techniques and also a chapter on altering patterns to fit the individual figure.

Part Five   illustrates the latest software offered by CAD suppliers for the menswear trade. The repetition of styles in this sector means that CAD is very applicable to the manufacture of men's clothing. CAD technology is now often integrated into design practices through product data management systems (PDM), which are often extended into product lifecycle management (PLM). Instant communication of procedures has become vital to companies designing in the UK but manufacturing overseas. The cost of CAD systems has reduced dramatically today, most clothing companies use some form of computer technology and the larger companies operate systems of considerable complexity.

This edition now separates quite clearly the sections useful to students beginning to be interested in menswear design, (Parts One and Two). It also offers more advanced sections aimed at students who wish to have a career working in the more formal sector of the menswear trade.

The book still remains true to its original concept, it aims to provide a simple flexible system of pattern cutting for menswear. It offers the student an opportunity to be inventive and to produce well-cut designs. The book includes many blocks (some revised) for traditional menswear shapes, for example, a variety of suit and shirt blocks, but it still concentrates on illustrating pattern adaptation. Rigid methods of pattern construction in the menswear trade often deterred many students from continuing their interest in designing for men. The book is written for students who have mastered the basic principles of pattern cutting for women; it allows them to transfer easily to exploring designs for men and to approach the subject in a creative way.

Special note – seam allowances A number of colleagues have queried this book's procedure of using blocks that include seam allowances and of retaining them during pattern adaptation. This seems to conflict with the method of working without seam allowances which is used in my two previous books written for women's wear and children's wear. There is a practical reason for this apparent lack of consistency. My books have not been written to promote some particular theoretical approach to clothing design, but to help students to become competent in the basics of pattern cutting and therefore gain the confidence to develop their own 'cut'. Many students are bewildered when they enter industry and find that they have to work with seam allowances added to the pattern. The patterns constructed in many clothing companies are derived from previous styles and it is just not practical to work with nett patterns. I believe that it is useful for students, usually in the second or third year of their course, to have a book which demonstrates the procedure of pattern cutting with seam allowances and illustrates the problems of working in this way. It is possible to use this book for pattern cutting without added seam allowances, an explanation of this process is given on page 17.

The introduction of CAD into the design rooms allows a company to work with nett patterns, but in practice this rarely happens as many companies modify previous styles. When the practice of nett pattern cutting on computers approaches a universal method, then this book will be revised accordingly.

Design and pattern cutting for menswear

The growth of fashion magazines for men has had a huge impact on male attitudes to fashion. They promote the image of the young affluent man, reflecting an aspiring lifestyle and a reference point for the current acceptable male image. *GQ*, a glossy magazine of almost three hundred pages, devotes less than one-third to features, the remainder is devoted to shopping, lifestyle and fashion. Fashion marketing for men is now accepted to the point where the weekend magazines of newspapers feature menswear in their mainstream fashion articles.

The classic garments worn by men have remained remarkably resilient through the decades. Fashion may appear to simply revolve around classic shapes but it is renewed by the differences in style, cut, colour and the combination of garments and accessories. Men are especially attracted to conventional pieces with eccentric twists. If this is discreet, it can offer fashion longevity. The majority of men steer away from complicated pieces and impracticality. More extremes of fashion that are shown by designers and displayed in the fashion journals may appear to be dismissed by High-street fashion, but ideas such as deconstruction or close fitting extremes are interpreted and infiltrate into a season's fashion style. The silhouette created is the signature of a style; subtle or extreme variations of the basic garment shapes can radically change the look of a season. A simple change of cut to the classic pea jacket, the bomber jacket or the formal overcoat can transform them into a new fashion style.

The mixing of sport and casual wear with formal wear has become accepted dressing in both the wearing of colour and in garment combinations. It has become conventional to wear polo shirts or tee shirts with a suit, or a formal jacket with jeans. This new acceptance of colour, print and new combinations of classic garments have produced a robust and acceptable fashion market for men. The past decade has seen a global perspective for men's fashion, with a growth in luxury brands and designer labels. Branded jeans are now a luxury item; customers will pay for the quality of the fabric, and most of all, the quality of the cut. The expansion of retail outlets that sell expensive garments and accessories may be halted as financial restraints impact on clothing sales.

The demise of the suit has often been predicted but appears to be irreplaceable. A well cut suit still demands respect in many areas of business. The bespoke tailor can still compete with the retailed 'designer' suit, and young radical designers are still entering the trade. A number of these who began their careers in the bespoke trade still seek to retain a high quality level with their own label or when developing a range for a manufacturer. The defined styling change to a closer fit that occurred in the late nineties has remained, together with length variations, one buttoned suits, lapel designs and explorations with new fabrics (particularly stretch components). This closer fit has expanded into shirts and knitwear. This will not necessarily remain; a new silhouette will appear and be accepted. Manufacturers have to respond with speed to these kinds of mercurial changes. British industry, which is dominated by large manufacturing groups, is not as responsive as its continental competition where small companies have the flexibility to respond. The middle and lower end of the market is highly influenced by the prediction companies.

The explosion of new fabrics has produced many problems for the mass-production market. The demands of the manufacturing process and the engineered garment have produced a rapid expansion of textile testing related to machinery use. This has also affected the cutting techniques that have to be employed when many of the new fabrics are used. New synthetics with a lack of tailorability require different cutting techniques. It is important to recognise that it is the handle of the fabric that is vital in the creation of garment shape. Mass-production and the engineered suit require quite different techniques from the bespoke suit.

High-level performance fabrics have had a significant impact in high-cost casualwear and sportswear. There has been an emergence of complex garments with breathable membranes, inner shells and complex constructions of many pieces. Sportswear, career and workwear designs have become increasingly technologically based. Designers have to consider the garment function and body actions, the study of the technological developments of fabrics and their impact on garment manufacture. Innovation can be driven by new fabric and construction techniques. The ability to handle the production of these garments in many variations of style and cloth has been largely due to the adoption of computer aided design by many manufacturing companies. CAD is now more affordable, thus lessening any technological advantages held by the larger suppliers.

The acceptance of changing shapes and proportions means that the fashion cycles and their themes are becoming as important in menswear as in women's wear. Designing for the male figure also holds attractions. It has motivated a number of top women's wear designers into bringing a fresh perspective to clothing collections for men.

Tools and equipment for constructing patterns

A student should aim to acquire a good set of equipment. However, some items are very expensive. The items marked with an asterisk denote those that are not essential immediately.

Working surface A flat working surface is required. However, a tracing wheel will mark any polished or laminated top, therefore some protection must be given to this type of surface.

Paper Strong brown or white paper is used for patterns. Parchment or thin card should be used for blocks that are used frequently.

Pencils Use hard pencils for drafting patterns (2H). Coloured pencils are useful for outlining complicated areas.

Fibre pens These are required for writing clear instructions on patterns.

Rubber

Metric ruler

Curved rules These are used for drawing long curves.

Metre stick

Set square A large set square with a 45° angle is very useful; metric grading squares can be obtained.

Metric tape measure

Tracing wheel

Shears Use separate shears for cutting cloth and paper as cutting paper will blunt the blades.

Sellotape

Pins

One-quarter and one-fifth scale squares These are useful for students to record pattern blocks and adaptations in their notebooks.

Stanley knife

Tailor's chalk This is used for marking out the final pattern onto the cloth and for marking alterations on the garment when it is being fitted.

Toile fabrics Calico is used for making toiles for designs in woven fabrics. Make sure the weight of the calico is as close to the weight of the cloth as possible. Knitted fabric must be used for making toiles for designs in jersey fabrics; the toile fabric should have the same stretch quality.

*Metric square This does not have to be the more expensive graduated tailor's square based on a chest scale. The system in this book is based on a range of standard body measurements so the graduated square is of limited use.

*Calculator The calculator is now a common tool in all areas of skill; it eliminates the hard work of calculating proportions and is accurate. If a calculator is not available, use the table of aliquot parts (page 8).

*French curves Plastic shapes and curves are available in a range of sizes; they are useful for drawing good curves. A flexicurve that allows a shape to be manipulated is also available.

*Pattern notcher This is a tool which marks balance points by snipping out a section of pattern paper.

*Pattern punch

*Pattern hooks

*Pattern weights These keep pieces of pattern in position on paper or cloth.

*Model stands Although not essential for a beginner, they are invaluable to the serious student for developing designs.

*Computer equipment A description of computer equipment is given in Chapter 14.

The equipment above can be obtained from:
Morplan, 56 Great Tichfield Street, London
  W1W 7DF. Tel: 020 7636 1887;
  Website: www.morplan.co.uk
Eastman Staples Ltd, Lockwood Road, Huddersfield
  HD1 3QW. Tel: 01484 888 888;
  Website: www.eastman.co.uk

Aliquot parts

If a calculator is not available for working out fractional parts, the following table can be used. (Figures in columns marked with an asterisk are calculated to one decimal place).

chest and seat (cm)

	*¹⁄₁₆	*¹⁄₁₂	⅛	*¹⁄₆	¼	*⅓	½
88	5.5	7.3	11	14.7	22	29.3	44
90	5.6	7.5	11.25	15	22.5	30	45
92	5.8	7.7	11.5	15.3	23	30.7	46
94	5.9	7.8	11.75	15.7	23.5	31.3	47
96	6	8	12	16	24	32	48
98	6.1	8.2	12.25	16.3	24.5	32.7	49
100	6.3	8.3	12.5	16.7	25	33.3	50
102	6.4	8.5	12.75	17	25.5	34	51
104	6.5	8.7	13	17.3	26	34.7	52
106	6.6	8.8	13.25	17.7	26.5	35.3	53
108	6.8	9	13.5	18	27	36	54
110	6.9	9.2	13.75	18.3	27.5	36.7	55
112	7	9.3	14	18.7	28	37.3	56
114	7.1	9.5	14.25	19	28.5	38	57
116	7.3	9.7	14.5	19.3	29	38.7	58
118	7.4	9.8	14.75	19.7	29.5	39.3	59
120	7.5	10	15	20	30	40	60
122	7.6	10.2	15.25	20.3	30.5	40.7	61
124	7.8	10.3	15.5	20.7	31	41.3	62
126	7.9	10.5	15.75	21	31.5	42	63

neck size (cm)

	¼	⅕
36	9	7.2
37	9.25	7.4
38	9.5	7.6
39	9.75	7.8
40	10	8
41	10.25	8.2
42	10.5	8.4
43	10.75	8.6
44	11	8.8
45	11.25	9

scye depth (cm)

	*⅕	¼	½
21.2	4.2	5.3	10.6
22	4.4	5.5	11
22.8	4.6	5.7	11.4
23.6	4.7	5.9	11.8
24.4	4.9	6.1	12.2
25.2	5	6.3	12.6
26	5.2	6.5	13
26.4	5.3	6.6	13.2
26.8	5.4	6.7	13.4
27.2	5.5	6.8	13.6

Glossary

Definitions of terms used when drafting patterns.

Back pitch/front pitch Points on body sections of the garment which match balance points on the sleeve, to ensure that the sleeve hangs correctly.

Balance Garment balance is the adjustment of the front and back lengths which, because of the stance of the figure, may become uneven.

Balance marks Marks or notches that denote positions where seams are joined together.

Bespoke tailoring The practice of cutting and making individual garments for customers.

Block See page 16.

Buttonstand The distance between the button line and the front edge of the garment.

Enclosed seams Seams that are hidden from view e.g. inside a collar, facing or cuff.

Fitting lines The lines along which a garment must be seamed when it is assembled.

Fly A flap to conceal buttons, often used with regard to the front fastening on men's trousers.

Forepart The front section of a jacket or coat.

Fork The seam line that joins the legs of the trousers, passing between the legs.

Girth A measurement around the body.

Gorge The front neck line of a garment.

Inlay See page 17.

Mass-production The practice of making a garment design in quantity by industrial methods.

Scye Armhole.

Seat angle The angle of the back fork line of trousers.

Seat wedge The wedge that is opened on back fork line of trousers to increase the seat angle.

Sidebody A side section of a jacket or coat.

Sleeve head The section of the sleeve from scye depth line to top of sleeve.

The definitions for the following terms: *Style line, Roll line, Stand, Fall, Break point, Break line* are given in the section on collars (page 86).

Chapter 1 The basic principles – sizing – using the blocks

Metric sizing and size charts

Measurement surveys

Some manufacturers undertake small-scale surveys of body measurements to gain information for their niche market. To obtain reliable measurements, costly surveys in which thousands of subjects are measured have to be carried out. The Ministry of Defence carried out this type of survey for aircrew in 1988. The government and retailers jointly funded the most recent British survey carried out by the Department of Computer Science, at UCL using computer body scanning. Companies that have borne all, or a proportion of the costs, see the information as commercially valuable and may withhold the raw data from public use. Some problems remain, but the scanners can now make reliable recordings of most of the principal body measurements required for clothing. The 3D body images also record the changing shape of the population.

British and European standards

The British Standards Institution has usually been a main guide to sizing, measurements and labelling. Their new Standards are now adopted from CEN, the European Committee for Standardization. Most European countries, including the UK, have signed to adopt the standards, the aim being to provide a coherent method of sizing and labelling. Three standards titled *The size designation of clothes* have been agreed and these are available from the British Standards Institution.

BS EN 13402-1:2001 *Terms, definitions and body measurement procedures*
BS EN 13402-2:2002 *Primary and secondary dimensions* (Used for garment labelling, example shown below)

Garment	Primary dim.	Secondary dim.
Jackets	Chest girth	Height Waist girth
Suits	Chest girth	Height Inside leg length
Overcoats	Chest girth	Height
Trousers	Waist girth	Inside leg length
Shirts	Neck girth	Height Arm length

BS EN 13402-3:2004 *Measurements and intervals*
The standard offers body measurement ranges in 4cm (chest 84-120cm) and 6cm (chest 12Q-144cm) intervals for use in size charts. The standard also shows a pictogram of a figure for use on garment labels.

A fourth standard BS EN 13402-4 designed to designate a coding system, was attempted but a draft paper could not be agreed. European coding divisions increase in 4cm and 6cm intervals whilst UK coding is still based on imperial divisions of two inches (5cm approx.).

Two new standards BS EN ISO 7250-1:2010 and BS EN ISO 7250-2:2010 *Basic human body measurements for technological design* offer measurement positions and international body size charts for ergonomic design. This information could be useful for manufacturers producing specialist workwear.

Comments on size labels (2010)

The use of standards by manufacturers is voluntary and explains the anarchic systems of sizing that are found in high-street fashion. Whilst some fashion outlets for younger men that sell European fashions have changed to metric sizing, most British manufacturers have retained imperial code sizing divisions and are showing approximate metric conversions. The different size intervals in European sized clothing can be confusing for UK customers. It often requires an interpretation from the salesman and this can vary. It is difficult to find any manufacturer using a pictogram to identify body measurement positions. Most of the major retail stores give metric conversions on inside labels, but still base their coding on the garment rails in imperial 2" size increments. This problem has probably been a factor in the growth of clothing marked SMALL, MEDIUM, LARGE and XLARGE.

Although size charts and conversion charts are lacking in the major retail stores, their sales websites appear to offer far more detailed information with body diagrams, size charts, and coding conversions.

Size charts

Manufacturers determine their size charts with reference to two main factors, the type of garment that they produce and their target market. It is also possible for manufacturers to purchase both national and international sizing information, some of which is from 3D body scanning data.

It is interesting to note that one major retailer states on their website that their size charts are derived from **centimetre body measurements** and are rounded up to the nearest inch.

Size charts of body measurements in this book

1. Standard body measurements: young men – athletic figures of regular height (4cm increments)
2. Standard body measurements: mature figures of regular height (4cm increments)
3. Standard body measurements: young men – athletic figures of regular height (5cm increments)
4. Body measurement chart for Small Medium Large Xlarge sizes: athletic figures of regular height (8cm increments)

Standard body measurements

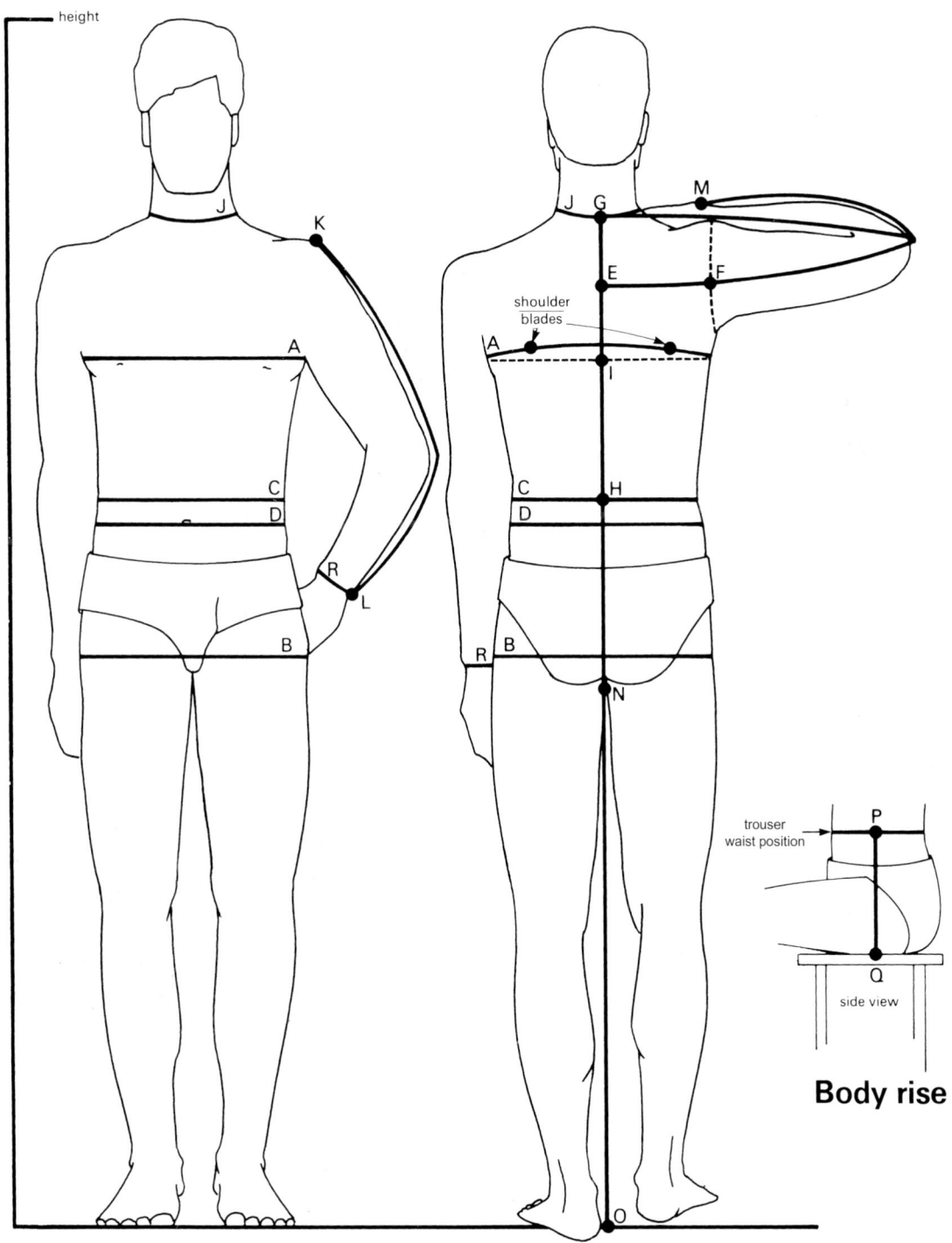

height

M

J G

E F

shoulder
blades

A I

A

C H

C

D

D

B

R B

R

N

trouser
waist position

P

Q

side view

Body rise

Standard body measurements: young men – athletic figures of regular height (4cm increments)

Height 173–180cm (5ft 8in–5ft 11in)

Size chart for overgarments and trousers

A	chest	88	92	96	100	104	108	112
B	seat	90	94	98	102	106	110	114
C	waist	74	78	82	86	90	94	98
D	trouser waist position (4–6cm below waist)	78	82	86	90	94	98	102
E–F	half back	18.5	19	19.5	20	20.5	21	21.5
G–H	back neck to waist	43	43.4	43.8	44.2	44.6	44.8	45
G–I	scye depth	22	22.8	23.6	24.4	25.2	25.6	26
J	neck size	37	38	39	40	41	42	43
K–L	sleeve length one-piece sleeve	63	63.6	64.2	64.8	65.4	65.7	66
E–M	sleeve length two-piece sleeve	79	80	81	82	83	83.8	84.6
N–O	inside leg	77	78	79	80	81	82	83
P–Q	body rise	27.2	27.5	27.8	28.1	28.4	28.7	29
R	close wrist measurement	16.6	17	17.4	17.8	18.2	18.6	19

Extra measurements (garments)

garment length	*varies with type of garment and with fashion*						
cuff size two-piece sleeve	27.4	28	28.6	29.2	29.8	30.4	30.8
trouser bottom width *(varies with fashion)*	21.4	21.8	22.2	22.6	23	23.4	23.8
jeans bottom width *(varies with style)*	21.4	21.8	22.2	22.6	23	23.4	23.8

Adjustments for short or tall figures

Size charts for tall or short men have each vertical measurement adjusted as follows

	SHORT 163–170cm (5ft 4in–5ft 7in approx.)	TALL 183–190cm (6ft–6ft 3in approx.)
back neck to waist	−2cm	+2cm
scye depth	−1cm	+1cm
sleeve length	−2.5cm	+2.5cm
garment length	−4cm	+4cm
inside leg	−4cm	+4cm
body rise	no change	+1cm

Standard body measurements: mature figures of regular height (4cm increments)

Height 173–180cm (5ft 8in–5ft 11in)

Size chart for overgarments and trousers									
A	chest	88	92	96	100	104	108	112	116	120
B	seat	92	96	100	104	108	114	118	122	126
C	waist	78	82	86	90	94	98	102	106	110
D	trouser waist position (4–6cm below waist)	82	86	90	94	98	102	106	110	114
E–F	half back	18.5	19	19.5	20	20.5	21	21.5	22	22.5
G–H	back neck to waist	43	43.4	43.8	44.2	44.6	44.8	45	45.2	45.4
G–I	scye depth	22	22.8	23.6	24.4	25.2	25.6	26	26.4	26.8
J	neck size	37	38	39	40	41	42	43	44	45
K–L	sleeve length one-piece sleeve	63	63.6	64.2	64.8	65.4	65.7	66	66.3	66.6
E–M	sleeve length two-piece sleeve	79	80	81	82	83	83.8	84.6	85.4	86.2
N–O	inside leg	77	78	79	80	81	82	82	83	83
P–Q	body rise	27.2	27.5	27.8	28.1	28.4	28.6	28.8	29	29.2
R	close wrist measurement	16.6	17	17.4	17.8	18.2	18.6	19	19.4	19.8

Extra measurements (garments)

garment length		*varies with type of garment and with fashion*								
cuff size two-piece sleeve *(varies with fashion)*		28.4	29	29.6	30.2	30.8	31.2	31.6	32	32.4
trouser bottom width *(varies with fashion)*		22.4	22.8	23.2	23.6	24	24.4	24.6	24.8	25
jeans bottom width *(varies with style)*		21.4	21.8	22.2	22.6	23	23.4	23.8	24.2	24.6

A size chart for shirts – mature and athletic figures

neck (collar size)		37	38	39	40	41	42	43	44	45
A	chest	88	92	96	100	104	108	112	116	120
G–I	scye depth	22	22.8	23.6	24.4	25.2	25.6	26	26.4	26.8
G–H	back neck to waist	43	43.4	43.8	44.2	44.6	44.8	45	45.2	45.4
E–F	half back	18.5	19	19.5	20	20.5	21	21.5	22	22.5
sleeve length for shirts		84	85	85	86	86	87	87	88	88
shirt length		78	78	80	81	81	82	82	82	82
cuff size for shirts		23	23.5	23.5	24	24	24.5	24.5	25	25

Standard body measurements: young men – athletic figures of regular height (5cm increments)

Height 173–180cm (5ft 8in–5ft 11in)

		Size chart for overgarments and trousers					
Imperial chest size approx. – inches		34	36	38	40	42	44
Imperial waist size approx. – inches		28	30	32	34	36	38
A	chest	87	92	97	102	107	112
B	seat	89	94	99	104	109	114
C	waist	73	78	83	88	93	98
D	trouser waist position (4–6cm below waist)	77	82	87	92	97	102
E–F	half back	18.4	19	19.6	20.2	20.8	21.4
G–H	back neck to waist	43	43.4	43.8	44.2	44.6	45
G–I	scye depth	22	22.8	23.6	24.4	25.2	26
J	neck size	36.8	38	39.2	40.4	41.6	42.8
K–L	sleeve length one-piece sleeve	63	63.6	64.2	64.8	65.4	66
E–M	sleeve length two-piece sleeve	78.8	80	81.2	82.4	83.6	84.8
N–O	inside leg	77	78.2	79.4	80.6	81.8	83
P–Q	body rise	27.2	27.6	28	28.4	28.8	29.2
R	close wrist measurement	16.5	17	17.5	18	18.5	19
Extra measurements (garments)							
garment length		*varies with type of garment and with fashion*					
cuff size two-piece sleeve		27.6	28.2	28.8	29.4	30	30.6
trouser bottom width *(varies with fashion)*		21	21.5	22	22.5	23	23.5
jeans bottom width *(varies with style)*		21	21.5	22	22.5	23	23.5

Adjustments for short or tall figures

Size charts for tall or short men have each vertical measurement adjusted as follows

	SHORT 163–170cm (5ft 4in–5ft 7in approx.)	TALL 183–190cm (6ft–6ft 3in approx.)
back neck to waist	−2cm	+2cm
scye depth	−1cm	+1cm
sleeve length	−2.5cm	+2.5cm
garment length	−4cm	+4cm
inside leg	−4cm	+4cm
body rise	no change	+1cm

Small Medium Large Xlarge XXLarge sizes

The actual measurements applied under the labels SMALL, MEDIUM, LARGE, XLARGE, XXLARGE depend on the breadth and the type of market that is being targeted. Retailers who see their market as the mature man will offer sizing under a particular label that is more generous in width than a retailer selling to the younger man.

Intervals working within the range of 8cm is suggested by British Standards and many British manufacturers are now using approximately this sizing interval. The following sizing examples are taken from the size charts of two large retailers.

Example 1: chest sizes (7–8cm intervals)

SML	MED	LGE	XLGE	XXLGE
up to 94	97–102	104–109	112–117	119–125

Example 2: chest sizes (7–8cm intervals)

SML	MED	LGE	XLGE	XXLGE
94–99	99–107	107–114	114–122	122–130

Body measurement chart for Small Medium Large Xlarge sizes (8cm increments)

This chart is useful for the younger (athletic) market. There is a small extra height differential between the sizes.

Chest sizes (cm) between		SMALL (88–96)	MEDIUM (96–104)	LARGE (104–112)	XLARGE (112–120)
A	chest	92	100	108	116
B	seat	94	102	110	118
C	waist	78	86	94	102
D	trouser waist position	82	90	98	106
E–F	half back	19	20	21	22
G–H	back neck to waist	43.4	44.2	45	45.8
G–I	scye depth	22.8	24.4	26	27.6
J	neck size	38	40	42	44
K-L	sleeve length one-piece sleeve	64	65	66	67
E–M	sleeve length two-piece sleeve	80	82	84	86
N-O	inside leg	78	80	82	84
P-Q	body rise	27.6	28.2	28.8	29.4
R	close wrist measurement	17	17.8	18.6	19.4
Extra measurements (garments)					
garment length		*varies with type of garment and with fashion*			
cuff size two-piece sleeve		28	29.2	30.4	31.6
trouser bottom width *(varies with fashion)*		21.8	22.6	23.4	24.2
jeans bottom width *(varies with fashion)*		21.8	22.6	23.4	24.2

Using block patterns

Block patterns

A block is a foundation pattern constructed to fit a specific figure. A block can be drafted to fit an individual figure using personal measurements. For this method see page 164.

In the clothing industry the blocks are constructed to the standard (average) measurements for specific groups of men, e.g. young men, regular sized men, tall men, etc. Size charts for these groups are based on the relationship of different measurements (e.g. chest to waist) of an average man in a particular group. The block is constructed to a set of standard measurements for a particular size. It is used as a basis for interpreting a design and producing a finished pattern. The design shape may change dramatically but the basic fit of the pattern will conform to the size of the basic block.

The blocks include the basic amount of ease required for the function of the block (e.g. a jacket has less ease than a coat).

Types of blocks

This edition of the book has been designed to separate two types of cutting that are used currently in the men's clothing industry. 'Flat' cutting is used for easy fitting garments and garments in stretch fabrics. It predominates in areas such as sportswear, nightwear, weatherwear and workwear.

Classic formal wear is based on 'form' cutting. It relies not only on fitting the body shape, the pattern shape is also a reflection of the particular garment's heritage, for example, the man's classic suit or the classic shirt.

Some casual garments are cut from 'form' blocks. They are usually more expensive because the pattern cutting, grading and manufacturing processes are more complex.

The 'flat' blocks

1. **The 'flat' trouser blocks** (page 20) Blocks for some casual wear, sportswear, weatherwear and workwear.
2. **The 'flat' shirt and overgarment blocks** (page 22) Easy fitting blocks for some casual wear, sportswear, weatherwear and workwear.
3. **The tee shirt and overgarment jersey blocks** (page 24) These blocks are very simple shapes constructed to be used for jersey fabrics only.
4. **The 'flat' kimono block** (page 26) A block adaptation for both woven and jersey fabrics.
5. **The basic jeans blocks** (page 40) A close fitting jeans block with easy fitting adaptation.
6. **The pyjama block** (page 58) The standard pyjama block.

The 'form' blocks

1. **The classic suit jacket block** (page 98) A basic suit block, to be used with rever collars and a two-piece sleeve. For more extreme designs use the casual jacket block, which is a simpler basic shape.
2. **The classic easy fitting jacket suit block** (page 100) An easy fitting version of the suit block with extended shoulder line, to be used with rever collars and a two-piece sleeve.
3. **The suit two-piece sleeve block** (page 102)
4. **The classic waistcoat block** (page 108).
5. **The classic trouser block** (page 110) A basic trouser block with parallel leg shaping.
6. **The classic shirt block** (page 120) To be used for standard easy fitting shirts. Includes its own sleeve block.
7. **The tailored shirt block** (page 122) Includes its own sleeve block and short sleeve adaptation.
8. **The casual shirt block** (page 124) A basic simple block to be used for styled casual shirts. Includes its own sleeve block.
9. **The basic jacket block** (page 130) A close fitting block to be used for casual jackets. The one-piece or two-piece sleeve can be used with the block.
10. **The easy fitting casual jacket block** (page 132) An easy fitting block with extended shoulder line, to be used for casual jackets. The one-piece or two-piece sleeve can be used with the block.
11. **The basic overgarment block** (page 134) A close fitting block to be used for overgarments and overcoats. The one-piece or two-piece sleeve can be used with the block.
12. **The easy fitting overgarment block** (page 136) An easy fitting block with extended shoulder line, to be used for easy fitting coats, anoraks and very loose jackets. The one-piece or two-piece sleeve can be used with the block.
13. **The one-piece sleeve block** (page 138)
14. **The two-piece sleeve block** (page 140)

Adapting the blocks – basic points

1. Choose the correct block, e.g. if an easy fitting shape is required select the easy fitting overgarment block or the easy fitting 'flat' block.
2. Decide the length; lengthen or shorten the block.
3. Decide if more ease is required in the armhole (ref. 8, page 70).

If this procedure is followed, any styling will be carried out on the required basic shape and therefore the proportions will be correct.

Seam allowances

The decision to include seam allowances in the blocks and to retain them during pattern construction was made so that students could gain some experience of working with added seam allowance. This is because they will encounter this method in the garment manufacturing industry.

The reasons for the decision to include seam allowances are discussed in more detail in the Special Note on page 5. It is recommended that this note be read before continuing with this section.

Working with seam allowances

A 1cm seam allowance is allowed on the blocks except where stated no seam allowance. Therefore if a seam is required at the centre back or side seam of the casual blocks or overgarment blocks, seam allowance must be added. The fitting line on the blocks is marked with a dotted line; this shows clearly which lines have seam allowance added. Where seam lines are drawn and the block is separated, seam allowances must be added.

The 1cm seam allowance allowed on the block is suitable for plain seams. Other seams usually require extra seam allowance, which must be added to the pattern. The extra width of seam allowance required will depend on the type of seam and the distance between the seam and the top stitching. Two examples are shown opposite.

For mass-production of lightweight garments, enclosed seams (e.g. collars, cuffs) may have their seam allowance reduced to 0.5cm.

Inlays

Inlays are extra material allowed on some seams in case an alteration is necessary. They are always allowed on garments cut for individual customers (bespoke tailoring). Most manufacturers allow inlays on certain seams.

Flat felled seam

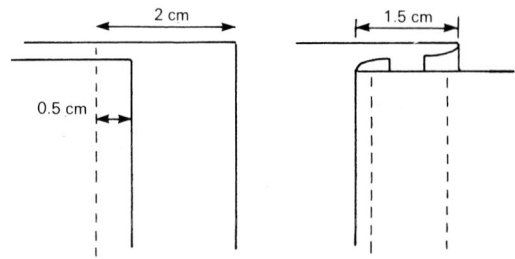

Welt seam

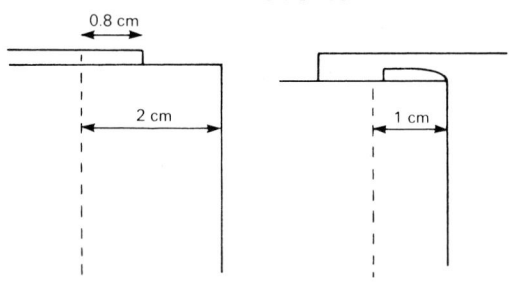

Working without seam allowances

If you wish to work without seam allowance during pattern adaptation, construct the blocks following the instructions given, then cut off the seam allowances where marked. You can then use them as nett blocks.

You will be able to follow the pattern procedures in the book, *but you must ignore any instruction that tells you to add seam allowances, and ignore any of the shaded sections of seam allowance on the diagrams.* When the pattern is completed, the appropriate seam allowances can be added where they are required.

Note. The construction of the kimono blocks (pages 26 and 66) should be based on a block that *includes* seam allowance.

Pattern instructions

The following instructions should be marked on patterns. Those marked with an asterisk are sometimes marked on an accompanying technical data sheet instead of the pattern.

1. The name of each piece.
2. Pattern size.
3. Centre back or centre front.
4. Fold lines (these are often marked by a fold symbol).
5. Balance marks (these are matching points marked by a notch).
6. Grain lines (these are usually marked by arrow lines).
7. Construction marks (these include darts, buttonholes, pocket placings, pleats. These lines are often marked by notches or punch holes).
8. * Seam allowances.
9. * The number of pieces to be cut (state if it is a single piece or a paired pattern piece.

PART ONE: 'FLAT' CUTTING
Chapter 2 The 'flat' blocks – woven and jersey fabrics

The 'flat' blocks are used for garments that are often flat packed, are easy fitting or are manufactured in jersey fabrics. Therefore cutting to a specific male shape is of less importance in these types of clothing.

Some 'flat' garment designs are divided into many sections; for example, weatherwear. In this case, it is often better to work without seam allowances (see page 17 for a description of the process).

Note: The jeans block has been placed in Chapter 3 and the pyjama block in Chapter 5.

The 'flat' trouser blocks
Useful 'flat' shapes for use in casual wear, sportswear, weatherwear and workwear

The one-piece trouser block (woven or jersey fabrics)

Measurements required to draft the blocks
(e.g. size MEDIUM) refer to the size chart (page 15)
for SMALL, MEDIUM, LARGE, XLARGE sizes.

Seat	102cm
Body rise	28.2cm
Inside leg	80cm

There is a 1cm seam allowance included in the
blocks except where stated *no seam allowance*.
The blocks are drafted to sit approximately 2–4cm
above the trouser waist position. This can be
adjusted during an adaptation. The main figures
will give a basic shape; the figures in brackets
will give an easier fitting shape.

The one-piece trouser block can be used as a simple
shape for a wide range of simple trousers, for
example, boxers and over trousers. The two-piece
block gives a better leg shape and is more suitable
for sportswear.

Front section
Square both ways from 0.
0–1   Body rise plus 2cm (plus 4cm); square across.
1–2   Inside leg measurement; square across.
1–3   ½ the measurement 1–2; square across.
1–4   ¼ seat measurement plus 4cm (8cm); square
up to 5.

5–6   1cm.
4–7   ¼ the measurement 4–5.
4–8   ¼ the measurement 1–4 minus 0.5cm
(plus 0.5cm).
Join 6–7 and 7–8 with a curve touching a point
3cm from 4 (3.25cm from 4).
2–9   ⅔ measurement 1–4 plus 2cm (plus 2.5cm).
Square up to 10 on the knee line.
10–11   = 2cm
Draw inside leg seam; join 9–11 with a straight line;
join 8–11 curving the line inwards 1cm.

Back section
6–12   3.5cm; square up 3.5cm (4.5cm) to 13.
Join 13–0.
4–14   ½ the measurement 4–5.
8–15   The measurement 4–8 plus 0.5cm (1cm).
15–16   1cm. Join 13–14 and 14–16 with a curve
touching a point 5.5cm from 4 (6cm from 4).
9–17   2cm.
11–18   3cm.
Draw inside leg seam; join 17–18 with a straight line;
join 16–18 curving the line inwards 2cm.

Creating the one-piece pattern
Trace round back section (heavy line).
Trace round front section (dotted line).
Mirror the front and place the side seams
together.

The two-piece trouser block (woven or jersey fabrics)

Front section
Square both ways from 0.
0–1   Body rise plus 2cm (plus 4cm).
1–2   Inside leg measurement; square across.
1–3   ½ the measurement 1–2; square across.
1–4   ¼ seat measurement plus 4cm (8cm); square
up to 5.
5–6   1cm.
4–7   ¼ the measurement 4–5.
4–8   ¼ the measurement 1–4 minus 0.5cm (plus
0.5cm).
Join 6–7 and 7–8 with a curve touching a point 3cm
from 4 (3.25cm from 4).
1–9   ½ measurement 1–4 plus 1cm; square down to
10 and 11.
11–12   ⅓ measurement 1–4 plus 1cm.
11–13   = 11–12.
Join 1–12; mark point 14 on the knee line.

10–15   = 10–14.
Draw inside leg seam; join 13–15 with a straight line;
join 8–15 curving the line inwards 1cm.

Back section
6–16   5cm.
16–17   4cm; 0–18 = 4cm (5cm).
Join 17–18.
4–19   ½ the measurement 4–5.
8–20   The measurement 4–8 plus 0.5cm (1cm).
20–21   1cm. Join 17–19 and 19–21 with a curve
touching a point 5.5cm from 4 (6cm from 4).
12–22   1cm. Join 18–22; mark point 23 on the
knee line.
13–24   1cm.
15–25   = 14–23.
Draw inside leg seam; join 24–25 with a straight line;
join 21–25 curving the line inwards 2cm.

21

Two-piece trouser block

Creating the one-piece pattern

One-piece trouser block

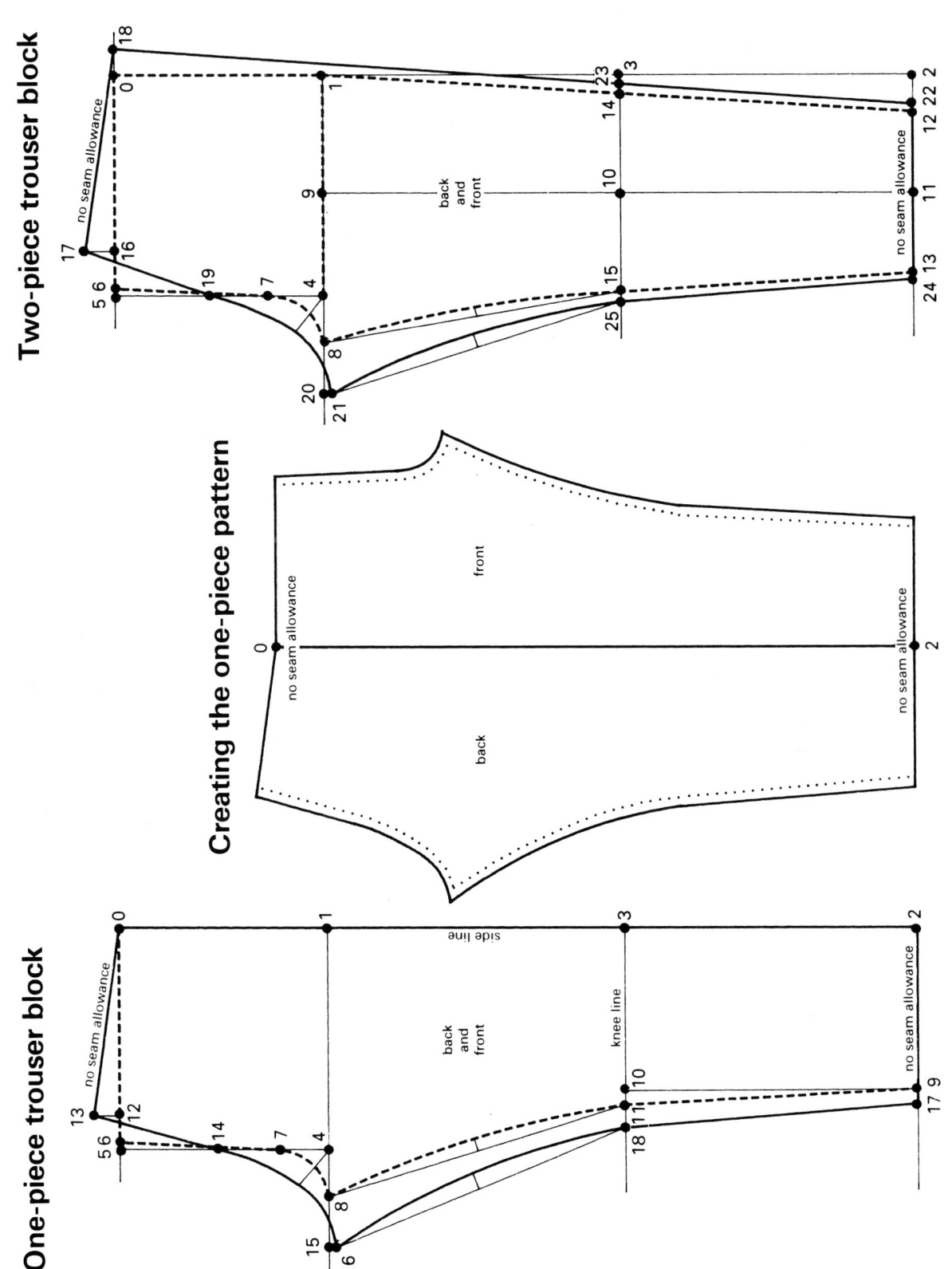

The 'flat' shirt and overgarment blocks
Useful blocks for casual wear, sportswear, workwear and weatherwear

The 'flat' shirt block (woven fabrics)

There is a 1cm seam allowance included in the blocks except where stated *no seam allowance*.

Measurements required to draft the blocks (e.g. size MEDIUM) refer to the size chart (page 15) for SMALL, MEDIUM, LARGE, XLARGE sizes.

Chest	100cm
Scye depth	24.4cm
Back neck to waist	44.2cm
Neck size	40cm
Half back	20cm
Garment length	varies with style
Sleeve length one-piece sleeve	65cm
Close wrist measurement	17.8cm

Body section
Square both ways from 0.
0–1 3cm.
1–2 Scye depth plus 4cm; square across.
1–3 Back neck to waist; square across.
1–4 Shirt length; square across.
2–5 ¼ chest plus 6.5cm; square up to 6 and down to 7 on waistline and 8 on hem line.

1–9 ⅕ neck size minus 0.6cm; square up 3cm to 10. Draw in neck curve to fitting line 1cm below 10.
1–11 ½ measurement 1–2; square out.
11–12 ½ back plus 5cm; square down to 13 on the scye depth line and up to 14.
1–15 ⅛ scye depth measurement minus 0.3cm; square out to 16.
16–17 1.5cm; join 10–17.
Draw in the armhole curve through points 17, 12, 5.
1–18 ⅕ neck size minus 2cm. Draw in front neck curve to fitting line 1cm below 10.

Sleeve – basic shape (machined on the flat).
Square down from 0.
0–1 ⅓ measurement 1–2 body block; square across.
0–2 Sleeve length minus 2cm.
0–3 The measurement of the diagonal 5–17 on the body block plus 3cm.
2–4 ½ close wrist measurement plus 5cm; join 3–4.
Divide 0–3 into five sections; mark points 5, 6, 7, 8.
Draw in sleeve head; hollow the curve 0.75cm at 5; raise the curve 1.5cm between 7–8.

The 'flat' overgarment block (woven fabrics)

The main figures will give a basic shape for jackets; the figures in brackets will give an easier fitting shape for wider overgarments.

Body sections
Square both ways from 0.
0–1 3cm.
1–2 Scye depth plus 5cm (9cm); square across.
1–3 Back neck to waist plus 1cm; square across.
1–4 Jacket length; square across.
2–5 ¼ chest plus 8.5cm (11.5cm); square up to 6; down to 7 on waistline and 8 on hem line.
1–9 ⅕ neck size plus 0.2cm (plus 0.5cm); square up 3cm to 10. Draw in back neck curve to fitting line 1cm below 10.
1–11 ½ measurement 1–2; square out.
11–12 ½ back plus 6.5cm (8.5cm); square down to 13 on the scye depth line and up to 14.
1–15 ⅛ scye depth measurement minus 0.3cm; square out to 16.
16–17 1.5cm; join 10–17.
Draw in the armhole curve through points 17, 12, 5.
1–18 ⅕ neck size minus 1.5cm.
Draw in front neck.

Sleeve – basic shape (machined on the flat).
Square down from 0.
0–1 ⅓ measurement 1–2 on body block; square across.
0–2 Sleeve length minus 2cm (minus 4cm).
0–3 The measurement of the diagonal 5–17 on the body block plus 3cm.
2–4 ½ the close wrist measurement plus 6cm (8cm); join 3–4.
Divide 0–3 into five sections, mark points 5, 6, 7, 8.
Draw in the sleeve head; hollow the curve 0.75cm at 5; raise the curve 1.5cm between 7 and 8.

'Raised' sleeve head (machined on the round) Alter the above instructions as follows:
0–1 ½ measurement 1–2 on body block minus 1cm; square across.
0–2 Sleeve length minus 2cm (minus 4cm). Divide 0-3 into six sections, mark points 5, 6, 7, 8, 9.
Draw in the sleeve head; hollow the curve 1cm at 5; raise the curve 2cm at 8.

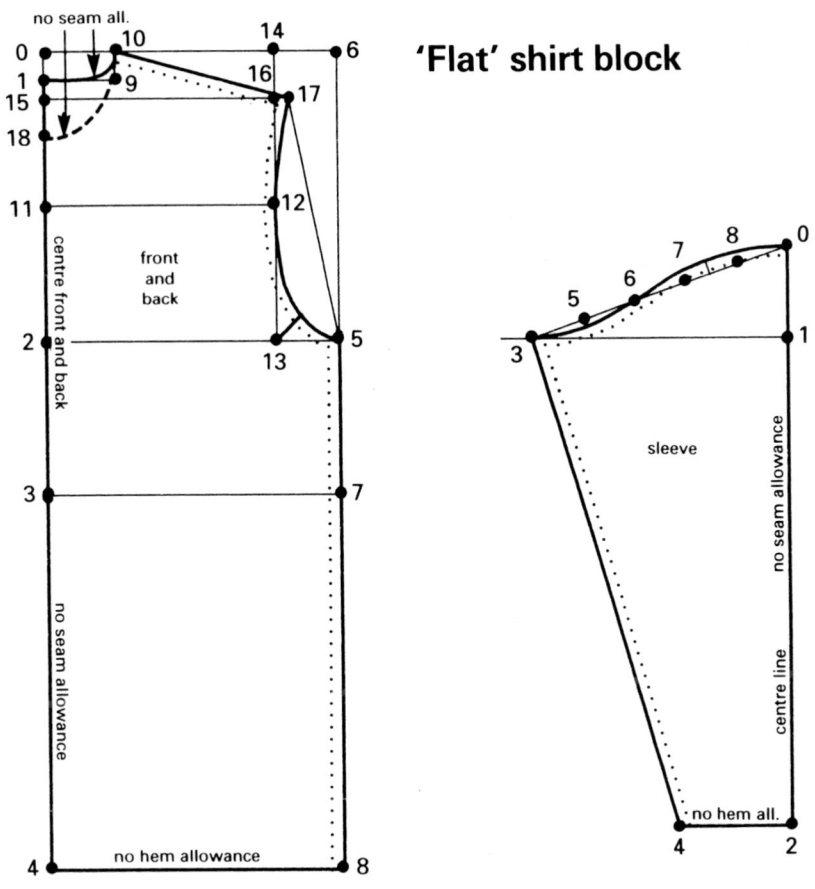

'Flat' shirt block

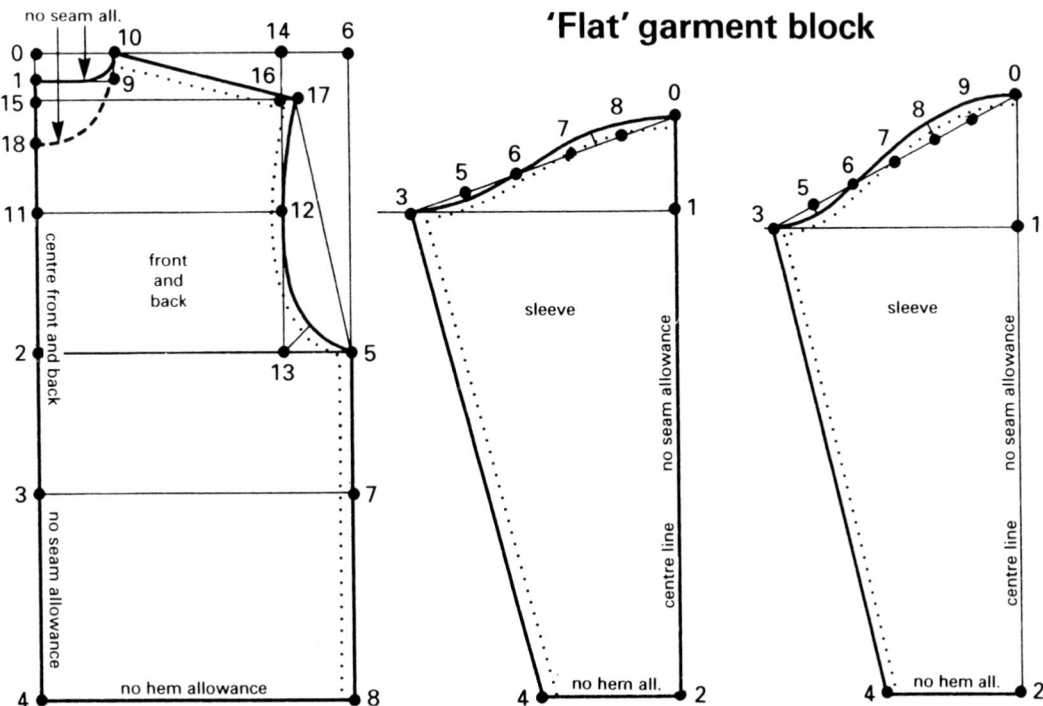

'Flat' garment block

The tee shirt and overgarment jersey blocks

The tee shirt and knitwear blocks (jersey fabrics)

There is a 1cm seam allowance on all the blocks except where stated *no seam allowance*.

The tee shirt blocks are drafted for jersey fabrics; they can also to be drafted for knitwear.

The first instructions given are for close fitting tee shirts or standard knitwear; those in brackets are the extra measurements required for easier fitting tee shirts or knitwear. For very close fitting jersey garments, construct the body sections as instructed but draft the sections without any ease allowance.

Note: The sleeve length for knitwear only can be reduced by 4–5cm approx. This is dependent on fabric stretch and relaxation.

Measurements required to draft the blocks
(e.g. Size MEDIUM)
Refer to the size chart (page 15) for SMALL, MEDIUM, LARGE, XLARGE sizes.

Chest	100
Half back	20
Back neck to waist	44.2
Scye depth	24.4
Neck size	40
Sleeve length one-piece sleeve	65
Close wrist measurement	17.8

Body sections
Square down and across from 0.

0–1 Back neck to waist plus 1cm; square across.
0–2 Finished length; square across.
0–3 Scye depth plus 1cm (2.5cm); square across.
0–4 ½ measurement 0–3; square across.
0–5 ¼ measurement 0–4; square across.
0–6 ⅕ neck size minus 1cm; square up.
6–7 1.5cm; draw in back neck curve.
3–8 Half back plus 1cm (2cm); square up to 9 and 10.
10–11 0.75cm; join 7–11.
3–12 ¼ chest plus 2.5cm (4cm); square down to 13.
Draw in armhole curve from 11 through 9–12.
0–14 ⅕ neck size minus 2cm; draw in front neck.
Back and front sections are the same shape except for the neck curves.

Sleeve
Square down from 15.
15–16 ½ measurement 0–3; square across.
15–17 Sleeve length required; square across.
15–18 Measurement of diagonal line from 11–12 on body section plus 2.5cm; square down to 19.
18–20 ⅓ measurement 18–15.
Draw in sleeve head; 18–20 curve in 0.75cm; 20–15 curve out 2cm.
17–21 ½ close wrist measurement plus 3cm (3.5cm); join 18–21 with a curve (close fitting block only).

Short sleeve
19–21 4cm; join 18 to 21 with a curve (close fitting block only).

The overgarment blocks (jersey fabrics)

The first instructions given are for a basic fit (e.g. track suits); the instructions in brackets are the extra measurements required to construct blocks for easier fitting jersey overgarments.

Body sections
Square down and across from 0.
0–1 Back neck to waist plus 1cm; square across.
0–2 Finished length; square across.
0–3 Scye depth plus 3cm (5cm); square across.
0–4 ½ measurement 0–3; square across.
0–5 ¼ measurement 0–4; square across.
0–6 ⅕ neck size; square up.
6–7 1.5 cm; draw in back neck curve.
3–8 Half back plus 2.5cm (3.5cm); square up to 9 and 10.
10–11 0.75cm; join 7–11.
3–12 ¼ chest plus 4.5cm (6cm); square down to 13.
Draw in armhole curve from 11 through 9–12.
0–14 ⅕ neck size minus 1.5cm; draw in front neck.
Back and front sections are the same shape except for the neck curves.

Sleeve
15–16 ½ measurement 0–3; square across.
15–17 Sleeve length required; square across.
15–18 Measurement of diagonal line from 11–12 on body section plus 2.5cm; square down to 19.
18–20 ⅓ measurement 18–15.
Draw in sleeve head, 18–20 curve in 0.75 cm; 20–15 curve out 2cm.
17–21 ½ close wrist measurement plus 6cm (7cm); join 18–21 with a curve if required.

25

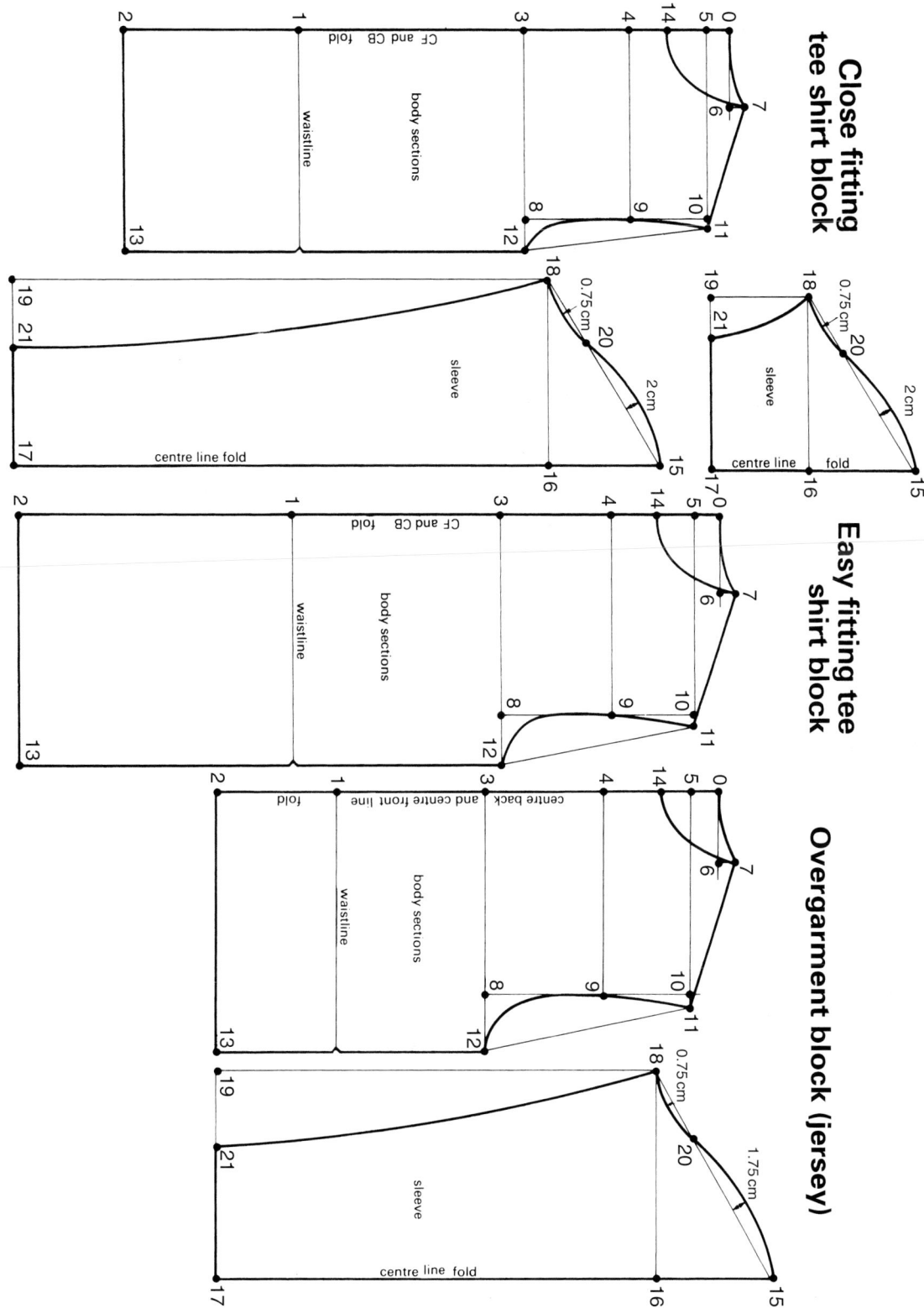

Close fitting tee shirt block

Easy fitting tee shirt block

Overgarment block (jersey)

The 'flat' kimono block (woven or jersey fabrics)

There is a 1cm seam allowance included in the block except where stated *no seam allowance.*

The 'flat' kimono block can be constructed by adapting any of the woven or jersey fabrics blocks. It is a very useful block that can be used for many kinds of 'flat' sleeve cutting processes, (see Chapter 6, Constructing sleeves).

Body sections
Trace round the basic body shape of the selected 'flat' block. Mark points 5, 9, 17.
Extend the line from 17–A the sleeve length minus 4cm.
Square out from A–B, ½ the close wrist measurement plus 4cm basic blocks (6cm easy fitting blocks).
5–C is 4cm. Join C–B.

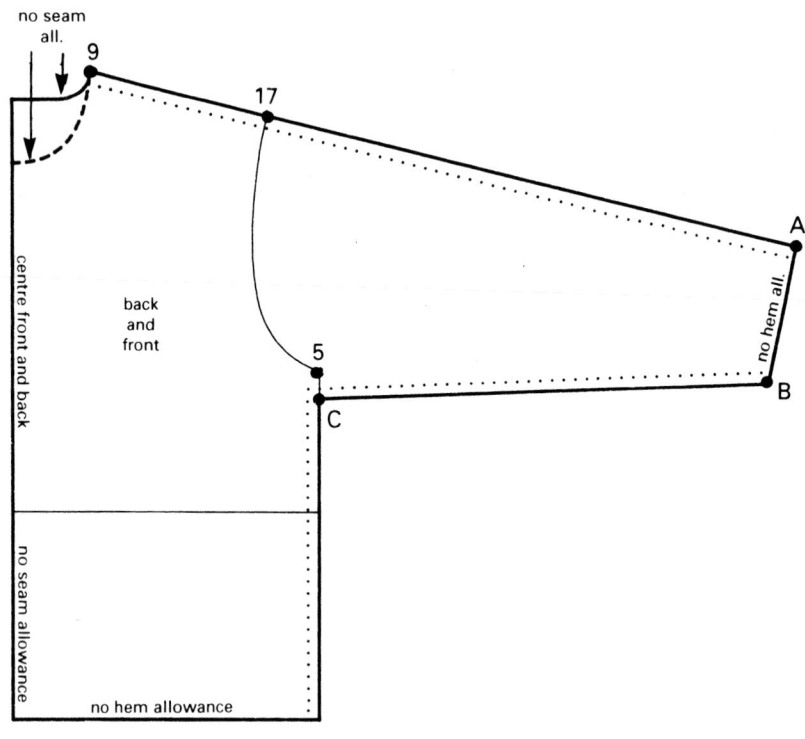

PART ONE: 'FLAT' CUTTING

Chapter 3 Leisurewear, weatherwear and sportswear

Special note: Some designers may find it useful to adjust the length of the back scye depth. This modification gives a better balance to the hang of a 'flat' jacket made in woven fabrics (see ref. 3 page 66). It is used mainly in more expensive 'flat' cutting because it can involve extra production costs, such as extra grade rules and lay planning costings.

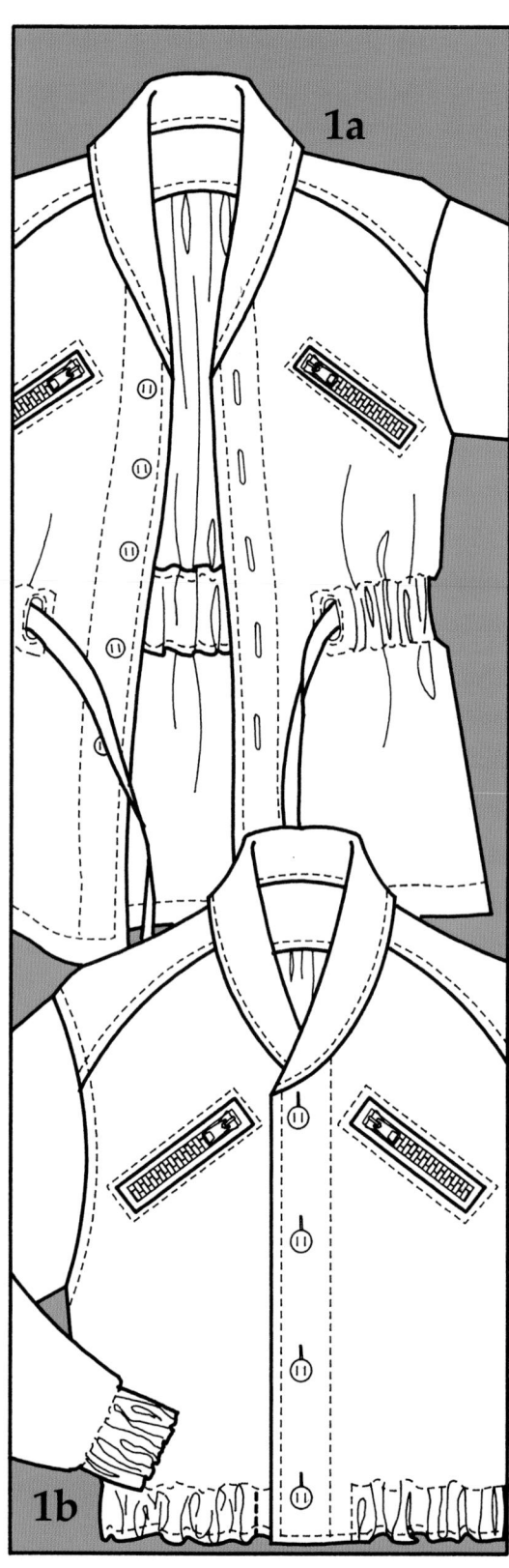

Leisurewear and weatherwear (woven fabrics)

A wide range of casual jackets can be constructed from the flat overgarment blocks. This page demonstrates how variations of a style can be made by the selection of the basic or easy fitting block.

Note The yokes are usually made up in double fabric for extra weather protection.

Many examples of sleeve and collar adaptations for jackets are shown in Chapters 6 and 7.

1a Casual overgarment

Trace off the 'flat' easy fitting overgarment block. Remove the seam allowance on the side seam. Mirror the front section and place sections together at the side seam to create draft. Curve the shoulder line down 1cm at shoulder point as shown.

Remove 1cm from the centre edge of the sleeve.

Body section Draw in finished jacket length.

Draw in stitch line 3cm in from centre front line.

Draw in button stand 3cm past centre front.

Mark point A on fitting line at neck point of shoulder; draw in neckline with slight curve. Mark buttonholes.

Mark B on centre front line at hem. B–C is 2cm.

Join C to side seam with a curve.

Draw in pocket opening and pocket bag.

Draw in casing to a point 10cm from centre front line; width 5cm. The top of casing is below waistline.

Trace off main body sections; cut up side seam.

Add 7cm to centre back line.

Add 6.5cm extended facing (ref. 1, page 80).

Add seam allowance to side seams, yoke lines, front neckline and edge of facing. Add 5cm hem allowance.

Yokes Trace off yokes. Add seam allowance along yoke lines and necklines.

Collar Place shoulder lines together on the fitting lines at A. Draft a flat collar (ref. 12, page 96).

Casing Trace off casing. Add 7cm to centre back.

Add seam allowance to all edges except centre back.

Tie belt Construct belt, required length and twice width plus seam allowance.

Pocket bag Trace off pocket bag. Add seam allowance.

Sleeve Mark point D at the underarm. D–E approx. 7.5cm: D–F approx 6cm.

Draw a diagonal line from E–F. Cut and open approx. 6cm. Re-draw the sleeve head.

Re-draw the underarm seam shaping in at the wrist.

Add 6cm for casing for an elasticated cuff.

1b Casual jacket

Trace off the 'flat' basic overgarment block.

Complete the adaptation above but cut off the body sections along line marked for the shorter jacket.

Add seam allowance.

Use the casing pattern for the lower edge of the jacket.

1a Casual overgarment

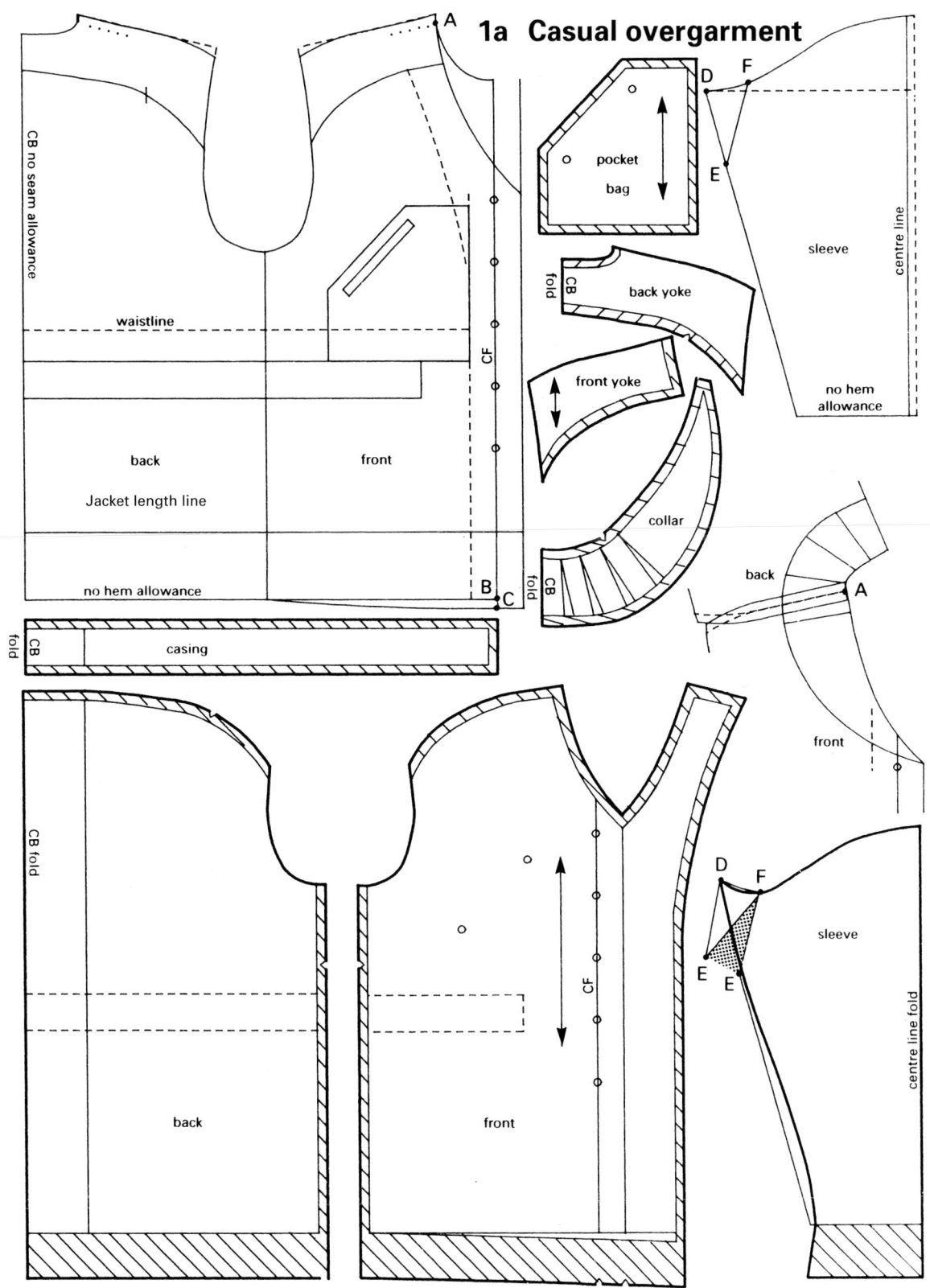

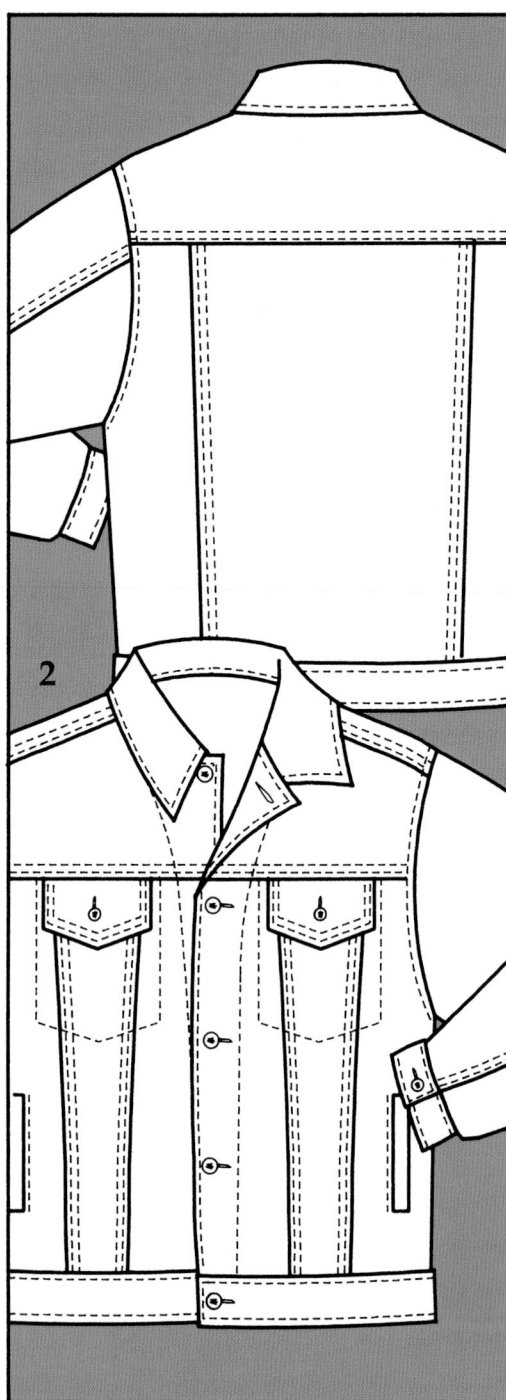

2 Jeans jacket

Body sections Trace off the 'flat' jacket block.
Extend to the length required.
Mirror the front block to create separate sections.
Mark A at the centre front hem line.
A–B = 2cm. Draw a curved line from point B to the side seam line. Add 2.5cm button stand.
Mark bottom button point on centre front line 1.75cm below hem. Mark top button point 2cm from top.
Divide the distance for a five button fastening.
Remove 2cm from front shoulder, add to back shoulder line. Place shoulder fitting lines together to make sure the neck is drawn accurately.
Draw front and back yoke line; mark points C D E F.
C–G is ¾ measurement C–D; square down.
Shape in back seam and side seam as required (example shown).
F–H is half the measurement E–F minus 1cm.
H–I and H–J = 4.25cm; square down.
Shape in front seams and side seam as required (example shown).
Draw in top pocket flap and pocket bag.
Draw in facing line.
Draw in side pocket positions and a pocket bag shape.
Mark point K on the original shoulder point.
Collar and facing Construct the draft for a standard convertible collar (ref. 2a, page 88). Trace off facing and complete (ref. 1, page 80).
Front panels Trace off front sections.
Add seam allowance to front line, panel lines, top line and bottom lines.
Front yoke Trace off front yoke. Add seam allowance to bottom edge, front edge and neckline.
Back Trace off back sections. Add seam allowance to panel lines, top line and bottom lines.
Back yoke Trace off back yoke. Add seam allowance to bottom edge and neckline.
Pockets Trace off pocket flap and welt. Add seam allowance. Trace off pocket bags; add seam allowance.
Sleeves Mirror sleeve. Shorten sleeve by 3.5cm.
Mark point L on top of sleeve head, M on hem. Measure the distance D–K on body draft; L–N is the distance D–K plus 2cm.
Mark O on the back sleeve line.
M–P is ⅓ the distance M–O. P–Q = 1cm.
Mark tuck positions. Trace off sleeve sections.
Add seam allowance to back seam lines and bottom edge.
Waistband Construct a waistband; width = 3cm; length is the measurement of the lower edge of the jacket plus 2.5cm button stand. Add seam allowance.
Cuff Construct a cuff width 3.5cm; length 29cm.
Add seam allowance.
Tab Construct a tab width 3 cm; length 12cm.
Add seam allowance.

2 Jeans jacket

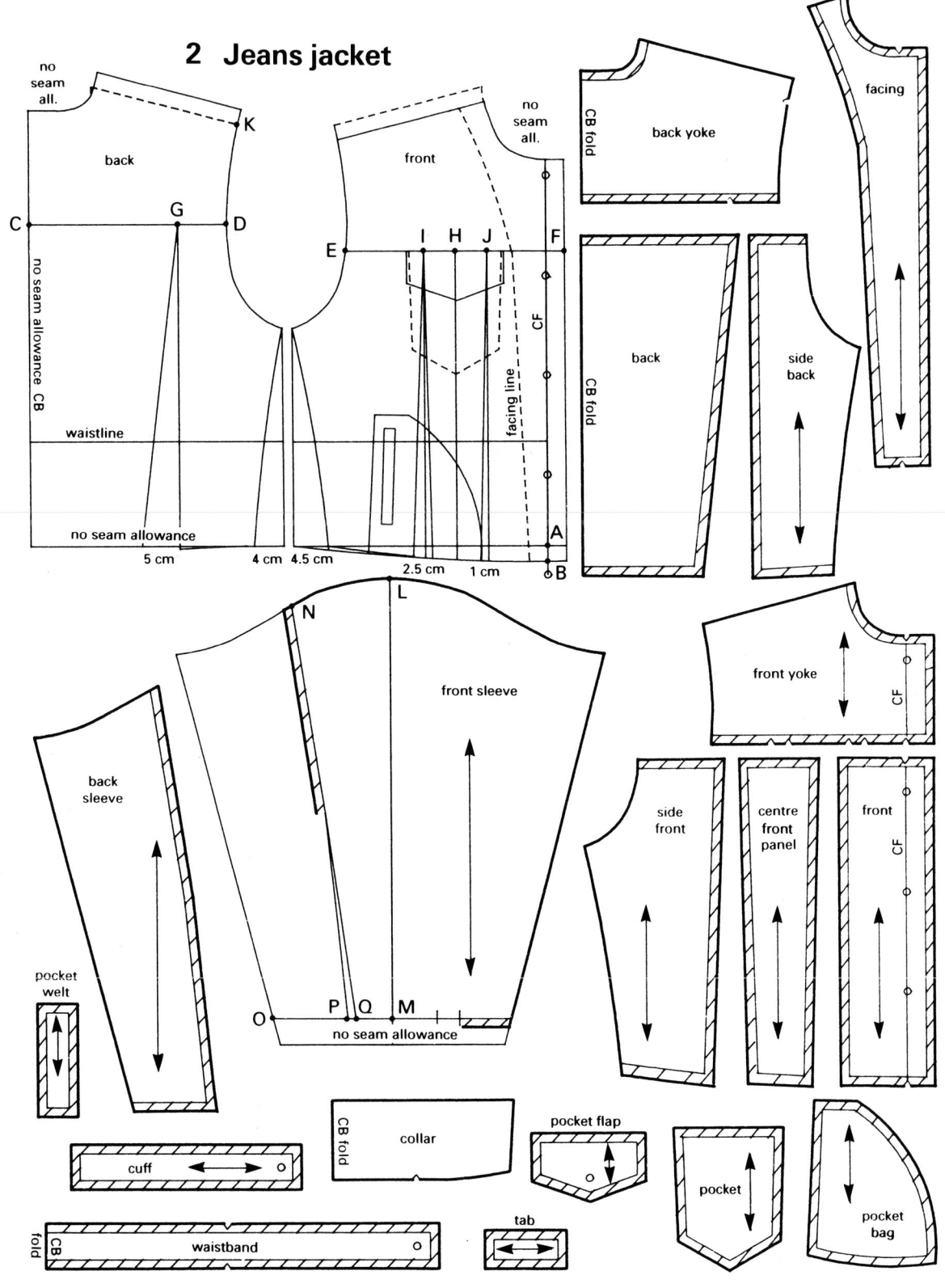

no seam all.

back

K

C   G   D

no seam allowance CB

waistline

no seam allowance

5 cm   4 cm   4.5 cm

front

no seam all.

E   I H J   F

CF

facing line

2.5 cm   1 cm

A
B

CB fold   back yoke

facing

back   side back

CB fold

N   L

front sleeve

back sleeve

pocket welt

O   P Q M
no seam allowance

front yoke

CF

side front   centre front panel   front

CF

cuff

CB fold   collar

pocket flap

pocket

pocket bag

tab

fold   CB   waistband

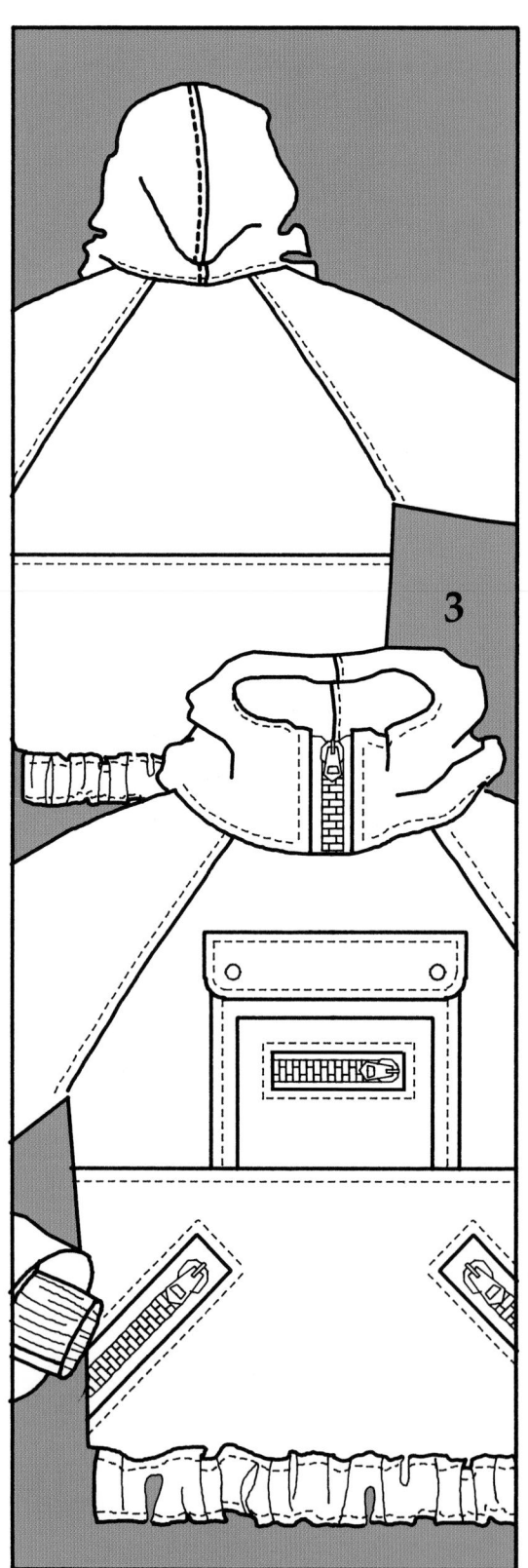

3

Weatherwear

Most designs of this type are based on flat shapes. The design illustrated is adapted from the 'flat' kimono (easy fitting overgarment) block. The sleeve underarm has extra movement by the inclusion of a hidden gusset. Some designers make this a feature by creating a 'patch' at the underarm which includes gusseting.

3 Anorak

Trace off the 'flat' kimono (easy fitting overgarment) block.

Draw in finished length required.

Mirror the front block to create separate sections.

Body sections Lower the neckline 2.5cm at A and B; 4cm at C and D. Draw in new neck curves.

Draw in raglan lines. On shaped styles some darting can be taken out along the raglan lines.

Draw in horizontal style lines.

Draw in any pockets, pocket flaps and pocket bags.

Top front and back Trace off top sections. Add seam allowance to seam edges and neckline.

Lower front and back Trace off lower sections.

Add seam allowance to seam edges.

Add 6cm casing to hem.

Pockets Trace off pockets, pocket flaps and pocket bags; add seam allowance to all edges except fold lines.

Hood E–F is the neckline measurement of front and back sections from A–C and B–D on fitting line (ref. page 86) plus 0.5cm. Square up.

E–G is 43cm; square across to H.

E–I is ¾ the distance E–G. I–J is 1.5cm. E–K is 6cm.

F–L is ⅓ distance F–H minus 2cm.

H–M is ½ measurement G–H.

H–N is ⅛ measurement G–H plus 1.5cm.

N–O is 0.5cm.

Draw in hood shape as shown in diagram.

Draw in facing line 5cm from front edge.

Add 2cm seam allowance to the centre front line.

Hood gusset Construct a triangular shape, width = 9cm, length = F–L. Add 2cm seam allowance.

Hood facing Trace off facing.

Add seam allowance to facing line.

Sleeve Mark point P at the underarm. P–Q and P–R are approx. 7.5cm. Draw a diagonal line from Q–R. Cut and open approx. 6cm. Re-draw the sleeve head as shown.

Re-draw the underarm seam shaping in at the wrist.

Draw in position of the undersleeve.

Add a shaped facing. The length is the distance of the undersleeve plus 1cm seam allowance.

Undersleeve Trace off undersleeve.

Remove knitted cuff distance plus 2cm from bottom of the undersleeve.

Add seam allowance to top and bottom edges.

3 Anorak

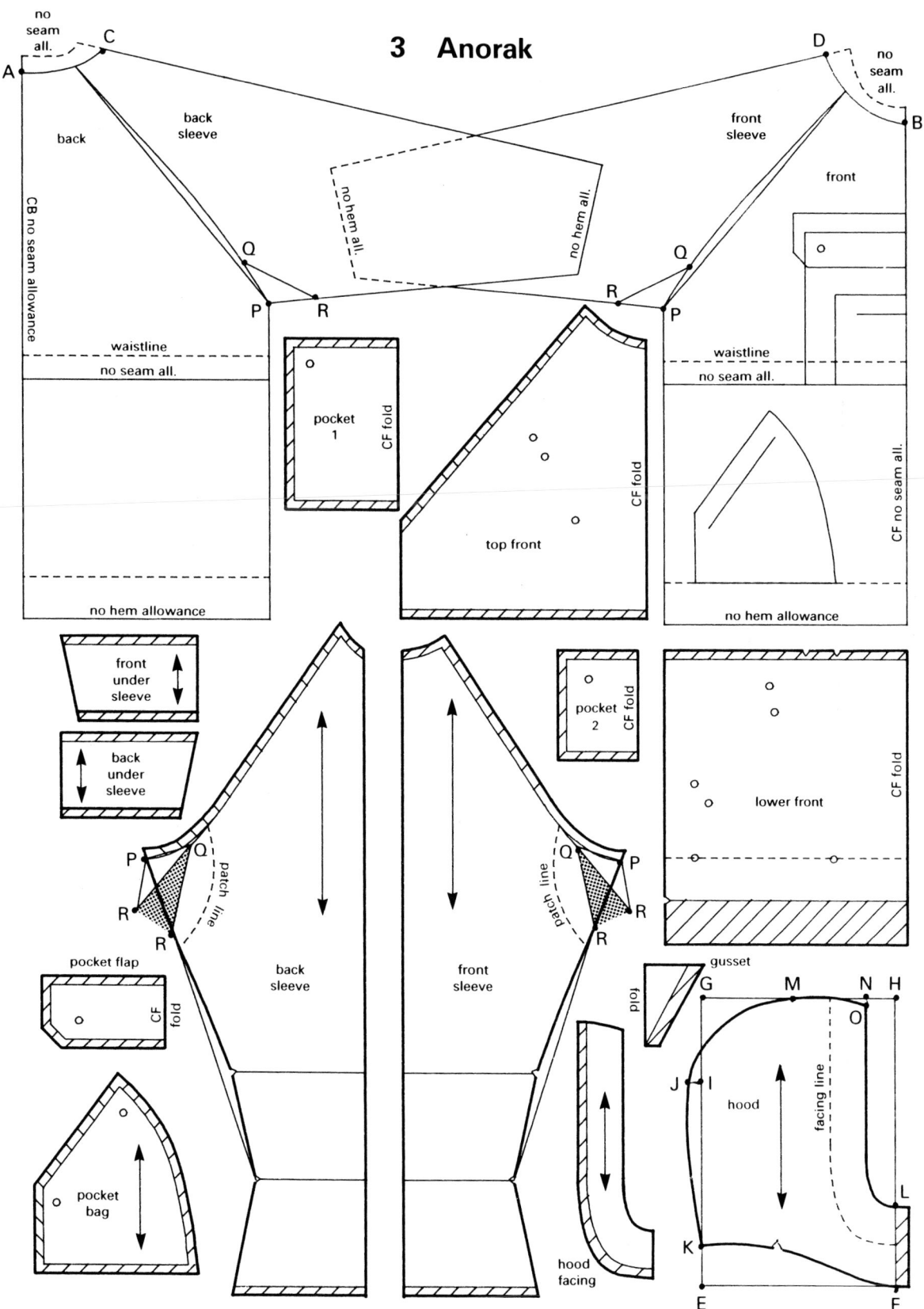

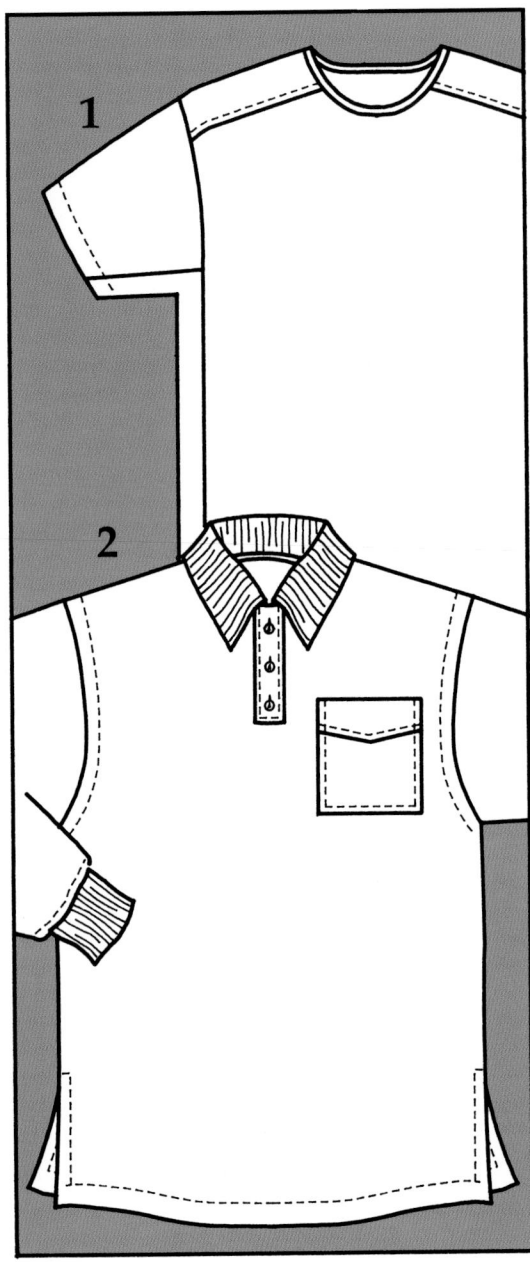

Leisurewear and sportswear (jersey fabrics)

Tee shirts

Print designs and logos dominate tee shirt design. These are printed on basic and easy fitting block shapes with sleeve length and neck variations.

1 Sports tee shirt adaptation

Body sections Trace round body and sleeve sections of basic tee shirt block to required length.
Remove seam allowance from shoulder seam.
Widen neck on back and front: 1.5cm at A; 2.5cm at B; 1cm at C.
Extend shoulder 2cm to D; join to armhole with curve.
Draw in 3cm shoulder strap lines.
Mark points E and F on body side seam; G, and H on sleeve seam.
Draw in panel lines on body and sleeve sections.
Panel widths should be equal at points E and G.
Mark point I at the sleeve head.
I–J is 2cm; draw in new sleeve head.
Back and front Trace off back and front sections along strap and panel lines.
Add seam allowance to shoulder lines and panel lines of body sections. Add 4cm hem allowance.
Sleeve Trace sleeve along panel line.
Add 1cm seam allowance to panel line.
Add 3cm hem allowance.
Shoulder strap Trace off back and front shoulder straps on *fitting line*.
Draw vertical line; place straps to line at points B and D. Add seam allowance to outer edges.
Side body and sleeve panel Draw vertical line.
Trace off body and sleeve panels omitting the side and sleeve seam allowances.
Place body panels to vertical line at point E and F.
Place sleeve panels to vertical line at points G and H.
Add 4cm hem allowance at H and 3cm sleeve hem allowance at J.
Note The tee shirt can be constructed using only the shoulder strap adaptation or the side body and sleeve panel adaptation.

2 Polo shirt

Back and front Trace round back and front sections of the easy fitting jersey block.
Draw in front gusset; approx. depth = 10cm, width = 3cm. Add 1cm seam allowance to the gusset line.
Add 4cm hem allowance to back and front.
Add 4cm vent allowance at hem line.
Sleeve Trace off sleeve, remove depth of rib cuff from base of sleeve. Add 1cm seam allowance.
Front gusset Construct a rectangle: width = 12cm; length = 10cm. Draw fold line down centre.
Draw in centre front line and button positions.
Add 1cm seam allowance to *fitting line*.
Collar and cuffs Construct ribbed collar and cuffs.

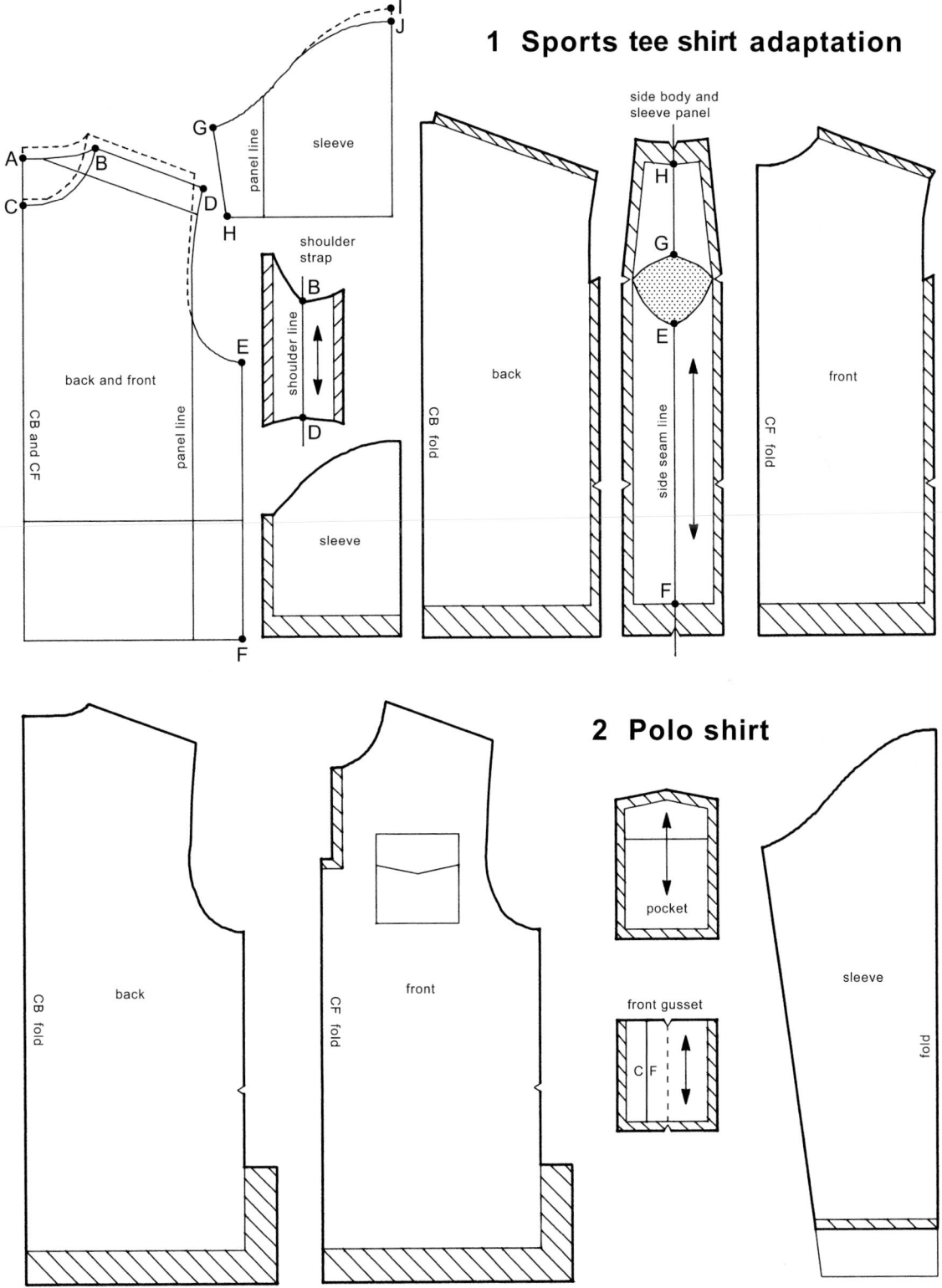

1 Sports tee shirt adaptation

side body and
sleeve panel

sleeve

panel line

G

I

J

H

A

B

C

D

shoulder line

shoulder
strap

B

D

E

back and front

CB and CF

panel line

F

sleeve

H

G

E

side seam line

F

back

CB fold

front

CF fold

2 Polo shirt

back

CB fold

front

CF fold

pocket

front gusset

C F

sleeve

fold

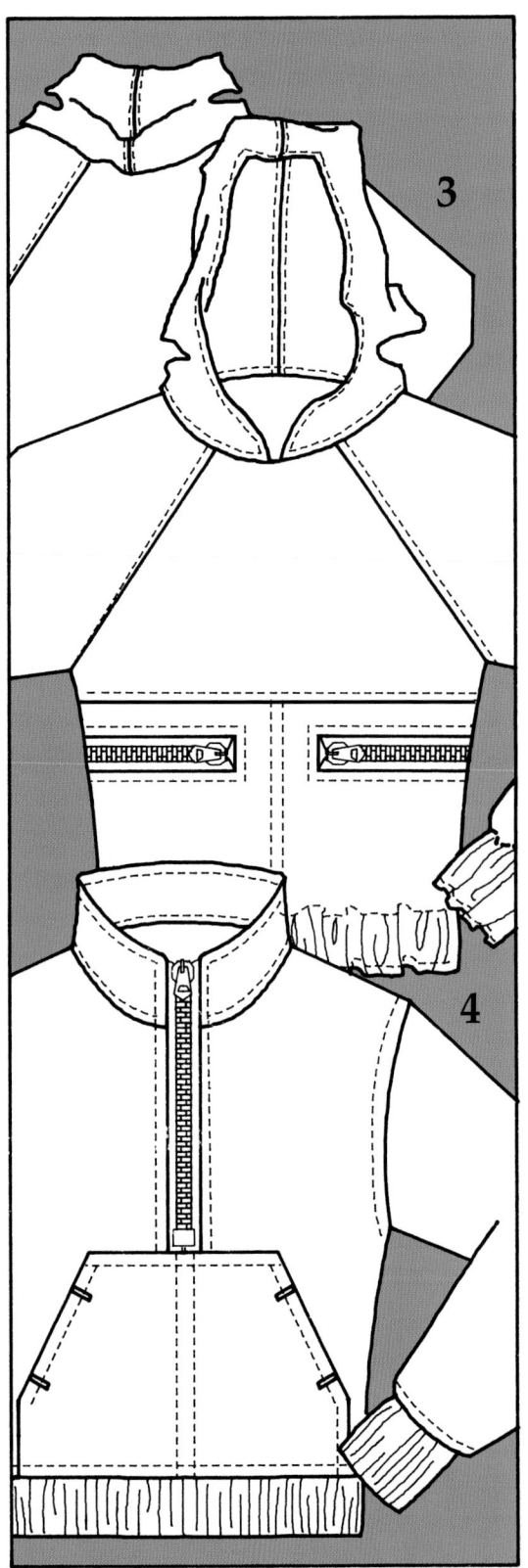

Jersey casual tops

Note: Both of these adaptations can be made with inset sleeves by ignoring the raglan instructions on the body sections and sleeve. Both adaptations can also be made with elaticated casings on the body and sleeves (ref. 3) or with a ribbed jersey hem and cuffs (ref. 4).

3   Raglan top with hood (track)

Trace off the selected jersey overgarment block. Mirror front section and front sleeve.

Mark points 9, 12, on the body section, 15, 18, 20 on the sleeve.

Body sections   Delete the armhole curves from 9–12. Square down from 9.

12–A and 12–B are the measurement 18–20 on sleeve. Curve the line inwards by 0.75cm.

Lower the neck 2cm at C and D; 4cm at E and F.

E–G is 4cm F–H is 4cm. Join G–A and H–B.

Cut off shaded sections.

Front   Draw in pocket line approx. 8cm below 12.

Draw in zip pocket; approx. width 12cm.

Back   Add 5cm to back hem for casing.

Front pocket   Trace pocket along pocket line.

Add 1cm seam allowance along top edge.

Add 5cm to hem for casing.

Sleeve   Extend centre line of sleeve from 15.

Draw parallel lines 5cm each side of this line.

20–I = A–G on back; 20–J = B–H on front.

Join I–J with curve.

Add 5cm allowance to hem for casing.

Hood   K–L is neck measurement from C–E and F–D on fitting lines plus 1.5cm.

K–M is 1.5cm; square up from L and M.

M–N is 40cm; square across to O.

M–P is two thirds the distance M–N.

K–Q is 6cm. R is midway between O–N; S is midway between M–L.

Draw hood shape as shown.

Mark centre front 1.5cm from L.

Add 5cm to front edge for casing.

4   Raglan top with collar (track)

Body sections   Complete body sections and sleeve as above but shorten by the depth of the hem rib.

Add 1cm seam allowance to hem.

Front   Draw zip line 2cm from the centre front edge.

Draw in a different pocket shape.

Draw in pocket facing.

Front pocket and facing   Trace off pocket. Add 1cm seam allowance where shown. Trace off pocket facing.

Add 1cm seam allowance to all edges.

Sleeve   Add 1cm allowance to cuff edge.

Collar   Measure the neckline along the *fitting line* (ref. page 87). Construct a stand collar without button stand (ref. 1a, page 86).

Add 2cm seam allowance to centre front edge.

3 Raglan top with hood (track)

4 Raglan top with collar (track)

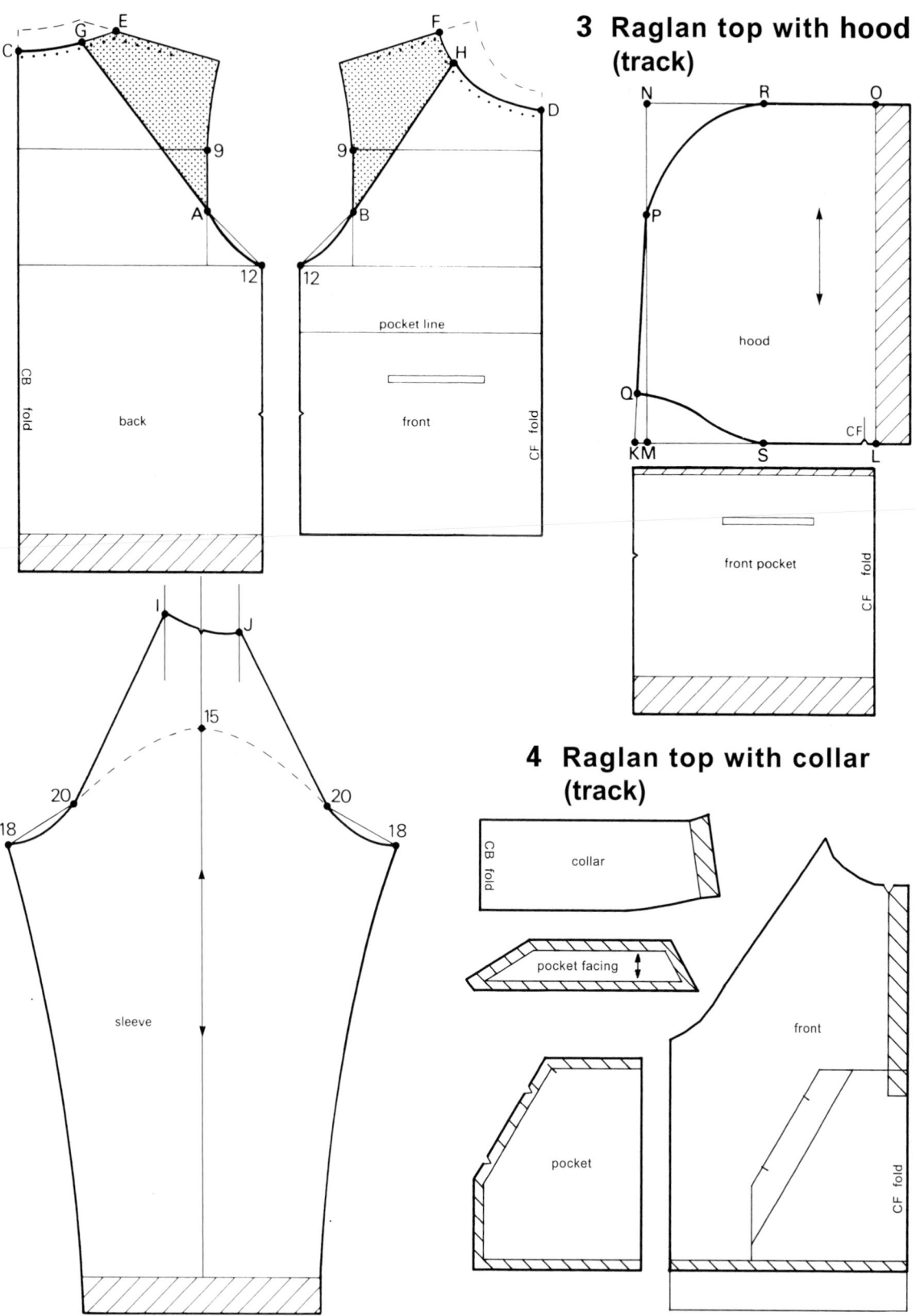

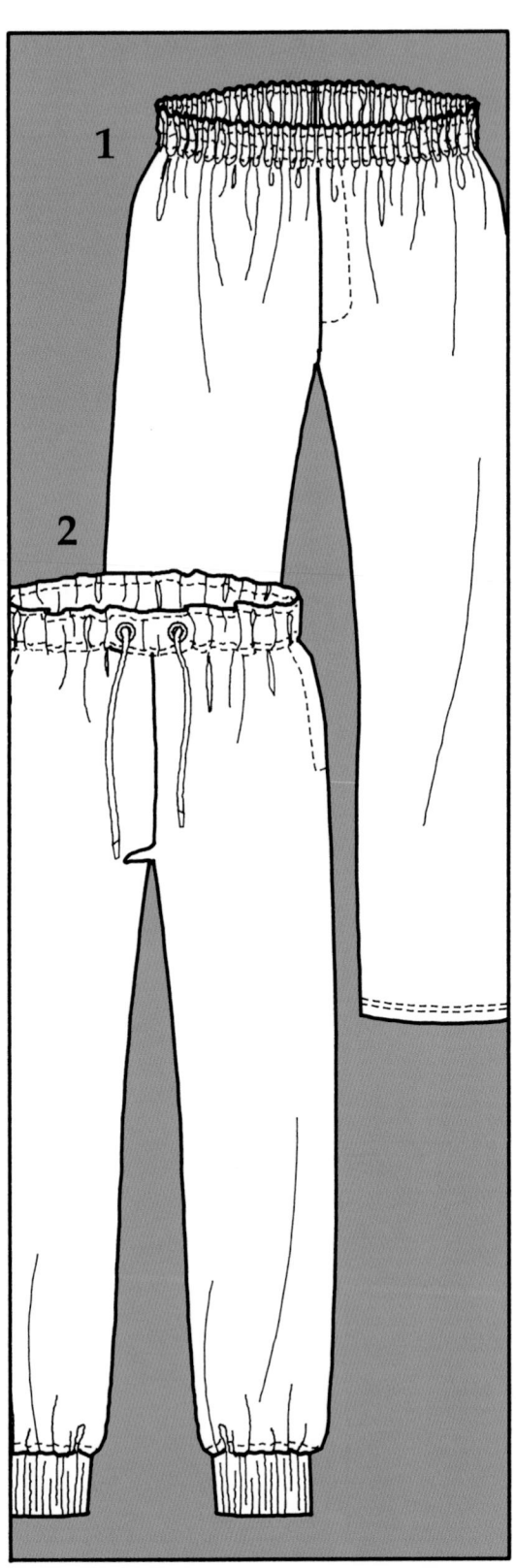

Casual trousers (woven and jersey fabrics)

1 Weatherwear trousers

Back and front   Trace off the easy fitting one-piece trouser block.

Mark point A at the front waistline.

A–B is 19cm.

Draw in fly piece: width = 7cm.

Add 5cm to the top edge for elasticated casing.

Add 4cm hem allowance.

2 Casual jersey trousers (track)

Trace off the easy fitting two-piece trouser block.

Front   Mark point A at the side seam.

Draw in pocket bag; length = approx. 22cm; width = approx. 12cm.

A–B is 17cm.

Draw in 4cm pocket extension.

Add 5cm to the top edge for elasticated casing.

Add 4cm hem allowance.

Back   Add 5cm to the top edge for elasticated casing.

Add 4cm hem allowance.

Pocket bag   Trace off pocket bag.

Trousers with ankle ribs   Shorten the leg length by the depth of the rib.

Add 1cm seam allowance.

39

2 Casual jersey trousers

1 Weatherwear trousers

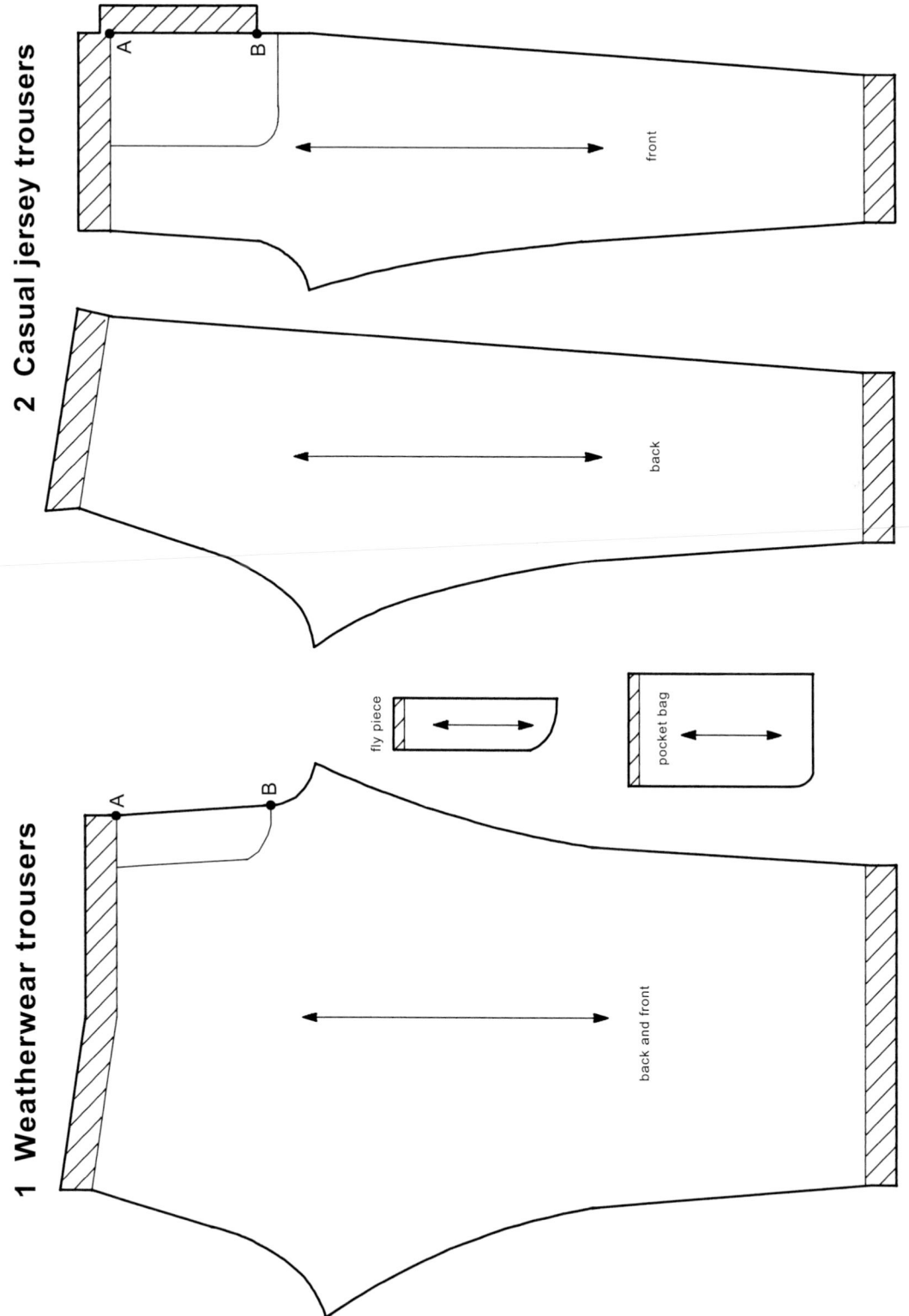

front

back

fly piece

pocket bag

back and front

The basic jeans blocks

The blocks

Jeans can be drafted for many different fits and styles. The main figures in this basic draft are given for a close fitting block shape and the figures in brackets will give an easier fitting, wider leg shape. Both block options will produce straight leg jeans, see illustrations page 42.

Special Note   Jeans sit in different positions on the body depending on the style. This block is drafted so that the top of the waistband sits approximately 2cm below the trouser waist position (see the diagram on page 11). The block draft therefore uses the trouser waist measurement (90cm).

Measurements required to draft the blocks
The sample illustrated is for the athletic figure (chest 100cm; trouser waist 90cm).
Refer to size chart (page 12) for standard measurements.

Trouser waist position	90cm
Seat	102cm
Body rise	28.1cm
Inside leg	80cm
Jeans bottom width	22.6cm
Waistband depth	4cm

Front

Square down and across from 0.
0–1 Body rise minus 5.5cm (4.5cm); square across.
1–2 Inside leg measurement plus 2cm; square across.
1–3 ½ measurement 1–2 plus 5cm; square across.
1–4 ¼ body rise measurement plus 1cm; square across.
1–5 ⅛ seat measurement plus 0.5 cm (1cm); square up to 6 on seat line, 7 on waistline.
6–8 ¼ seat measurement plus 2cm (3cm).
5–9 ¹⁄₁₆ seat measurement minus 0.5cm (plus 0.5cm).
7–10 1.5cm.
Join 10–6; draw in front curve 6–9 to touch a point 3.5cm from 5.
10–11 ¼ trouser waist measurement plus 2.5cm.
2–12 ½ jeans bottom width measurement (plus 1cm).
2–13 ½ jeans bottom width measurement (plus 1cm).

Square up from 12 and 13 to 14 and 15 at knee line.
Draw side seam: join 11, 8, 14, 12; curve 8–11 out 0.2cm; on close fitting jeans only curve 8–14 in 0.5cm.
Draw inside leg 9, 15, 13; curve 9–15 in 1cm.

Back

5–16 ¼ measurement 1–5; square up to 17 on the seat line and 18 on the waistline.
19 Midway between 16–18.
18–20 2cm.
20–21 1cm.
9–22 ½ measurement 5–9 plus 0.5cm (1cm).
22–23 0.5cm.
Join 21–19; draw in back fork 19–23 to touch a point 5cm from 16.
21–24 ¼ trouser waist measurement plus 3.5cm.
25 Midway between 21 and 24; square down; on this line construct a dart 5cm long, 1cm wide.
17–26 ¼ seat plus 3cm (4cm).
12–27 2cm.
13–28 2cm.
14–29 2cm.
15–30 2cm.
Draw side seam: join 24, 26, 29, 27; curve 26–29 in 0.75cm on close fitting jeans only.
Draw inside leg seam 23, 30, 28; curve 23–30 in 1.5cm.

Block completion

Front   Trace off front block.
Mark points 10 and 11.
10–A is 1cm; join A–11.
Back   Trace off back block.
To insert crutch ease: mark point 26 and new point B on the fork seat line.
Cut across the seat line to point 26; open a 3.5cm (5cm) wedge at the fork line.
B–C is 1.5cm; draw in a new fork line.
Re-draw the side seam from the waistline to 12cm below the crutch line to create a smooth curve.

Jeans adaptation

The following pages 42–43 demonstrate how to construct a jeans pattern from the basic jeans block. A traditional style is demonstrated, but many variations can be made.

Block completion

Jeans block

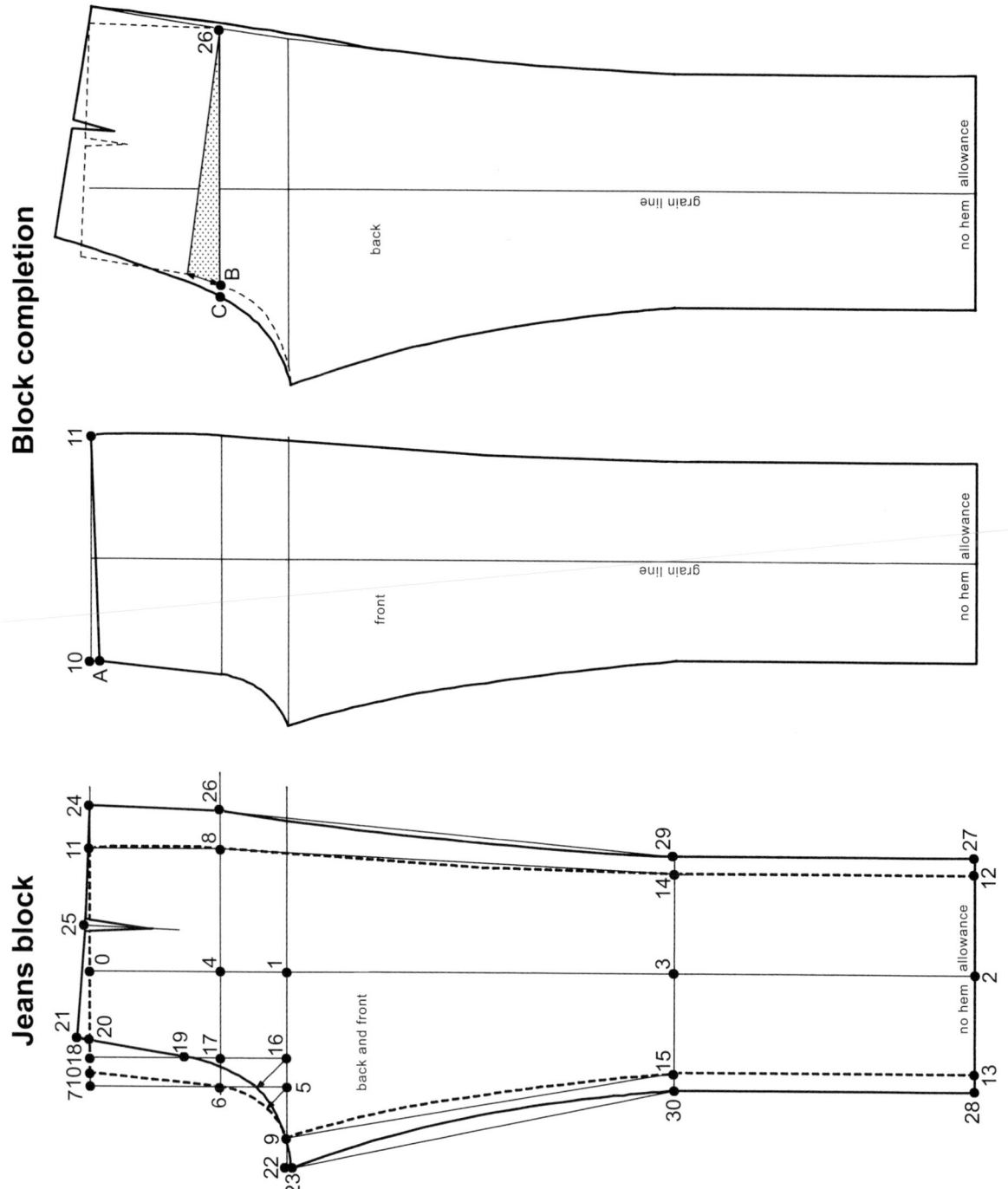

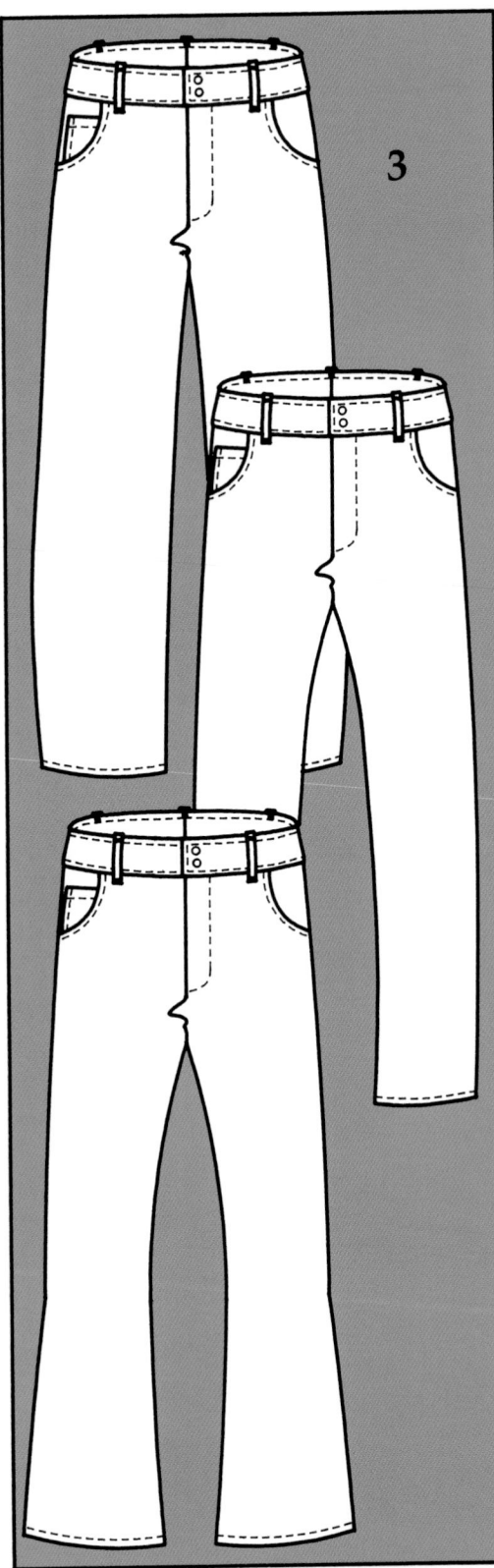

3   Jeans adaptation

Front   Draw in front pocket line mark points A and B.
Draw in pocket bag.
Draw in fly piece on front fork as shown: length = 19cm;
width = 6cm.
Trace off front along the pocket line, add 2cm seam
allowance.
Add 3cm hem allowance.
Side piece   Trace off side piece along pocket line, add 5
cm from A–B.
Fly piece   Trace off fly piece.
Add seam allowance to outer edges.
Pocket bag   Trace off pocket bag 1 along pocket line.
Trace off pocket bag 2 along waistline, mark pocket line.
Back   Draw in back yoke.
Draw in back pocket design.
Trace off back along yoke line.
Add seam allowance to yoke edge.
Add 3cm hem allowance.
Back yoke   Trace off yoke section, extend dart to touch
yoke edge; close dart.
Add seam allowance to edge of yoke line.
Back pocket   Trace back pocket.
Add 2cm to top of pocket and 1cm seam allowance on all
other edges.
Waistband   Construct a double cloth waistband:
length = trouser waist measurement plus 2cm ease;
width = 8cm. Add a 4cm overlap to one end.
Mark fold line down centre.
Add seam allowance to all edges.

Jeans shorts

For jeans shorts cut across jeans draft at length required.
Add 4cm hem allowance.

Adaptation for boot cut jeans

The 'boot cut' jean is adapted from the close fitting block.
To obtain a 'boot cut' leg shape the jeans bottom width is
extended.
Front   Add approximately 2cm to the hem width at
points 12 and 13 on the front jeans block.
Join the new hem points to the original knee points
14 and 15.
Back   Add approximately 2cm to the hem width at points
27 and 28 on the back jeans block.
Join the new hem points to the original knee points
29 and 30.

3 Jeans adaptation

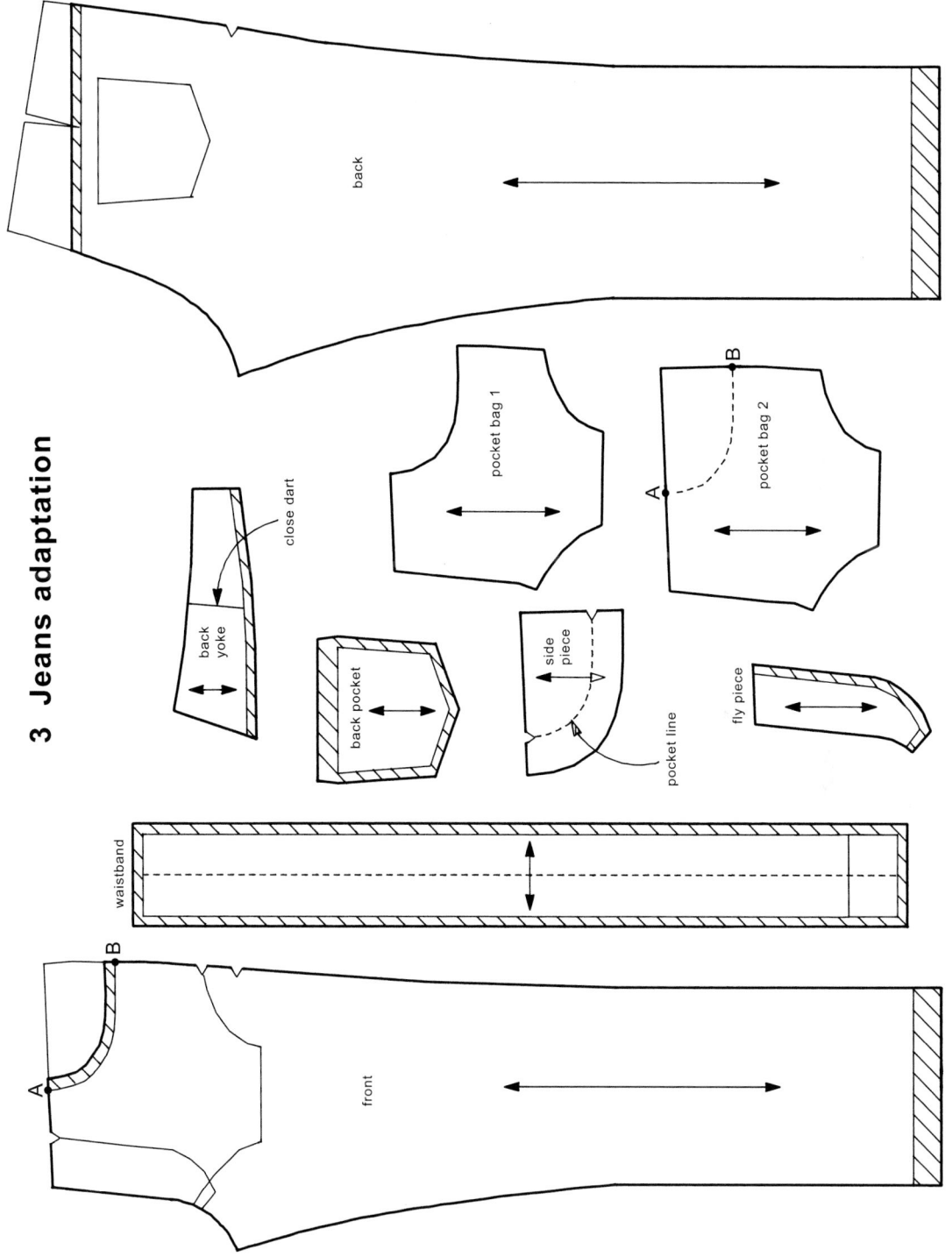

back

pocket bag 1

B

A

pocket bag 2

close dart

back
yoke

back pocket

side
piece

pocket line

fly piece

waistband

B

A

front

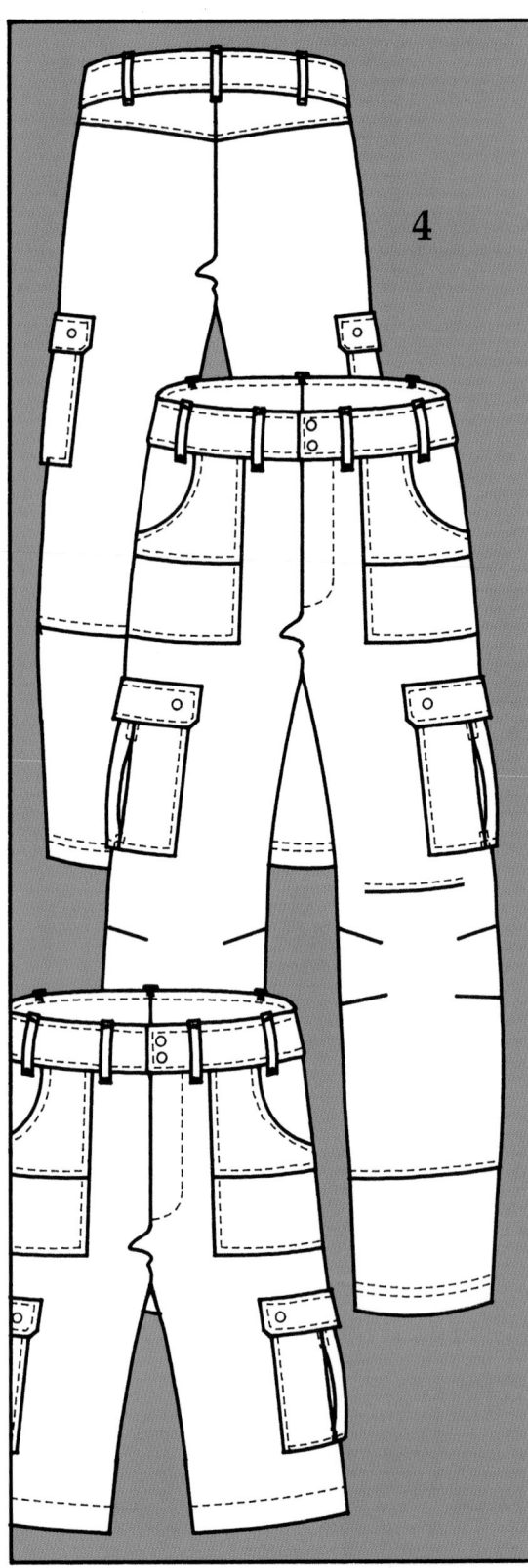

Fashion cargo trousers are usually cut from the easy fitting jeans block (ref. page 40). For a 'baggy' look use either the basic or easy fitting 'flat' trouser block, depending on the fit required. (ref. page 20).

4   Combat trousers

Front   Mark point A at the inside crutch line and B at the hem line.
B–C is ½ measurement A–C minus 4cm; square across to D.
Cut across the line and open 3cm.
Draw in four darts as shown, approx. 4.5cm each side of C and D: length = 6cm; width = 1.5cm.
Draw in lower panel line.
Draw in front pocket and front pocket facing.
Draw in side pocket, side pocket facing and pocket flap.
Draw in fly piece on front fork as shown: length = 19cm; width = 6cm.
Trace off front along the lower panel line.
Add seam allowance to lower panel line.
Front lower panel   Trace off the front lower panel.
Add seam allowance to the top edge.
Front pocket and facing   Trace off front pocket and pocket facing.
Add seam allowance to the top and inside edges of the pocket and pocket facing.
Side pocket   Trace off side pocket, cut up the centre; insert 4cm to create an inverted pleat.
Add seam allowance to all edges.
Side pocket facing   Trace off side pocket facing.
Add seam allowance to all edges.
Side pocket flap   Trace off side pocket flap; mirror pattern and mark the fold line.
Add 2cm seam allowance to top edge; 1cm seam allowance to side edges.
Fly piece   Trace off fly piece.
Add seam allowance to outer edges.
Back   Draw in back yoke.
Trace off back on yoke line and lower panel line.
Add seam allowance to yoke edge.
Add seam allowance to lower panel line.
Back yoke   Trace off yoke section, extend dart to touch yoke edge; close dart.
Add seam allowance to edge of yoke line.
Back lower panel   Trace off the back lower panel.
Add seam allowance to the top edge.
Waistband   Construct a double cloth waistband: length = trouser waist measurement plus 2cm ease; width = 8cm. Add a 4cm overlap to one end.
Mark fold line down centre.
Add seam allowance to all edges.

Combat shorts

For combat shorts cut across draft at length required.
Add 4cm hem allowance.

45

4 Combat trousers

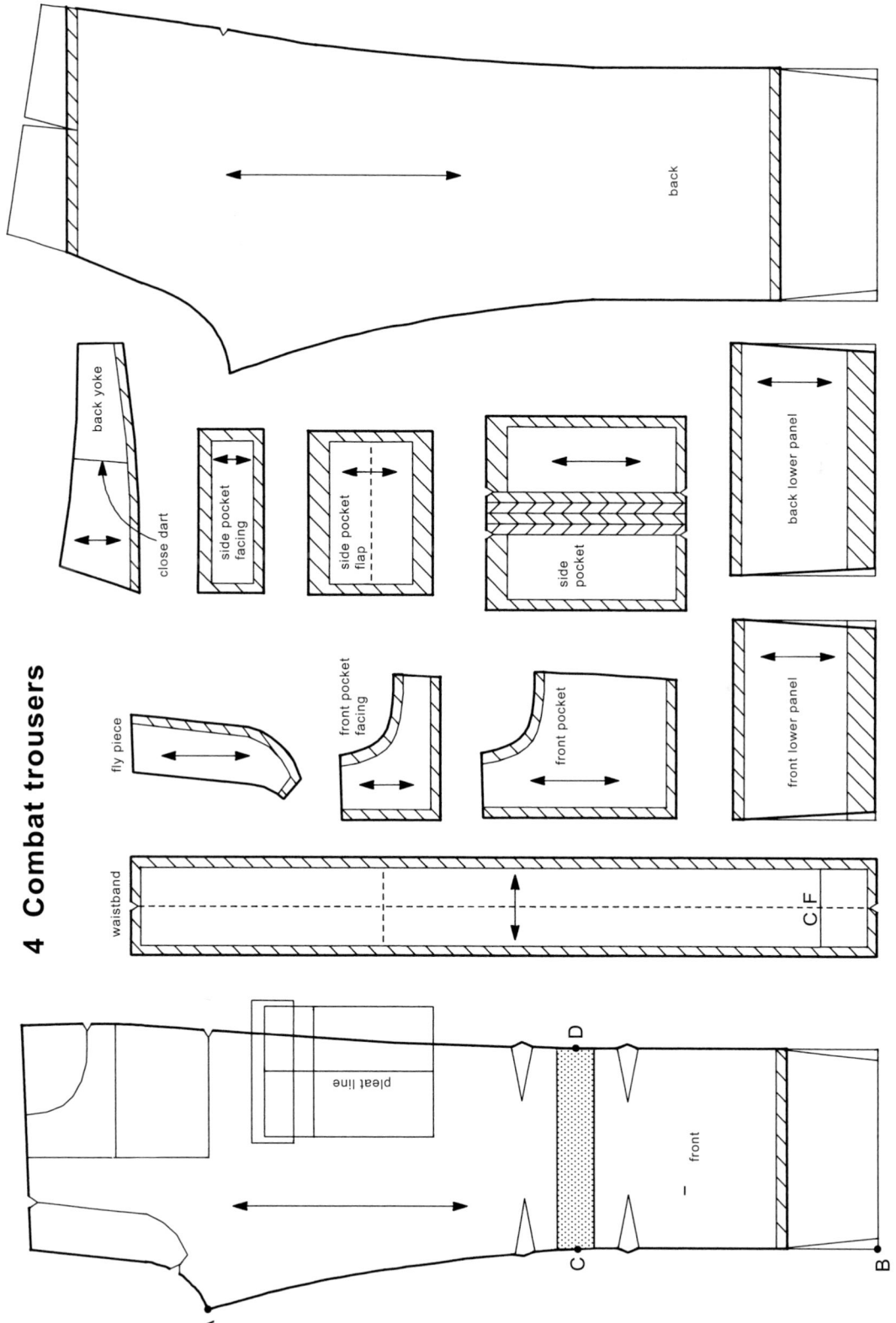

back

back yoke

close dart

side pocket facing

side pocket flap

side pocket

back lower panel

fly piece

front pocket facing

front pocket

front lower panel

waistband

C F

pleat line

front

A

B

C

D

5 Boxer shorts

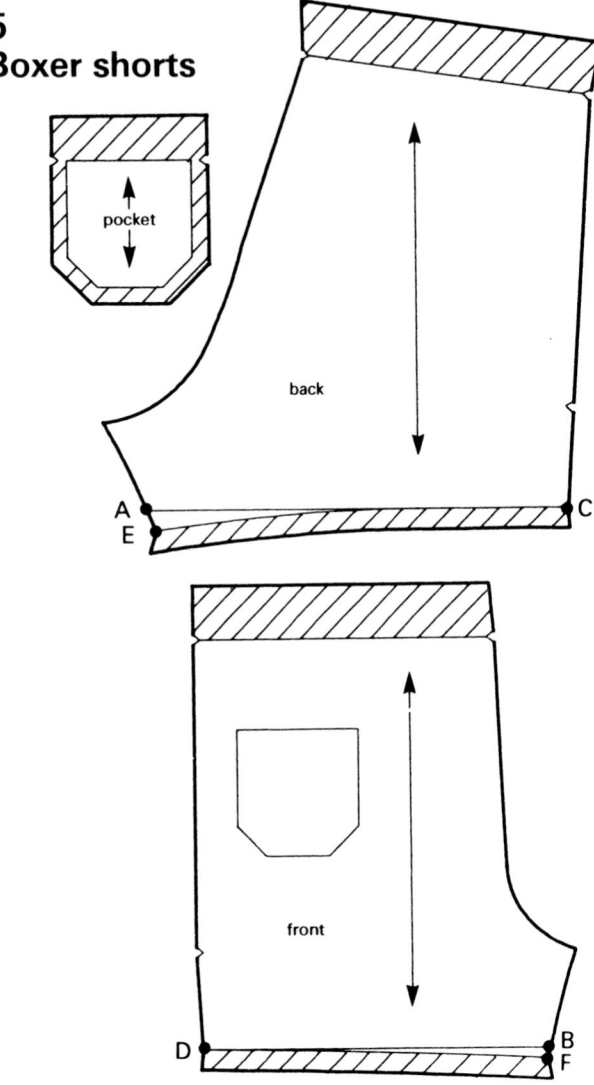

5 Boxer shorts

Back and front sections   Trace off the back and front sections of the 'flat' trouser block.
Reduce the block's crutch depth meas. by 3cm.
Draw in the length of shorts. Mark points A B C D.
A–E = 2cm. B–F = 1cm. Join C–E and D–F with curves.
Add 5cm casing to the top edge of the trousers.
Add 3cm hem allowance to the hem of the trousers.
Draw in pocket shape.
Pocket   Trace off pocket shape. Add 4cm to top edge.
Add seam allowance to remainder of the edges.
Note   For a separate waistband, remove the waistband depth measurement from the top edge of the shorts. Construct a waistband (ref. page 118).

6 Swimming trunks (stretch fabric)

0–1 varies with the amount of 'stretch' in the fabric.
The draft includes 0.5cm seam allowance.
Back   Square up and across from 0.
0–1   ¼ seat less 3cm.
1–2   16cm can be varied (dependent on design); square across to 3.
2–4   2.5cm; join 4–1 with a curved line.
3–5   3cm for casing; square across to 6.
0–7   ⅙ seat measurement plus 0.5cm; square across.
7–8   7cm; 8–9 is 2.5cm; join 9–1.
9–10   ⅓ the distance 9–1.
Draw in leg shaping. Curve inwards 0.5cm from 9–10; curve outwards 0.5cm from 10–1.
Front   Square up and across from 11.
Construct points 11–17 as for back (points 0–6).
11–18   ⅙ seat meas. less 1.5cm; square across.
18–19   10cm; square across.
18–20   8.5cm; square up to 21; join 21–12.
18–22   1.5cm; 22–23 is 1cm; join 23–19; join 23–20.
Curve 12–21 inwards 1cm, 21–20 0.5cm.
24 is midway between 20 and 21.
Draw curved line from 24–19; cut across this line.
Trace front and front gusset. Add seam allowance.

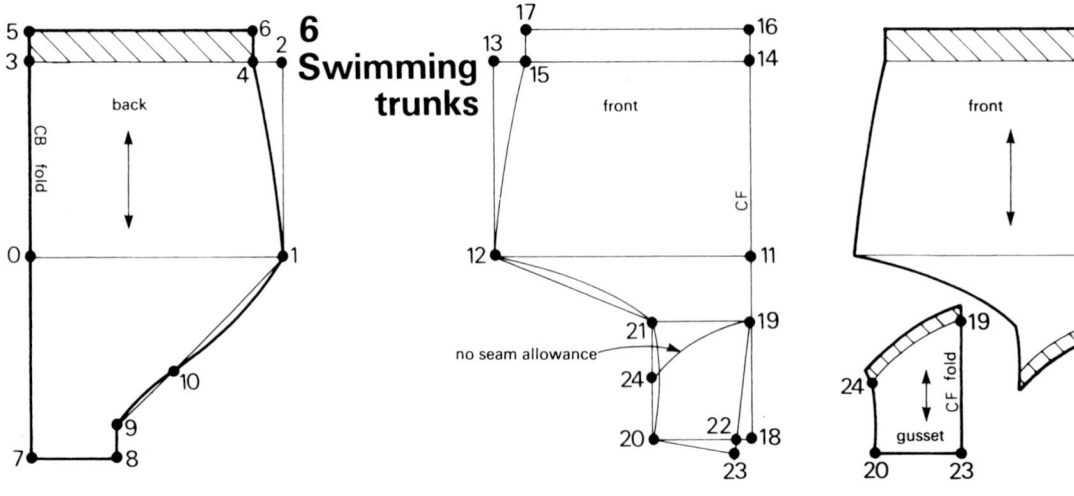

PART ONE: 'FLAT' CUTTING

Chapter 4 Workwear

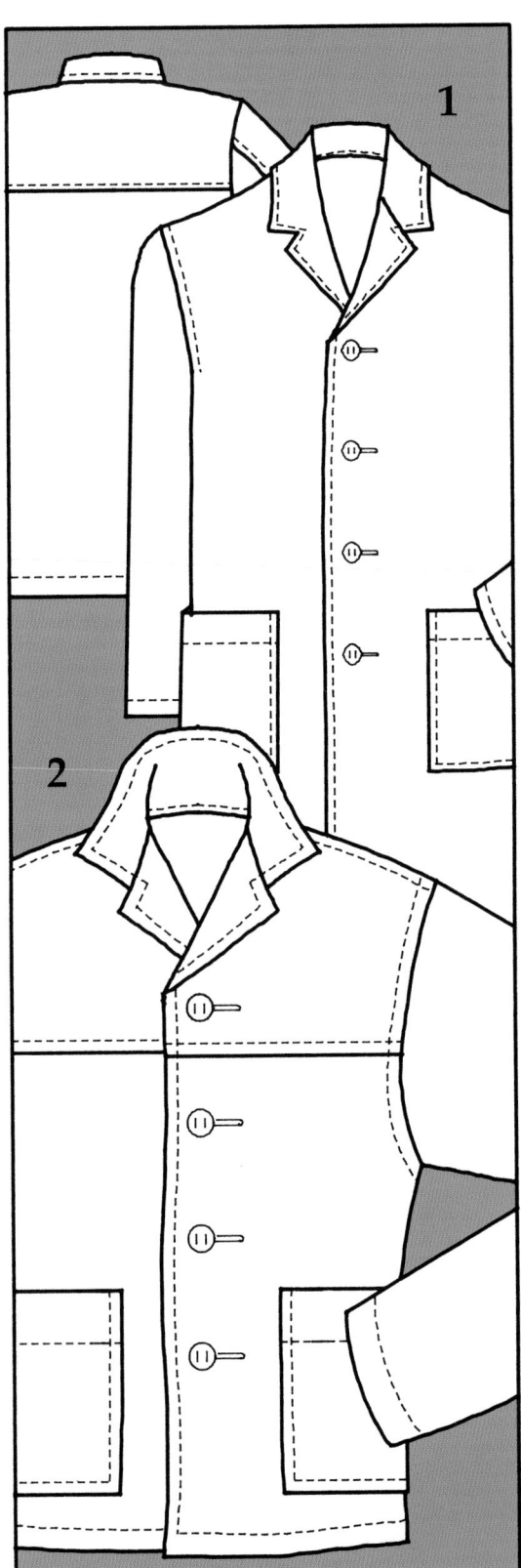

These adaptations demonstrate the flexibility of 'flat' blocks for cutting all forms of work overjackets and coats. For example, they can be used for indoor medical wear, warehouse protection and for all forms of outdoor work. Use the basic or easy fitting block options where appropriate.

1 Indoor work jacket or coat

Body sections   Trace off the basic overgarment block. Extend to the length required.

Mirror the front block to create separate sections.

Mark A at the centre front hem line.

A–B = 1cm. Draw a curved line from point B to the side seam line. Add 2.5cm button stand.

Mark buttonholes.

Draw in facing line. Draw in pocket shape.

Front   Construct an extended facing (ref. 1, page 80).

Add 4cm hem allowance.

Add seam allowance to facing edge and neckline.

Back   Trace off back section.

Add 4cm hem allowance, add seam allowance to neckline.

Collar   Construct a standard convertible collar (ref. 2a, page 88).

Pocket   Trace off pocket. Add 4cm facing to top edge. Add seam allowance to the remaining edges.

Sleeves   Mirror sleeve. Draw in elbow line midway between underarm and hem.

Mark point C on top of sleeve head, D and E on hem.

D–F is ½ the distance D–E. F–G = 2cm.

Mark H at back sleeve position on the sleeve head.

Join H–F and H–G with curves, curving out 0.7cm at the elbow line. Trace off sleeve sections.

Add 3cm hem allowance and 1cm seam allowance to back seam line.

2 Easy fitting overjacket or coat

Complete as above with the following extra instructions.

Body sections   Remove 2cm from front shoulder, add to back shoulder line. Place shoulder fitting lines together to make sure the neck line is drawn accurately.

Draw in back and front yoke lines.

Front   Trace off front sections.

Add 4cm hem allowance.

Add seam allowance to facing edge and top edge.

Front yoke Trace off front yoke.

Add seam allowance to facing edge, bottom edge and neckline.

Back   Trace off back section. Add 4cm hem allowance, add seam allowance to top edge.

Back yoke   Trace off back yoke.

Add seam allowance to bottom edge and neckline.

Sleeve   Add 4cm extra ease in the underarm before dividing the sleeve (ref. 1, page 64).

1 Indoor work jacket or coat

2 Easy fitting overjacket or coat

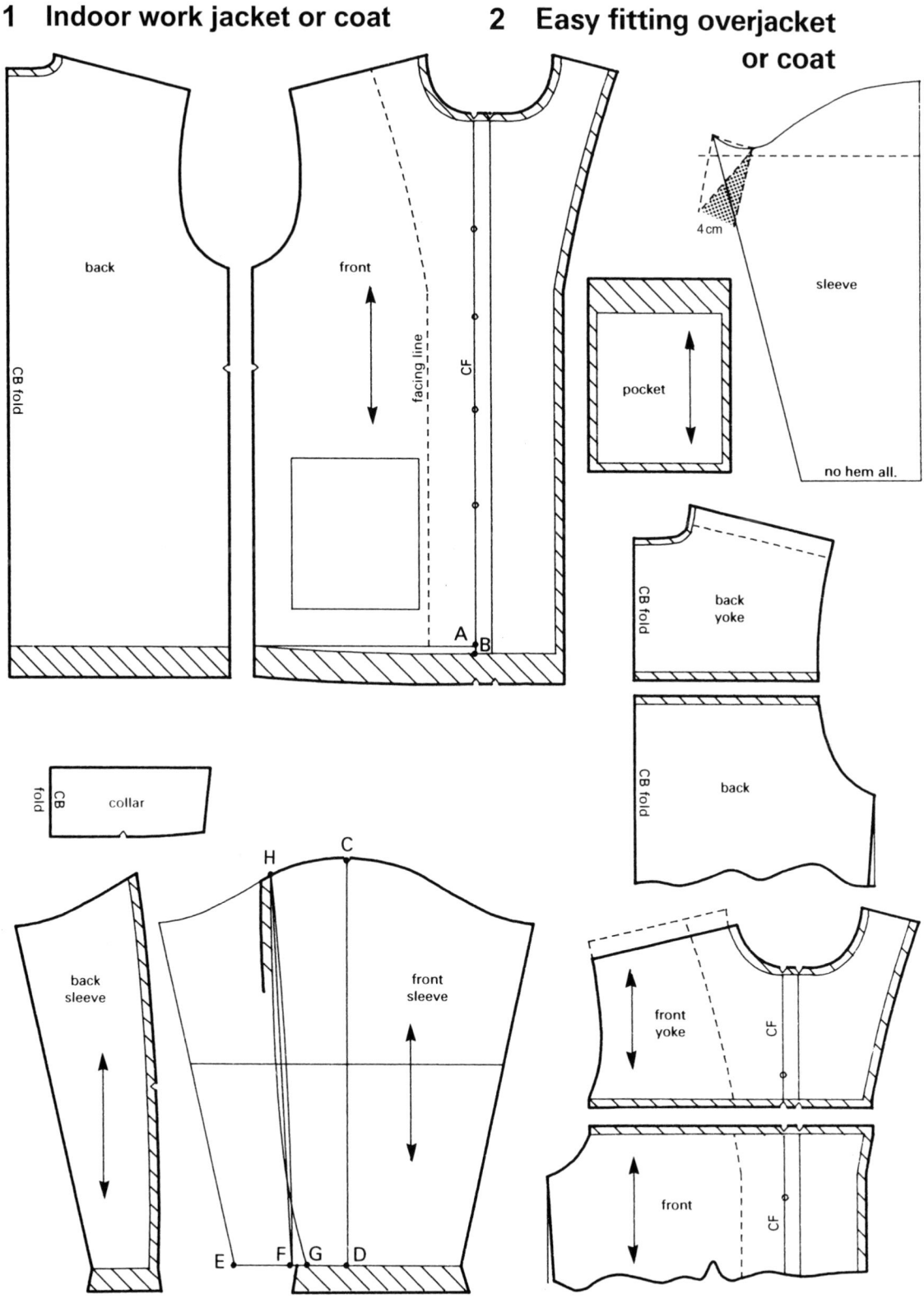

back

CB fold

front

facing line

CF

A B

collar

CB fold

back sleeve

H C

front sleeve

E F G D

sleeve

4 cm

no hem all.

pocket

back yoke

CB fold

back

CB fold

front yoke

CF

front

CF

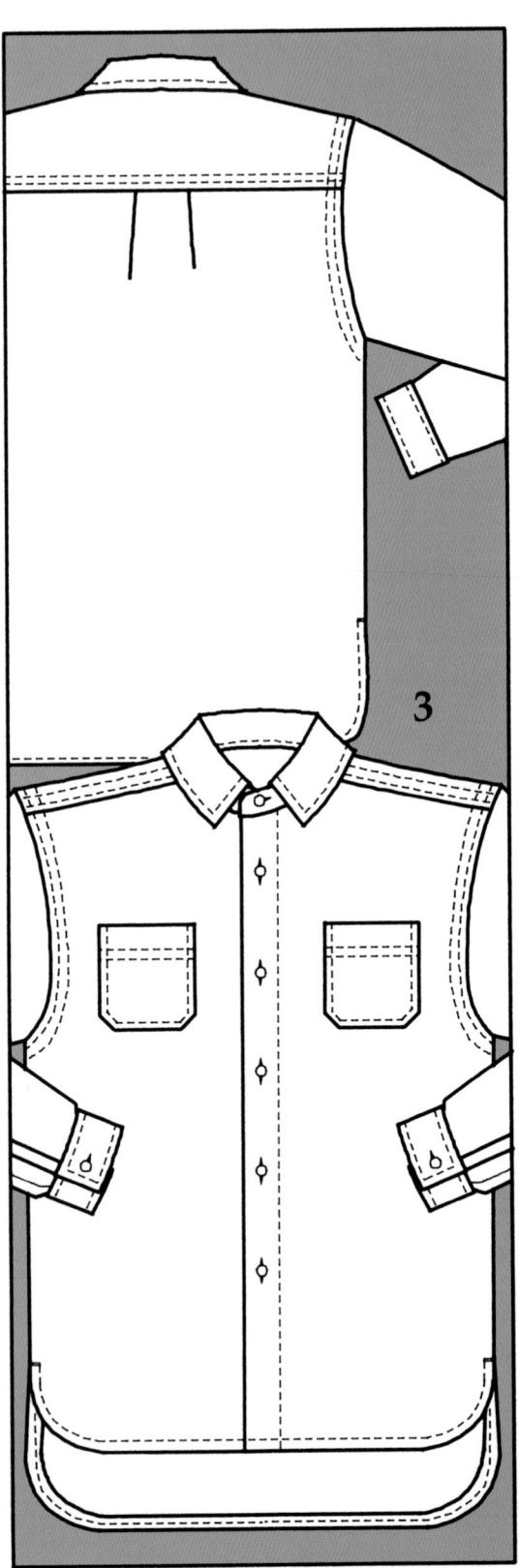

The 'flat' shirt block can be used for a wide range of work or casual shirts. Its simple shape allows the possibilities for many complex pockets, seams, pleats and other decorative features. The example shows the adaptation for a conventional type of work shirt.

3 Basic work shirt

Body sections   Trace off the 'flat' shirt block.
Mirror the front block.
Extend the shirt to the length required: make the back length 5cm longer than the front length.
Curve the side seams at the hem edge.
Remove 2.5cm from front shoulder, add to back shoulder line; (place shoulder fitting lines together to make sure the neckline is drawn accurately).
Add 1.5cm button stand. Mark buttonholes.
Add an extended facing of 3cm.
Draw in the back yoke line.

Front   Trace off front section.
Add 1.5cm seam allowance to bottom edge and 1cm to facing edge and neckline.

Back   Trace off back section.
Add 2.5cm to the centre back; mark tuck positions.
Add 1.5cm seam allowance to bottom edge and 1cm to the yoke line.

Back yoke   Trace off the back yoke.
Add 1cm seam allowance to yoke line and neckline.

Collar   Construct the draft for a shirt collar (ref. 3a, page 88).

Pockets   Trace off pocket. Add 3cm facing to top edge and 1cm seam allowance to the remaining edges.

Sleeves   Mirror sleeve. Shorten sleeve by 6cm.
Mark point A on top of sleeve head, B and C on hem.
C–D is ½ the distance E–C; mark sleeve placket line.
Mark tuck positions.
Add seam allowance to bottom edge.

Cuff   Construct a rectangle: width = 6cm; length = cuff size for shirts (ref. page 13) plus 2cm. Add seam allowance to all edges.

3 Basic work shirt

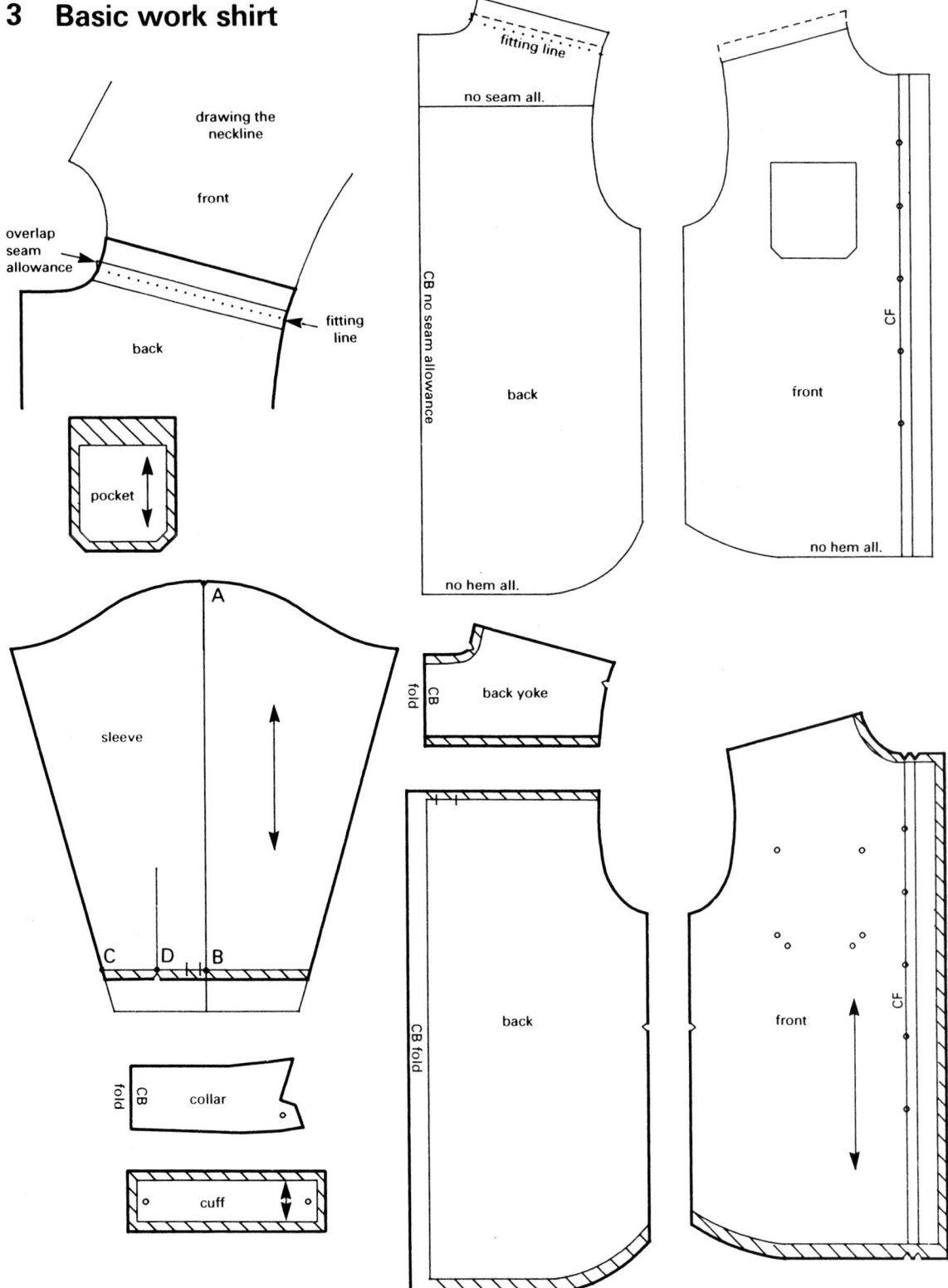

drawing the neckline

front

overlap seam allowance

fitting line

back

pocket

fitting line

no seam all.

CB no seam allowance

back

front

CF

no hem all.

no hem all.

sleeve

A

C D B

back yoke

CB fold

back

front

CF

fold CB collar

cuff

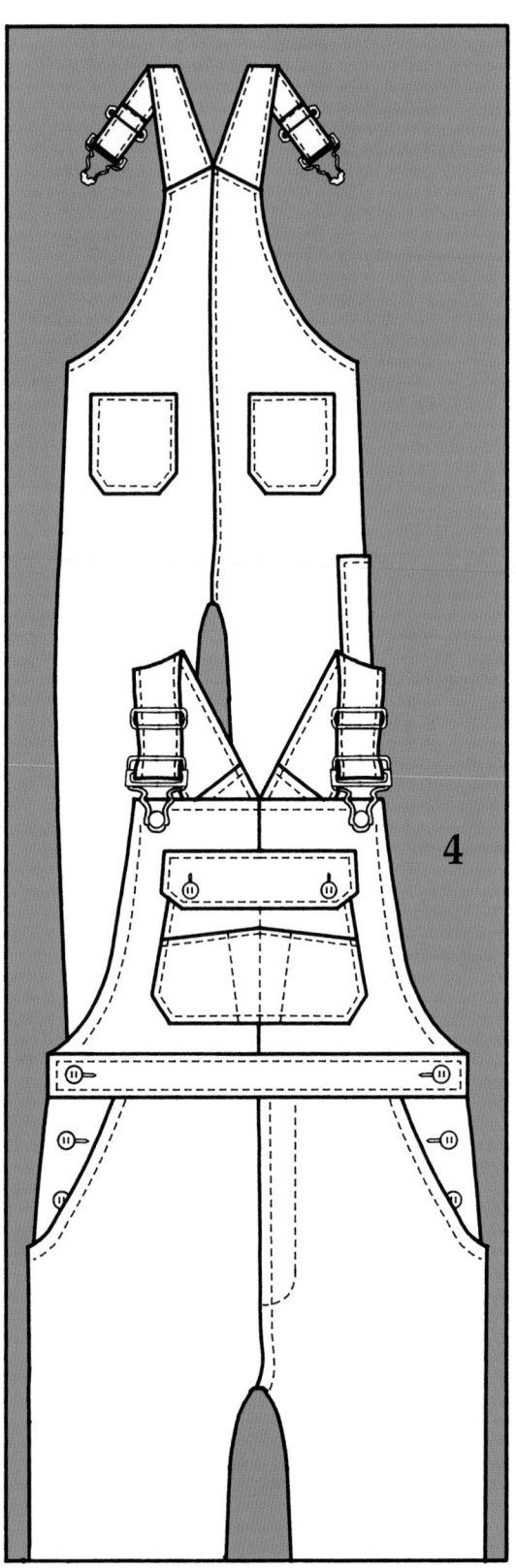

Dungarees can be constructed to be worn over other garments or as close or loose fitting garments depending on the block selected. The basic 'flat' two-piece trouser block was used for this adaptation.

4 Dungarees

Trace off the two-piece 'flat' trouser block.
Insert 5cm at the seat line to give extra body length.
Front trousers Trace off front section.
Mirror front trouser section.
Mark A at the centre front waistline. A–B = 23cm.
A–C = 6cm.
Draw in curved fly piece to the front edge from B–C.
Draw in front pocket lines. Draw in pocket bags. Trace off front section and side front.
Add 3cm hem allowance.
Add 1cm seam allowance to the top of the trousers.
Add 2cm seam allowance to pocket line.
Side front Trace off side front with pocket bag.
Add 4cm extension to the side edge.
Add 1cm seam allowance to top edge.
Front waistband Construct front waistband:
width = 3.5cm; length = the finished measurement of the top of the front trousers.
Add seam allowance to all edges.
Bib front Construct a shaped bib front approx.
27cm deep; top width approx. 30cm.
Draw in any pocket shapes required.
Add 2cm seam allowance to side and top edges.
Add 1cm seam allowance to bottom edge.
Front bib pockets Trace off pockets.
Add 2cm facing to top edge.
Add seam allowance to the remaining edges except the centre front fold line.
Pocket flaps Trace off pocket flaps, add seam allowance to all edges except the centre front fold line.
Back trousers Trace off back section.
Extend the side seam at the waist vertically 3.5cm.
Extend a shaped back approx. 30cm long to a top width of approx. 10cm.
Draw side seam extensions: width = 8cm; length = 21cm.
Draw in back pockets and a rule pocket at side seam.
Add 2cm seam allowance to side and top edges.
Add 3cm hem allowance.
Back pockets Trace off pockets. Add 2cm facing to top edge. Add seam allowance to the remaining edges.
Strap Construct a strap: width = 3.5cm shaping out to approx. 10cm (width of back top edge);
length = 50cm approx.
Add 2cm seam allowance to all edges.

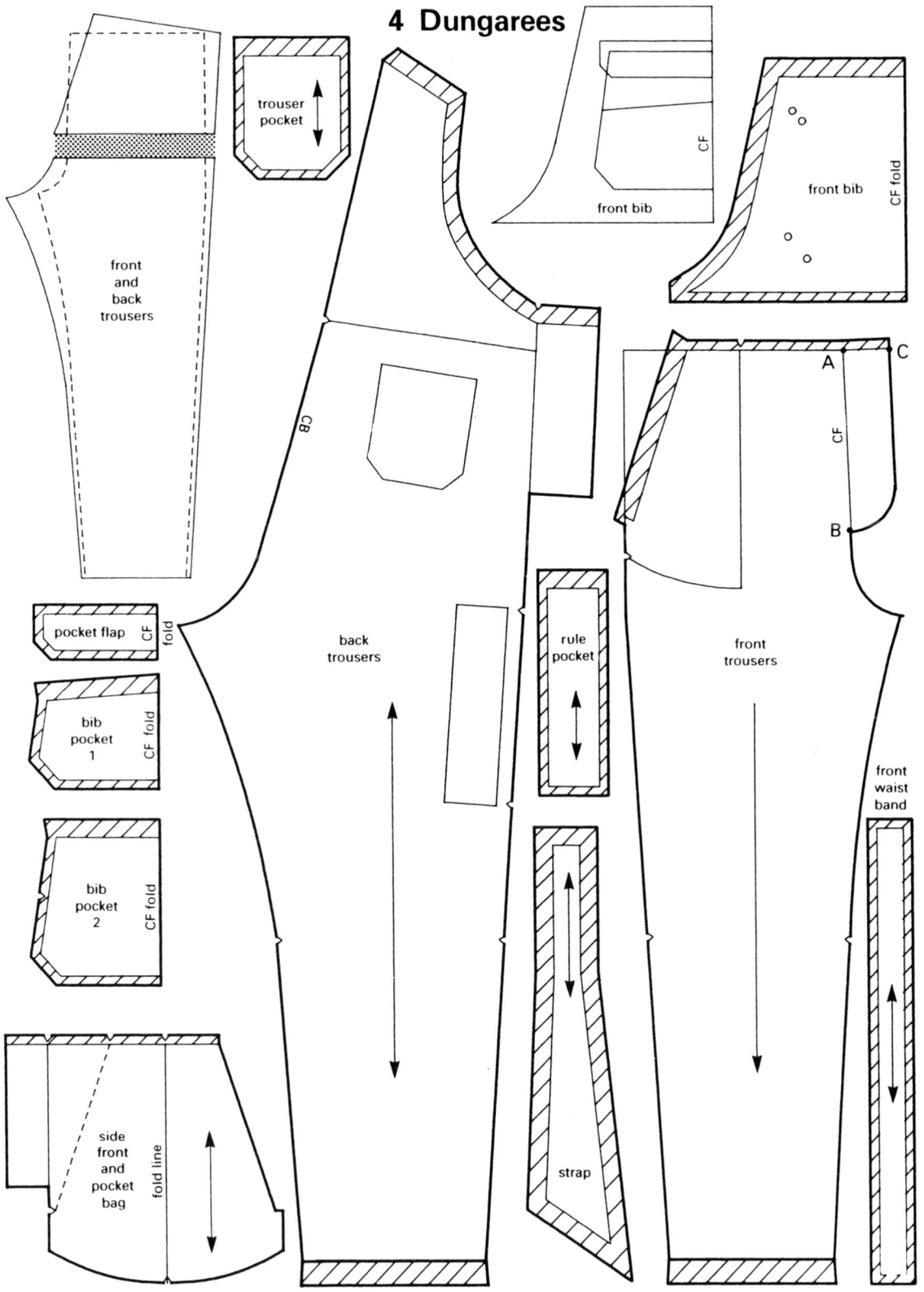

53

4 Dungarees

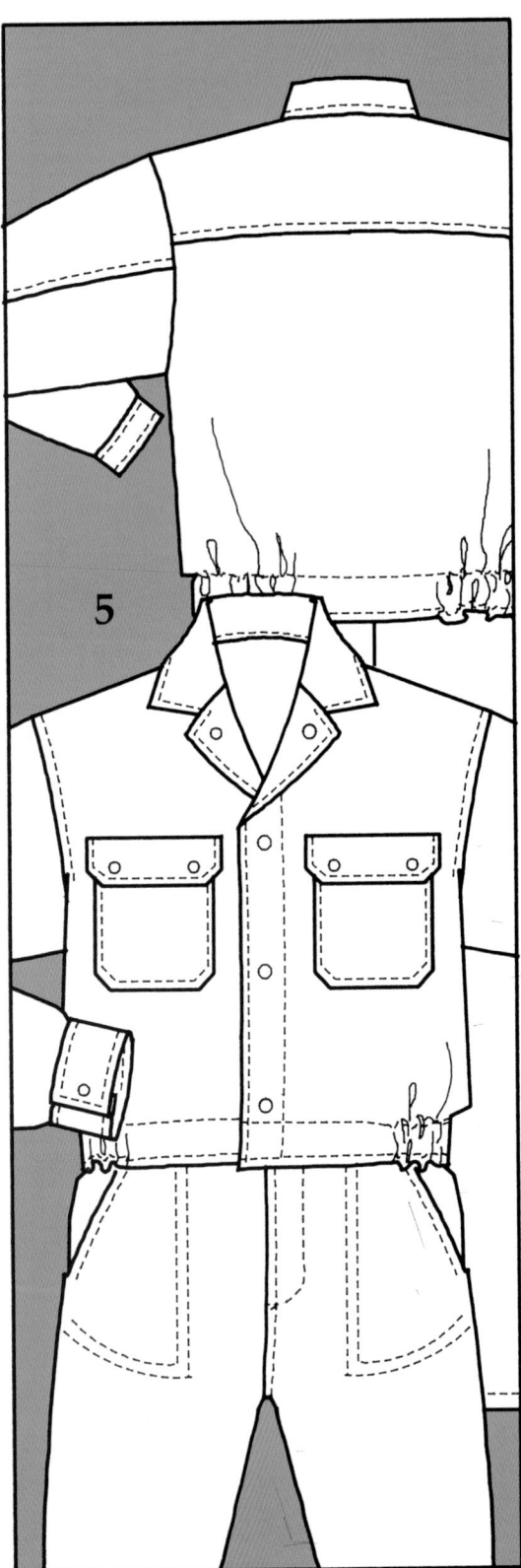

Overalls can be constructed to be worn over very different garments. Select the basic or easy fitting overgarment block.

5 One-piece overalls

Body and trouser sections   Trace off the selected block to waist length. Add 8cm of extra length to the body section below waistline.

Trace off the two-piece 'flat' trouser block.

Mirror front body and front trouser sections.

Insert 5cm at the seat line to give extra body length; (see jeans block page 40), 'crutch ease insertion'.

Insert 1.5cm ease down the centre of front and back trouser sections. Add 1cm to the side seam waist of the back trousers.

Adjust side seams of body sections to fit the measurement of the top of the trousers.

Construct a 7cm casing to this measurement.

Body sections

Front   Add 2cm button stand.

Mark stud positions. Draw in facing line.

Construct an extended facing (ref. 1, page 80).

Draw in pocket shape and pocket flaps.

Add seam allowance to facing, lower edge and neckline.

Back   Mark in back yoke line. Trace off back section.

Add seam allowance to top edge and waistline.

Back yoke   Trace off back yoke.

Add seam allowance to bottom edge and neckline.

Collar   Construct a convertible collar (ref. 2a, page 88).

Pocket   Trace off pocket. Add 2cm facing to top edge.

Add seam allowance to the remaining edges.

Pocket flaps   Trace off pocket flaps.

Add seam allowance to all edges.

Sleeves   Mirror sleeve. Shorten sleeve by 4cm.

Draw elbow line midway between underarm and hem.

Mark point A on top of sleeve head, B and C on hem.

B–D is ½ the distance B–C. D–E = 2cm.

Mark H at back sleeve position on the sleeve head.

Join H–D and H–E with curves, curving out 0.7cm at the elbow line. Mark tuck position.

Trace off sleeve sections. Add 1cm seam allowance to back seam lines and bottom edges.

Cuff   Construct a rectangle: width = 5cm; length = cuff size for shirts (ref. page 13) plus 2cm.

Add seam allowance to all edges.

Trouser sections

Front trousers   Mark F at the centre front waistline.

F–G = 23cm. F–H = 2cm. Join G–H.

Add 6cm extended facing to front edge from G–H.

Draw in front pocket line and pocket bags.

Trace off front and side front with pocket bag.

Add 1cm seam allowance to the top of both trouser sections. Add 3cm hem allowance.

Back trousers   Trace off back section.

Add 1cm seam allowance to the top of the trousers.

Add 3cm hem allowance.

5 One-piece overalls

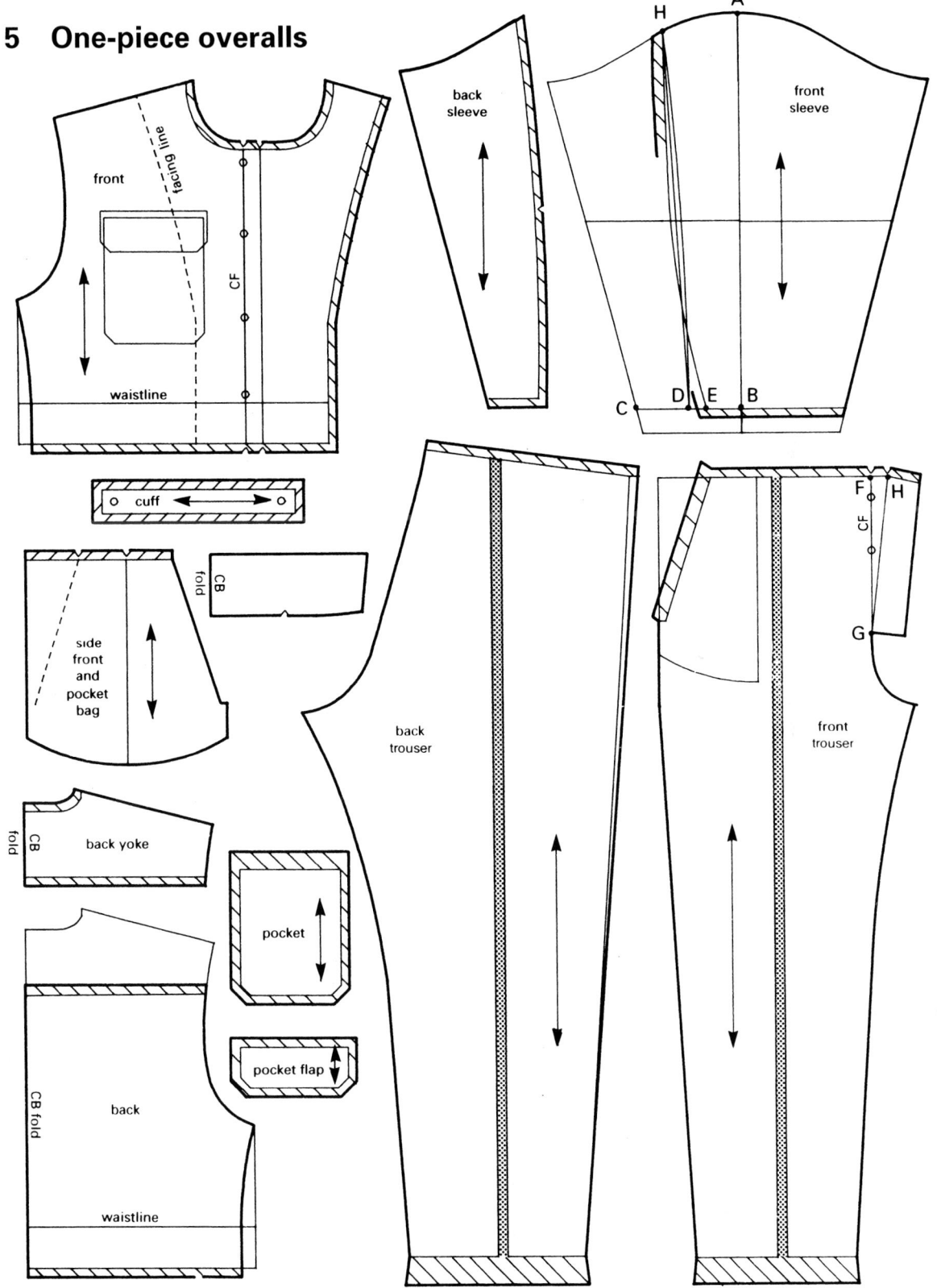

Two-piece overalls

The one-piece overalls can be manufactured as
two separate garments.

6　Work jacket

The top section can be constructed as for a
one-piece overall.
Add 5cm to the length of the back and front sections.
Add 7cm to the hem line of back and front sections
for an elasticated facing.

7　Work trousers

Separate work trousers can be constructed.
The two-piece or one-piece 'flat' trouser blocks
can be used for a wide range of work trousers.

For example, medical wear or for more robust forms
of workwear.
Select either the basic or easy fitting blocks where
appropriate.
The blocks are drafted to sit approximately 2–4cm
above the trouser waist position. This can be
adjusted if required.
To add hem and waist casings, trouser fly or side
pockets see the trouser adaptations on page 38.
Waistbands　If a waistband is required remove 4cm
from the top of the trousers.
Construct a double cloth waistband for the trouser
waist measurement required (ref. 1c, page 118).

PART ONE: 'FLAT' CUTTING

Chapter 5 Basic nightwear

A 'form' cut classic dressing gown adaptation with a two-piece sleeve has been placed in Chapter 11, Classic and casual overgarments.

The pyjama block

Measurements required to draft the block
(e.g. size MEDIUM) refer to the size chart (page 15
for SMALL, MEDIUM, LARGE, XLARGE sizes.

Chest	100cm
Scye depth	24.4cm
Back neck to waist	44.2cm
Neck size	40cm
Half back	20cm
Sleeve length one-piece sleeve	65cm
Seat	102cm
Trouser waist position	90cm
Body rise	28.2cm
Inside leg	80cm

A 1cm seam allowance is included in the block
except where stated *no seam allowance.*

Pyjama jacket
Body section   square both ways from 0.
0–1   scye depth plus 3.5cm; square across.
0–2   back neck to waist plus 1cm; square across.
0–3   pyjama jacket length plus 1cm; square across.
1–4   ½ chest plus 10cm; square up to 5, down to 6.
0–7   ⅕ measurement 0–1 less 2cm; square across.
0–8   ⅕ neck size plus 0.2cm; square up.
8–9   2.5cm; draw in neck curve.
1–10   half back plus 3.5cm; square up to 11.
11–12   0.5cm; join 9–12.
10–13   ½ measurement 10–11.
5–14   ⅕ neck size minus 0.5cm.
5–15   ⅕ neck size minus 0.5cm; draw in neck curve.
11–16   1.5cm; square across.
14–17   the measurement 9–12.
1–18   ⅓ chest plus 2.5cm.
18–19   2.5cm; join 17–19.
17–20   ½ measurement 17–19.
20–21   1.5cm.
18–22   ½ measuremnt 10–18; square down
to 23, 24.
Draw in armhole 12, 13, 22, 19, 21, 17.
6–25   1cm; join 24–25.

Sleeve   Square down from O.
0–1   ¼ arm scye measurement (see page 139
measuring a curve); square across.
0–2   sleeve length plus 1cm; square across.
0–3   ½ arm scye measurement plus 1cm; square
down to 4.
0–5   ½ arm scye measurement plus 1cm; square
down to 6.
Divide 0–3 into four sections, mark 7, 8, 9.
Divide 0–5 into four sections, mark 10, 11, 12.
Draw sleeve head; raise 1cm at 8, 2cm at 9; raise 1cm
at 10, hollow 1cm at 12.
4–13   6cm; 6–14 is 6cm; join 3–13, 5–14.

Pyjama trousers
Front   Square down and across from 0.
0–1   body rise plus 1cm; square across.
1–2   inside leg measurement; square across.
2–3   ½ measurement 1–2 plus 6cm; square across.
1–4   ¼ seat measurement plus 4cm; square up to 5,
down to 6 and 7.
4–8   ¼ measurement 4–5.
4–9   ¹/₁₂ seat measurement minus 0.5cm; draw
in front fork through points 9, 8, 5.
7–10   4cm. Draw inside leg seam 9, 6, 10; curve
in 9–6 1.5cm.

Back
5–11   2.5cm; square up.
11–12   4cm.
4–13   ½ measurement 4-5.
9–14   ¹/₁₂ seat measurement minus 0.5cm.
14–15   1cm. Join 12–13; join 13–15 with a curve.
Join 12–0 with a slight curve.
6–16   4cm.
10–17   3cm.
Draw inside leg seam 15, 16, 17, curve in 15–16
1.75cm.
2–18   2.5cm. Draw in new side seam line.
Note   Front and back of pyjama trousers are usually
cut in one piece; side seam line 0–18 becomes the
grain line.

To complete a pattern for pyjama jacket
Add 2cm button stand, mark buttonholes.
Add 7cm extended facing. Draw in pocket shape.
23-A is 1.25cm; 23-B is 1.25cm; square down
from A and B.
Shape side seam from 22 to A and B.
Add 2cm hem allowance. Add seam allowance
to side seam.
Collar   construct convertible collar (ref. 2a, page 88).
Pocket   trace off pocket, add 3cm facing to top edge.
Add seam allowance to remainder of the edges.
Sleeve   add 2.5cm hem allowance.

To complete a pattern for pyjama trousers (elasticated waistline)
Add 6cm to front fork for fly piece to point 8.
5–19   8cm.
Add 4.5cm to top of waistline from 19 to outer
edge of fly piece.
Add 2cm hem allowance.
Construct a casing for the waistline: length = top of
trouser measurement; width = 7cm.

Nightshirt adaptation
Trace off the pyjama jacket to the length required.
Make back length 8cm longer than the front length.
Curve hems as for a shirt (ref. 3, page 50).

Pyjama jacket

Pyjama trousers

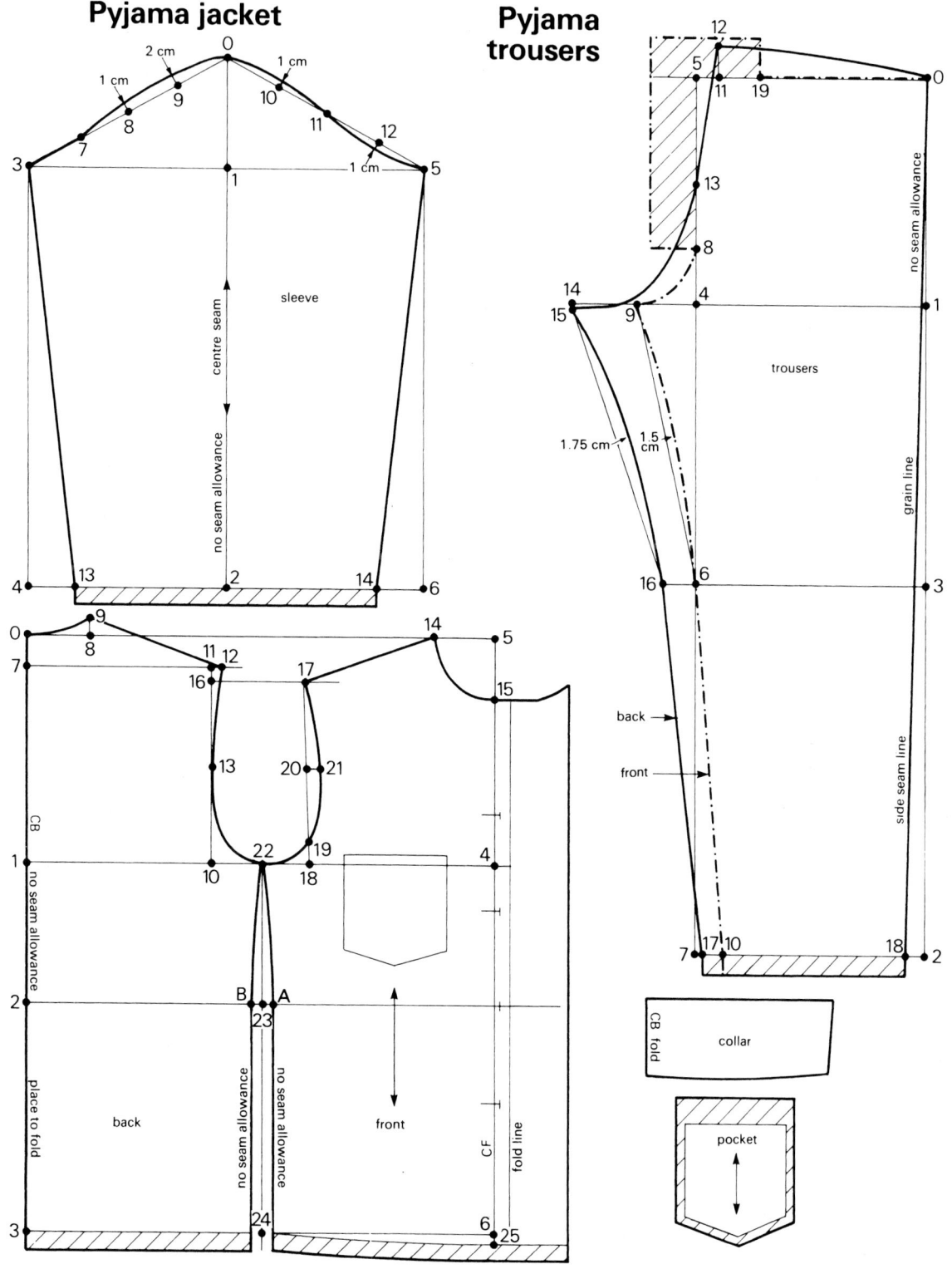

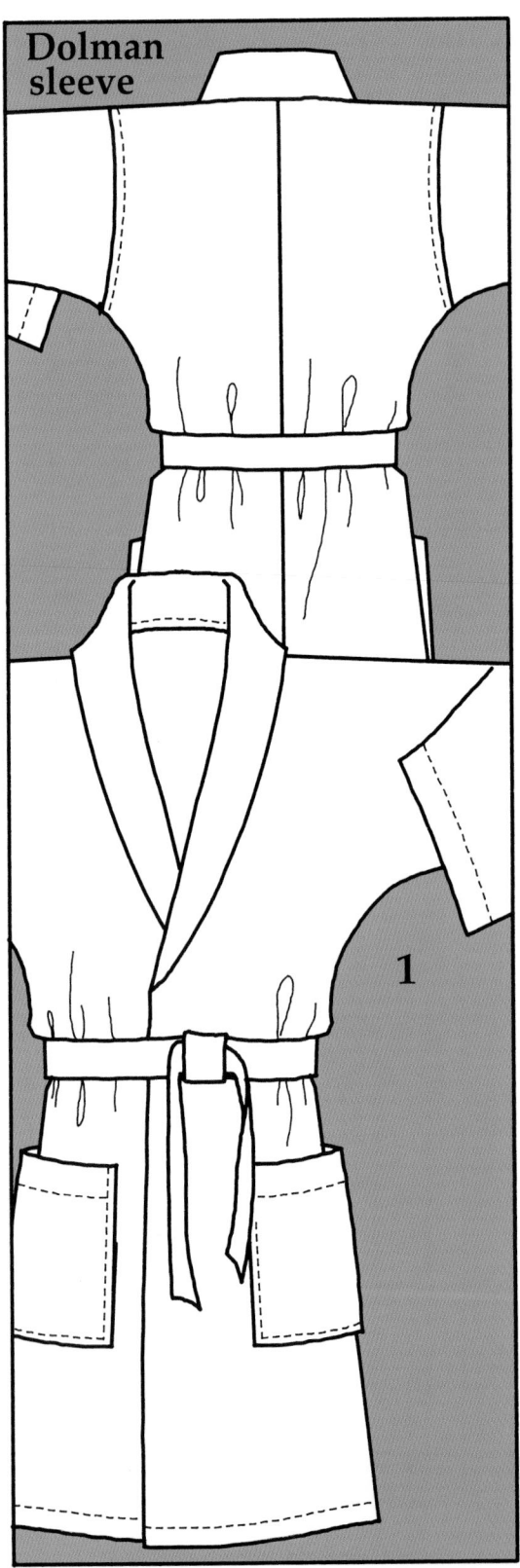

Dolman sleeve

1

1 Bathrobe

Back and front sections
Trace off the 'flat' easy fitting overgarment block.
Construct the 'flat' kimono block (ref. page 26).
Draw in finished length.
Shorten sleeve length approx. 12cm if required.
Mark A at underarm point, B at waistline, C at sleeve hem.
A–D ¼ measurement A–B.
C–E 1.5cm; join D–E.
B–F 4cm square down to hem and up to the line D–E.
Curve underarm seam as shown.
Add 3cm flare at hem.
Back   Trace off the back section.
Add seam allowance to the centre back line.
Add 5cm allowance to hem and sleeve hem.
Front   Trace off and mirror the front section.
G–H is 1cm.
Mark I at side seam hemline.
Join H–I with a curved line.
Add 6cm button stand.
Mark point 1 at break point.
Mark point 2 at neck point on fitting line.
Construct a standard roll collar (ref. 4, page 90).
Draw in required pocket shape 6cm below waistline.
Add 5cm allowance to hem and sleeve hem.
Lower and upper facings   Complete the instructions for the facing and top collar (ref. 4, page 90).
Add required seam allowances for that adaptation.
Pocket   Trace off pocket shape.
Add 4cm to top edge for facing.
Add seam allowance to remainder of the edges.
Belt   Construct belt, length 200cm and twice width required plus 2cm.

Dolman Sleeve adaptation   More efficient lay plans can be made if there is a sleeve seam in the bathrobe. Use the Dolman Sleeve adaptation (ref. 1, page 64) to create a sleeve seam.

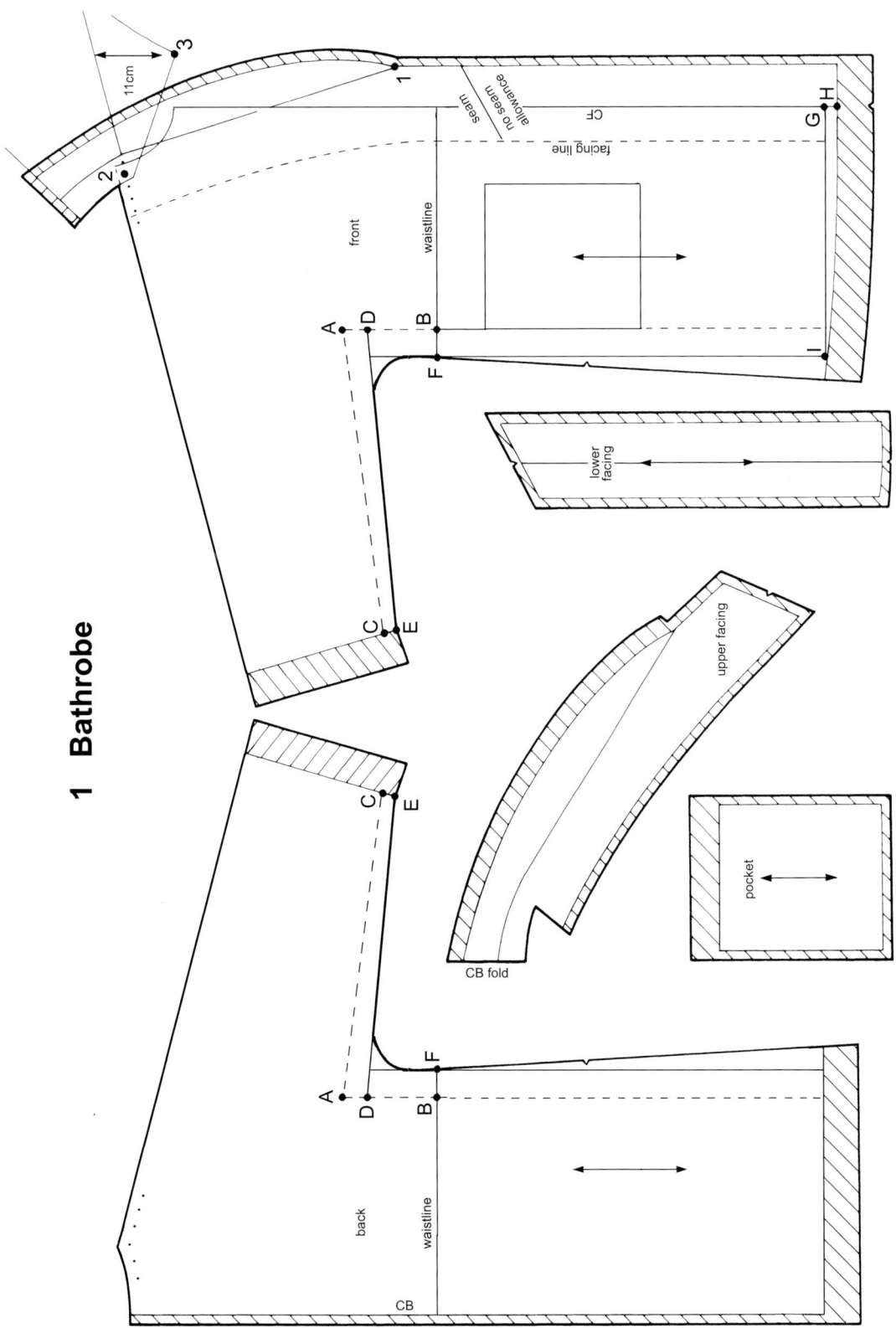

1 Bathrobe

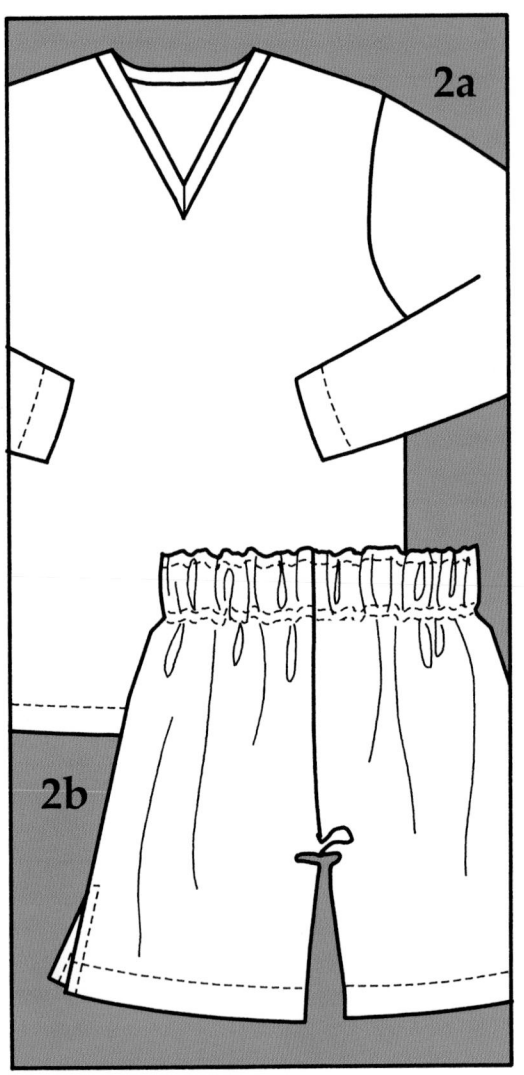

Jersey nightwear

2a   Jersey nightwear – tops
These tops are very standard shapes. Trace off the easy
fitting tee shirt block or the basic jersey overgarment block
depending on the garment fit required.
Style the neckline as required.
Add 4cm hem allowances to sleeve and hemlines.

2b   Jersey nightwear – pants
Trace off either the basic or easy fitting two-piece trouser
block depending on the garment fit required.
Reduce the body rise measurement by 2cm.
Use the adaptation instructions for casual jersey trousers
(ref. 2, page 38).

Shorter length pants
Complete adaptation as above.
Make inside leg seam length approx. 24cm.
Add 4cm hem allowance.
Add 4cm side vent allowance; length = 10cm.

PART TWO: STANDARD PATTERN CUTTING PROCESSES

Chapter 6 Constructing sleeves

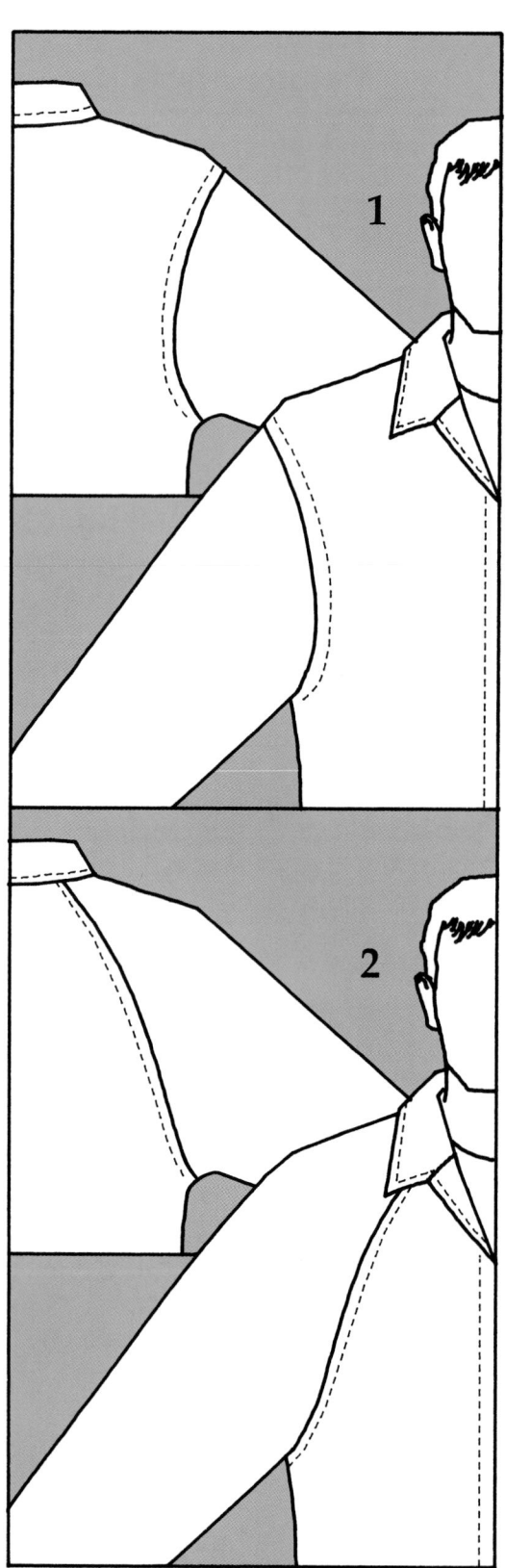

Sleeves – 'flat' cutting

Using the 'flat' kimono block

The 'flat' kimono block (page 26) can be used for many easy fitting 'flat' sleeve adaptations.
For the following adaptations a curved underarm shape is required.
Mark point A at the underarm point B at the waistline.
B–C is ½ the measurement A–B.
A–D is the measurement A–C.
Draw a curved line from C–D.

1 Dolman Sleeve ('flat' kimono block)

Body sections   Trace round the selected kimono block with curved underarm seam (see the instructions at the top of this page).
Draw in the armhole shape required to centre of the underarm curve.
Mark points A and B on armhole line.
B–C is ½ measurement A–B.
Draw a curved dart from B–C approx. 1cm wide.
Trace off back and front body sections.
Add seam allowance to armhole seams.
Sleeve   Trace off sleeve section.
B–D is ½ the measurement B–C.
B–E = B–D.
Cut along the line D–E, open approx. 3cm.
Re-draw the underarm sleeve seam with a smooth curve.
Raise the sleeve head at A approx. 1cm.
Re-draw the sleeve head curving the line.
Add seam allowance to sleeve head.

2 Raglan sleeve ('flat' kimono block)

Body sections   Trace round the selected kimono block with curved underarm seam (see the instructions at the top of this page).
Draw a shaped raglan line from neckline to centre of underarm curve.
Mark points A at neckline, B at underarm point.
B–C is ⅓ measurement A–B.
From C draw a curved dart on raglan line; width 1cm.
Mark points D and E on shoulder seams.
Trace off body sections; mirror the front section.
Add seam allowance to raglan seams.
Sleeve   Trace off back and front sleeve sections.
Mirror the front sleeve.
Draw a perpendicular line.
Place the sleeve points D and E to the line.
On front and back sleeve:-
B–F is the measurement B–C.
B–G is approx. 7cm.
Cut along the line G–F, open approx. 4cm.
Re-draw the underarm sleeve seams with a smooth curve.
Re-draw the raglan seams with a smooth curve.
Add seam allowance to raglan sleeve seams.

65

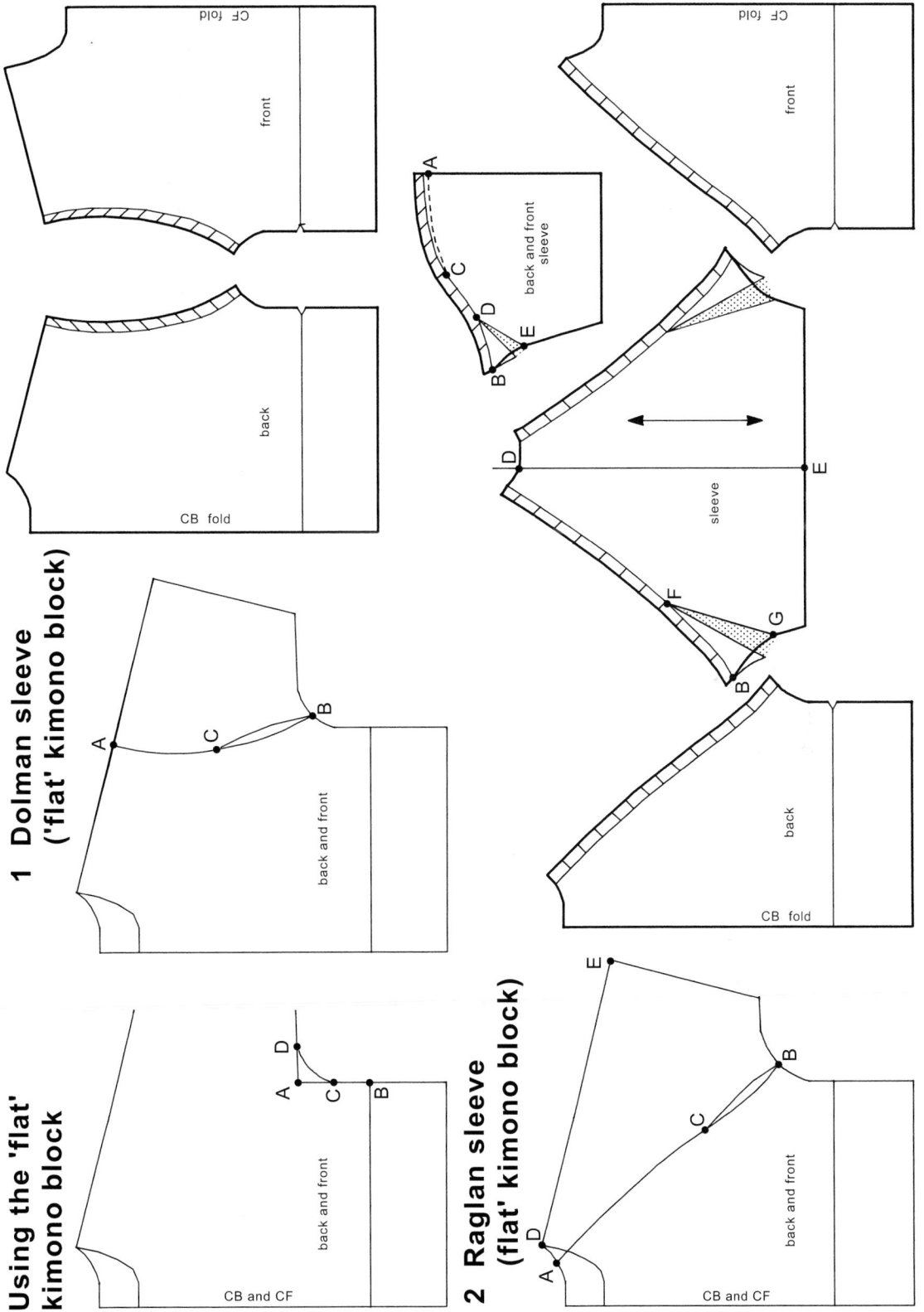

Using the 'flat' kimono block

1 Dolman sleeve ('flat' kimono block)

2 Raglan sleeve ('flat' kimono block)

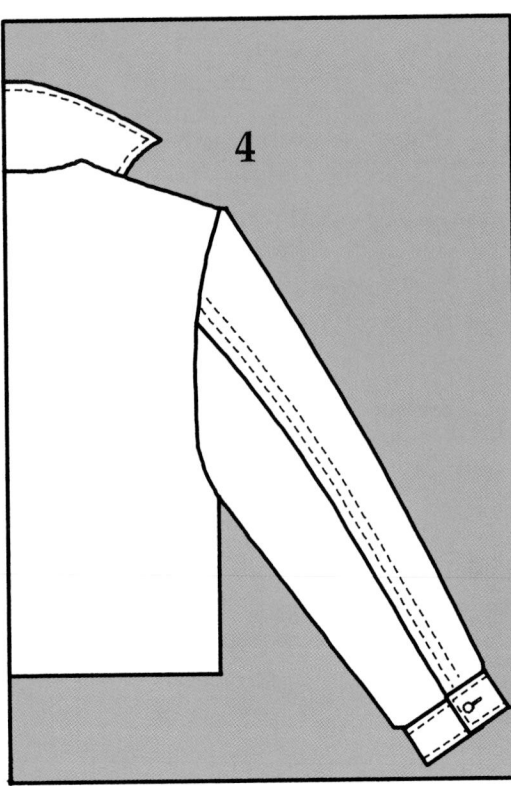

Sleeves – 'flat' or 'form' cutting

3 Modification to 'flat' blocks (menswear shaping)

This adaptation creates extra length to the back armhole. It reflects the male stance and extra muscle development of the back shoulders.

Back Trace round back section of block required.
Mark point A on armhole mid-way between shoulder and armhole depth line. Square across to B.
Cut across the line A–B and open 1.5cm.
Re-draw the back armhole making a smooth curve.

Sleeve Mirror front sleeve, to create a one-piece sleeve.
Mark point C at back underarm point. Square across to D on the centre line.
C–E is midway between C–D.
Square up to F and down to G.
Cut up the line G–F and open 1.5cm.
Re-draw the back sleeve head making a smooth curve.

4 Shaped sleeve with back seam

Sleeve Trace round a one-piece sleeve block. (Mirror sleeve if using a flat block without modification).
Mark point A at back underarm point B at wrist point.
Square across from A to C on centre line.
D is midway between A–B; square across.
A–E is ½ measurement A–C plus 2cm; square up to F, and down to G and H.
H–I is 2.5cm. H–J is 1.5cm.
Draw front sleeve curve from F to I, curving the line outwards 0.75cm at G on elbow line.
Draw back seam curve from F to J curving the line outwards 0.75cm at G on elbow line.
Trace off back and front sections.
Add seam allowance to sleeve seams.

5 Closer fitting kimono blocks

The block is used for designs based on a kimono shape but require a closer fit around the armhole. Any 'flat' or 'form' inset sleeve block can be used.

Back Trace back section of the block required.
Mark points 1 and 2 on the side seam.
1–3 is 5cm; square across.
3–4 is 3.5cm; square down to 5.
Mark point 6 at shoulder point, 7 at neck point.
Divide sleeve from balance point at sleeve head.
Place back sleeve to back body section. Place underarm point of sleeve to point 6. (Depending on the block used the sleeve may not touch this point exactly.)
6–8 is 1.5cm. Join 7–8 and 8–9 at wrist point.

Front Construct the front as for the back.

3 Modification to the 'flat' blocks

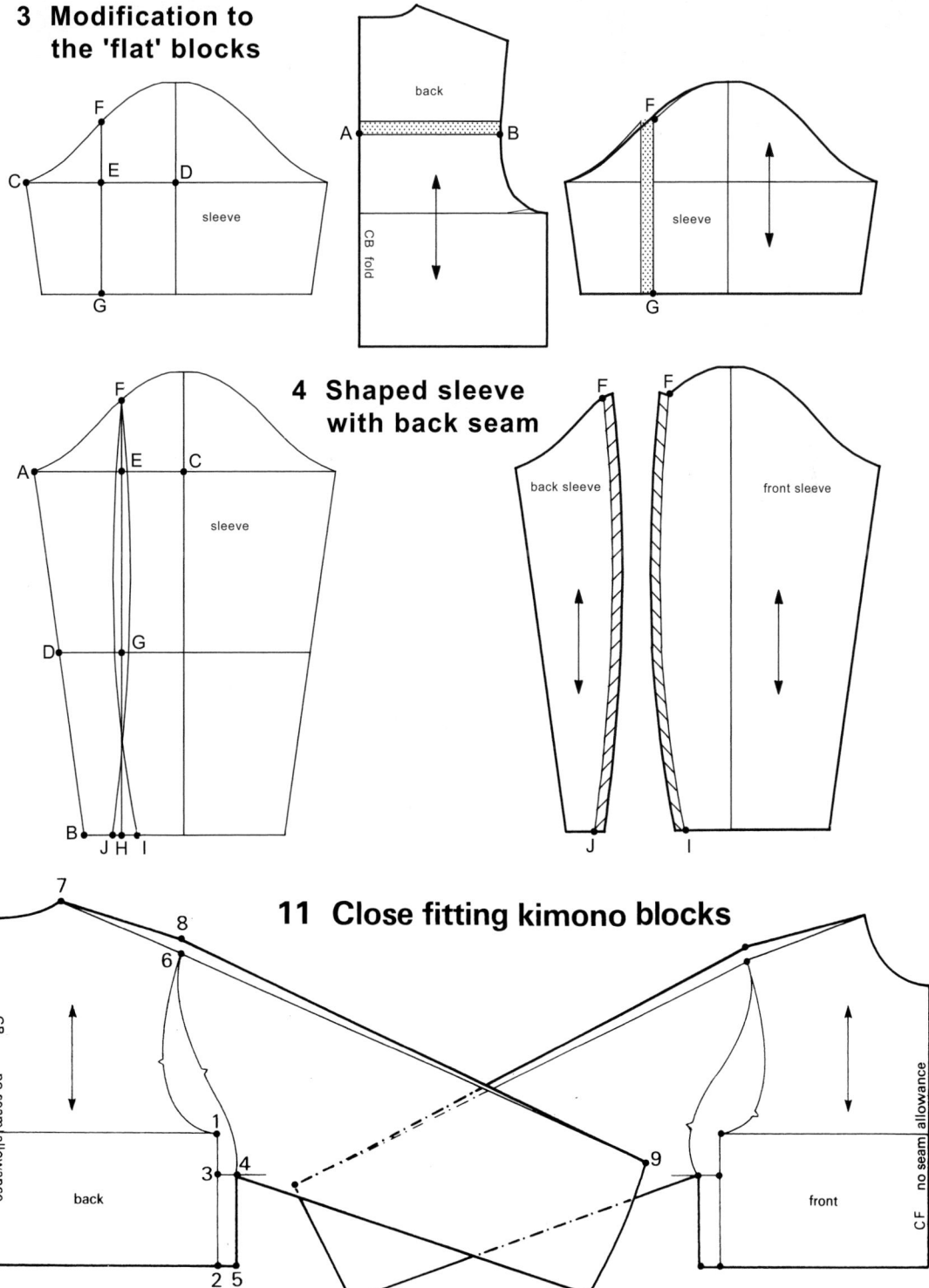

back

A ⋯⋯ B

CB fold

F
C E D
sleeve
G

F
sleeve
G

4 Shaped sleeve with back seam

F
A E C
sleeve
D G
B
J H I

F
back sleeve
J

F
front sleeve
I

11 Close fitting kimono blocks

7
8
6
CB
no seam allowance
1
3 4
back
2 5

9
front
CF no seam allowance

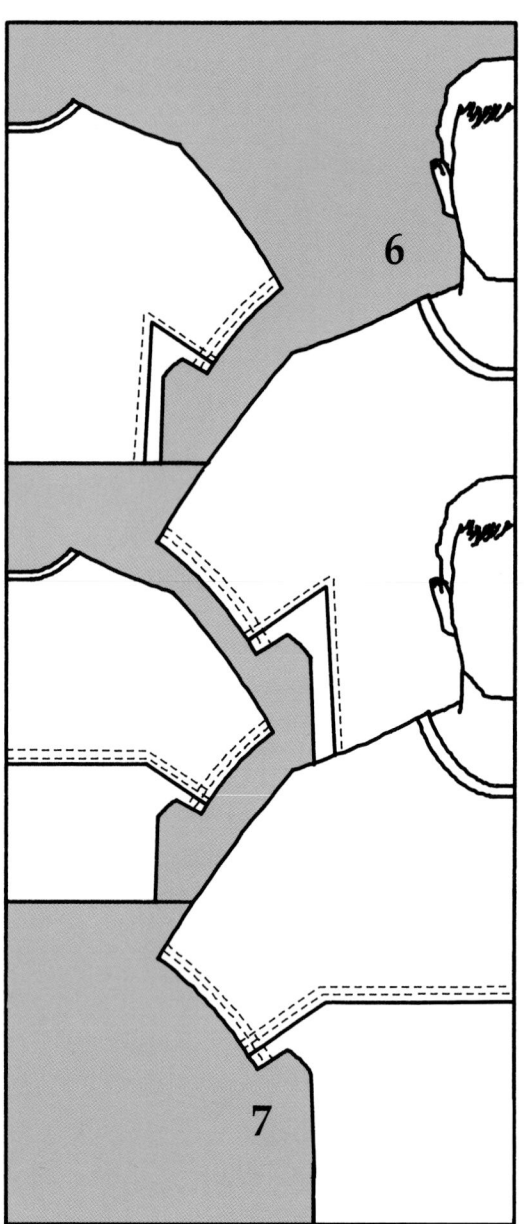

6 Simple gusseting (closer fitting kimono blocks)

Back and front Trace round kimono block, mark points A and B approximately 40cm from wrist points. Join A–B. Mark C at underarm, D at waistline of side seam.
A–E is 5cm; draw a line parallel to A–C.
D–F is 5cm; square up to G on the line from E.
Side panel Draw a vertical line from point H.
Cut away back section F, G, E.
Cut up line from C–G.
Open the line C–G so that C–A and C–D can be placed to the vertical line.
Cut away front section. Place to vertical line as for the back to make a diamond shaped gusset and to complete side panel.
Add seam allowance to outer seams as shown.
Seam allowance will be required along panel seams on back and front body sections.

7 Seam styling with gusset (closer fitting kimono blocks)

Back and front Trace round kimono block, mark points A and B approximately 40cm from wrist points.
Join A–B.
Mark C at underarm, D at waistline of side seam.
A–E is 5cm; draw a line parallel to A–C.
D–F is 5cm; square up with a dotted line to touch the line from E at point G.
Square across to centre back line at H.
Lower back and front panel Cut along back and front yoke lines (e.g. E, G, H).
Draw a vertical line from point J.
Cut up line from C–G on lower back section; place the line C–D to vertical line from J.
Open the line C–G so that C–A and C–D can be placed to the vertical line.
Take lower front section and repeat instructions as for back, to make a diamond shaped gusset and to complete lower panel.
Add seam allowance to yoke seams (E–G and G–H) of lower back and lower front panel.
Add seam allowance to yoke seam of top back and front sections.

6   Simple gusseting

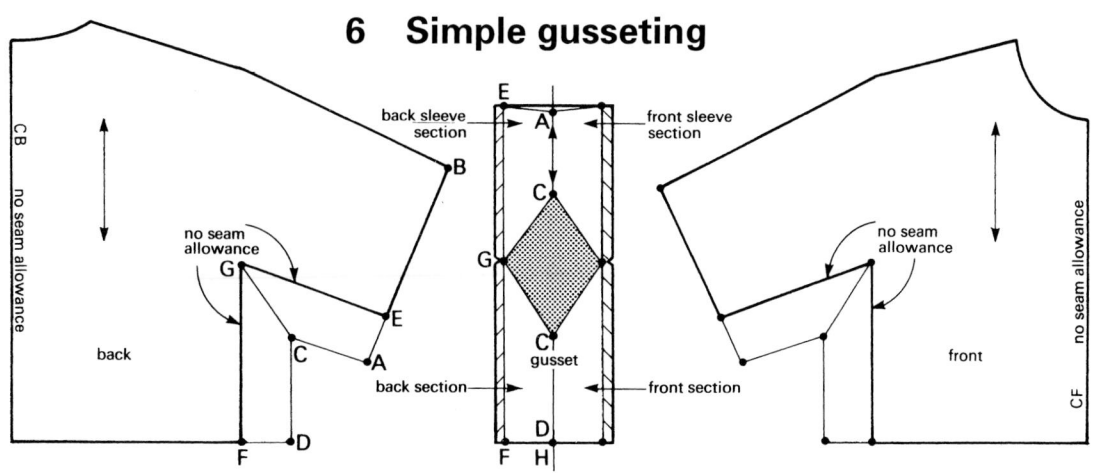

7   Seam styling with gusset

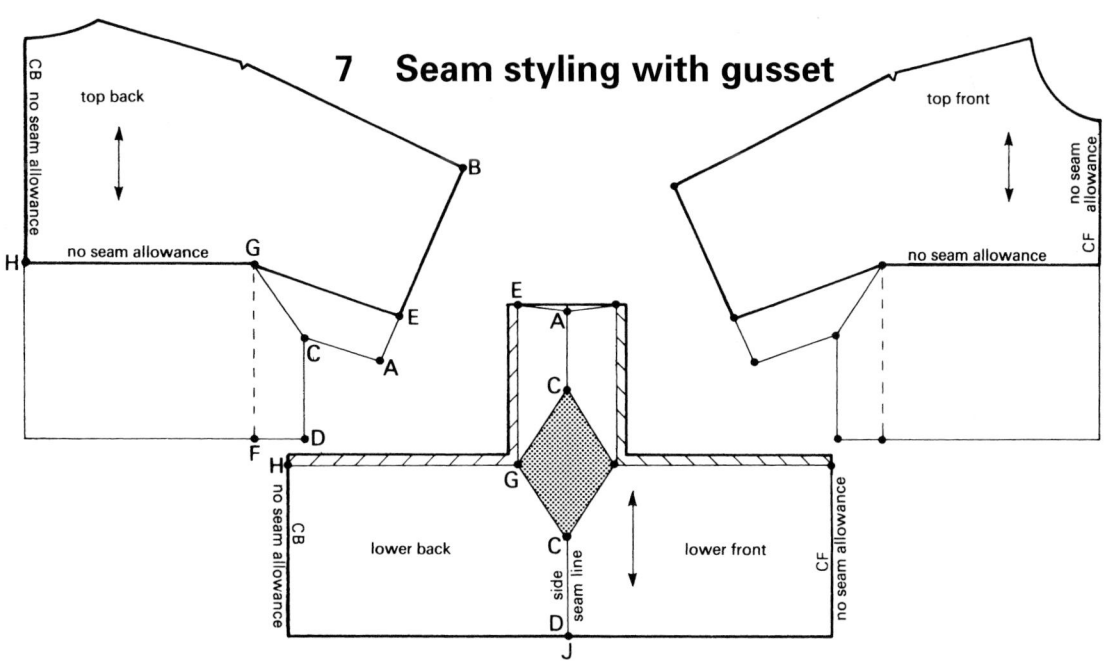

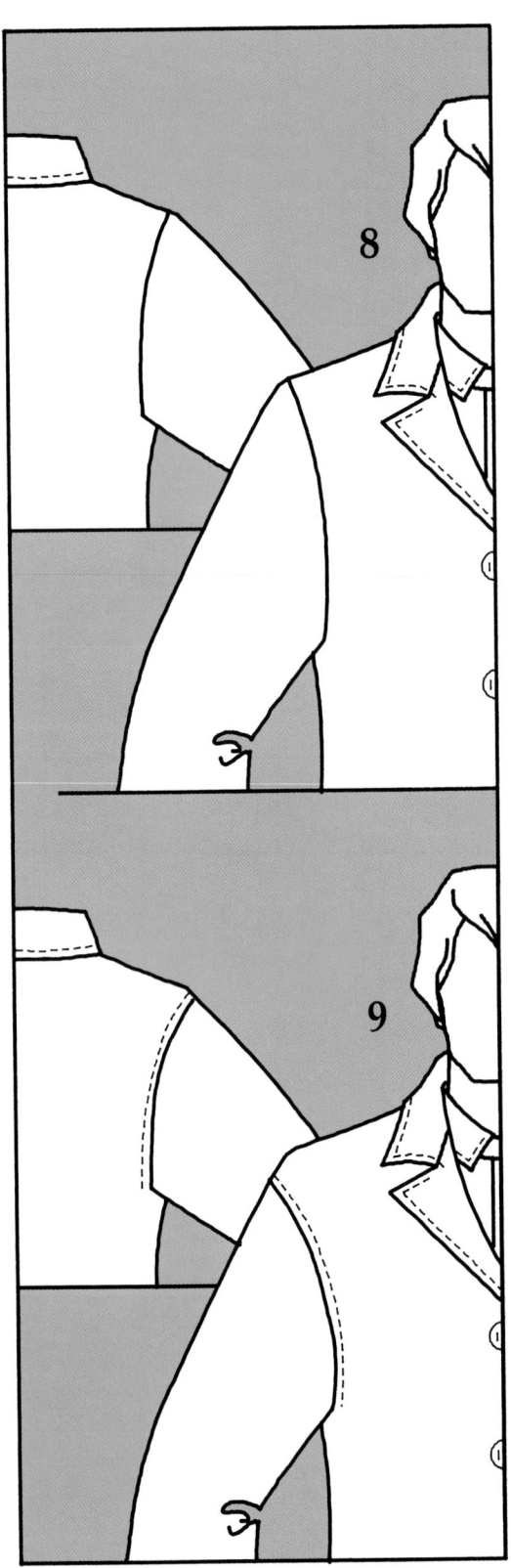

Sleeves – 'form' cutting

Easy fitting armhole (scye) shapes

'Form' cut blocks produce a better tailored shape; but it is important that you choose the correct type of block. It is necessary to select easy fitting versions of the blocks for easier fitting shapes. Ways of creating shapes with even greater ease are given below.

In most cases, lower the armhole first before proceeding with a sleeve adaptation. If the armhole is part of the new design line of the sleeve, e.g. extended shoulder, work the adaptations together to achieve a good armhole shape.

8 Lowered armhole (scye)

Body section   Trace body section of block required. Cut up side seam, open 4cm and mark new side seam down centre.
Lower scye depth line 3.5cm, mark A. Mark B and C at back and front pitch points.
Draw in new armhole shape as shown.
Sleeve   Trace one-piece sleeve block, below underarm points draw parallel lines; the distance is half the measurement the armhole was lowered.
Mark D and E at the back and front pitch points.
Draw curve D–F, it equals measurement B–A plus 1cm (seam allowance).
Draw curve E–G, it equals measurement C–A plus 1cm (seam allowance).
Draw underarm seams, narrow at wrist if required.
Note   The amount the block is widened and the armhole lowered can be varied but the proportions should remain constant.

9 Extended shoulder

Body section   Mark A at underarm point, mark B and C at back and front pitch points; extend shoulder to F and G as shown.
Sleeve   Mark D and E at back and front pitch points; H at sleeve head point, H–K is the amount shoulder is extended. Draw new sleeve head D, K, E.
Note   Check the measurements along fitting lines of new sleeve head; D–K should equal B–F, K–E should equal C–G.
If sleeve head is too small, split sleeve from K, open required amount (see diagram).

With lowered armhole – easy fitting

Body section   Cut up side seam, widen required amount, draw new scye depth line (ref. 1, lowered armhole). Extend shoulder line, raise 0.5cm.
Draw in new armhole shape, mark new back pitch point at X where old and new armhole shapes touch.
Sleeve   Mark new pitch point Y. Y–D = X–B.
Adapt underarm of sleeve Y–F and E–G as for lowered armhole; head of sleeve Y–K and K–E as for dropped shoulder.
If sleeve head is too small, split sleeve from K, open required amount (see diagram).

8   Lowered armhole

9   Extended shoulder

With lowered armhole

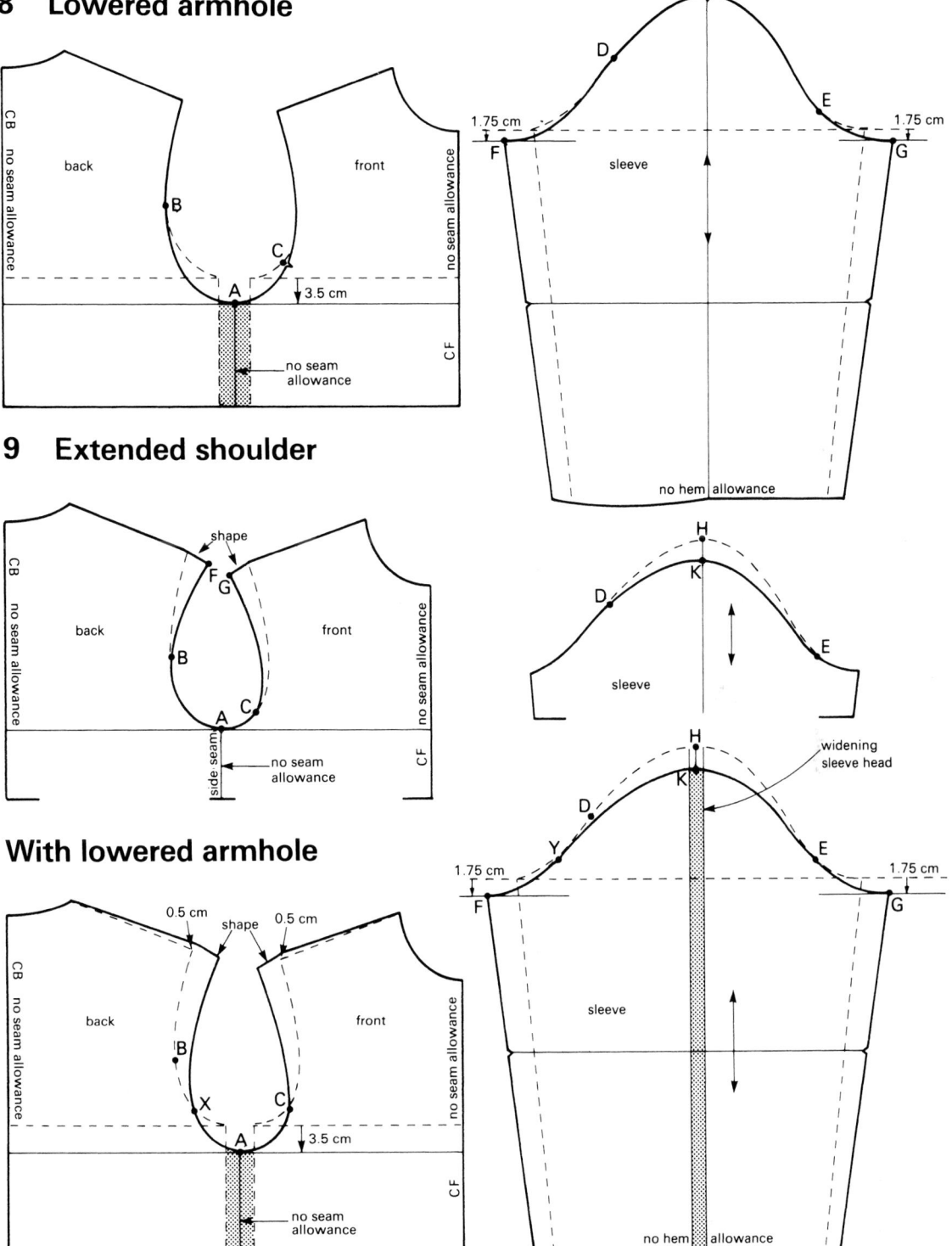

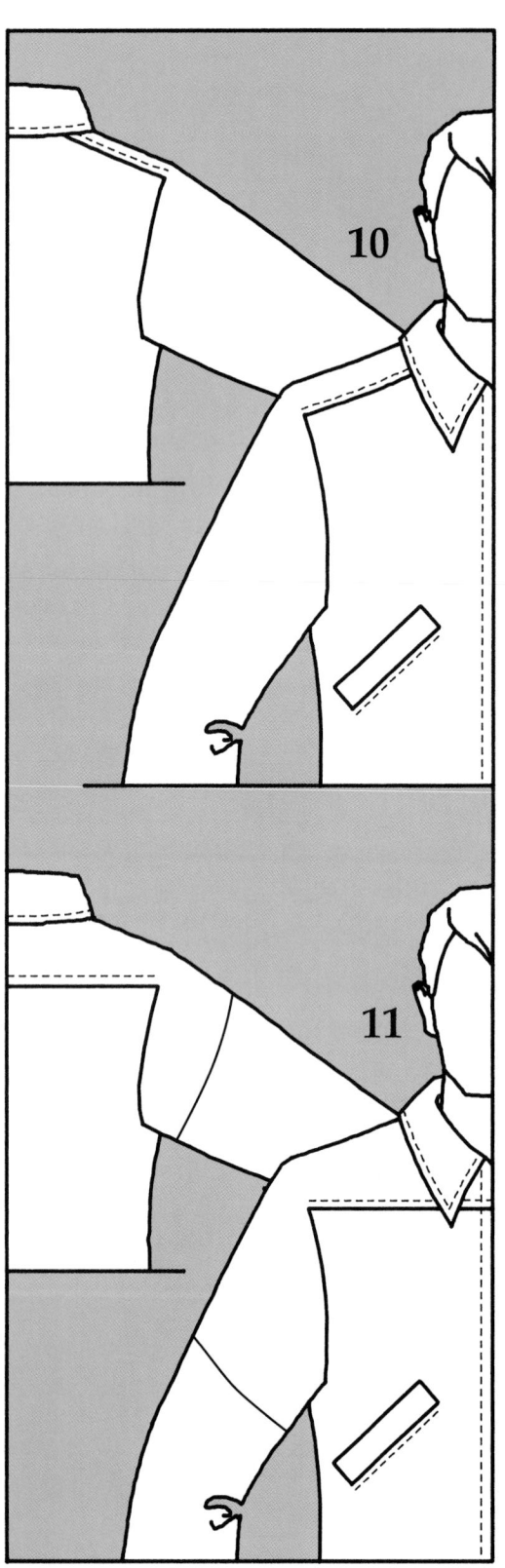

10 Strap shoulder

Body section Trace body section of block required.
Take 1cm seam allowance off back and front shoulders.
Mark points A and B at front shoulder points, mark points
C and D at back shoulder points.
Cut 3cm sections from back and front shoulders; place
together along shoulder line, cut away back shoulder ease.
Leave the 1cm ease on back shoulder of body section, add
1cm to front shoulder of body section, shape to armhole
line as shown.
Add seam allowance to shoulder seam.
Sleeve Trace one-piece sleeve block; mark point E on
fitting line at sleeve head.
Place shoulder section to sleeve head, place points D and B
to point E.
Add seam allowance to shoulder section.
Note If a wider shoulder strap is required, the shoulder
line of both body sections has to be extended to ensure
that seam lines fit.

11 Extended yoke sleeve

Body section Trace body section of block required. Mark
points A and B.
Draw in yoke lines; mark points C and D.
Cut off yoke sections.
Add seam allowance to body section along yoke lines.
Extend 1cm outwards from points C and D, shape to
armhole line as shown.
Sleeve section Trace one-piece sleeve block, mark point
E on fitting line of back balance point; mark point F on
fitting line of front balance point; mark point G at sleeve
head point.
E–H equals the measurement A–C on body section.
F–K equals the measurement B–D on body section.
Cut across sleeve 8cm below underarm points.
Divide upper sleeve along the line from G.
Upper Sleeves Place yoke sections to upper sleeves,
place C to point H, D to point K and shoulder points to
outer edge of sleeve (they will not reach G).
Add seam allowance to centre sleeve seams curving
inwards to touch point G, then join to neck points
L and M.
Add seam allowance along yoke lines, centre back line and
lower edge of sleeves.
Lower sleeve Add seam allowance to the top edge.

10 Strap shoulder

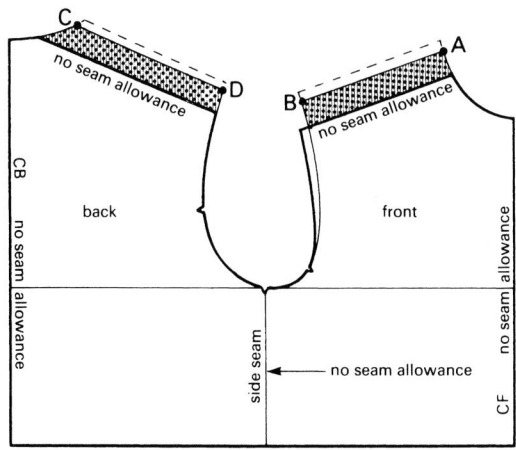

11 Extended yoke sleeve

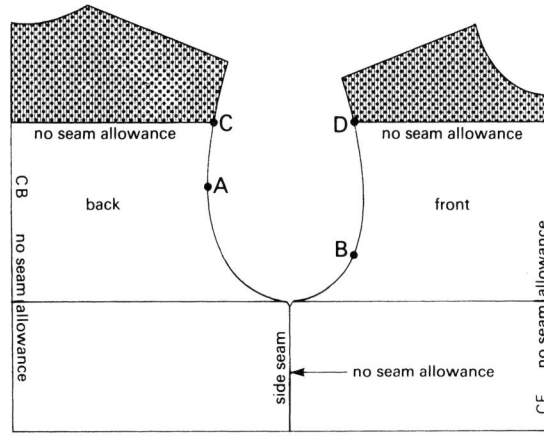

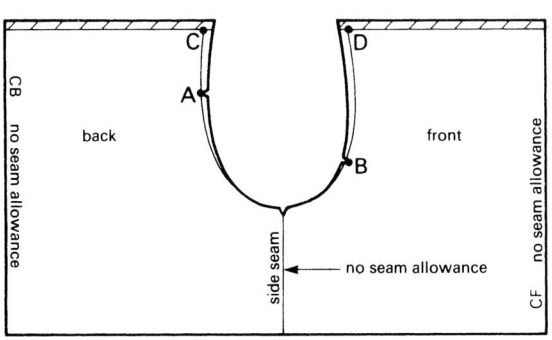

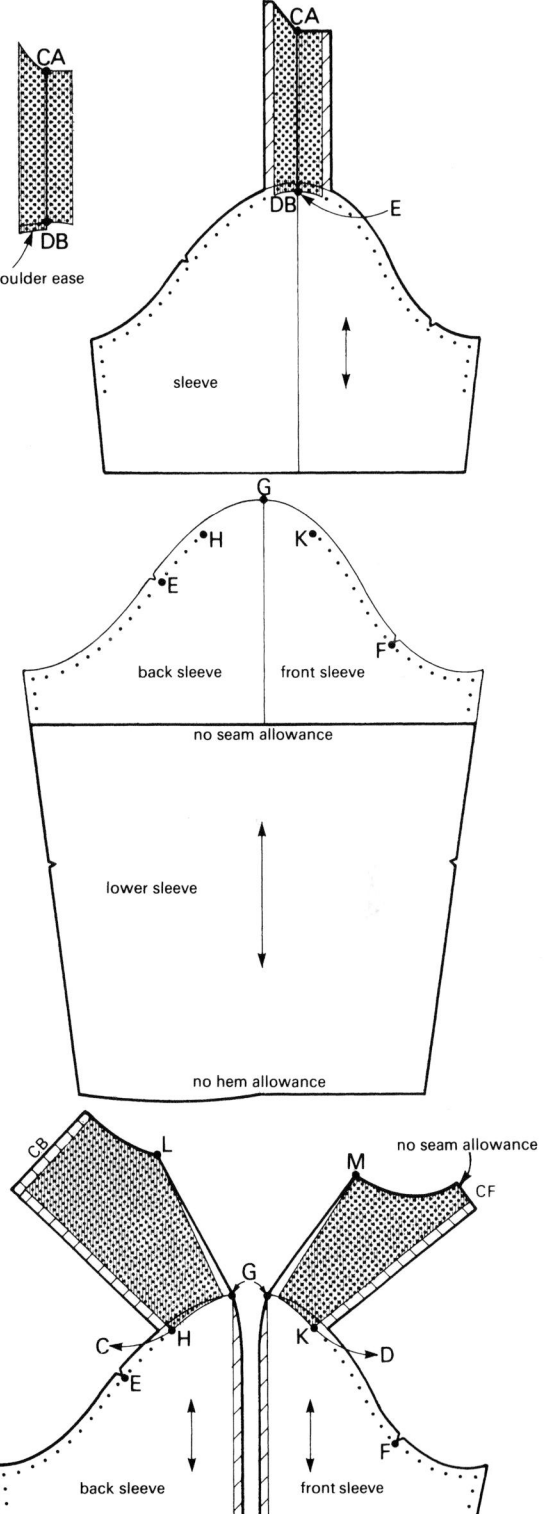

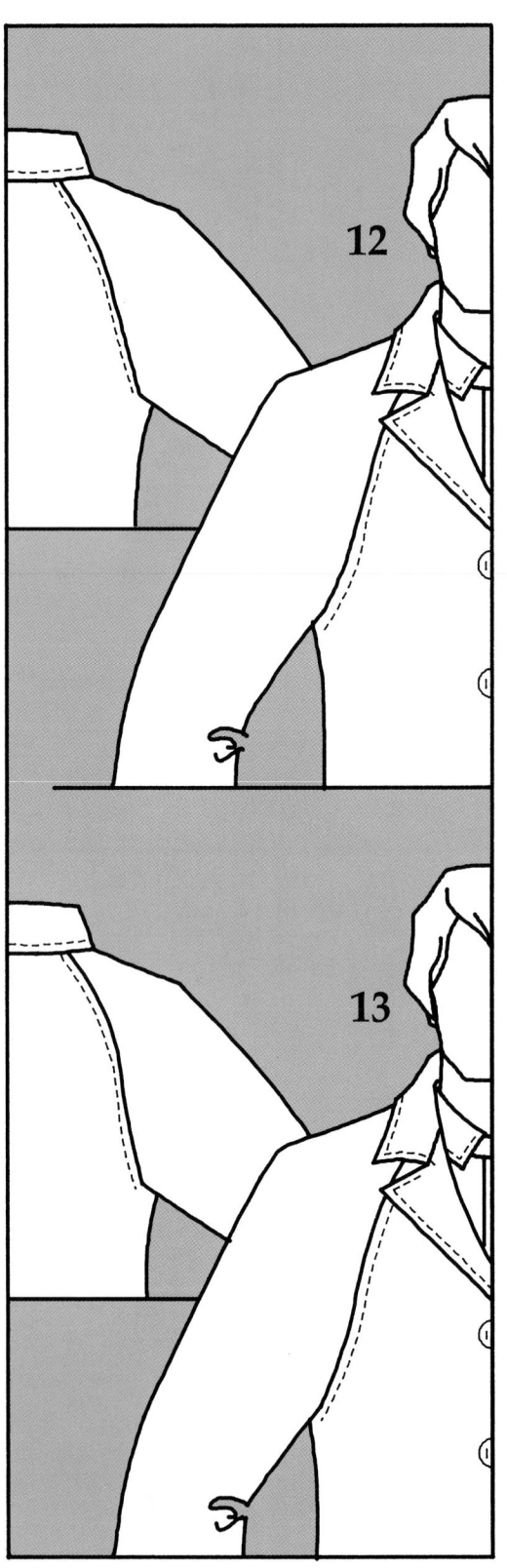

12 Classic raglan sleeve

Body section Trace body section of block required. Take 1cm off front shoulder line; add 1 cm to back shoulder line.

Mark points A and B, 4cm in from new shoulder points; mark C on *fitting line* 2.5cm below back pitch point; mark D directly opposite on *fitting line* on front armhole; mark E on *fitting line* of front pitch point.

Draw curved lines from A–C and B–D; draw in 1cm dart on back shoulder.

Cut off shaded sections.

Close back shoulder dart.

Separate front and back body sections.

Add seam allowance to side seam and raglan seams from A–C and B–D.

Sleeve Trace one-piece sleeve block, draw centre line of sleeve 1cm forward.

Mark point F at new sleeve head point; mark G on *fitting line* 2.5cm below back pitch point, H on *fitting line* at front pitch point.

H–K = E–D on body section.

Separate sleeve vertically from F.

Place back body section to back sleeve; place C to touch G, place shoulder point to F.

Place front body section to front sleeve, place D to touch K, place shoulder point to F.

Depending on the block used the body sections may not touch the sleeve points exactly.

Add seam allowance from A–G and B–K.

Add seam allowance to centre seams curving inwards to touch F as shown.

13 Easy fitting raglan sleeve

Use an easy fitting block or a pattern adapted for a lowered armhole (ref. 8, page 70).

Body section Take 1cm off front shoulder line; add 1cm to back shoulder line.

Mark points C and D on *fitting lines* at front and back pitch points; mark point E directly opposite on *fitting line* of back armhole.

Sleeve Mark F, 1cm forward from sleeve head point.

Mark points G and H on *fitting line* at pitch points.

G–K = C–E.

Now work the adaptation for the classic raglan using the new lower pitch points.

12 Classic raglan sleeve

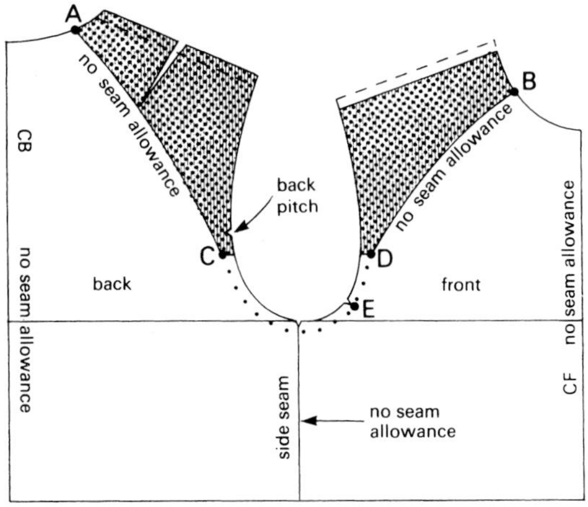

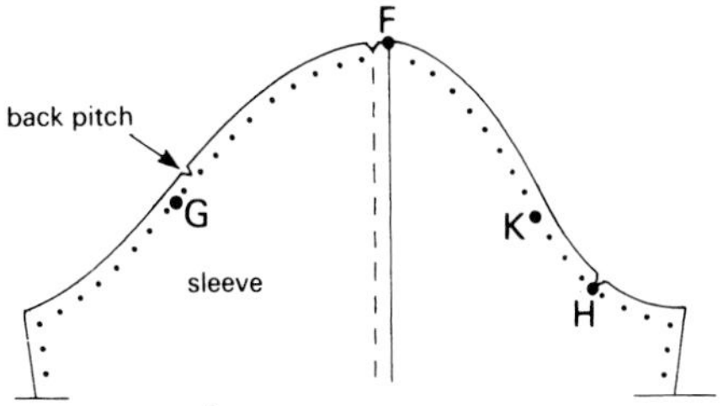

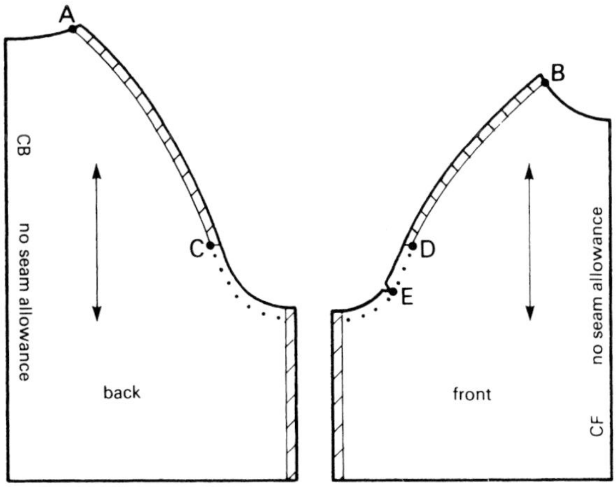

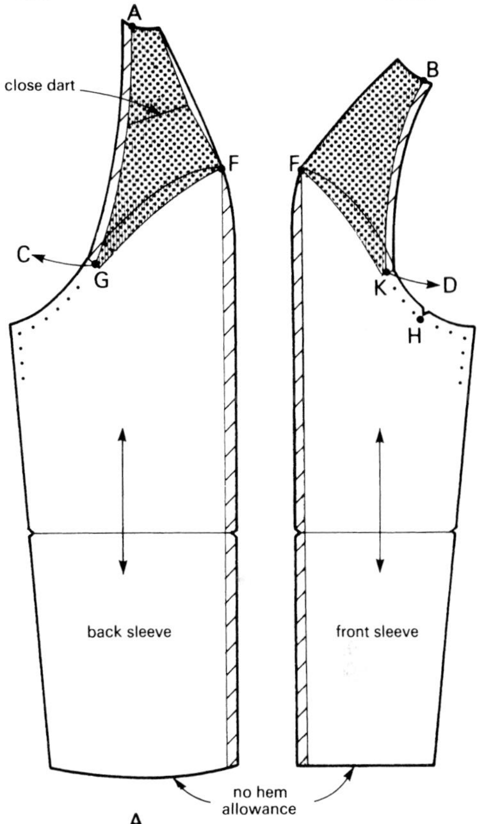

back pitch

sleeve

CB

no seam allowance

back

back pitch

no seam allowance

no seam allowance

side seam

no seam allowance

CF

close dart

CB

no seam allowance

back

no seam allowance

front

CF

back sleeve

front sleeve

no hem allowance

13 Easy fitting raglan sleeve

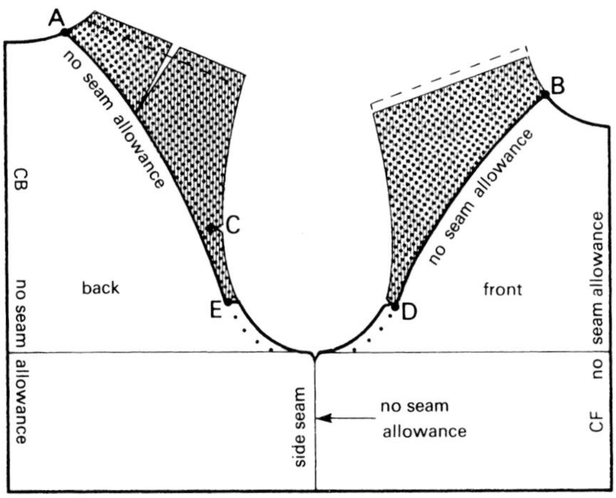

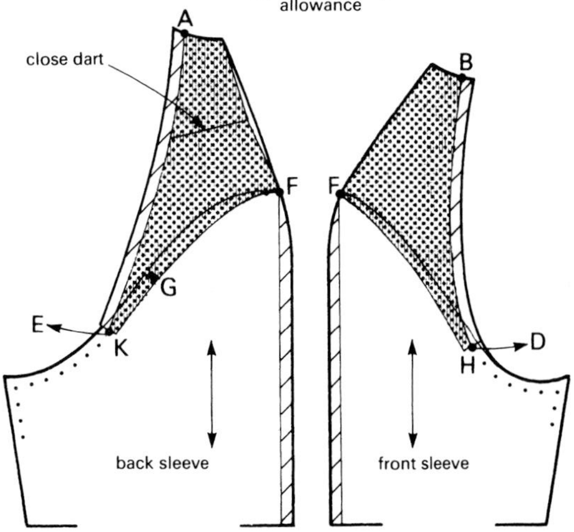

CB

no seam allowance

back

no seam allowance

side seam

no seam allowance

front

CF

no seam allowance

close dart

back sleeve

front sleeve

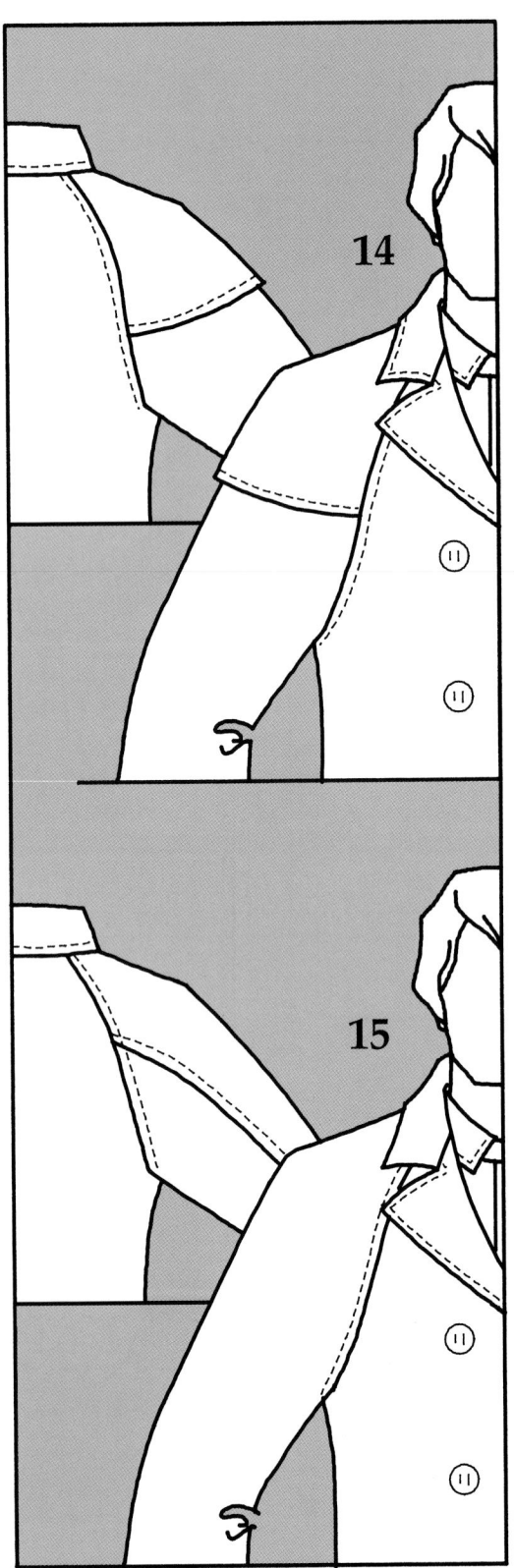

14 Oversleeve – raglan

Trace standard or deep raglan adaptation (e.g. shows easy fitting raglan (ref. 13, page 74). Mark pitch points A and B on body sections, C and D on sleeves.
Back Draw in yoke line; mark point E on armhole. Trace back yoke, add seam allowance to lower edge.
Sleeves C–F equals the measurement A–E on back section.
From point F draw in oversleeve lines; mark point G.
Trace off oversleeves; add seam allowance to lower edge.
Add 0.5cm ease to shoulder seam.
Front Mark point H on front armhole, B–H equals the measurement D–G.

15 Raglan sleeve (two-piece sleeve)

Body section Trace body section of block required. Mark point 14 on armhole line.
Take 1cm off front shoulder line; add 1cm to back shoulder line.
Mark points A and B, 4cm in from new shoulder points; mark C on *fitting line* 4cm below point 14; mark E on *fitting line* at front pitch point.
Mark point D, 5cm above E on *fitting line*.
Draw curved lines from A–C and B–D; draw in 1cm dart on back shoulder.
Cut off shaded sections. Close back shoulder dart. Separate back and front sections, add seam allowance as shown for classic raglan (ref. 12, page 74).
Sleeves Trace off from two-piece sleeve block the top sleeve and the under sleeve from point 21 to point 13. Mark in elbow line. Mark point 5.
Top sleeves Mark F, 1cm forward from balance point on sleeve head. Extend back of sleeve head 4cm from 5–G^1.
Mark G on *fitting line*; mark H on *fitting line* of front pitch point.
H–K = E–D on front body section. 13–L is 1cm.
Join G^1 to L with a curved line.
Mark M and N on elbow line.
Place back body section to back of sleeve, place C to touch G, place shoulder point to F.
Place front body section to front of sleeve, place D to touch K, place shoulder point to F.
Add seam allowance from A–G and B–K.
Mark O at front wrist point. P is midway between L and O. Mark Q midway between M and N.
Draw a curved line from F through Q to P.
Trace off top sleeve and separate along this centre seam line.
Add seam allowance to centre seams curving inwards to touch shoulder line at F as shown.
Under sleeve Square across from G^1 on sleeve block. On back body section mark V at armhole edge.
21–R is meas. of the armhole curve V to underarm point (U.P.) plus 0.5cm. (21–R is measured straight.)
Draw line from 21–R curving in 1.75cm.
R–S is 1.5cm, 13–T is 1cm. M–U is 5.5cm; join S–T with curved line.
Extend back seam line 0.5 cm above S, and underarm seam 0.75cm above R for seam step.

14 Oversleeve – raglan

15 Raglan sleeve (two-piece sleeve)

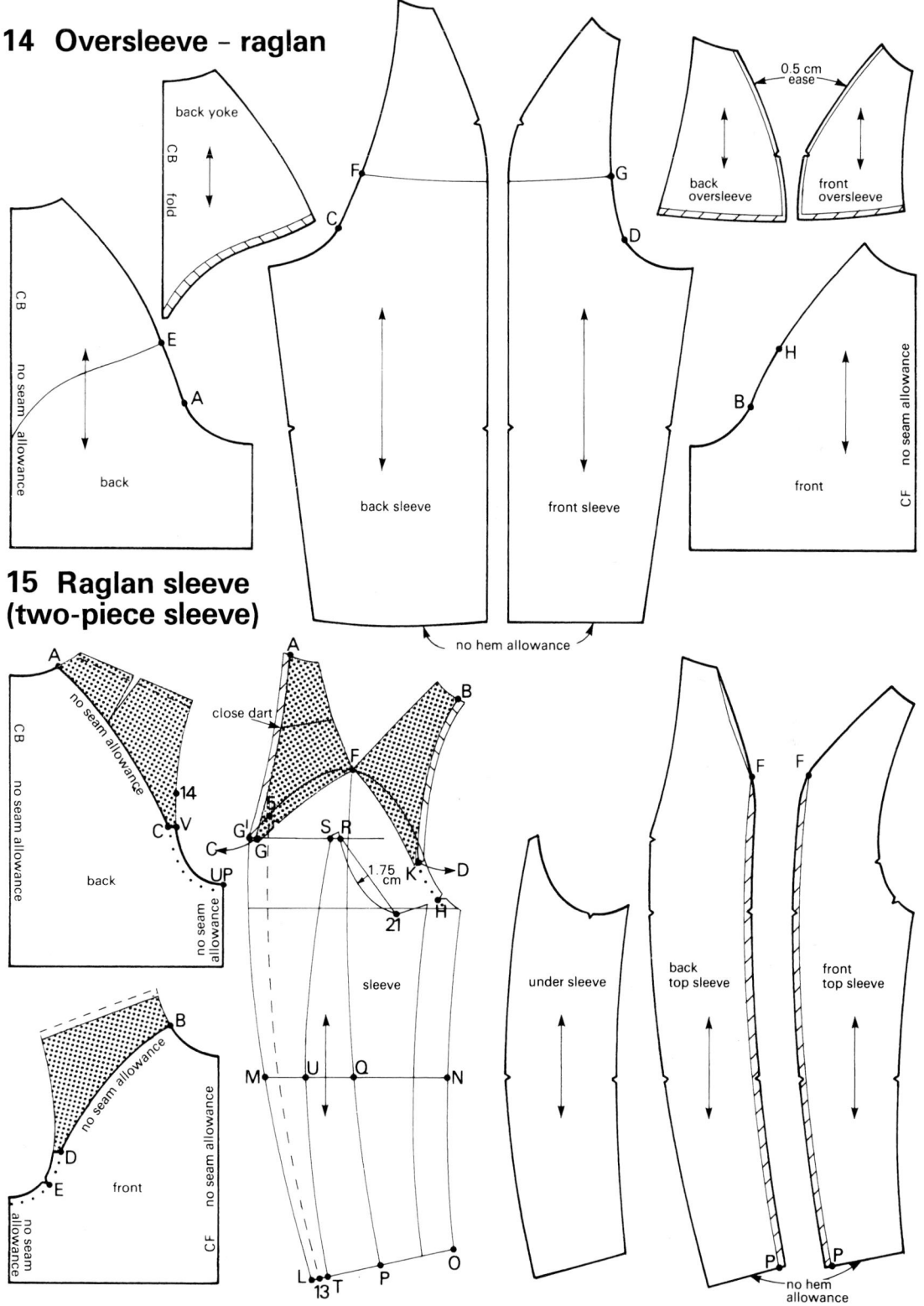

78

16 High padded shoulders

For a design with a high padded shoulder, cut across from armhole to shoulder point and open the required amount.

Cut across the sleeve head above back pitch point and vertically to top of sleeve; open and raise sleeve head.

The distance of A plus B must equal C.

17 Cuffs

Instructions for cuffs include a 1cm seam allowance.

Single folded cuffs   A–B is cuff size plus 4cm.
B–C is twice cuff depth plus 2cm.

Shaped single cuffs   A–B is cuff size plus 4cm.
B–C is cuff depth plus 2cm (shape lower edge).

Shaped double cuffs   A–B is cuff size plus 4cm.
B–C is twice cuff depth plus 2cm (shape lower edge).

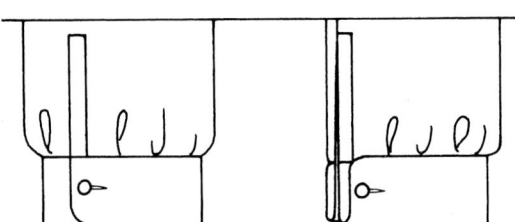

16 High padded shoulders

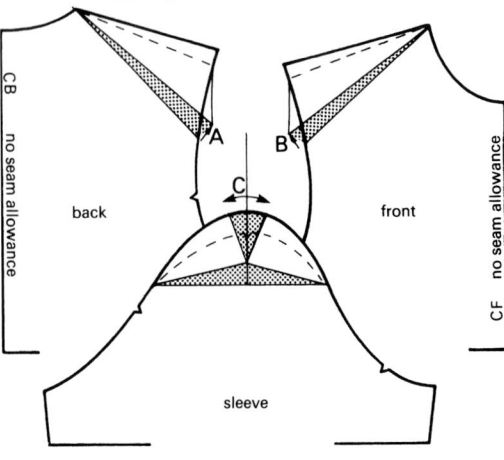

17 Cuffs

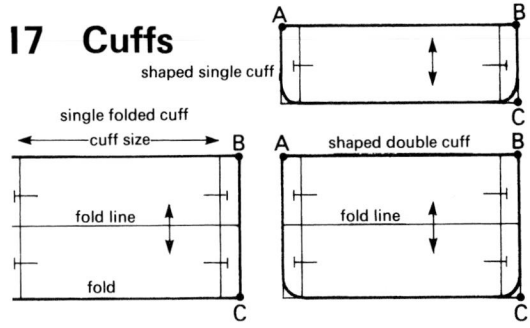

PART TWO: STANDARD PATTERN CUTTING PROCESSES

Chapter 7 Constructing openings and collars

Front openings

There are many types of openings designed for the fronts of shirts, jackets and coats.

Ten basic adaptations are illustrated based on standard manufacturing techniques.

However, all designs should follow the basic principle that the centre front on a pattern is a stable position and cannot be moved or the fit of the jacket will alter. Therefore care must be taken when button stands and straps are added to patterns.

If the neckline requires lowering or altering in any way, it must be completed before working the instructions for front openings.

1 Standard front

Mark buttonholes on centre front line (buttonholes overlap the line by 0.2cm). Add button stand, approximately 2.5cm (varies with size of button).

Draw in facing line with a dotted line.

Trace round front edge of pattern and trace through facing line to construct facing pattern.

Add seam allowance to front edge of body section and vertical edges of facing pattern.

Extended facing Mark buttonholes, add button stand. Fold front edge line, trace through facing line and neckline to construct an extended facing.

Add seam allowance to facing edge.

2 Double breasted front

The example shows neckline lowered before front is constructed.

Draw in two button lines at equal distances each side of centre front. Mark buttonholes, button placings and add button stand.

Construct facing as for a standard front.

Add seam allowance to front edge of body section and vertical edges of facing pattern.

3 Single strap front

Decide width of strap. Add button stand to centre front, half width of strap.

Draw strap line in from centre front, half width of strap. Trace off strap pattern, mark centre front line; mark buttonholes.

Add seam allowance to front edge of body section.

Add seam allowance to both outer edges of strap.

4 Double strap front

Decide width of strap.

Add button stand to centre front half width of strap.

Draw strap line in from centre front, half width of strap.

Trace off strap pattern, make it double the finished width, repeating slight curve at neck edge.

Mark centre front line, buttonholes, fold line.

Add seam allowance to both outer edges.

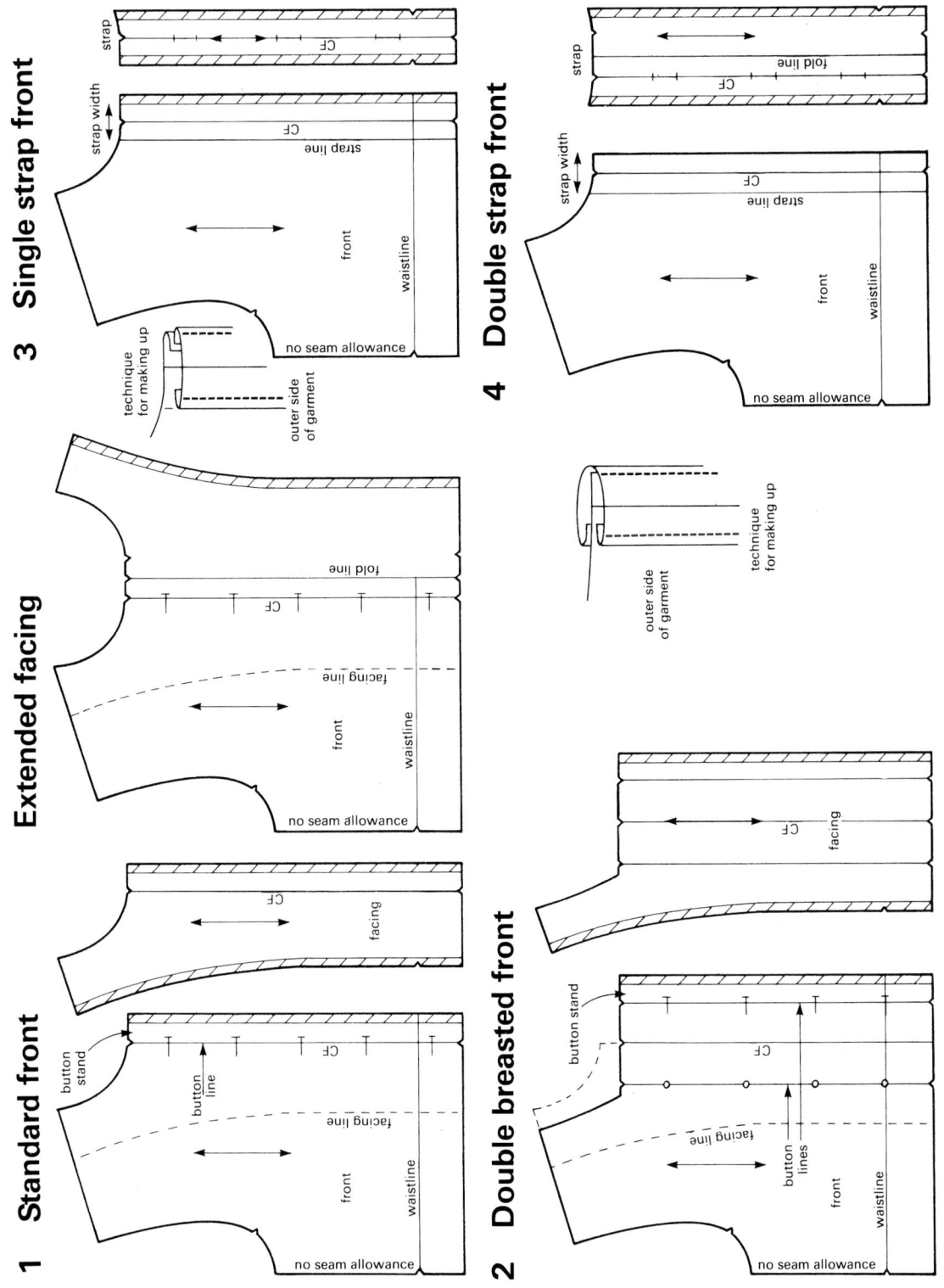

3 **Single strap front**

strap

CF

strap width

strap line

CF

front

waistline

no seam allowance

technique for making up

outer side of garment

Extended facing

fold line

CF

facing line

front

waistline

no seam allowance

1 **Standard front**

CF

facing

button stand

button line

CF

facing line

front

waistline

no seam allowance

4 **Double strap front**

strap

fold line

CF

strap width

CF

strap line

front

waistline

no seam allowance

technique for making up

outer side of garment

2 **Double breasted front**

facing

CF

button stand

button stand

CF

facing line

button lines

front

waistline

no seam allowance

5 Standard zip front

Measure width of zip that will be shown on front
of jacket.

Mark in from centre front half this distance and mark this
line 'front edge line'.

Rub out centre front line.

Draw in facing line with a dotted line.

Trace round front edge of pattern and facing line to
construct facing pattern.

Add seam allowance to front edge of body section and to
vertical edges of facing pattern.

6 Standard zip front with extension

The standard zip front pattern can be used with an
extension added to one or both fronts.

Extension Draw a vertical line the same length as the
front edge of body section; mark this line *'fold line'*.

Draw parallel lines 4cm each side of this line.

Add seam allowance to each edge.

7 Concealed zip front

Draw in facing line with a dotted line, trace round centre
front edge of pattern and trace facing line to construct
facing pattern.

Add a seam allowance of 2cm to centre front edge of
body section and to front edge of facing.

Add seam allowance to inside edge of facing.

8 Concealed zip front with extension

This zip fastening requires a left and a right front pattern.

Left front Draw in stitch line 2.5cm in from centre
front line.

Draw in fold line of front edge 2.5cm out from centre
front line.

Add a 5cm extended facing.

Add seam allowance to front edge of extended facing.

Right front Mark in stitch line 2.5cm in from centre
front line.

Draw in zip edge line 1cm out from centre front line
(this gives 1.5cm allowance for the zip).

Add seam allowance.

Right front facing with extension Draw vertical line
from A, mark centre front.

Construct parallel lines 2.5cm each side of line.

Add 1.5cm extension to front edge line.

Add seam allowance to both outer edges.

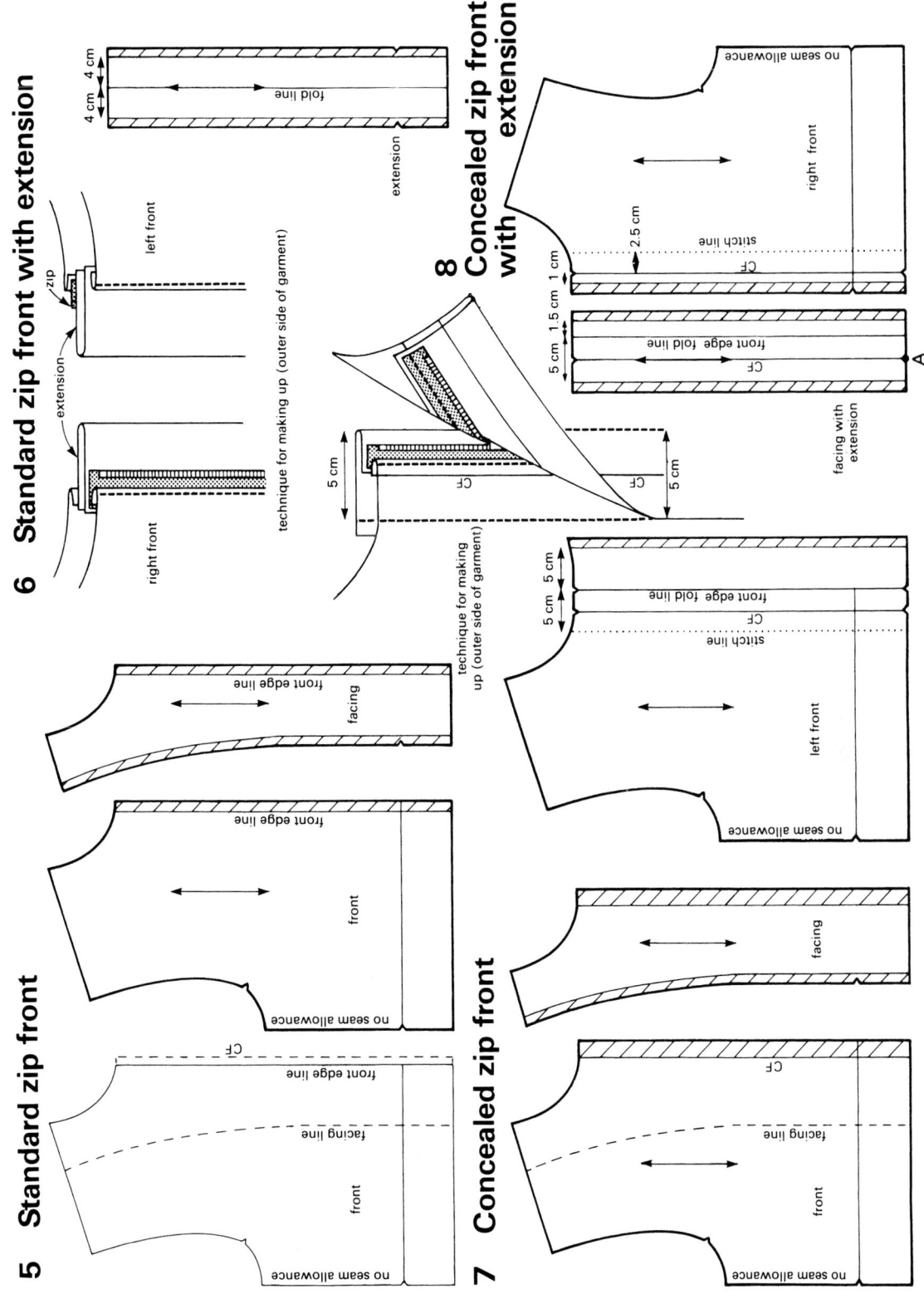

5 Standard zip front

6 Standard zip front with extension

7 Concealed zip front

8 Concealed zip front with extension

9 Standard fly front

Front Add 3cm button stand to centre front line; mark stitch line 3cm in from centre front line; mark A.
Draw facing line with a dotted line.

Left front facing Trace off facing from front pattern; mark point A.
Draw in a 1cm step 15cm down from neck to 4cm above point A; mark buttonholes.

Fly piece B Cut a strip: length=step length plus 5cm, width=5cm.
Mark centre front line 2cm in from front edge.

Fly piece C Cut a strip: length=step length plus 5cm, width=6cm.
Mark centre front line down centre of both fly pieces.

Right front facing Trace off a standard facing.
Add seam allowance to front edges of front body sections.
Add seam allowance to vertical edges of both facing patterns and all edges of fly pieces.

10 Strap fly front

Left front Add 2.5cm button stand to centre front line.
Mark in fly strap line 2.5cm in from centre front line.
Add 5cm to front edge line for facing.

Right front Construct as left front, but add seam allowance to front edge.

Fly strap for left front Draw a vertical line from A; length equals measurement of front edge.
Mark line 'fold line'; draw parallel lines 5cm each side of the line. Curve neckline.
Mark centre front; mark buttonholes.
Add seam allowance to left edge.

9 Standard fly front

10 Strap fly front

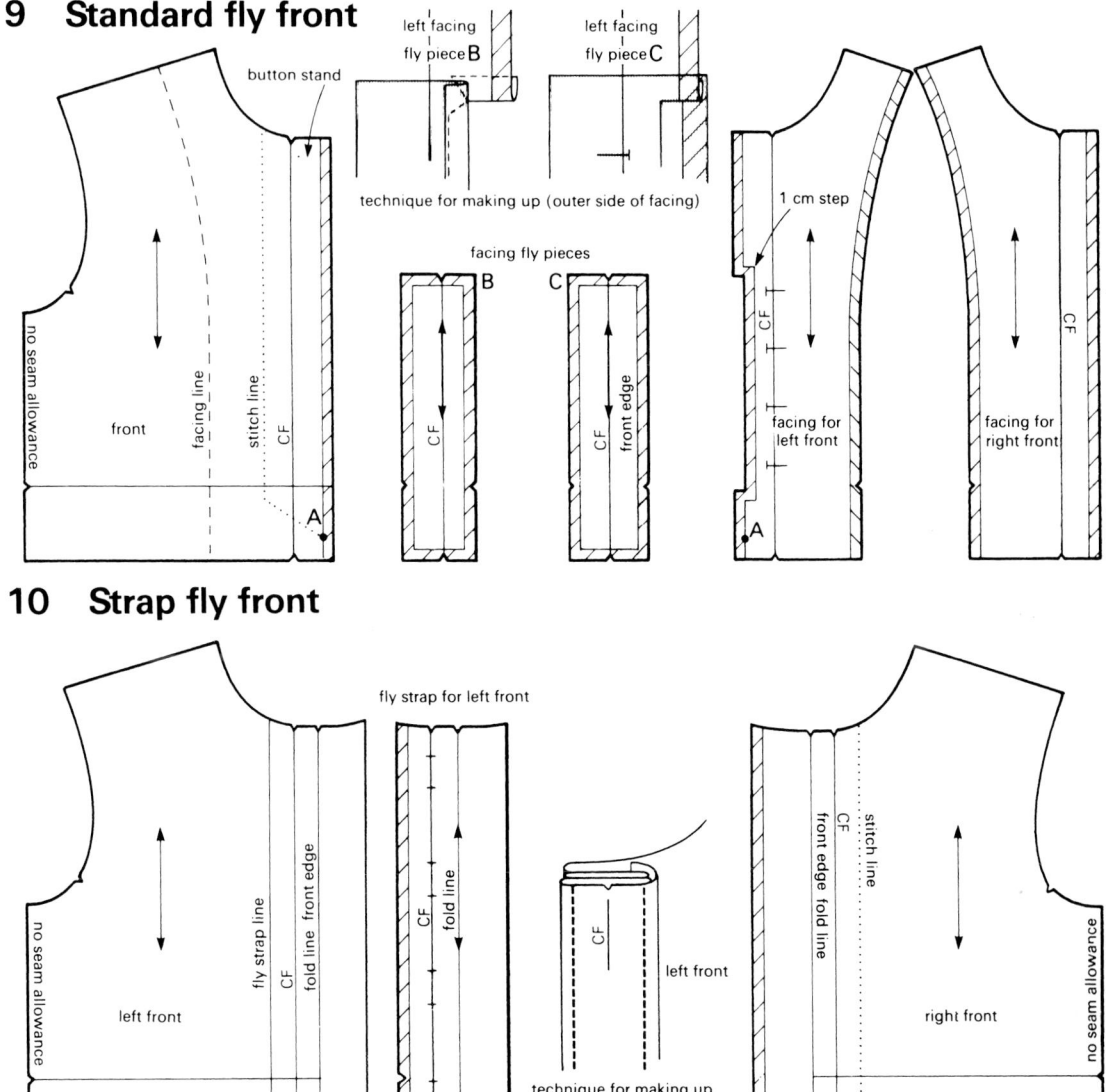

9 Standard fly front (labels)

left facing
fly piece B

left facing
fly piece C

technique for making up (outer side of facing)

facing fly pieces

B   C

CF   CF   front edge

button stand

no seam allowance

front

facing line

stitch line

CF

A

1 cm step

CF

facing for left front

facing for right front

CF

A

10 Strap fly front (labels)

fly strap for left front

no seam allowance

left front

fly strap line

CF

fold line   front edge

CF

fold line

CF

left front

technique for making up
(outer side of garment)

A

stitch line

CF

front edge   fold line

right front

no seam allowance

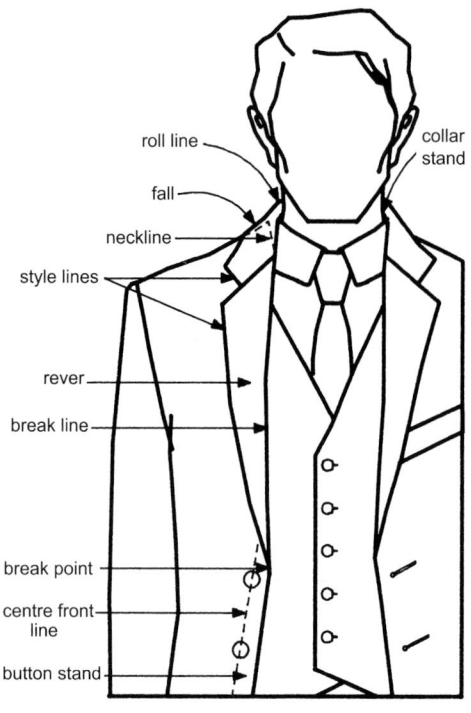

roll line
collar stand
fall
neckline
style lines
rever
break line
break point
centre front line
button stand

Collars – basic principles

Terms used for collar construction

Neckline   Line where the collar is joined to the neck.
Style line   Outer edge of collar or rever.
Roll line   The line where the collar rolls over.
Stand   Rise of the collar from neckline to roll line.
Fall   Depth of the collar from roll line to style line.
Break point   The point where the rever turns back.
Break line   Line along which rever rolls back.
Note   The break line and the roll line are sometimes referred to as *crease lines*.

Before drafting a collar

Adjust neckline if required; mark any button lines, buttonholes and button stands.

Collar shapes

Although the style line determines the shape of the outer edge of the collar, the length of the outer edge determines where it sits on the body.

Top collars

Add approximately 0.25cm (depending on thickness of fabric) to outer edge of top collars from A–B.
Some collar designs will require 0.25cm at back neck edge from C–D.

Standing Collars

The standing collar drafts on pages 86 and 88 can be used for all blocks except suit drafts. The depth of a collar or stand will vary with the type of garment.
Seam allowances   A 1cm seam allowance is included in all standing collar drafts.
The neckline measurement of a pattern   Place back shoulder to front shoulder on *fitting line*. Measure accurately from centre front to centre back along the *fitting line* with the tape upright as in diagram.
(If the neckline is to be lowered, complete this first.)

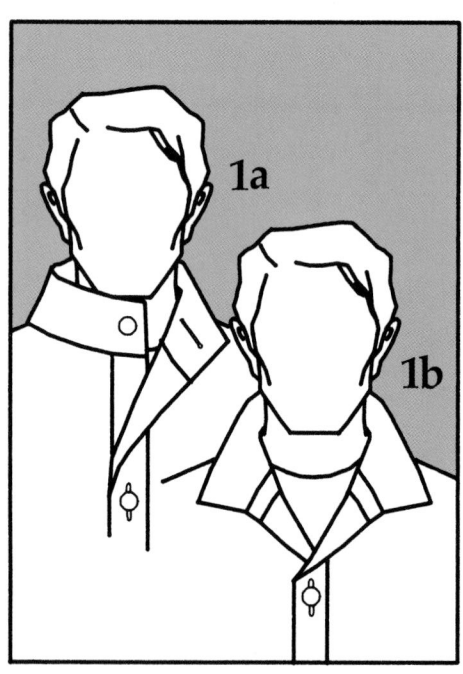

1a

1b

1a   Standard straight collar

1–2   neck measurement, (measured on *fitting line*).
2–3   meas. of button stand plus 1cm; square up.
1–4   collar depth plus 2cm; square across to 5.
5–6 is 1.5cm; 6–7=2–3. Join 2–7.
1–8   ¾ meas. 1–2.
3–9 is 1.5cm; join 6–9. Join 8–9 with a curve.
Mark any buttonholes.

1b   Standard straight collar with stand

Stand   Construct stand as for the standard straight collar but make 1–4 stand depth plus 2cm.
Collar   10–11=4–6; square up from 10 and 11.
10–12 collar depth required plus 2cm; square across to 13. 11–14=6–7.

Collar shapes

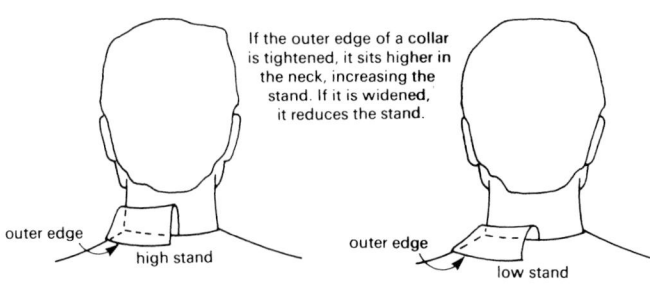

If the outer edge of a collar is tightened, it sits higher in the neck, increasing the stand. If it is widened, it reduces the stand.

outer edge
high stand

outer edge
low stand

Top collars

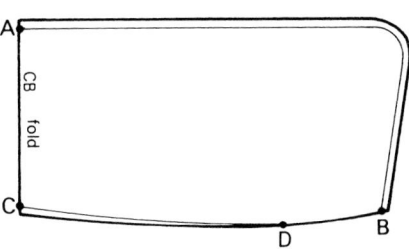

Neckline measurement

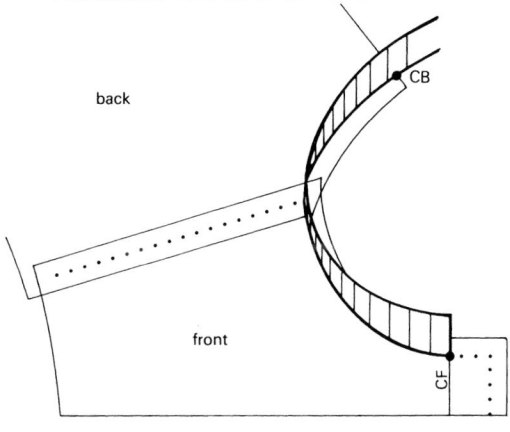

back

front

1a   Standard straight collar

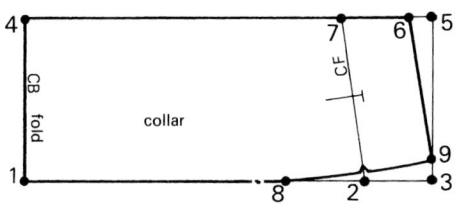

1b   Standard straight collar with stand

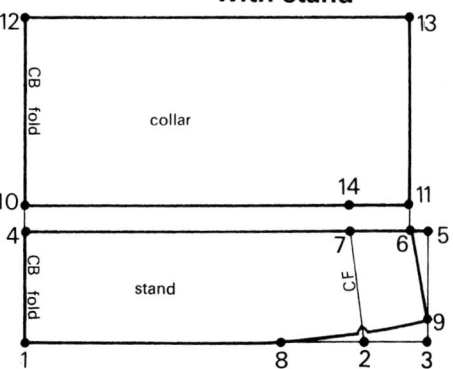

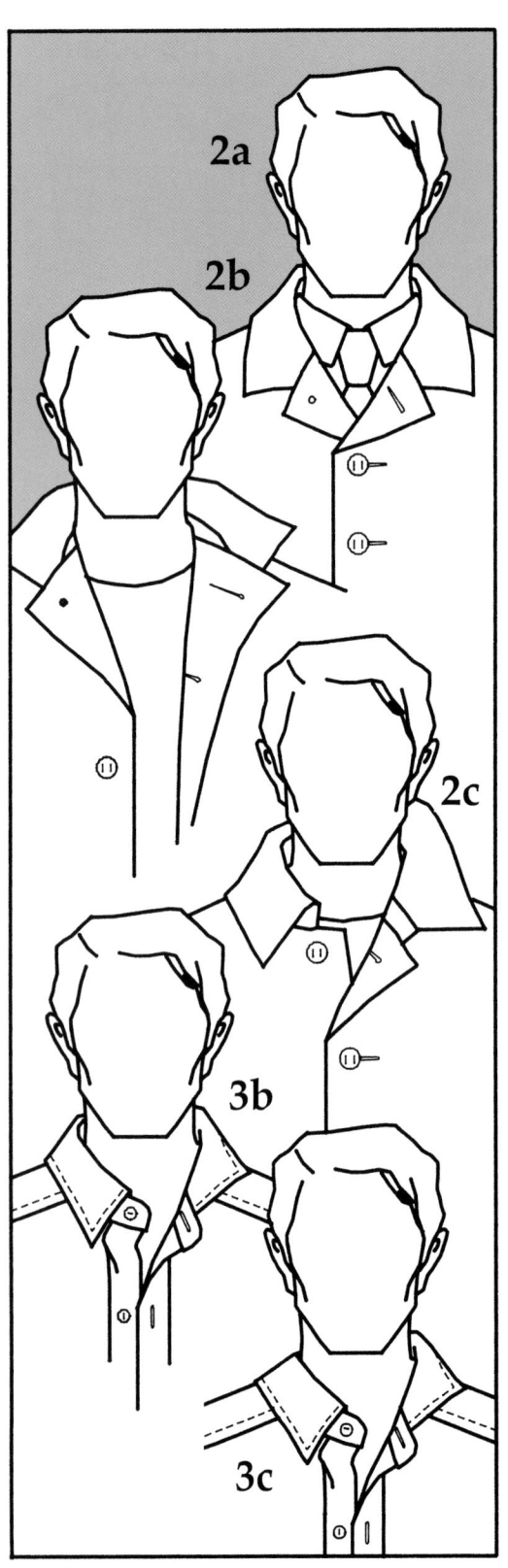

2a Standard convertible collar

1–2 neck measurement (see diagram page 87) plus 1cm; square up.
1–3 ¾ measurement 1–2 minus 1cm.
1–4 collar depth plus 2cm; square across to 5.
1–6 is 0.6cm.
2–7 is 1cm; shape neckline of collar from 6–7.
Draw in style line of collar from 5–7.
Note If depth of collar exceeds 10cm the outer edge is cut and spread to sit lower on the shoulder line.

2b Shaped convertible collar – hidden stand

Trace standard convertible collar, omit point 6.
1–8 is 4.5cm (can vary).
Draw curved line from 8–3.
Divide measurement 1–3 into four sections; square up.
Cut out collar and stand. Cut up lines.
Overlap stand at outer edge 0.3cm at each line.
Open outer edge of collar 0.4cm at each line.
Cut 0.9cm from fold line at centre back of collar.
Trace collar and stand.
Add 1cm seam allowance from 8–3 on collar and stand.

2c Shaped convertible collar with stand

Trace standard convertible collar omitting point 6.
1–8 is 4.5cm (can vary); square across to 9.
Divide measurement 1–3 into four sections; square up.
9–10 is 0.5cm; square up from 3–11.
Draw a curved line from 10–11.
Cut out collar and stand.
Divide and shape as collar 2b.
Add 1cm seam allowance from 8–9 on collar and 8–10 on stand.

3a Shirt collar

1–2 ½ neckline measurement (see diagram page 87).
2–3 is button stand plus 1.25cm.
1–4 ¾ measurement 1–2; square up from 1, 2, 3.
1–5 collar and stand depth plus 2cm; square across.
1–6 ½ depth 1–5; square across to 7 and 8.
8–9 is 1cm, join 3–9.
3–10 and 9–11 are 0.75cm. 1–12 is 0.5cm.
Draw in style line from 5–7; complete outline of collar.

3b Shirt collar with stand

Trace shirt collar outline.
13 is midway between 6 and 7.
7–14 and 11–15 are 1cm; join 13–15 with a curve.
Join 14–16 at collar point.
Separate collar and stand.
Seam allowance is required on lines 6–14 and 6–15.

3c Shaped shirt collar with stand

Trace shirt collar with stand.
Divide 12–4 into four sections.
Shape stand and collar as for 2c.
Add 1cm seam allowance from 6–14 and 6–15.

2a Standard convertible collar

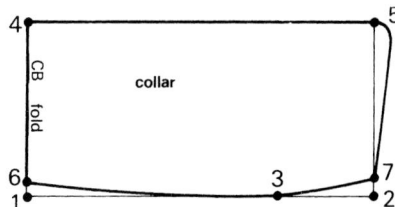

3a Shirt collar

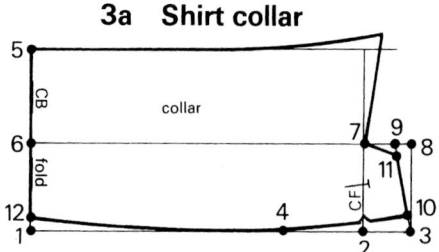

2b Shaped convertible collar – hidden stand

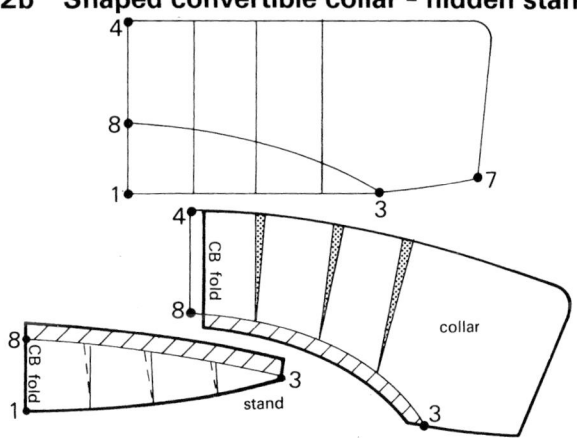

3b Shirt collar with stand

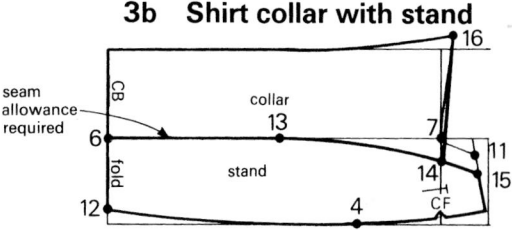

3c Shaped shirt collar with stand

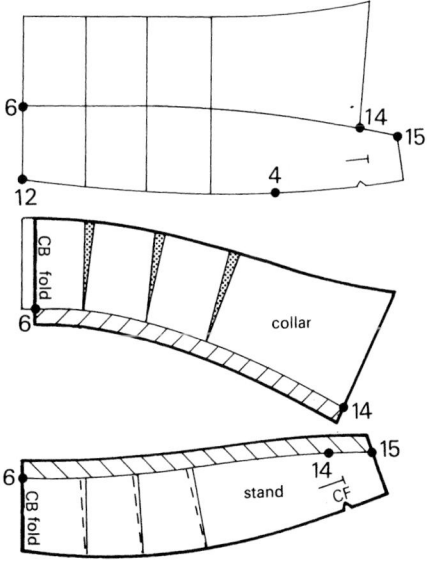

2c Shaped convertible collar with stand

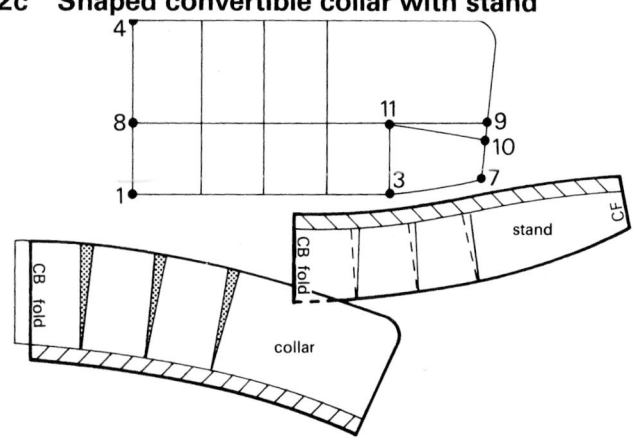

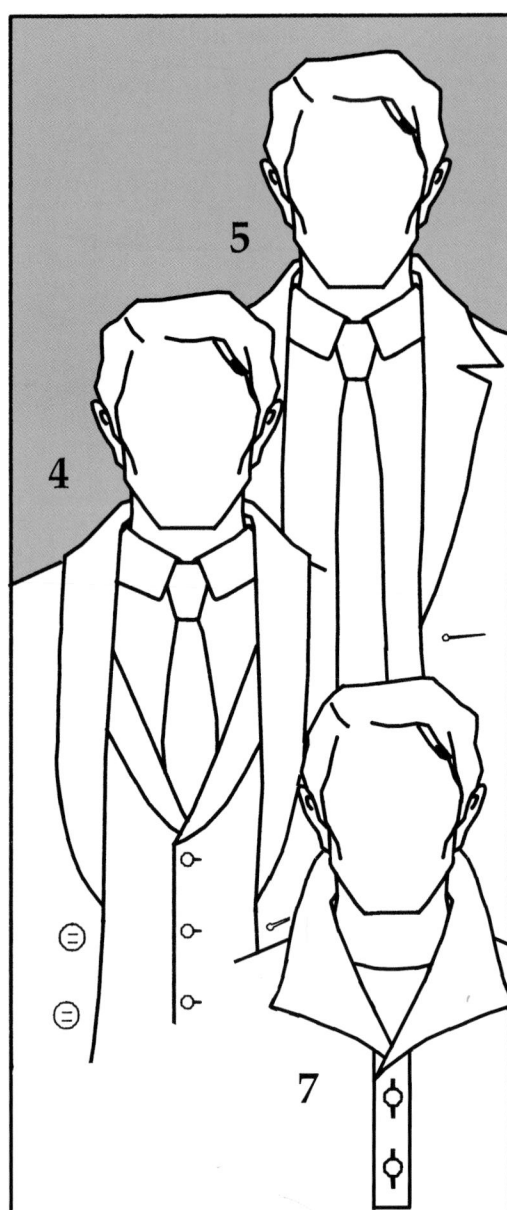

Collars cut in one with the garment

Seam allowances   The roll collar drafts are drafted to include 1cm seam allowance except where marked.

4   Standard roll collar
Body section   Trace round front body section; mark buttonholes, add button stand.
Mark point 1 at break point; mark point 2a at neck point of *fitting line* on front shoulder section.
Extend fitting line of front shoulder.
Mark 2b at neck point, 3 at shoulder point on *fitting line* of back body section.
Place reversed back body section to front body so that points 2a and 2b meet; swing back so that point 3 is 11cm (measured vertically) from extended shoulder line.
Mark 4 at back neck on *fitting line*.
4–5 is 3cm; 5–6 is 4.5cm; 2–7 is 2.5cm.
Draw crease line from 5 through 7 to break point at 1.
Draw in style line from 6 to 1. Draw in facing line.
Facing   Trace off facing. Draw a line across facing below rever. This allows the facing to be cut in two parts, the lower half on the straight grain of fabric; the top half can then have centre back line placed to a fold of the fabric to avoid a back seam.
Add 2cm seam allowance to front edge from 6–1; add 1cm seam allowance from point 1 and on facing line.
Add standard 1cm seam allowance to body section along front edge and back seam of collar.

5   Changing the style line
Changes can be made to the style line, and front edge.
Collars that have extra depth (points 4–6) are drafted with a reduced swing at point 3 so that the outer edge of the collar becomes wider and will allow the collar to sit lower around the shoulders.

6   Standard roll collar with stand
Trace round roll collar block, remove seam allowance from back neck seam and back seam of collar.
Mark points 4, 5, 6, 2.   Join 5–2 with a curved line; cut along this line to remove back collar stand.
Divide stand into 3 sections, cut up lines, overlap edges 0.3cm. Add seam allowance from 5–2 and 4–2.
Remove 0.6cm from back seam of collar.
Add 1cm seam allowance to this seam and back neckline.

7   High shaped collar
Trace roll collar draft with centre front line and to point 6 at back neck. Mark 2 at shoulder point.
Mark point 1 approx. 20cm down from neck point.
1–3 is 2.5cm; square up to 5 at neckline. 1–4 is 2.5cm.
Draw in style line of collar from point 6 to 4.
Trace off collar from point 6 round outer edge, through points 4 and 3, along *fitting line* to point 2 then around outer edge to point 6.
Add seam allowances to the body section from points 5–1 and to all edges of collar from points 2–6.

4 Standard roll collar

5 Changing the style line

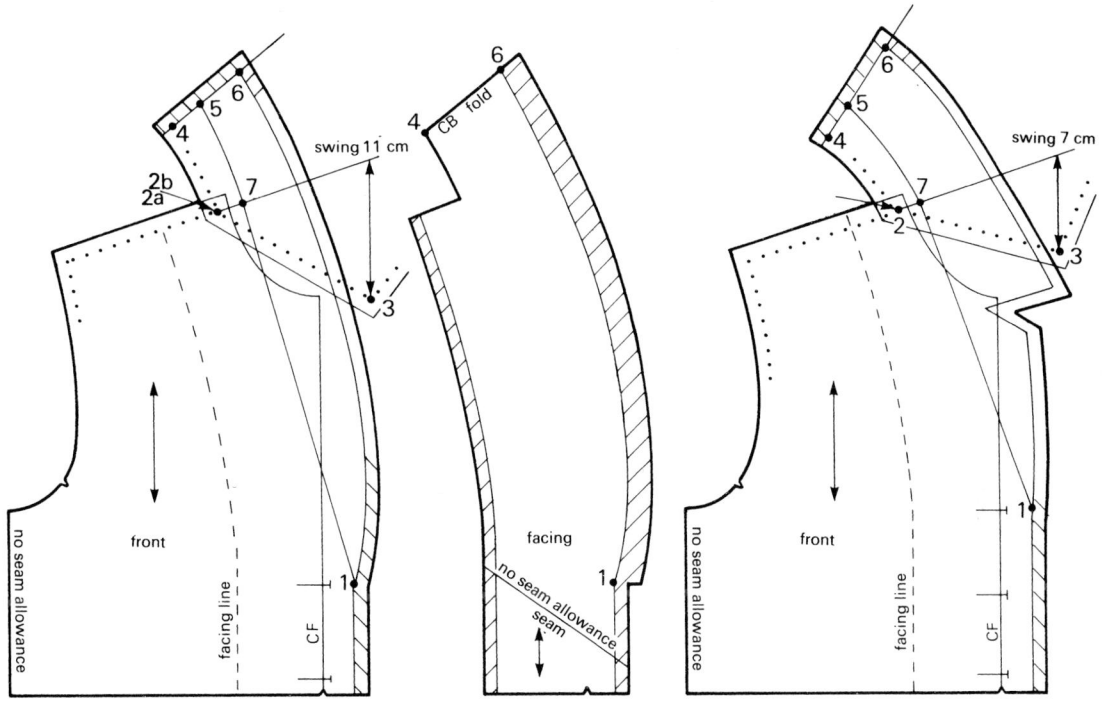

6 Standard roll collar with stand

7 High shaped collar

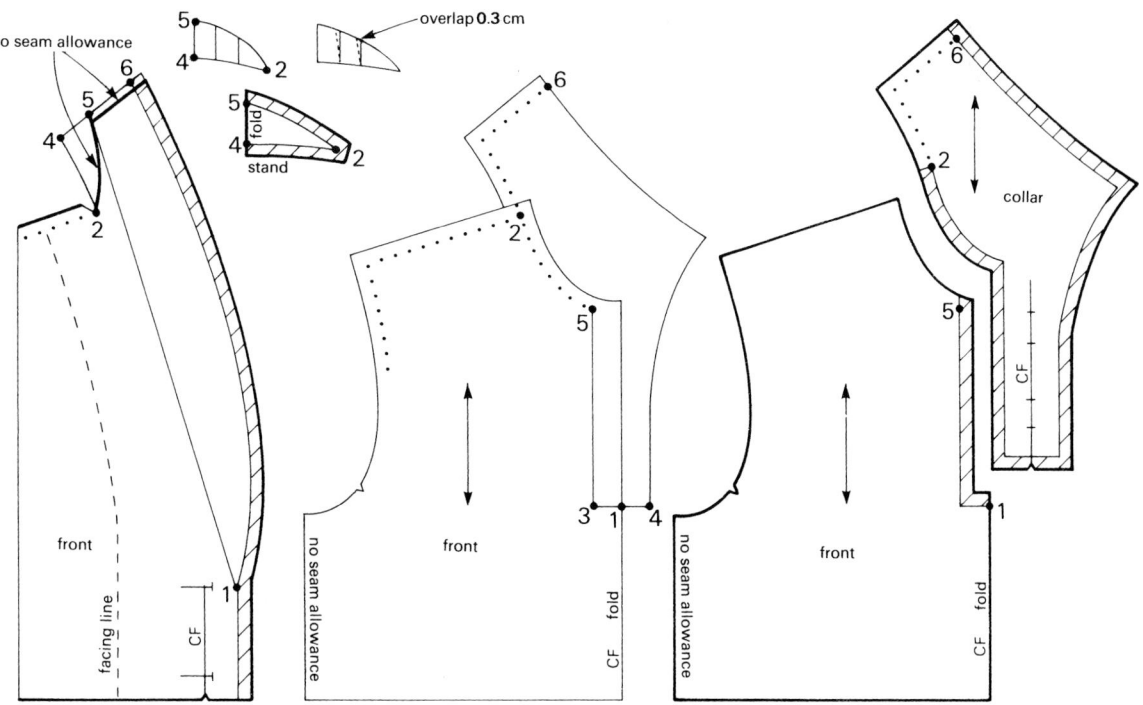

Collars and revers

Bespoke collars and revers

'Bespoke' collars and revers are constructed for tailored garments where the shaping is done by hand methods of steaming and stretching. These collar drafts are constructed for bespoke suits.

For patterns for top collars and facings see page 104.

Engineered collars and revers   Manufacturers use engineered pattern methods to create the shaping for collar and rever styles (see instructions on page 94).

8   Bespoke gents collar

Trace block required.

Draw in facing line. Mark point 1 at break point, 2 at neckline of shoulder point; square down from 2.

2–3   ⅛ neck size plus 1cm.

3–4 is 1.5cm; square across to 5 on centre front line.

Join 3–5; extend rever line from 5.

Mark in and extend *fitting line* of shoulder, mark 6 at neck point. 6–7 is 2.5cm.

Draw break line from point 1 through 7, extend this line.

7–8 is measurement of back neck plus 0.5cm, measured along *fitting line*. 8–9 is 2cm; join 7–9.

(If the break point is near the waistline, 8–9 is 1.5cm; if the break point is very high make 8–9, 2.5cm.)

Using the line 7–9, square across both ways from 9.

9–10 is 3cm; 9–11 is 4cm.

Draw a line from 10 parallel to the line 7–9 to touch the line 3–5 at 12.

Mark collar point 13 (e.g. 2cm in from 5).

Draw style line of collar and rever.

Mark point 14 at collar edge.

Curve outer edge of collar slightly.

Add seam allowance to the body section from neck point 2 to break point 1 and remainder of front edge.

Add seam allowance to under collar at centre back edge and top edge.

Note   When constructing different collar and rever styles based on this draft:

a.   the depth of 3–4 can vary;

b.   the shape and angle of the rever can vary;

c.   the position of the collar point can also vary.

9   Bespoke reefer collar

The example opposite shows the reefer collar used with a double breasted jacket.

Trace off block required.

Mark in both button lines, buttonholes, button stand.

Complete instructions for gents collar but change style line of rever from 13.

Bespoke collars and revers

8 Bespoke gents collar

9 Bespoke reefer collar

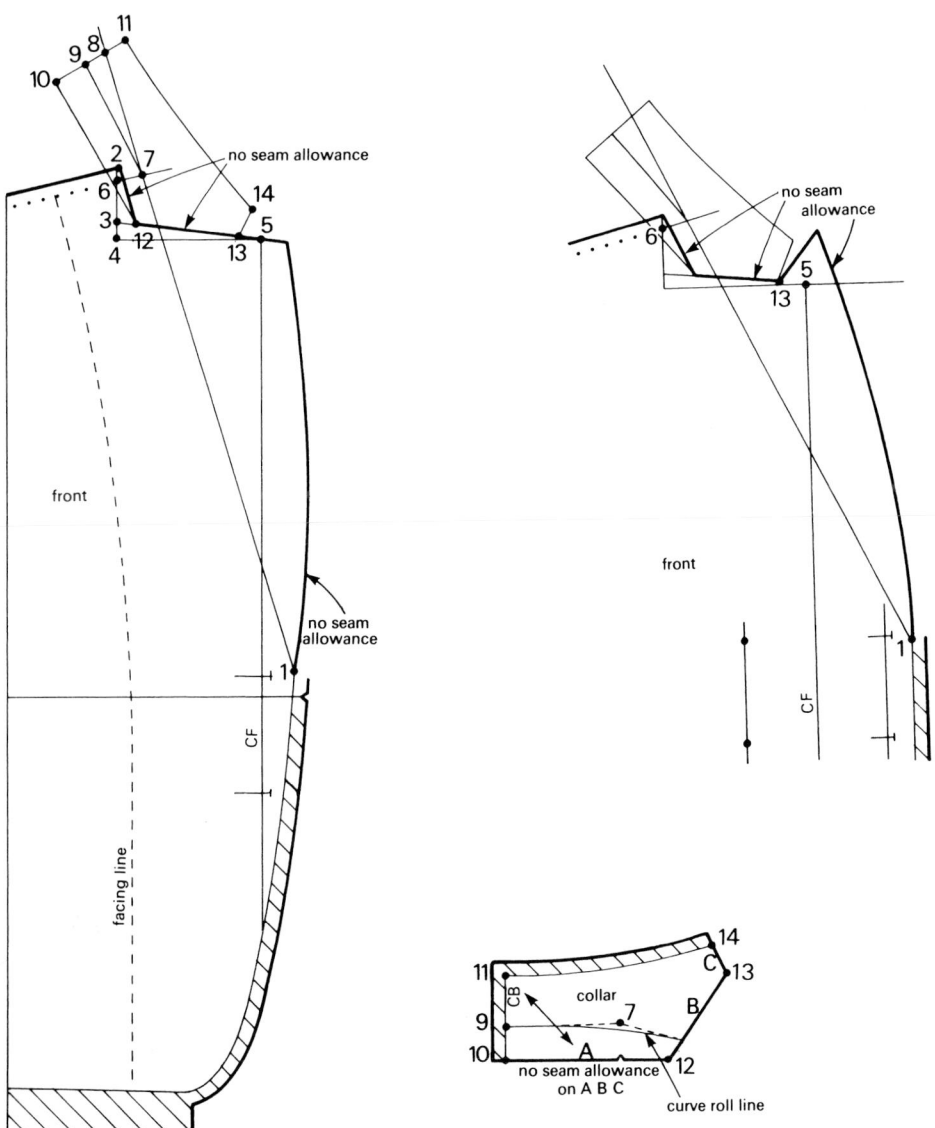

10a
Gents collar

Standard
collar

11

Engineered collars and revers
Manufactured suit and overgarments have engineered collars and revers.
For patterns for top collars and facings see page 104.
Garments constructed from casual or 'flat' blocks.
Remove seam allowance and fitting line from front neckline, add buttonstand and buttonholes.

10a Basic collar and rever draft
Trace block required.
Draw in facing line. Mark point 1 at break point 2 at neckline of shoulder point; square down from 2.
2–3 ⅛ neck size plus 1cm.
3–4 is 1.5cm; square across to 5 on centre front line.
Join 3–5; extend rever line from 5.
Mark in and extend *fitting line* of shoulder, mark 6 at neck point. 6–7 is 2.5cm.
Draw break line from point 1 through 7, extend line.
7–8 is measurement of back neck plus 0.5cm, measured along *fitting line*. 8–9 is 2cm; join 7–9.
(If the break point is near the waistline, 8–9 is 1.5cm. If the break point is very high make 8–9, 2.5cm.)
Using the line 7–9, square across both ways from 9.
9–10 is 3cm; 9–11 is 4cm.
Draw a line from 10 parallel to the line 7–9 to touch the front shoulder line; draw a curved front neckline.
Draw style line of collar and rever. The main style line shows a gents collar (mark gent's collar points 13 and14), the dotted line a standard collar.
Note When constructing different collar and rever styles based on this draft:
a.   the depth of 3–4 can vary;
b.   the shape and angle of the rever can vary;
c.   the shape of the collar and the position of the collar point can also vary.

10b Shaping the collars
Trace off the required under collar.
Divide the collar into four sections at the stand line.
Open the sections slightly at points A B C (the amount varies with type of manufacture and whether the under collar is to be cut on the cross or the straight).

10c Collar with hidden stand
Trace off the required under collar.
Draw new stand line below original stand line.
Divide collar and stand at points A B C.
Shape collar and stand as for shaped convertible collar – hidden stand (ref. 2b, page 88).
Add seam allowance where shown.

11 Collar with visible stand
Construct collar as 10a, but draw collar outline to touch the neck at point A.
Continue the line from 9 to point B.
Trace off collar; divide along the line 9–B.
Divide and shape the collar and stand as for a shaped convertible collar with stand (ref. 2c, page 88).
Add seam allowance where shown.

Engineered collars and revers

10a Basic collar and rever draft

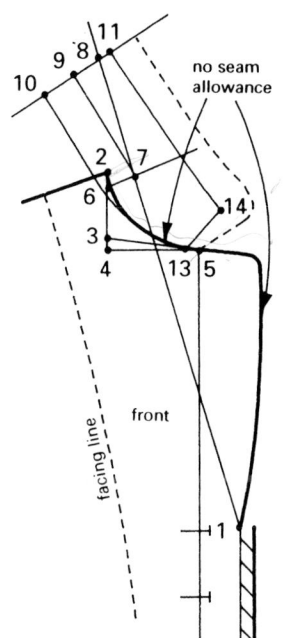

10b Shaping the collars

Gents collar

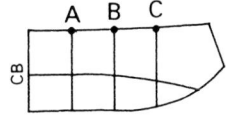

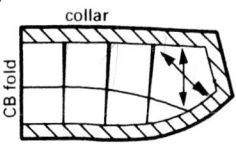

Standard collar

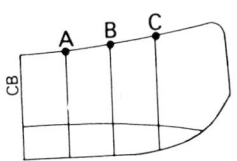
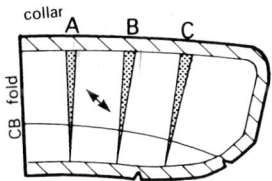

10c Collar with hidden stand

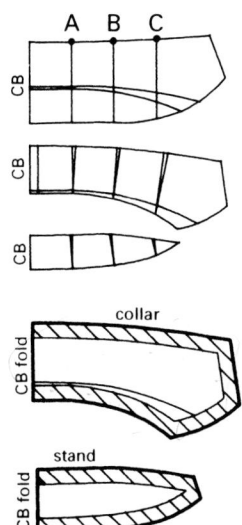

11 Collar with visible stand

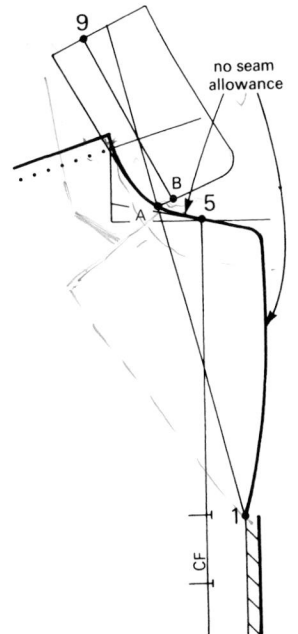
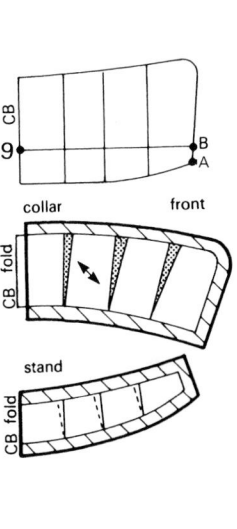

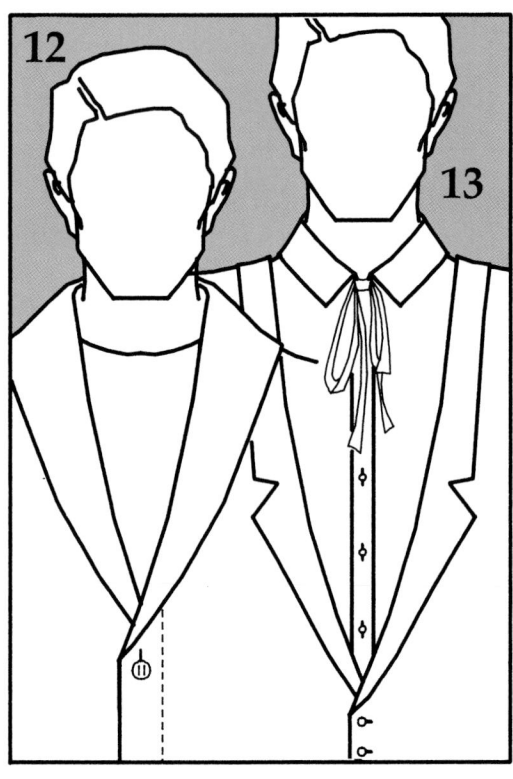

Flat collars

Many flat collars have the appearance of roll collars. For garments with strap or fly fronts construct the collar from a flat collar draft where the collar is a separate pattern piece.

12 Standard flat collar

Trace round front body section. Mark in button stand and buttonholes. Place shoulder of back body section to shoulder of front body section along *fitting lines*.
Draw in *fitting line* of new front neckline.
Draw in collar shape.
Draw four lines at A, B, C, D as shown in diagram.
Trace off collar along *fitting line* of back and front neck, along style line and centre back line.
Cut up lines A, B, C, D; overlap 1cm. Trace collar.
Add seam allowance to neckline and collar style line.
Add seam allowance to front neckline and front edge of front body section.

13 Half collar

Trace front body section. Mark button stand, buttonholes.
Mark A on *fitting line* at neck point.
Draw in *fitting line* of new front neckline.
Draw in collar shape. Trace off collar shape.
Add seam allowance to neckline and style line of collar.
Add seam allowance to front neckline.

12 Standard flat collar

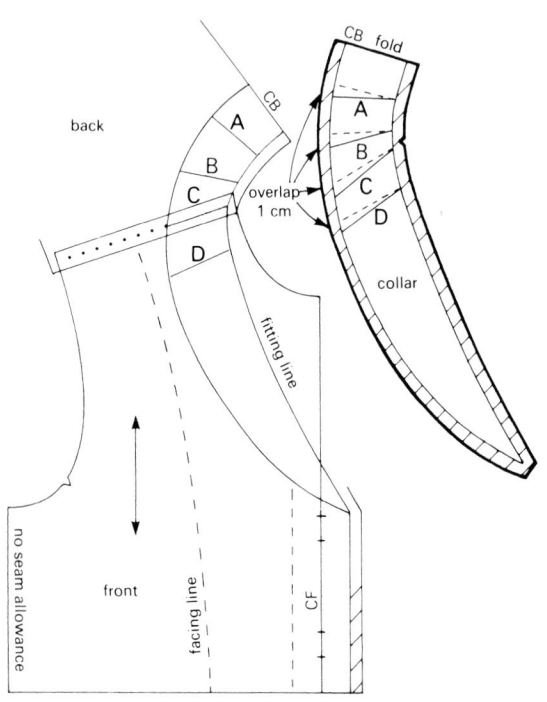

13 Half collar

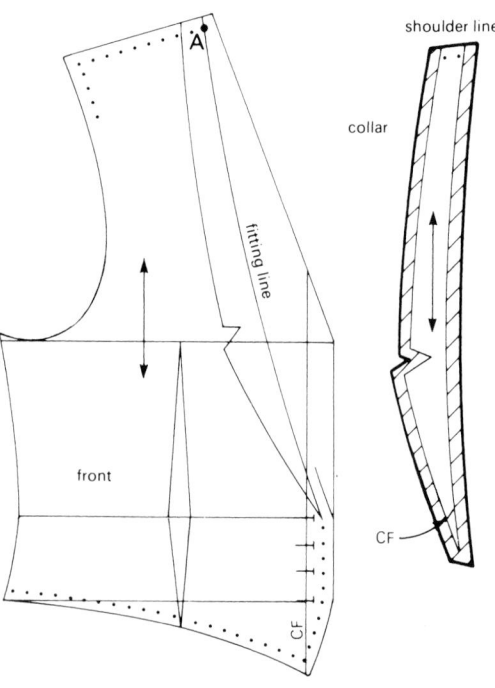

PART THREE: 'FORM' CUTTING – CLASSIC AND CASUAL MENSWEAR

Chapter 8 Classic suit jackets

Classic suit jacket

High cut revers

Classic easy fitting suit jacket

Classic suit jackets

The classic suit jacket block

Measurements required to draft the block
The sample illustrated is for the athletic figure (chest 100cm). Refer to the size chart (page 12) for standard measurements.

Chest	100cm
Scye depth	24.4cm
Back neck to waist	44.2cm
Neck size	40cm
Half back	20cm
Jacket length – varies with fashion	76cm

A 1cm seam allowance is included in the block except where stated **no seam allowance.**

Body section
Square both ways from 0.
0–1 scye depth plus 1cm; square across.
0–2 ½ measurement 0–1; square across.
0–3 ¼ scye depth; square across.
0–4 back neck to waist; square across.
4–5 21cm (seat line); square across.
0–6 jacket length; square across.
4–7 1.5cm; square down to 8 and 9; join 7–1 to complete back seam line.
0–10 ¼ neck size minus 0.5cm; square up.
10–11 2cm; draw in neck curve.
1–12 half back plus 2.5cm; square up to 13 and 14.
14–15 2.25cm.
15–16 2cm; draw lightly hollowed shoulder line.
12–17 ¼ armhole depth minus 1cm. 17–18 is 0.5cm.
18–19 1cm; square down to 20. 19–21 is 1cm.
12–22 2.5cm; square down to 23 and 24.
1–25 ½ chest plus 10cm; square down to 26 and 27.
27–28 2cm; join 28–24.
12–29 ⅙ chest minus 1.5cm; square up 2cm to 30.
29–31 ½ measurement 29–25 minus 1cm; square up to 32. Join 32 to 14.
32–33 the measurement 11–16. Square down 1cm to 34. Join 34 to 30.
Join 34 to 32 with a slight curve.
30–35 ⅓ measurement 30–34; 35–36 is 1.5cm.
29–37 4cm; square down to 38 and 39.
Draw in armhole shape; make a step of 0.5cm at 19.
24–40 3.5cm. Draw in back seam 19, 23, 40.
Draw in back seam of side body 19, 20, 24.
39–41 0.5cm.
39–42 2cm. Draw in front seam of side body 37, 38, 41.

Draw in front seam of forepart 37, 38, 42; curve in 37–38 by 1cm.
29–43 2.5cm; square down to 44, 8cm below the waistline (centre of pocket); square across.
44–45 8.25cm. 44–46 is 9.5cm. 46–47 is 1cm; join 45–47.
45–48 1.5cm; square up to 49 and 50, 6cm below the scye depth line.
Draw in 1cm front dart from 50.
25–51 1.25cm; join 30–51.
30–52 4cm, 52–53 is 10cm; square up from 52 and 53; draw in breast pocket.
26–54 1.5cm; top buttonhole position; square out.
54–55 10cm; lower buttonhole position.
54–56 2.5cm.
28–57 6cm; join 56–57 as shown.
29–58 ½ measurement 12–29 minus 1cm; mark underarm point (UP).
Mark back pitch (BP) 1.5cm below 13; mark front pitch (FP) at 30.

Draw in *fitting line* of shoulder; extend *fitting line*.
The diagram shows points (1) (6) (7) from the collar and rever draft to show position of break line.
See refs. 8–10 pages 92 and 94 to complete the collar and rever draft.

Complete the two-piece sleeve block on page 102. See pages 104–105 for the completion of a suit pattern.

Closer fitting alterations
If a suit with a closer waist, armhole and sleeve fitting is required, complete the instructions for the block above, but with the following alterations. These alterations must be made before drafting the sleeve.
0–1 scye depth measurement; square across.
Remove 0.5cm from the side body side seam (37, 38, 41).
Shape in front side seam (37, 38, 42) 0.5cm at point 37, 1cm at point 38 and 0.5cm at point 42.
From point 50, construct a 1.5cm dart.

High cut revers
High cut revers and button placements require a narrower neck gorge.
Make the following alterations to the draft.
32–32a 2cm; join 32a to 14.
32a–33 the measurement 11–16; square down 0.75cm to 34. Join 34–32a with a slight curve.

99

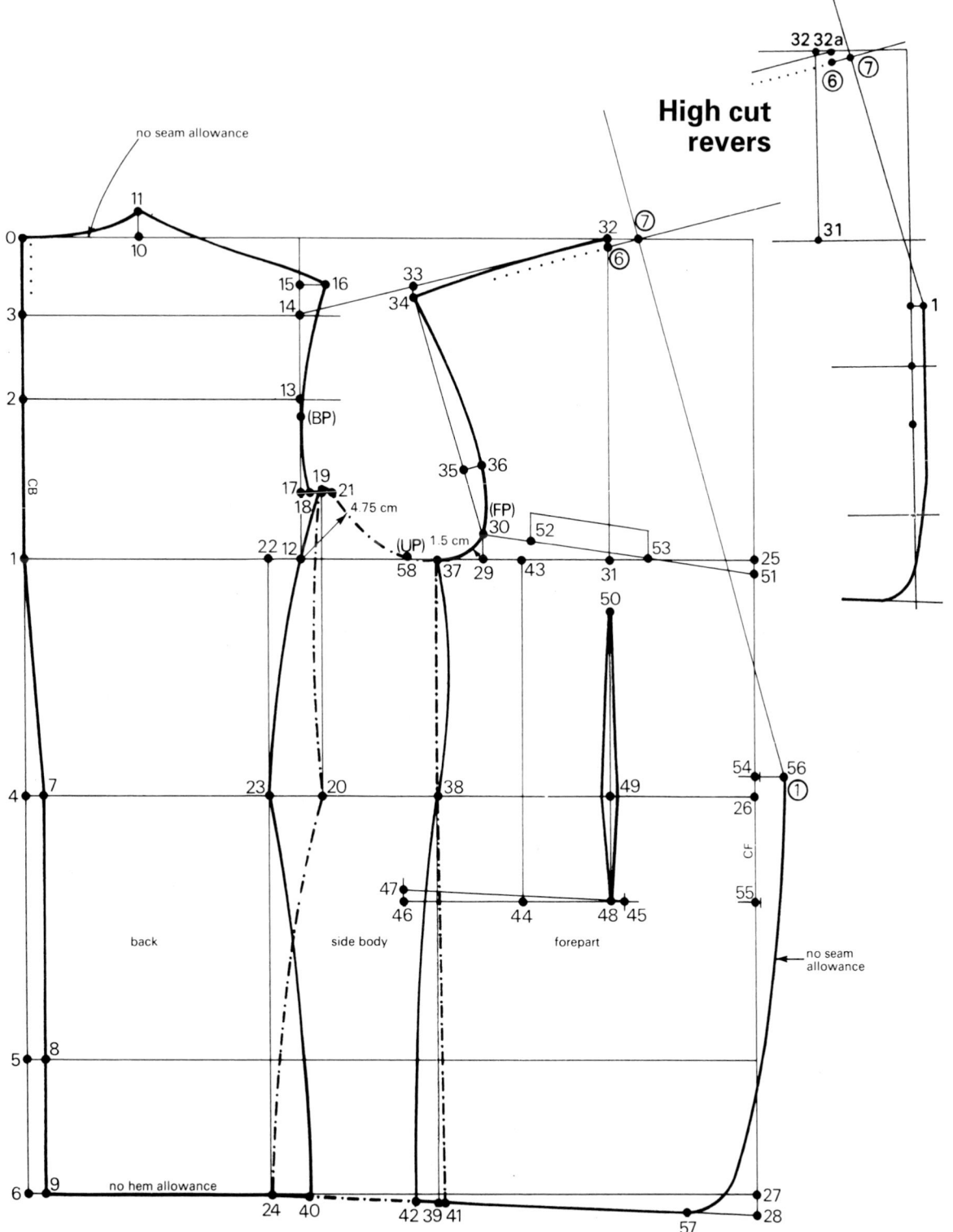

High cut revers

WATFORD LRC

The classic easy fitting suit jacket block

This block is for an easy fitting suit with a widened shoulder.

Measurements required to draft the block
The sample illustrated is for the athletic figure (chest 100cm). Refer to the size chart (page 12) for standard measurements.

Chest	100cm
Scye depth	24.4cm
Back neck to waist	44.2cm
Neck size	40cm
Half back	20cm
Jacket length – varies with fashion	76cm

A 1cm seam allowance is included in the block except where stated **no seam allowance**. There is 0.7cm ease on the back shoulder.

Body section
Square both ways from 0.
0–1 scye depth plus 5cm; square across.
0–2 ½ scye depth plus 1.5cm; square across.
0–3 ¼ scye depth minus 0.5cm; square across.
0–4 back neck to waist; square across.
4–5 21cm (seat line); square across.
0–6 jacket length; square across.
4–7 1.5cm; square down to 8 and 9; join 7–1 to complete back seam line.
0–10 0.25cm; join 10–3 with a curve.
10–11 ¼ neck size minus 0.5cm; square up.
11–12 2cm; draw in neck curve.
1–13 half back plus 4cm; square up to 14 and 15.
15–16 3cm; square out.
16–17 3cm; square down 1.75cm to 18; join 12–18 through 16 with a hollowed curved line.
13–19 ½ measurement 13–14 plus 0.5cm.
19–20 0.5cm.
20–21 1cm; square down to 22. 21–23 is 1cm.
13–24 2.5cm; square down to 25 and 26.
1–27 ½ chest plus 15cm; square down to 28, 29 and up to 30.
29–31 2cm; join 31–26.
13–32 ⅙ chest plus 1cm; square up 3cm to 33.
30–34 ¼ neck size plus 2.5cm; join 34–15.
34–35 the measurement 12–16 minus 1cm (minus 0.5cm for less ease on back shoulder); square down 1.75cm to 36; square out.
36–37 3cm.
37–38 2cm; join 34–38 through 36, with a curved line as shown.
33–39 ⅓ measurement 33–38.

39–40 1.5cm.
32–41 4.5cm; square down to 42 and 43.
26–44 1.5cm; draw in back seam 21, 25, 44.
26–45 0.5cm; draw in back seam of side body 21, 22, 45.
43–46 0.5cm; draw in front seam of forepart 41, 42, 46; curve in 41–42 by 0.75cm.
Draw in side body seam 41, 42, 43.
32–47 ½ measurement 32–27 minus 1cm; square down to 48, 8cm below the waistline.
48–49 1cm; square across.
49–50 measurement of pocket (16.5cm). Add to this measurement, the 2cm seam allowance of the side seam minus any overlap of the side seam.
50–51 1cm; join 49–51.
47–52 2cm; mark point 53 on waistline. Draw in 1cm front dart from 52–48.
27–54 1.25cm; 32–55 2cm; join 54–55.
55–56 5cm.
56–57 10cm; square up from 56 and 57; draw in breast pocket.
28–58 1.5cm; top buttonhole position; square out.
58–59 10cm; lower buttonhole position.
58–60 2.5cm.
31–61 6cm; join 60–61 with a curve as shown.
32–62 ½ measurement 13–32 minus 1cm; mark underarm (UP).
Mark back pitch (BP) 2.75cm below 14; mark front pitch (FP) at 33.
Draw in armhole shape; make a step of 0.5cm at 21.
Draw in *fitting line* of shoulder; extend *fitting line* 2.5cm. Join to point 60 for the break line.
See refs. 8–10 pages 92 and 94 to complete the collar and rever.

Complete the two-piece sleeve block on page 102. A larger but not deeper shoulder pad is required to give a smooth shoulder line.
See pages 104–105 for the completion of a suit pattern.

High cut revers

High cut revers and button placements require a narrower neck gorge.
The diagram shows points (1) (6) (7) from collar draft to show position of break line (see refs. 8–10 pages 92 and 94).
Make the following alteration to the draft.
30–34 ¼ neck size plus 0.5cm. Join 34–15.
34–35 the measurement 12–16 minus 1cm (minus 0.5cm for less ease on the back shoulder); square down 1.5cm to 36; square out.

High cut revers

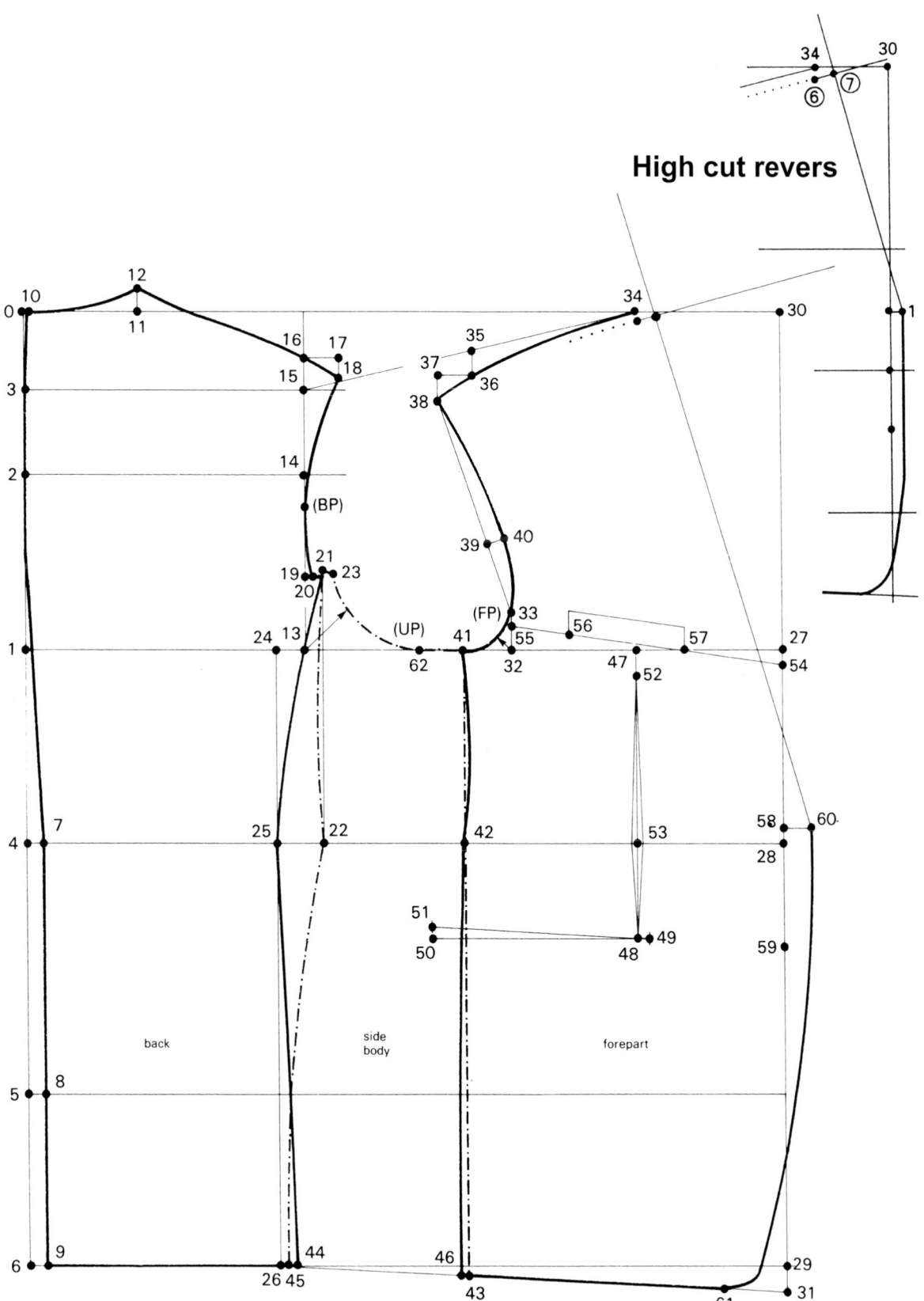

The suit two-piece sleeve block

Measurements required to draft the block
The sample illustrated is for the classic suit jacket block for the athletic figure (chest 100cm). Refer to the size chart (page 12) for standard measurements.

Sleeve length two-piece sleeve	82cm
Cuff size two-piece sleeve	29.2cm

Note
1. Instructions for the sleeve which will fit the easy fitting suit block are shown in brackets.
2. If constructing a sleeve for the close fitting version of the classic suit, make the cuff size 28.2cm.

A 1cm seam allowance is included in the block.

Top sleeve
Mark point 0, square across, up and down.
0–1   2cm (3cm) mark FP.
0–2   the measurement 12–BP (13–BP) on body block; square across.
0–3   ⅓ measurement 16–18 plus 21–34 (18–20 plus 23–38) on armhole of body block measured in a curve; square across.
1–4   is measured straight to touch the line from 3. The measurement is: 34–FP (38–FP) on body block, measured in a *curve* plus 2cm (1.75cm).
4–5   is measured straight to touch the line from 2. The measurement is: 16–BP (18–BP) on body block, measured in a *curve* plus 1cm.
0–6   2cm; square down with a dotted line.
7   is midway between 5 and 4.
4–8   ⅓ measurement 4–1.
Draw in sleeve head through points 5, 4, 1, 6 as shown in diagram.

5–9   1.5cm.
9–10   sleeve length minus half back plus 1cm; square out.
10–11   ½ measurement 1–10; square across.
10–12   3.5cm; square across.
12–13   ½ cuff size plus 2cm (3cm).
10–14   2cm; join 13–10.
Join 6–14; curve line inwards 1cm at elbow line. Join 5–13 with a dotted line: mark 15 on elbow line.
15–16   3cm.
Join 5–13 curving the line through point 16.

Undersleeve
0–17   2cm: square down with a dotted line.
17–18   0.5cm.
10–19   2cm; join 18–19. Curve the line inwards 1cm at elbow line.
0–20   the measurement 29–58 (32–62) on the body block plus 0.3cm.
21–22   is measured straight to touch the line from 2–5.
The measurement is: BP–18 plus 21–58 (BP–20 plus 23–62) on body block, measured in a *curve*, plus 0.5cm.
23   midway between 21 and 22.
23–24   1.75cm; draw a curved line through the points 22, 24, 21, 18.
22–25   1.5cm: join 25–13. Mark point 26 on elbow line.
26–27   ½ measurement 16–26 plus 0.8cm.
Join 25–13 curving the line through point 27.
Extend back seam line 0.25cm above 25 to 28.
Extend underarm seam line 0.75cm above 22 to 29.
Join 28–29.

Classic suit block

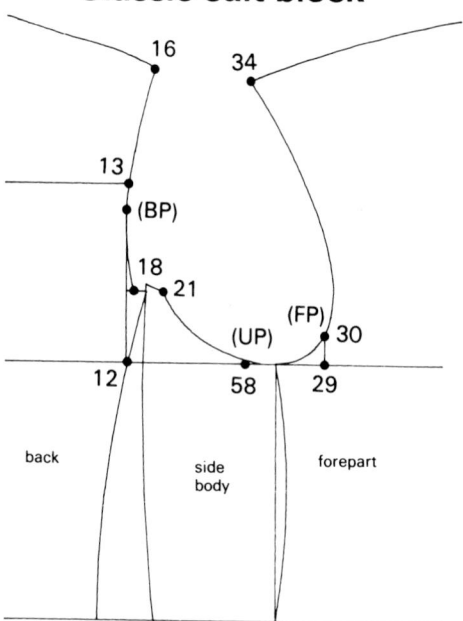

Easy fitting suit block

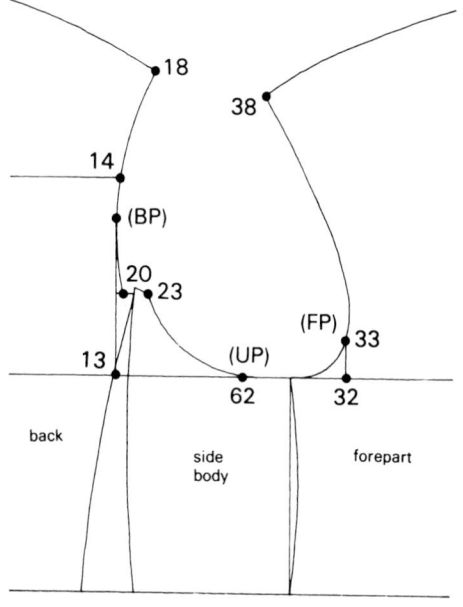

Two-piece sleeve

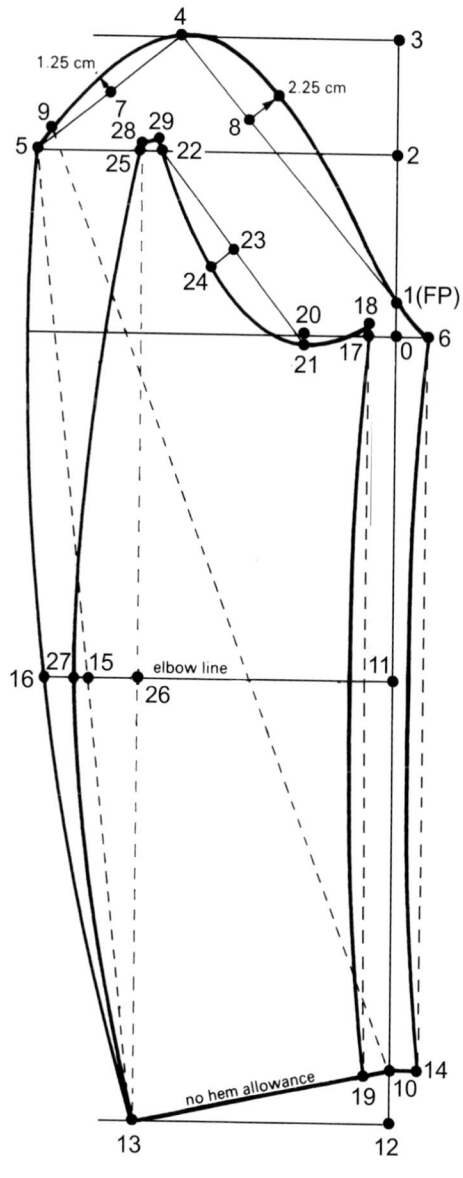

To complete suit jacket patterns

Back and side body Trace off back and side body. Add vents: example shows side body seam vents; 24cm long 4cm wide. Add 4cm hem allowance. Add seam allowance to back neck.

Forepart Trace off forepart.
Add seam allowance from neck point A to point B on hemline on forepart. Add 4cm hem allowance. Stretch armhole from C–D.

Facing Trace off facing. Add 1cm seam allowance to all edges except the shoulder line.

Under collars See the instructions on pages 92 and 94.

Top collars – bespoke The top collar is cut after the under collar has been shaped. Add 1cm seam allowance to neck and outer edge of collar and 1.5cm to front edge.

Add ease (0.25cm–0.5cm) to the edges shown in the diagram.
Top collars – manufacture Add 1cm seam allowance to all edges. Add ease (0.25cm–0.5cm) to the edges shown in the diagram.
Sleeves Trace off top sleeve and under sleeve. Add vents to back seams 10cm long, 2.5cm wide. Add 6cm seam allowance.
Pockets Construct pocket flap: 16.5cm long, 7cm wide. Add seam allowance to all edges. Trace off breast pocket: add 2cm seam allowance to top edge, 1cm to the remainder of the edges.

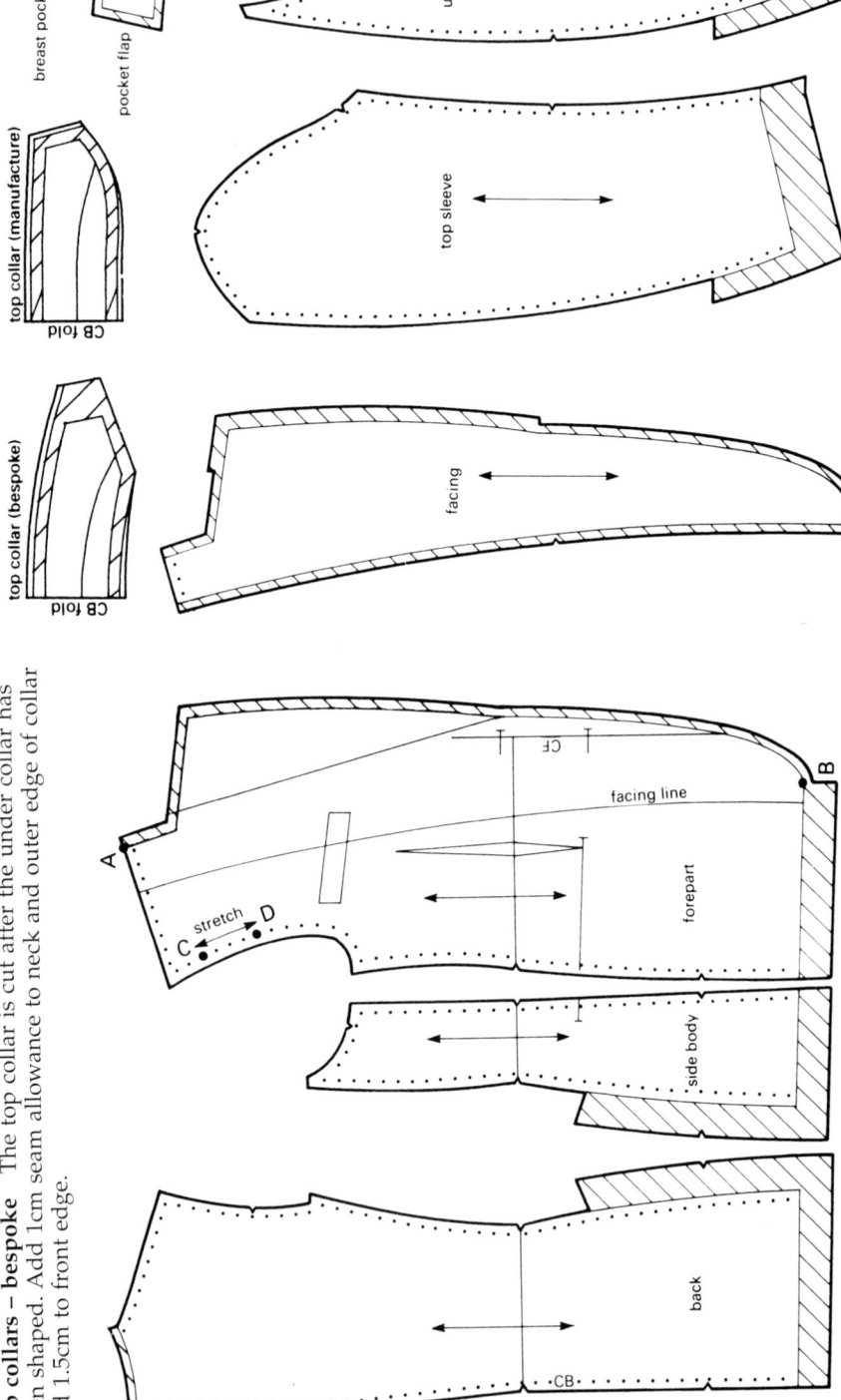

Lining the suit jackets

Ease allowance is required on linings for two reasons.
1. Cloth garment pieces 'spread' a little when they are cut out. Extra ease allowance is required on linings because lining fabrics do not relax in the same manner. The amount of ease required will vary depending on the cloth used for the garment.
2. The linings should also be loose enough to prevent the garment being pulled out of shape when the lining is inserted. Particular stress points are the armholes and the centre back.

Note Some bespoke tailors cut linings from the cloth pieces of the garment, specific ease is then added at the stress points. Body and sleeve lining hems are cut 2cm above cloth hemlines.

Back Add 2cm at A for a centre back pleat. Add 1.5cm out and up at B: 1cm out and 0.5cm up at C: 0.3cm out at D and E.
Side body Add 0.5cm up and out at F and G. Add vent allowance.
Forepart Add 2cm up at H for front pleat: 1.5cm out at I. Add 1cm out at J: 1cm out and 0.5cm up at K. Add 0.3cm out at L and M. Add 2cm for seam at N.
Top sleeve Add 1.5cm up and 0.8cm out at O and P: 1.5cm up at Q.
Under sleeve Add 0.8cm out and 1.5cm up at R and S: Add 1.5cm at underarm point T; re-shape the under-arm curve as shown. Add vent allowance.

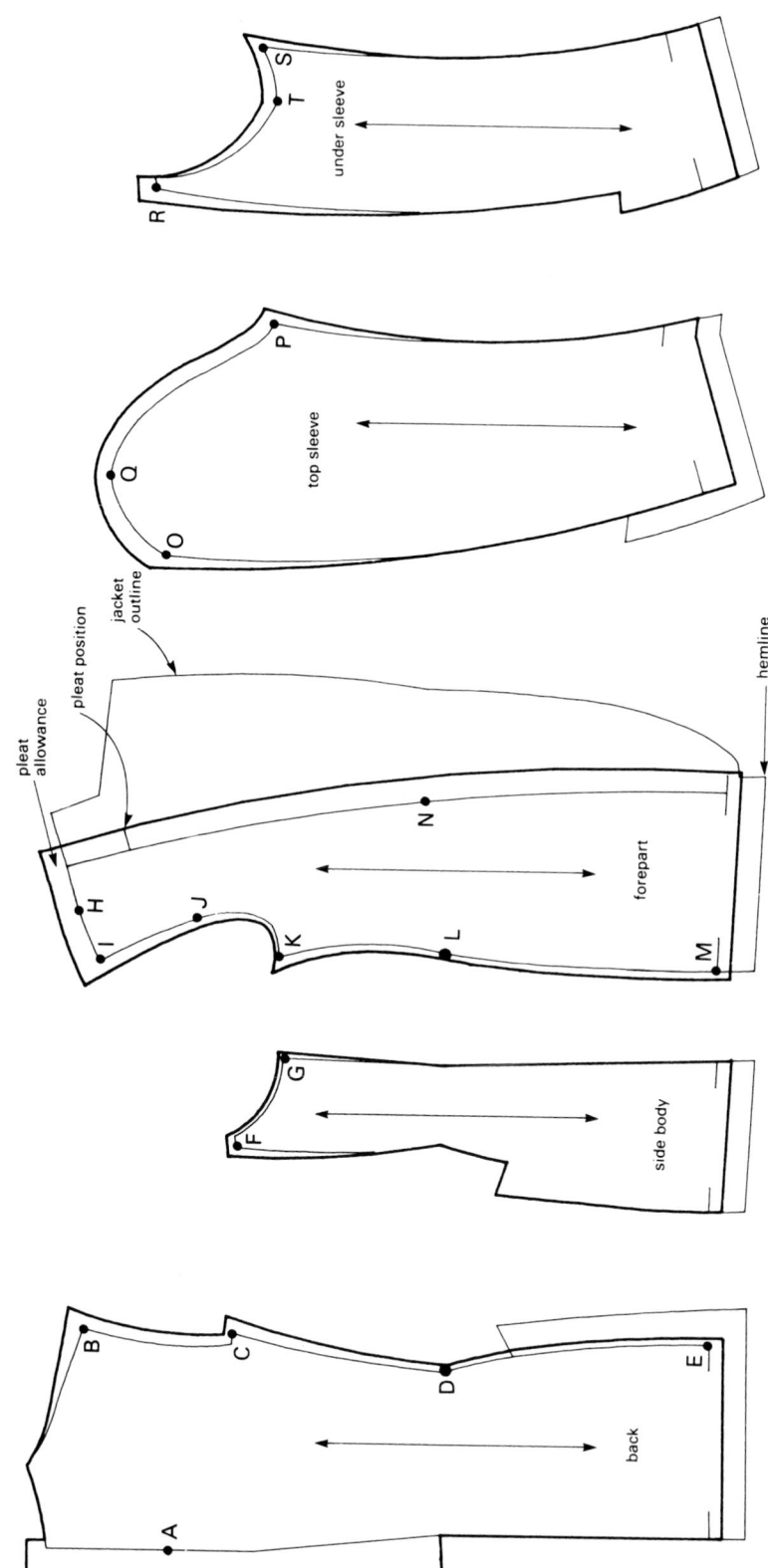

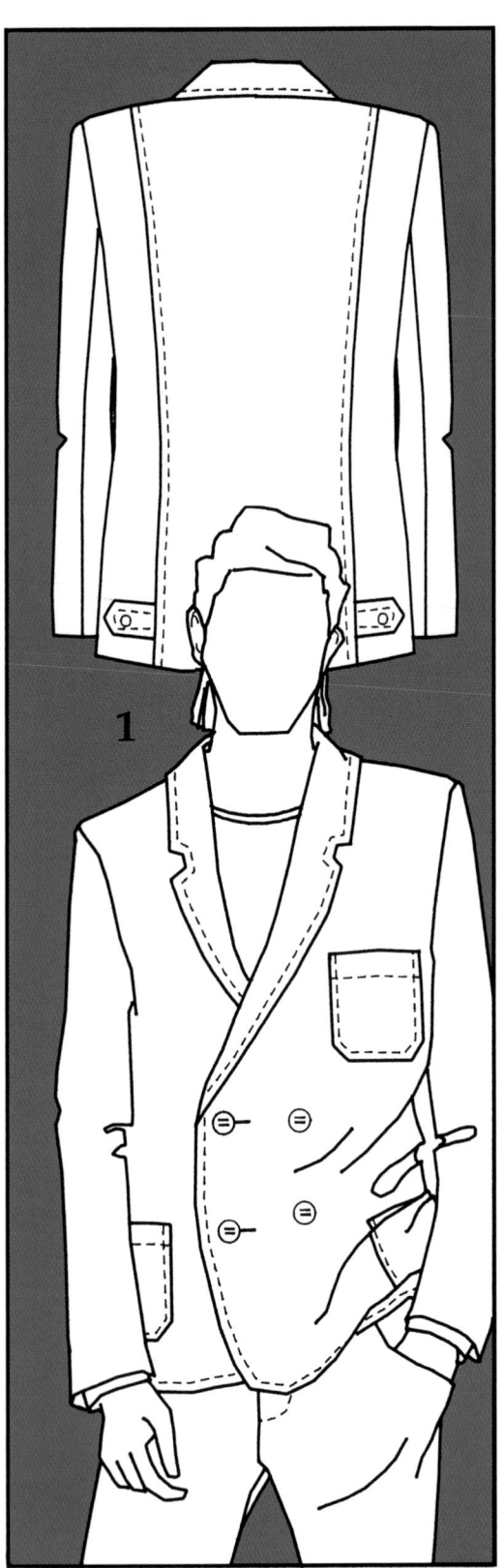

1 Suit jacket design

This design has a double breasted front. panel back and notched roll collar. Seam allowances for a welt seam are given for the back panel seam.

Trace off the classic suit block at length required to the centre front line. Omit break line and centre back shaping. Trace off suit jacket two-piece sleeve.

Mark points 19, 29, 37, 41, 42, 45, 47.

Points 1, 2, 3, 7 are from the roll collar adaptation.

Body section   Square down from point 19.

Mark in 1cm seam allowance each side of line.

Remove the seam allowance from the centre back line.

Draw in back style line to waistline, mark points A and B (B is 12cm from CB); square down to C on hem line.

A–D is 1cm: B–E is 3cm; C–F is 3cm.

Draw in scye depth line. Mark point 29.

Draw in button lines 6cm each side of centre front line.

Add 2.5cm button stand. Mark buttonholes 5cm above and below waistline. Mark break point.

Draw diagonal shaping at front hem, as in diagram.

Construct roll collar (ref. 4, page 90), draw in notch on style line. Draw in facing line.

29–G is 3cm; G–H is 13cm; G–I is 1cm: join I–H.

Square down 13cm from H–J and I-K; draw in shaping at base of pocket.

Draw in pocket line 45–47; extend to 19cm.

Square down 19cm from 45 to L.

Draw lower edge of pocket parallel to the hem line.

Back   Trace off back section along A, B, F.

Add seam allowance to neck edge and panel seam.

Add 4cm hem allowance.

Side body   Trace off side body along D, E, C and along the line 37–41.

Remove the seam allowance from the seam at point 19; rejoin pattern piece.

Add 2cm seam allowance to panel seam.

Add 4cm hem allowance.

Forepart   Trace off forepart section.

Seam allowance is added to the front edge and back neckline. Add 4cm hem allowance.

Facing   Trace off facing and complete as for standard roll collar (ref. 4, page 90).

Remove seam allowance from centre back neck seam.

Pockets   Trace off top pocket.

Add 4cm facing to top edge, add seam allowance to remainder of the edges.

Trace off the three sides of lower pocket.

Make 45–M 18cm; square down to N on lower line.

N–O is 1cm: join M–O. Shape lower edge of pocket.

Add 4cm facing to top edge.

Add seam allowance to remainder of the edges.

Tab   Construct tab; add seam allowance to all edges.

Sleeves   Add vents to back seams; length = 10cm, width = 2.5cm. Add 6cm hem allowance.

1 Suit jacket design

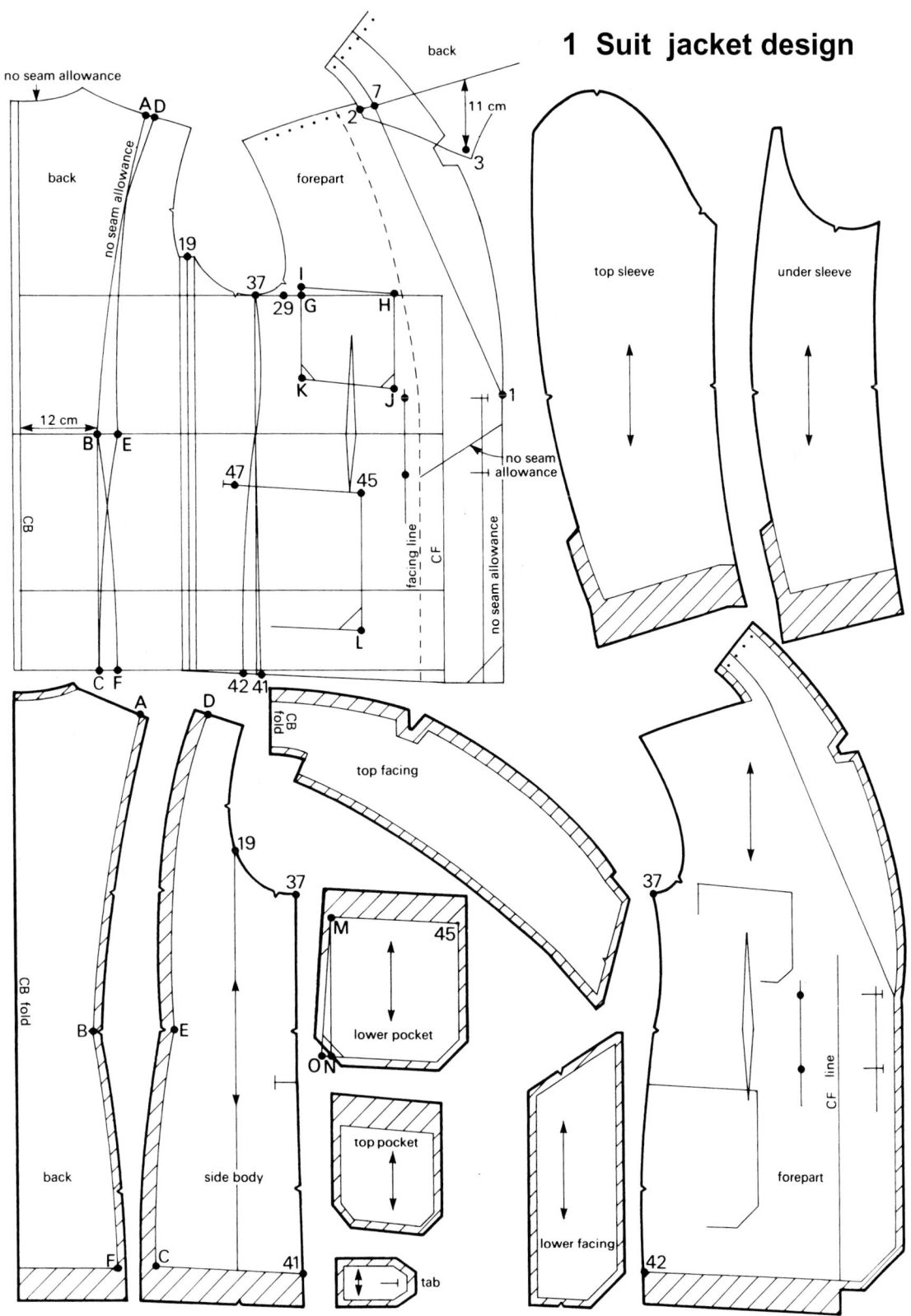

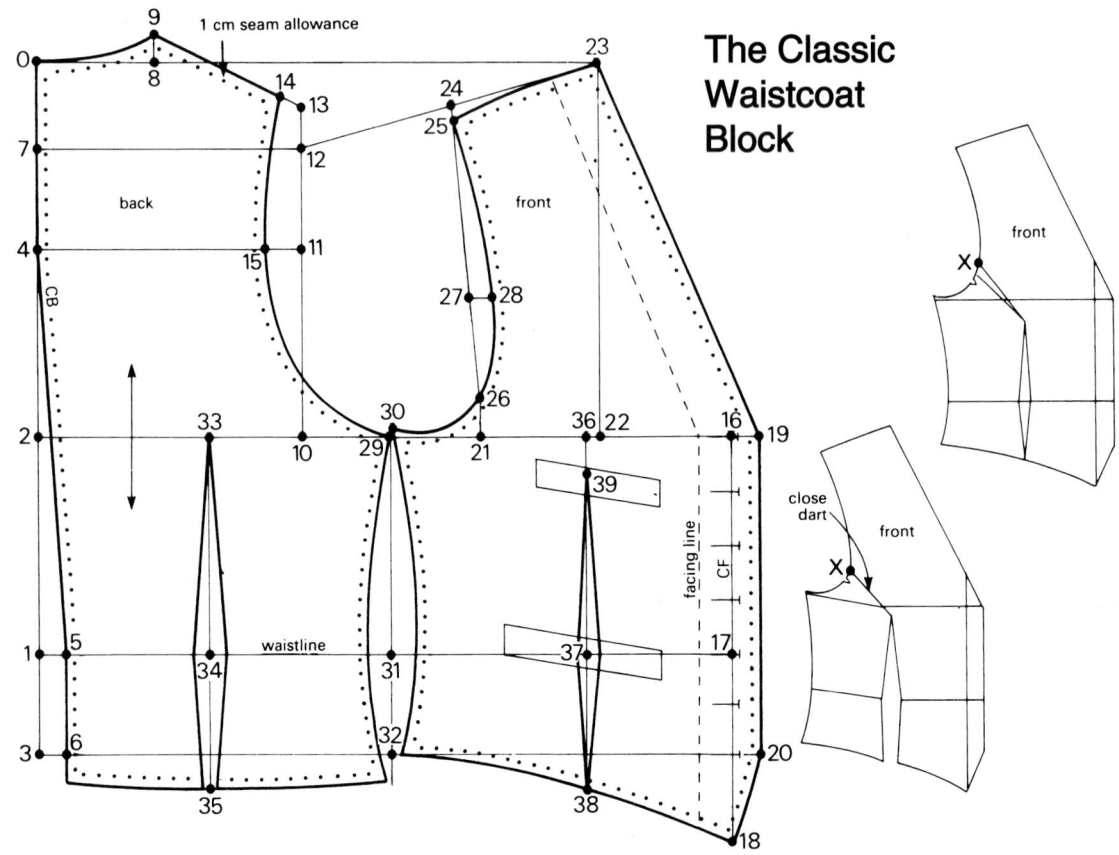

The Classic Waistcoat Block

The classic waistcoat block

Measurements required to draft the block
The sample illustrated is for the athletic figure (100cm chest). Refer to size chart (page 12) for standard measurements.
A 1cm seam allowance is included in the block.

Chest	100cm
Back neck to waist	44.2cm
Scye depth	24.4cm
Half back	20cm

Square both ways from 0.
0–1   nape to waist plus 1cm; square across.
0–2   scye depth plus 4cm; square across.
1–3   7.5cm; square across.
0–4   ½ measurement 0–2; square across.
1–5   2cm; square down to 6. Join 4–5.
0–7   ¼ scye depth; square across.
0–8   ¼ neck minus 1cm. 8–9 is 2cm; draw in neck curve.
2–10   half back plus lcm; square up to 11 and 12.
12–13   2.5cm; join 9–13. 13–14 is 2cm. 11–15 is 3cm.
2–16   ½ chest plus 5cm; square down to 17 on waistline. 17–18 is 14cm.

16–19   2.5cm; square down to 20.
10–21   ⅙ chest measurement minus 2.5cm.
16–22   ½ measurement 16–21 plus 0.5cm; square up to 23. Join 23–12.
23–24   The measurement 9–14 plus 0.5cm.
24–25   1cm; join 23–25.
21–26   3cm; join 25–26.
26–27   ⅓ measurement 25–26; 27–28 is 1.5cm.
10–29   ½ measurement 10–21; square up 0.5cm to 30, down to 31 and 32.
Draw back armhole through points 14, 15, 29.
Draw front armhole through points 25, 28, 26, 30.
Draw front edge 23, 19, 20, 18.
Draw lower edge of front from 32 as shown.
Add 2cm to lower edge of back, draw with slight curve.
2–33   ½ measurement 2–10 plus 2.5cm: square down to 34 and 35.
Construct back dart from 33; shape 2.5cm at 34, 1cm at 35.
22–36   1cm; square down to 37 and 38.
36–39   2.5cm.
Construct front dart from 39; shape 1.5cm at 37.
Shape side seam 4cm at 31, 1cm at 32.
Standard placings for pockets are shown.
Note   Close fitting armhole – take 0.75cm dart at X.

PART THREE: 'FORM' CUTTING – CLASSIC AND CASUAL MENSWEAR

Chapter 9 Classic and casual trousers

The 'flat' trouser blocks in Part two are used for garments that are often flat packed, are very easy fitting or are manufactured in jersey.

The classic trouser block

Measurements required to draft the block

The sample illustrated is for the athletic figure (trouser waist 90cm, seat 102cm, chest 100cm). Refer to the size chart (page 12) for standard measurements.

Seat	102cm
Trouser waist	90cm
Body rise	28.1cm
Inside leg measurement	80cm
Trouser bottom width	22.6cm
Waistband depth (the example uses a 4cm waistband).	

1cm seam allowance is included in the block. There is no hem allowance.

Special Note Most trousers sit 4cm below the natural waistline, therefore:
1. For basic trousers use the trouser waist measurement.
2. For trousers that sit high on the natural waist, use the waist measurement and add 5cm to body rise measurement.
3. For trousers that sit well below the waistline see page 116.

Front

Square down and across from 0.

0–1 body rise plus 1cm minus waistband depth; square across.

1–2 inside leg measurement; square across.

2–3 ½ measurement 1–2 plus 5cm; square across.

1–4 ¼ body rise measurement; square across.

1–5 ⅛ seat measurement minus 1cm square up to 6 on seat line, 7 on waistline.

6–8 ¼ seat measurement plus 2cm.

5–9 ¹⁄₁₆ seat measurement plus 0.5cm.

7–10 1cm.

Draw in front fork 9, 6, 10 to touch a point 3cm from 5 as shown in diagram.

10–11 ¼ trouser waist plus 2.5cm.

2–12 ½ bottom width.

2–13 ½ bottom width.

3–14 the measurement 2–12 plus 1.5cm.

3–15 the measurement 2–13 plus 1.5cm.

Draw side seam through points 11, 8, 14, 12. Curve hipline outwards 0.5cm.

Draw inside leg seam; join 13–15, join 9–15 curving the line inwards 0.6cm.

Back

5–16 ¼ measurement 1–5; square up to 17 on the seat line and 18 on the waistline.

19 midway between 16 and 18.

18–20 2cm.

20–21 1cm.

9–22 ½ measurement 5–9 plus 0.5cm.

22–23 0.5cm.

Draw in back fork 23, 19, 21 to touch a point 4.5cm from 16 as shown in diagram.

21–24 trouser waist plus 4.5cm.

25 midway between 21 and 24: square down from this line.

Construct a dart on this line; length = 12cm, width = 2.5cm.

17–26 ¼ seat measurement plus 3cm.

12–27 2cm.

13–28 2cm.

14–29 2cm.

15–30 2cm.

Draw side seam through points 24, 26, 29, 27; but curve the line from 26–29 inwards 0.3cm.

Draw inside leg seam; join 28–30, join 23–30 curving the line inwards 1.2cm.

Curve hem line of trousers down 1cm.

Block completion

Front Trace off front block.

Mark points 10 and 11.

10–A is 1cm; join A–11 with a slight curve.

Back Trace off back block.

To insert crutch ease: mark point 26 and new point B on the fork seat line.

Cut across the seat line to point 26; open a 2.5cm wedge at the fork line.

B–C is 1cm; draw in a new fork line 23, C, 21.

Altering the leg shape

Trouser legs can be widened or narrowed. However, this must take place evenly on each side of the leg or the 'stride' of the trousers will be affected.

Widened trousers

If trousers need to be generally widened for a straight shape 'baggy' effect. Cut up the centre grain line and open the required amount.

Alter the leg shape if required.

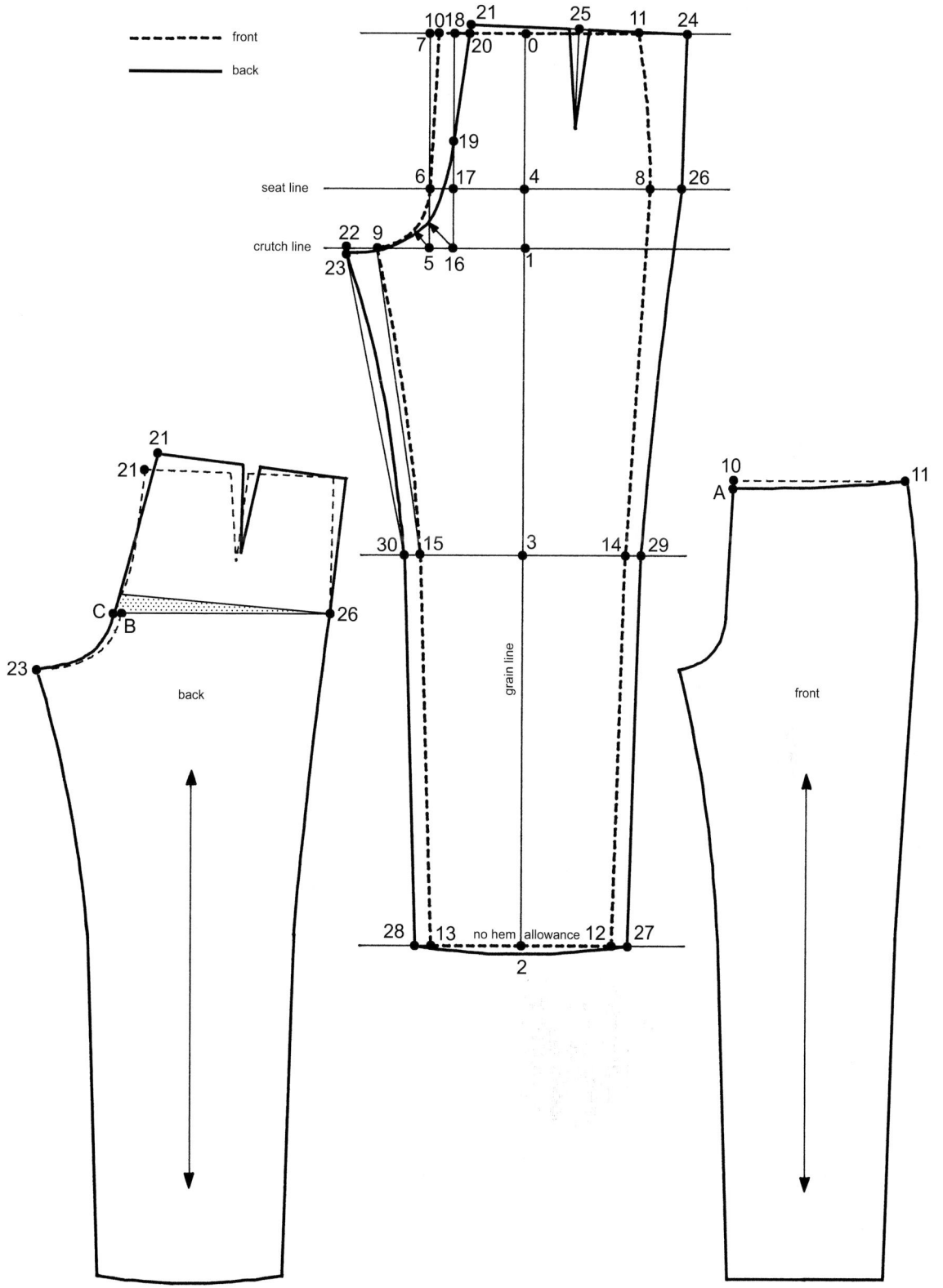

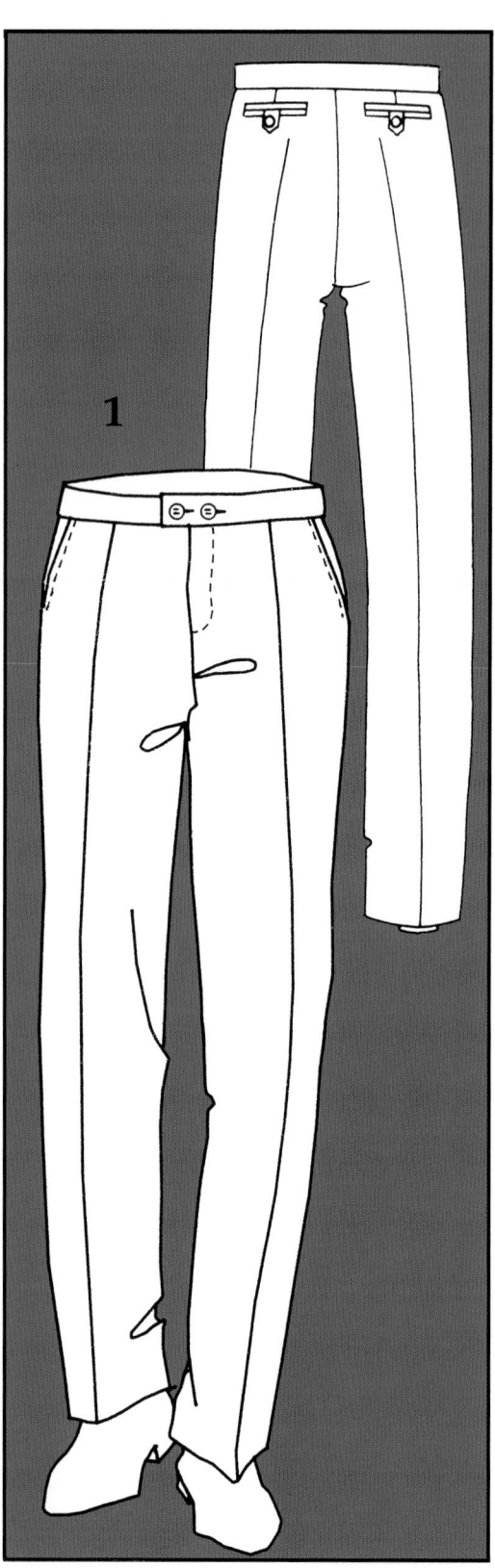

1 Basic trousers

Front and side piece Trace off front trouser block.
Draw in fly piece on front fork as shown; length = 24cm, width = 5cm.
Mark point A on fitting line of side seam; A–B is 5cm.
Draw pocket line; join B–C on fitting line of side seam, length = 19cm.
Cut off side piece; add 5cm extension from B–C.
Add seam allowance to base of side piece.
Add seam allowance from B–C on body section.
Add 5cm hem allowance.

Back Trace off back trouser block.
Mark in point 25. 25-D is 6cm.
D is the centre point of pocket mouth, pocket width = 14cm.
Add 5cm hem allowance.

Fly piece Trace off fly piece.
Add seam allowance to outer edge.

Front pocket facing Trace off pocket facing from side piece; place on the straight grain.
Add seam allowance to edges shown.

Front pocket bag Trace off pocket bag with pocket line placing it to a fold.
Open pocket bag; cut off pocket line piece.
Add seam allowance to places shown.

Back pocket facing Cut a rectangle: width = pocket width plus 4cm; depth = approx. 5cm.

Back pocket bag Cut a rectangle: width = pocket width plus 4cm; depth (placed to a fold) = approx. 12cm.

Waistband Construct a single cloth waist band (ref. 1a, page 118).

1   Basic trousers

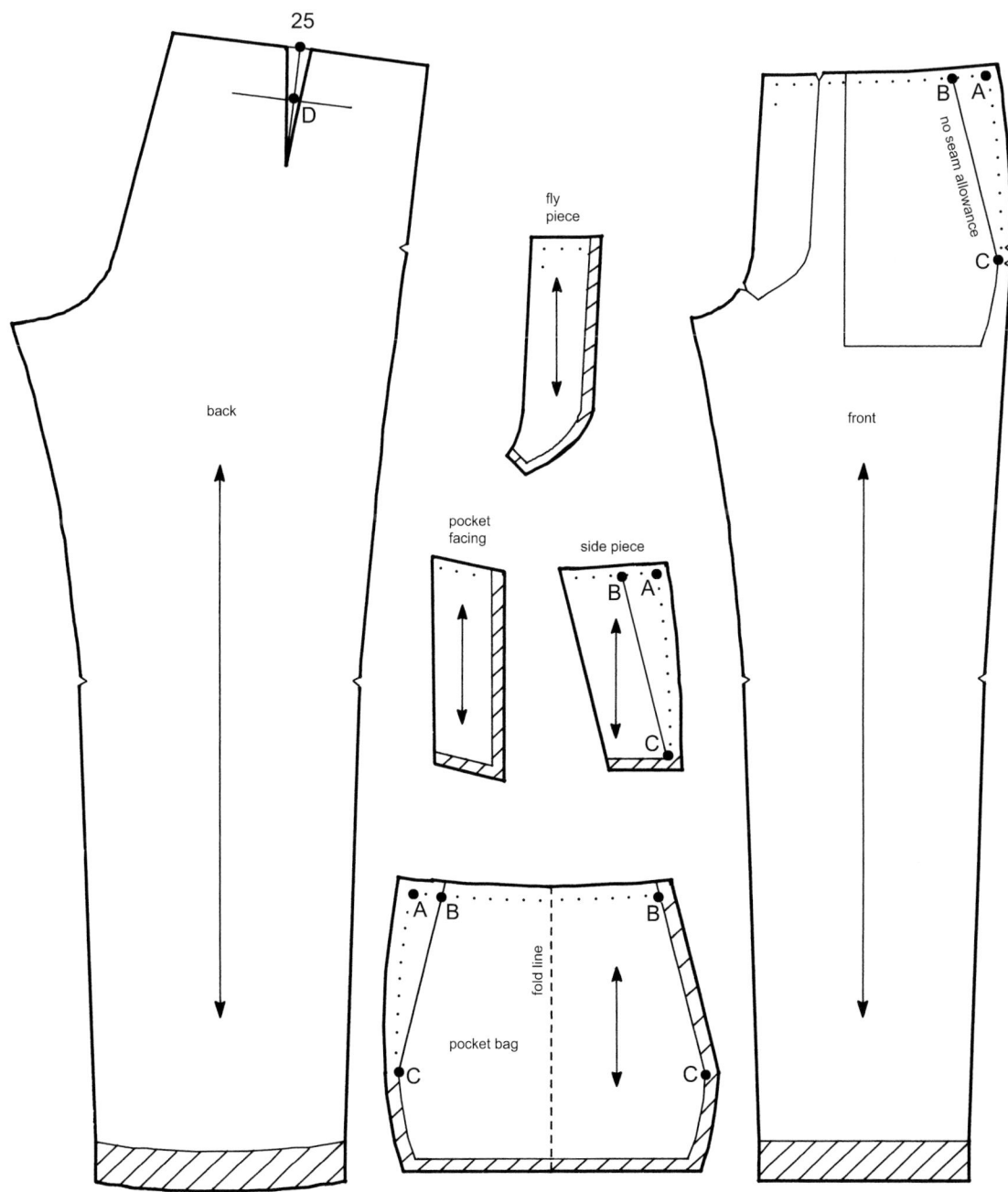

25

D

back

fly
piece

front

no seam allowance

B A

C

pocket
facing

side piece

B A

C

A B

C

pocket bag

fold line

A B

B

C

C

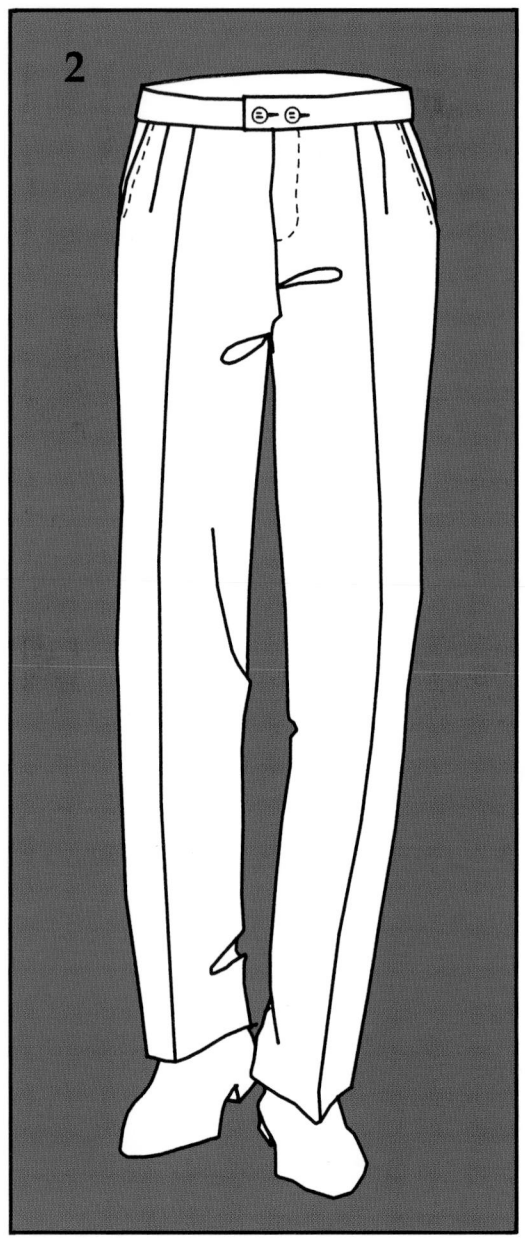

2 Trousers with pleated waistline

Back Trace off back trouser block and complete adaptation for basic trousers (ref. 1, page 112).

Front Trace off front trouser block.

Draw a line midway between the knee line and hem line. Mark points A and B.

Cut across line; divide top section along the grain line. Open 3.5cm at waistline.

Extend waistline by 2.5cm to C at side seam.

Join C–B. Trace round front.

Make a first 3cm pleat at the grain line and a second 3cm pleat with a spacing between of approx. 4cm.

Add 5cm hem allowance.

Waistband Construct the selected waistband ref. page 118.

Pockets and fly piece Construct as for the basic trousers (ref. 1, page 112).

Turn-ups

If turn-ups are required, add to hem line twice the depth of the turn-up required plus 5cm hem allowance.

2 Trousers with pleated waistline

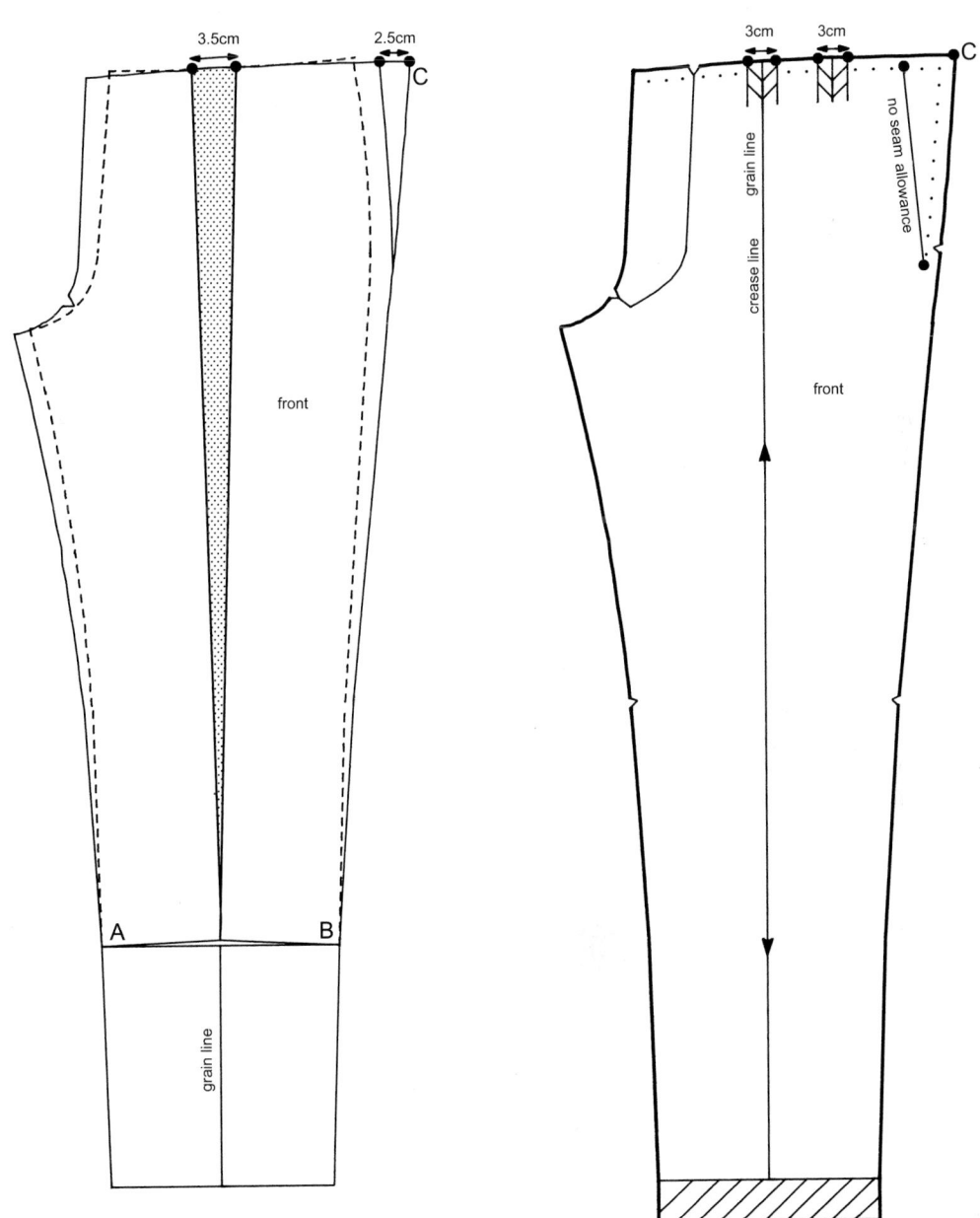

3.5cm   2.5cm   C

front

A   B

grain line

3cm   3cm   C

crease line   grain line   no seam allowance

front

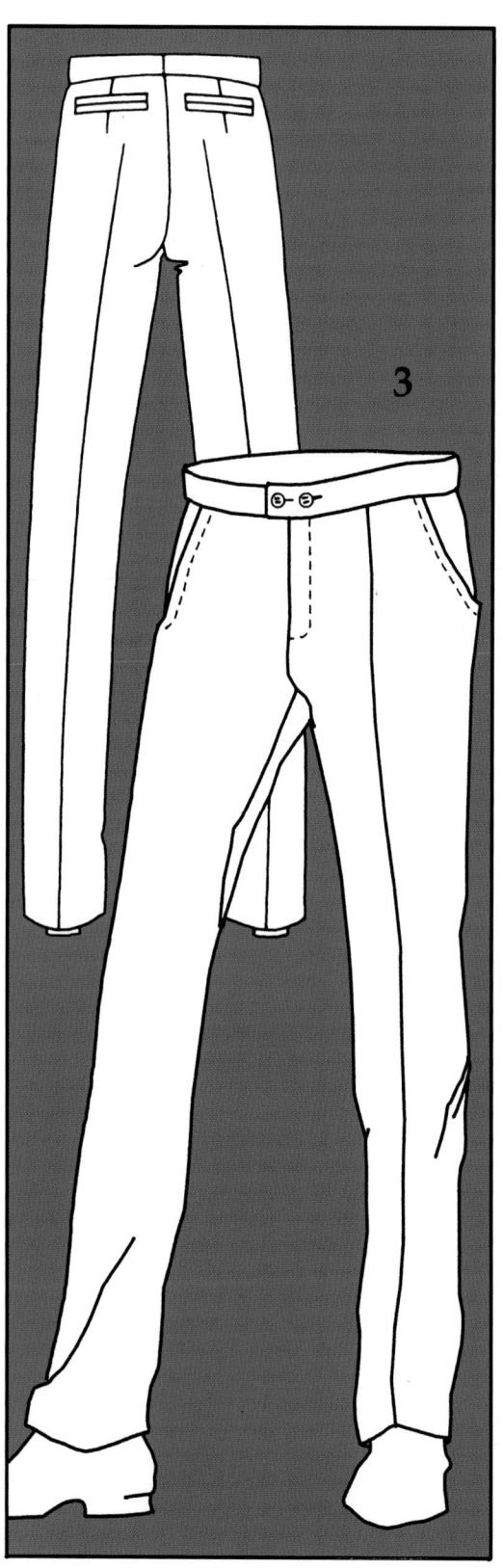

3

3 Trousers – slimline

If the waistband sits lower than the trouser waist position, the amount is taken from the top of the trousers.

Any narrowing of the trouser legs must take place evenly on each side of the leg or the 'stride' of the trousers will be affected.

Both sections   Trace off the basic trouser block.

On the knee line mark A, B, C, D at the width that the trousers are required to be reduced.

Reduce the width at the hemline by the same amount as shown.

Back   Mark points E and F on the crutch line.

Join E–B with a slightly curved line.

F–G is 1.5cm; join G–A with a curved line.

Add 5cm hem allowance.

Front   Mark points H and I on the crutch line.

Join H–D.

I–J is 1cm; join J–C with a curved line.

Mark point K on side seam waist.

K–L is 1.5cm; draw new side seam from point L to H.

Mark point M at grain line.

Construct a dart at M: length = 7cm long, width = 1.5cm.

Add 5cm hem allowance.

Waistband   Construct the selected waistband ref. page 118.

Pockets and fly piece   Construct as for the basic trousers (ref. 1, page 112).

3 Trousers - slimline

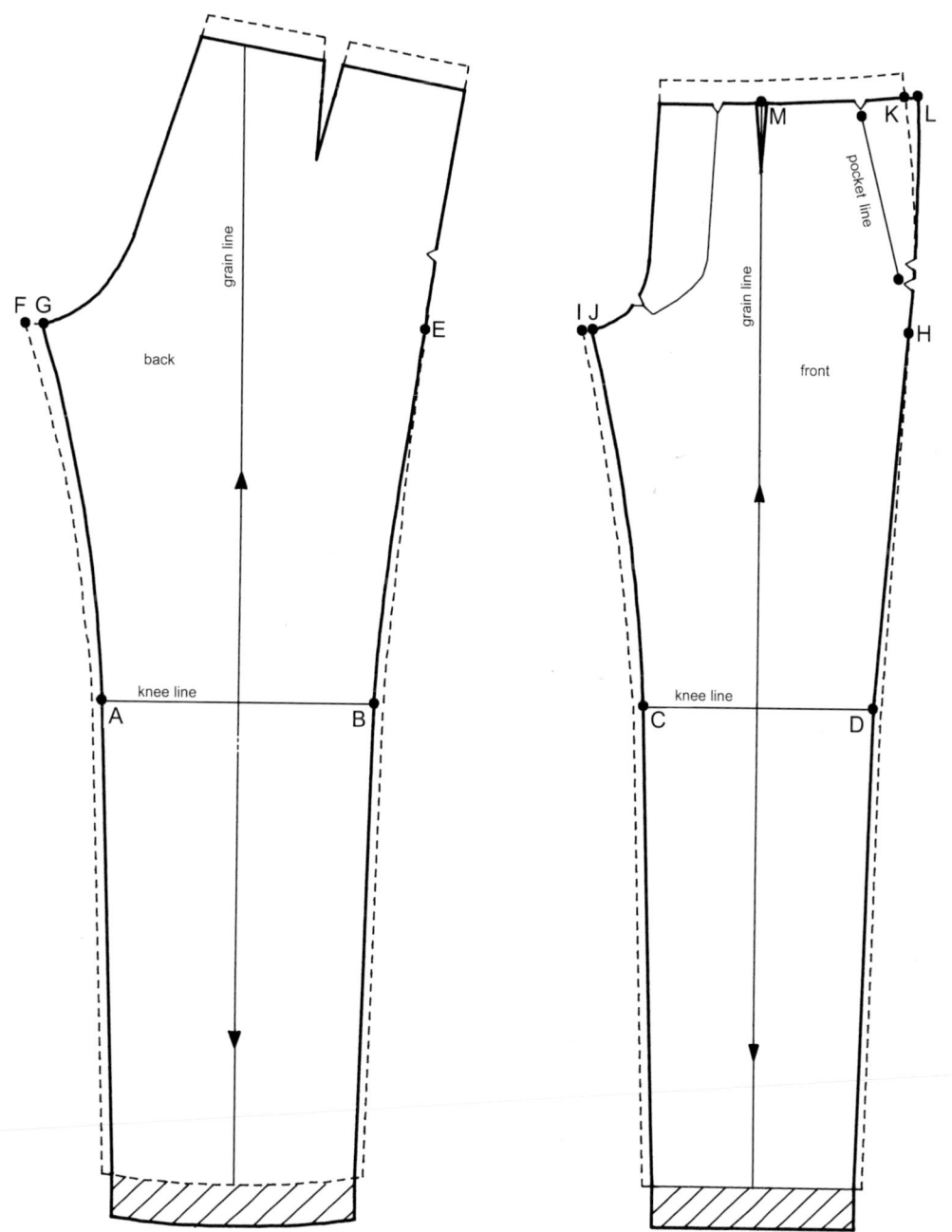

Waistbands

Waistbands – length and depth

The waistband length to the centre front (CF) depends on where the waistband sits on the body (use the waist or trouser waist measurement). On trousers with elasticised waistbands, the length will be determined by the waist measurement of the pattern. The waistband depth can vary but it is usually approximately 4cm.

The waistband of formal trousers usually has a back seam. There is often a 3cm seam allowance (inlay) on this seam; this inlay means that a trouser waistline can be altered.

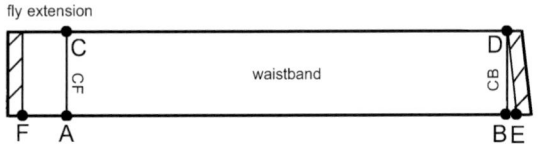 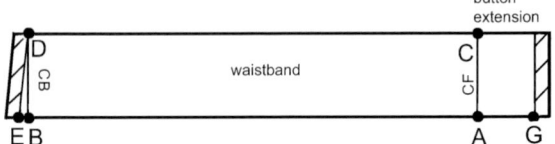

1a   Single cloth waistband

Draw two rectangles: A–B is ½ waistband length required; B–D is the waistband depth plus 2cm for seam allowance.
B–E 0.5cm; join D–E.
A–F is the width of fly extension.

A–G is the width of button extension.
Add seam allowances to edges where shown.
A single cloth waistband has a top seam and is usually self-faced. Some formal trousers are faced with a 'shirt-gripper' band. In this case, cloth facings are cut for the fly and button extensions.

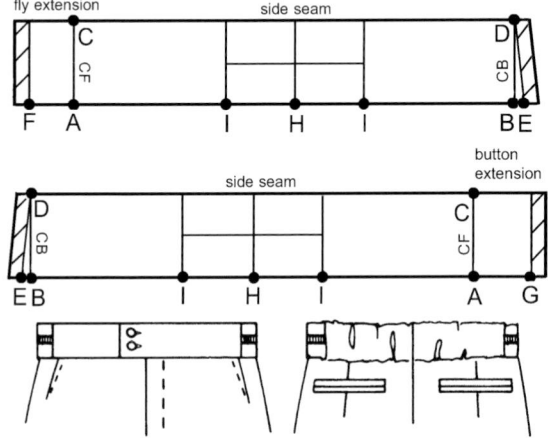 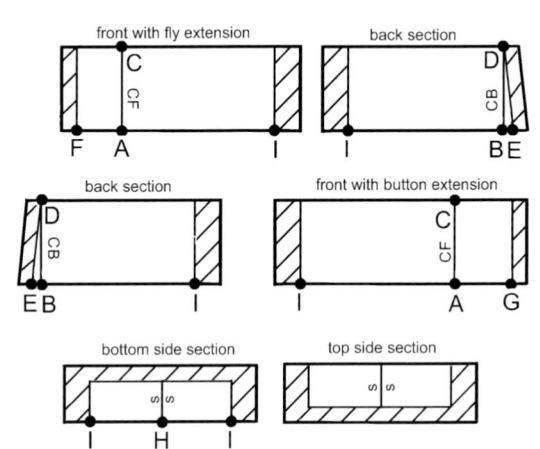

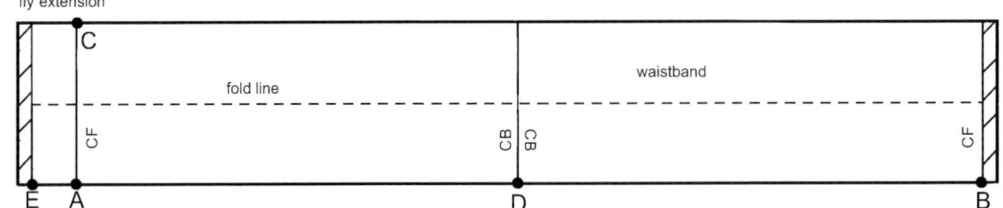

1b   Tailored waistband with slide adjusters

The waistband is cut from the single cloth waistband. Construct the waistband 1a, but add 2.5cm to measurement A–B.
A–H is ½ measurement A–B; square up.

Mark side seam.
H–I is 5cm each side of side seam; square up.
Cut up seams.
Add 2cm seam allowance to back and front sections.
Divide the side sections horizontally. Add seam allowance to the divided seams as shown.

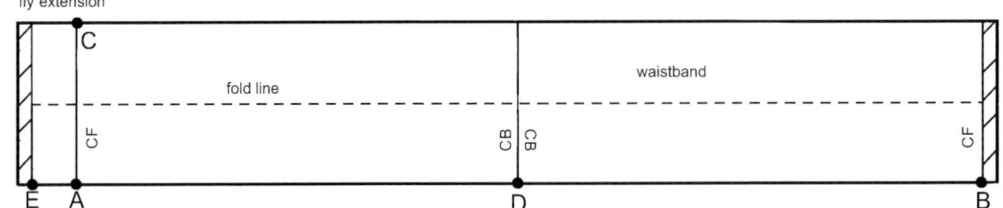

1c   Double cloth waistband

This waistband has no button extension.
Draw a rectangle; A–B is waistband length required; A–C is twice the waistband depth plus 2cm seam allowance.

A–E is the width of the fly extension.
Draw a fold line down the centre.
Add seam allowance to both front edges.

PART THREE: 'FORM' CUTTING – CLASSIC AND CASUAL MENSWEAR

Chapter 10 Classic and casual shirts

The 'flat' shirt block in Part two is used mainly for workwear, simple shirts or shirts manufactured in jersey.

The classic shirt block

Measurements required to draft the block
The sample illustrated is for the athletic figure (neck size 40cm chest 100cm). Refer to the *shirt* size chart (page 13) for standard measurements.

Neck size	40cm
Chest	100cm
Scye depth	24.4cm
Back neck to waist	44.2cm
Half back	20cm
Shirt length – varies with fashion	81cm
Sleeve length for shirts	86cm
Cuff size	24cm

A 1cm seam allowance is included in the block.

The measurements shown in brackets are for an easier fitting shirt.

Body sections
Square both ways from 0.
0–1 scye depth plus 4cm (7cm); square across.
0–2 natural waist length plus 3cm; square across.
0–3 shirt length plus 8cm; square across.
1–4 ½ chest plus 12cm (16cm); square up to 5 and down to 6 on hem line.
0–7 ⅕ neck size minus 0.5cm; square up.
7–8 4.5cm; draw in neck curve.
0–9 ⅕ measurement 0–1 plus 2cm; square out.
9–10 ½ back plus 4cm (5cm); square down to 11 on scye depth line and up to 12.
12–13 0.75cm; join 8–13 with slight curve.
10–14 10cm.
10–15 0.75cm; join 14–15 with a slight curve.
1–16 ½ measurement 1–4 plus 0.5cm; square down to 17 and 18.
5–19 4.5cm; square out.
19–20 ⅕ neck size minus 1cm.
19–21 ⅕ neck size minus 2.5cm; draw in neck curve.
10–22 1.5cm; square out.
20–23 the measurement 8–13 plus 0.5cm; join 20–23 with a slight curve.
1–24 ⅓ chest plus 4.5cm (7.5cm).
24–25 square up 3cm from 24; join 23–25.
23–26 ½ measurement 23–25.
Draw in armhole shape through points 13–10 and 15, 16, 25, 23; curve inwards 1cm at 26.
21–27 1.5cm button stand; square down.
27–28 3.5cm facing; square down; shape top edge at neckline.

17–29 2cm.
17–30 2cm.
18–31 20cm; square across.
31–32 1cm.
31–33 1cm; draw in side seams.
34 midway between 6–18; square up.
35 midway between 3–18.
34–36 4cm; square across to the front edge.
Draw shaped curves as shown from 33–35 and 32–36.
If pleats are required at the back yoke line. 9–37 is 2cm; square down.

Sleeve
Square down from 0.
0–1 ¼ arm scye measurement; square across. Measure outer edge of body block (see diagram on page 139, measuring a curve).
0–2 sleeve length plus 6cm; minus cuff depth and yoke width (0–13); square across.
1–3 ½ measurement 1–2; square across.
0–4 ½ arm scye measurement; square down to 5.
0–6 ½ arm scye measurement; square down to 7.
Divide 0–4 into four sections; mark points 8, 9, 10.
Divide 0–6 into four sections; mark points 11, 12, 13.
Draw in back sleeve head; join 4–8, raise 1cm at 9, 2cm at 10, touch point 0.
Draw in front sleeve head; raise 1cm at 11, touch point 12, hollow 1cm at 13; join to 6.
5–14 ⅓ measurement 2–5.
7–15 ⅓ measurement 2–7.
16 midway 5–14; join 4–16.
17 midway 7–15; join 6–17.
Draw underarm seams as shown.
18 midway 2–14; square up 15cm to 19.
18–20 1cm; join 2–14 with a curve.

Cuff
Construct a rectangle: cuff size plus 5cm, cuff depth plus 2cm.

Collar
Construct shirt collar with stand (ref. 3b, page 88). Depth of shirt collar and stand approx. 8cm.

Short sleeve adaptation
Join 4–14 and 6–15 with straight lines.
Complete the adaptation shown on page 122.
Note The easy fitting shirt option (shown in brackets) is not suitable for short sleeve shirts.

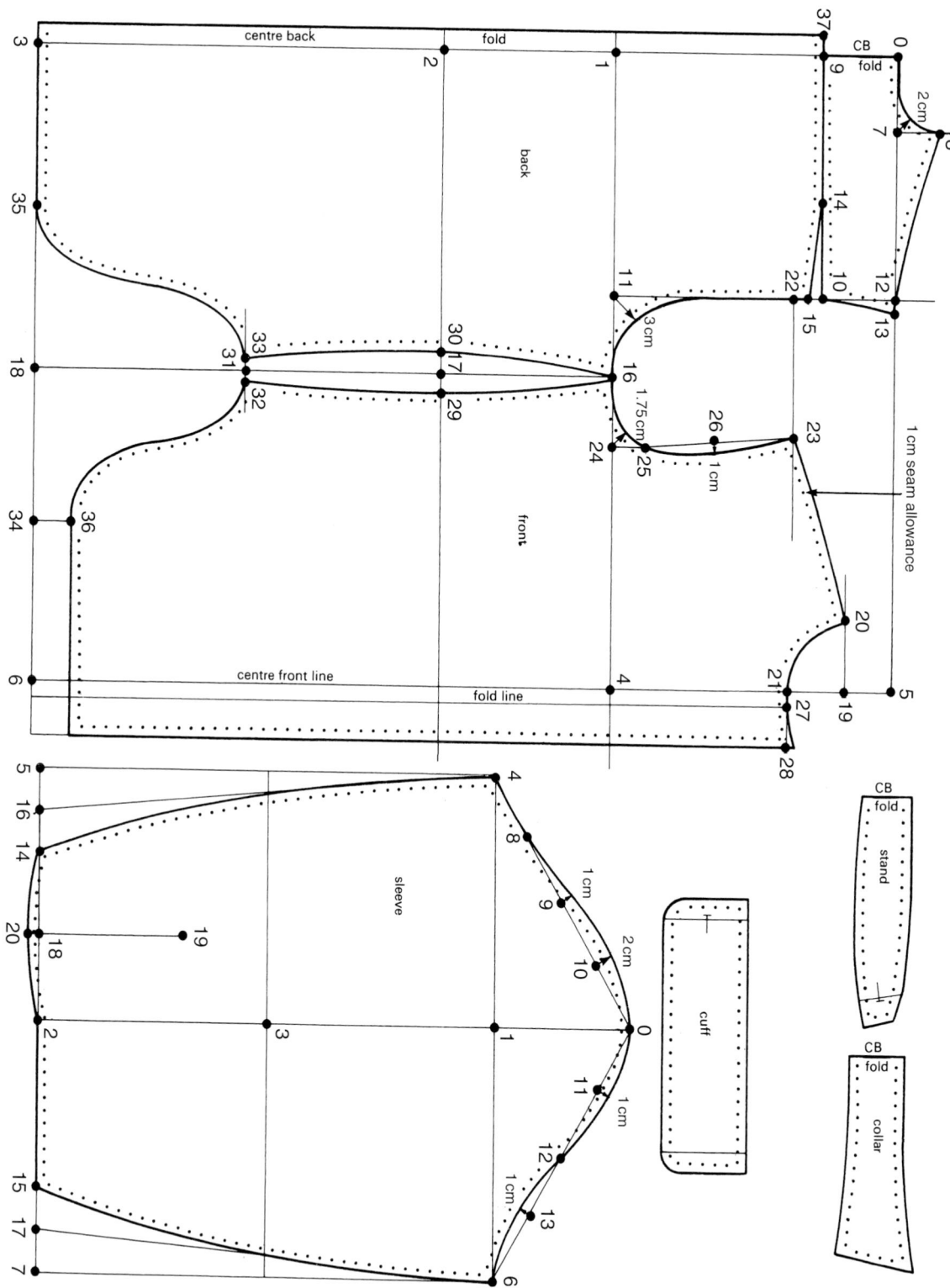

The tailored shirt block

Measurements required to draft the block
The sample illustrated is for the athletic figure (neck size 40cm chest 100cm). Refer to the **shirt** size chart (page 13) for standard measurements.

Neck size	40cm
Chest	100cm
Scye depth	24.4cm
Back neck to waist	44.2cm
Half back	20cm
Shirt length – varies with fashion	81cm
Sleeve length for shirts	86cm
Cuff size	24cm

A 1cm seam allowance is included in the block.

Body sections
Square both ways from 0.
0–1 scye depth plus 6cm; square across.
0–2 natural waist length plus 2.5cm; square across.
0–3 shirt length plus 4cm; square across.
1–4 ½ chest plus 10cm; square up to 5 and down to 6 on hem line.
0–7 ⅕ neck size minus 0.5cm; square up.
7–8 4.5cm; draw in neck curve.
0–9 ⅕ measurement 0-1 plus 4cm; square out.
9–10 ½ back plus 4cm; square down to 11 on scye depth line and up to 12.
12–13 1.5cm; square up 2cm to 14. Join 8–14.
10–15 10cm.
10–16 0.75cm; join 15–16 with slight curve.
1–17 ½ measurement 1–4 plus 0.5cm; square down to 18, 2.5cm below waistline and 19 on hemline.
5–20 4.5cm; square out.
20–21 ⅕ neck size minus 1cm.
20–22 ⅕ neck size minus 2.5cm; draw in neck curve.
10–23 1.5cm; square out.
21–24 the measurement 8–14 plus 0.5cm.
1–25 ⅓ chest plus 4cm.
25–26 square up 4cm from 25; join 24–26.
24–27 ½ measurement 24–26.
Draw in armhole shape through points 14–10, and 16, 17, 26, 24; curve arm scye inwards 1cm at 27.
22–28 1.5cm button stand; square down.
28–29 3.5cm facing; square down; shape top edge at neckline.
18–30 2.5cm.
18–31 2.5cm.
19–32 8 cm; square across.
32–33 1.5cm.
32–34 1.5 cm; draw in curved side seams.

35 midway between 6–19; square up 3cm to 36; square across to front edge.
37 midway between 3–19.
Draw shaped curves as shown from 33–36 and 34–37.
1–38 ½ measurement 1–11 plus 2cm.
If added waist shaping is required, construct a dart in the back section:
38–39 4cm; square down to 40, 2.5cm below waistline.
40–41 16cm. Draw a 1.5cm dart on the line 39–41.

Sleeve
Square down from 0.
0–1 ¼ arm scye measurement plus 1.5 cm; square across.
Measure outer edge of body block (see diagram on page 139, measuring a curve).
0–2 sleeve length plus 6cm; minus cuff depth and yoke width (0–13); square across.
1–3 ½ measurement 1–2; square across.
0–4 ½ arm scye measurement minus 0.5cm; square down to 5.
0–6 ½ arm scye measurement minus 0.5cm; square down to 7.
Divide 0–4 into four sections; mark points 8, 9, 10.
Divide 0–6 into four sections; mark points 11, 12, 13.
Draw in back sleeve head; hollow 0.5cm at 8, raise 1.25cm at 9, 2.25cm at 10, touch point 0.
Draw in front sleeve head, raise 1.5cm at 11, touch point 12, hollow 1.25cm at 13; join to 6.
5–14 ⅓ measurement 2–5 minus 0.75cm.
7–15 ⅓ measurement 2–5 minus 0.75cm.
Join 4–14 and 6–15.
Draw underarm curves shaping out 0.5cm at elbow line.
2–16 midway between 2–14; square up 15cm to 17.

Cuff
Construct a rectangle; cuff size plus 5cm, cuff depth plus 2cm.

Collar
Construct shirt collar with stand (ref. 3b, page 88). Depth of shirt collar and stand approx. 8cm.

Short sleeve adaptation
0–A short sleeve length (example 25cm).
Mark points B and C on the straight construction lines from 4 and 6.
Trace off short sleeve.
Curve lines 4–B and 6–C inwards 0.3 cm.
Add 4cm hem facing.

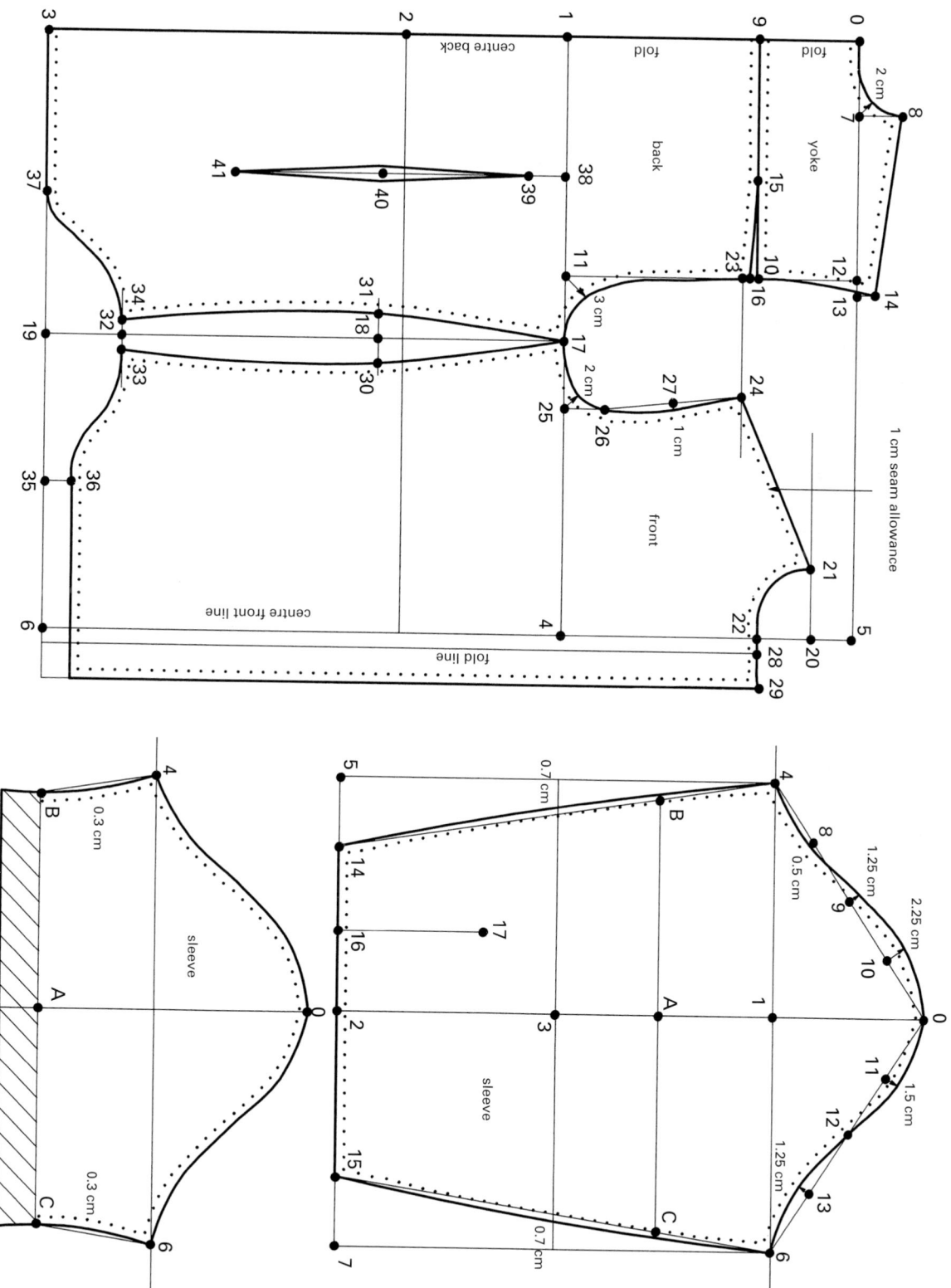

123

The casual shirt block

Measurements required to draft the block
The sample illustrated is for the athletic figure (100cm chest) using the size chart on page 12 for standard measurements. For SMALL, MED, LARGE, XLARGE sizing, use the size chart on page 15.

Chest	100cm
Scye depth	24.4cm
Back neck to waist	44.2cm
Neck size	40cm
Half back	20cm
Shirt length – varies with fashion	80cm
Sleeve length one-piece sleeve	64.8cm

A 1cm seam allowance is included in the block, except where stated **no seam allowance**.

The measurements shown in brackets are for an easier fitting casual shirt.

Body section
Square both ways from 0.
0–1 scye depth plus 2.5cm (5cm); square across.
0–2 natural waist length plus 1cm: square across.
0–3 shirt length plus 1cm; square across.
1–4 ½ chest plus 8cm (11.5cm); square up to 5 and down to 6 on hem line.
0–7 ½ scye depth plus 1cm; square out.
0–8 ½ measurement 0–7; square out.
0–9 ⅕ neck size minus 0.5cm; square up.
9–10 2cm; draw in neck curve.
1–11 half back plus 2.5cm (3.5cm); square up to 12 and 13.
13–14 3.5cm; square out.
14–15 1.5cm; join 10–15.
1–16 ⅓ chest plus 1.5cm (3.5cm).
5–17 ⅕ neck size minus 1cm.
5–18 ⅕ neck size; draw in neck curve.
15–19 2cm; square out.

17–20 the measurement 10–15 plus 0.5cm; join 17–20.
16–21 square up 3.5cm from 16; join 20–21.
21–22 ⅓ measurement 20–21.
16–23 ½ the measurement 11–16 minus 0.5cm; square down to hem line.
Draw in armhole shape through points 15, 12, 23, 21, 20; curve inwards 1.25 cm at 22.

For yet further ease in the body shape, see the adaptation on page 70.

Sleeve
Square down from 0.
0–1 ¼ arm scye measurement plus 1.5cm; square across.
Measure outer edge of body block (see diagram on page 139, measuring a curve).
0–2 sleeve length one-piece sleeve plus 2cm; square across.
1–3 ½ measurement 1–2; square across.
0–4 back arm scye measurement plus 1.5cm; (measure outer edge of body block); square down to 5.
0–6 front arm scye measurement plus 1.5cm. (measure outer edge of body block); square down to 7.
Divide 0–4 into three sections; mark points 8 and 9.
9–10 2cm.
Divide 0–6 into four sections; mark points 11, 12, 13.
Draw in back sleeve head: hollow 0.6cm from 4–8, raise 1.75cm at 10, touch point 0.
Draw in front sleeve head, raise 1.75cm at 11, touch the line at 12, hollow 1.25cm at 13, join to point 6.
5–14 ⅓ measurement 2–5 minus 1.5cm.
7–15 ⅓ measurement 2–5 minus 1.5cm.
Join 4–14 and 6–15.

Short sleeve adaptation
Complete the adaptation described on page 122.

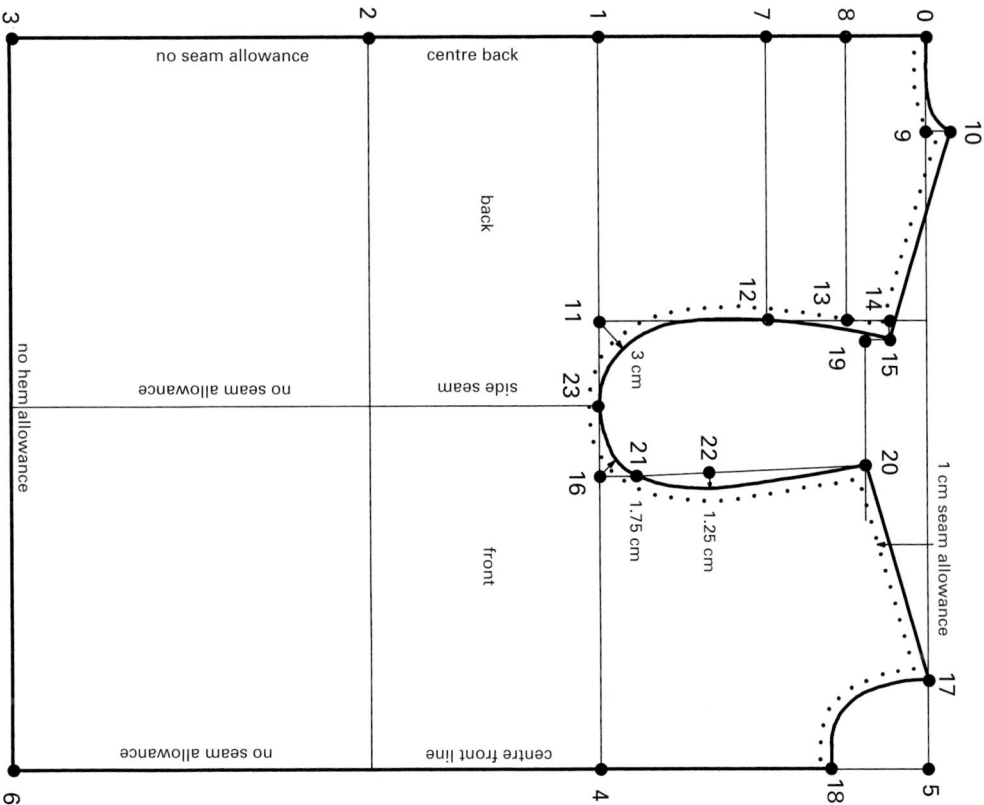

no seam allowance

centre back

back

no seam allowance

side seam

3 cm

1.75 cm

1.25 cm

front

1 cm seam allowance

centre front line

no seam allowance

no hem allowance

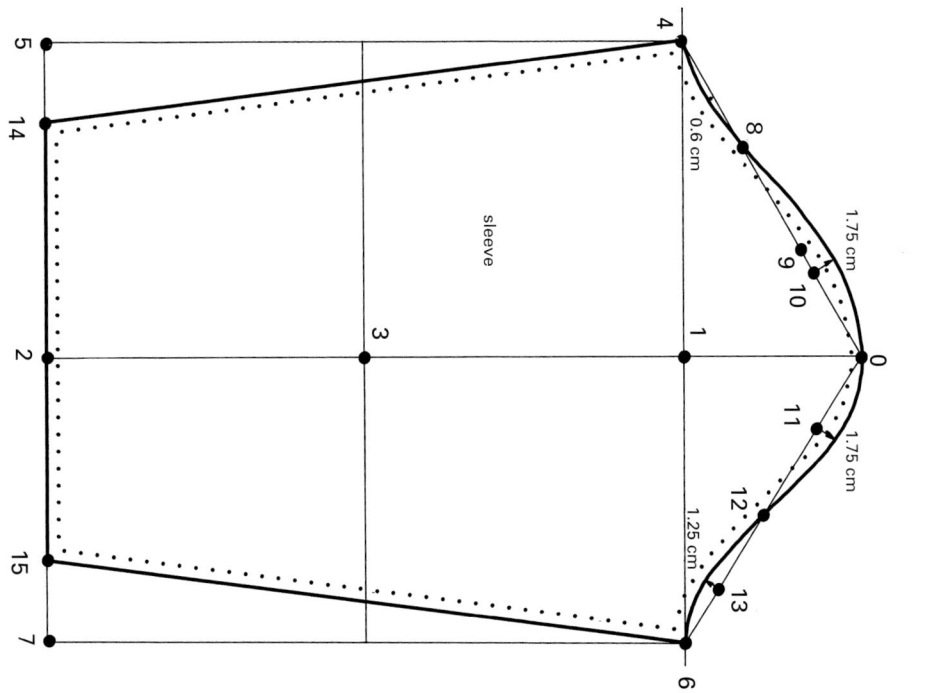

sleeve

0.6 cm

1.75 cm

1.75 cm

1.25 cm

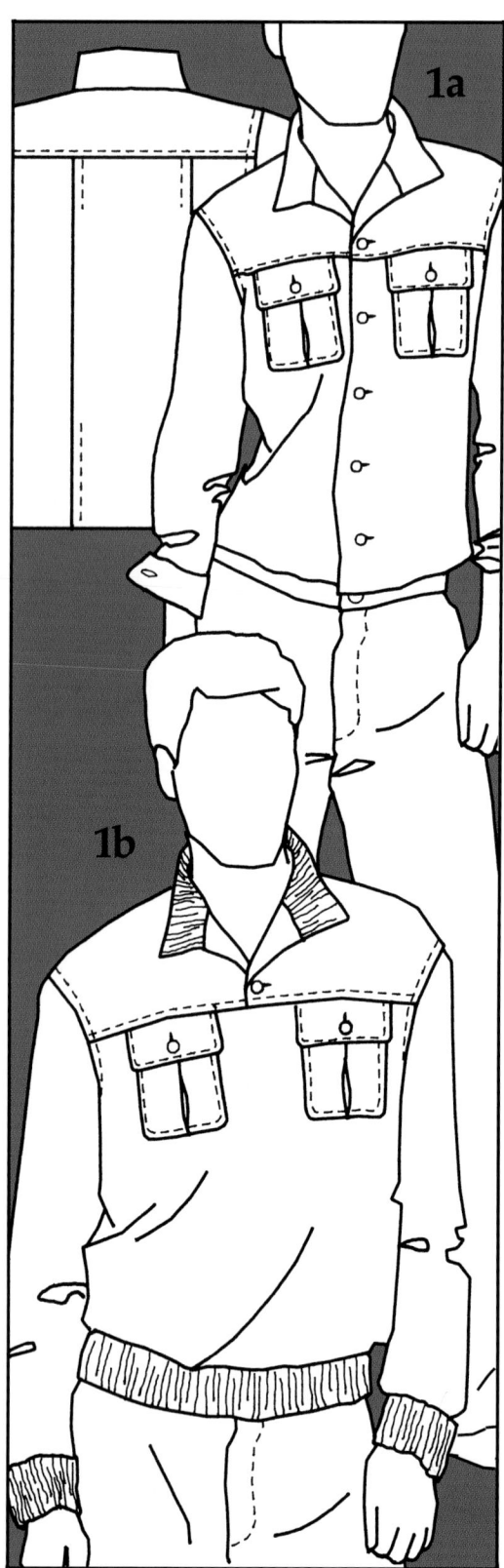

Classic and fashion casual shirts

The casual shirt block (which has the men's balance and shaping and a one-piece sleeve with a high sleeve head) is a very useful block for styled close fitting fashion shirts. The easy fitting version can be used on a wide range of styled casual shirts in which men's shaping is important.

1a   Casual shirt

Trace off casual shirt block with sleeve.
Body section   Draw in finished length.
Lower neckline. Add button stand; mark buttonholes.
Draw in facing line.
Draw in yoke line and back pleat line.
Draw in front pocket shape and pocket flap.
Back   Trace off back section along yoke line; insert required amount for pleat, e.g. 6cm.
Add seam allowance to side seam and top edge.
Add 2cm hem allowance.
Front   Trace off front section along yoke line.
Trace pocket position. Add extended facing.
Add seam allowance to side seam, top edge and facing line.
Add 2cm hem allowance.
Yokes   Trace off back and front yokes.
Add extended facing to front yoke.
Add seam allowance to lower edge of yokes and facing line.
Collar   Construct a standard straight collar (ref. 1a, page 86).
Pocket   Trace pocket shape, insert 8cm for pleat at centre of pocket.
Add seam allowance to outer edges.
Add 2cm to top of the pocket.
Trace off pocket flap; add seam allowance to all edges.
Sleeve   Shorten sleeve length by cuff depth (7cm) less 1cm.
Shape in underarm seam of sleeve 2.5cm at wrist line.
Cuff   Construct shaped single cuff (ref. 17, page 78).

1b   Easy fitting casual shirt

Body and sleeve sections   Trace off the easy fitting version of the casual shirt block to length required minus rib depth. Add 1cm seam allowance.
Complete the adaptation for the extended shoulder with the easy fitting armhole (ref. 9, page 70).
Front and back   Complete the style adaptation listed above for yokes and pockets.
Below the yoke line on the front section, place centre front to a fold line.
Sleeve   Shorten sleeve by rib depth.
Add seam allowance.
Rib sections   Create ribs for hemline, collar and cuffs.

1a   Casual shirt

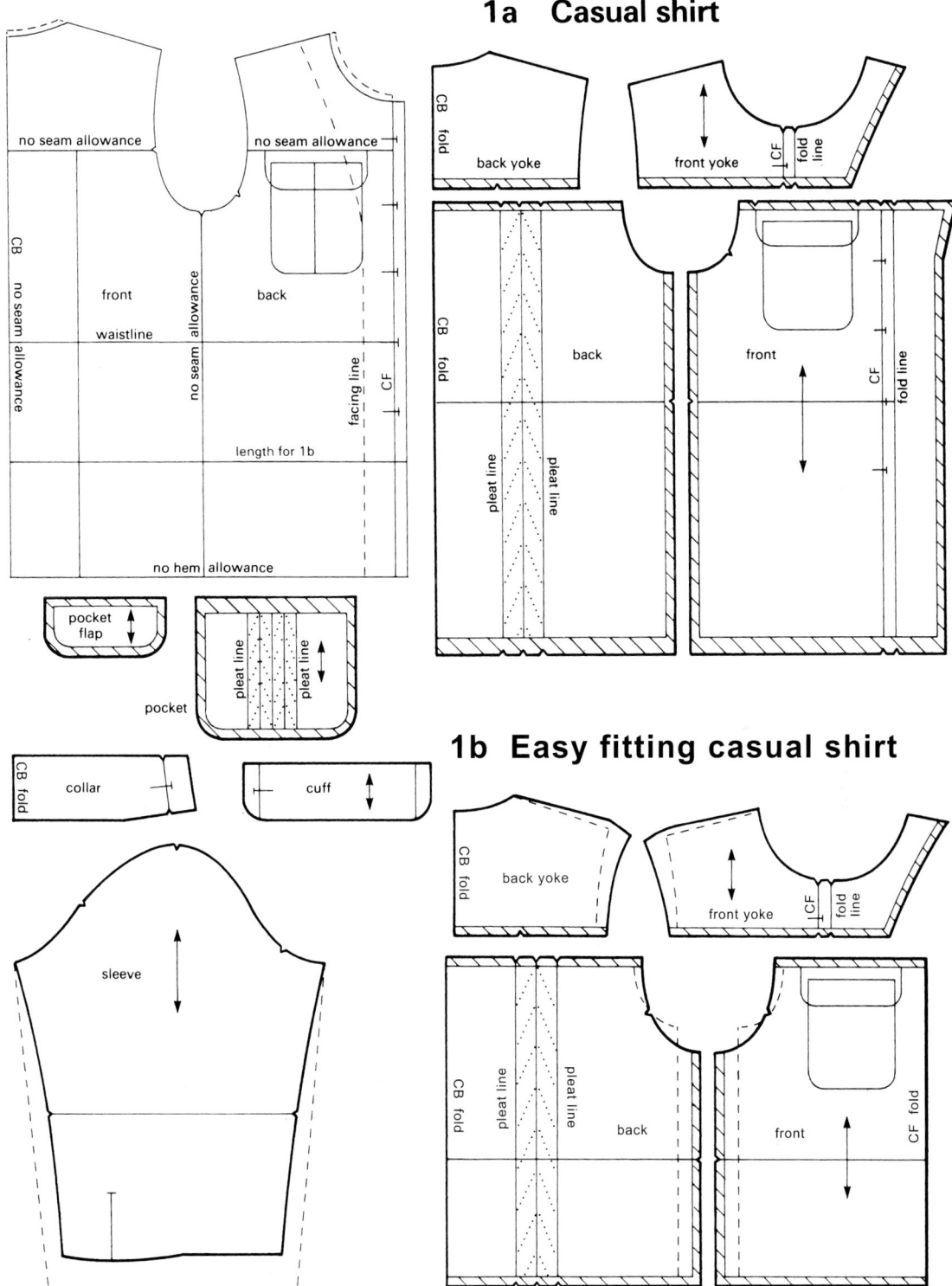

1b   Easy fitting casual shirt

PART THREE: 'FORM' CUTTING – CLASSIC AND CASUAL MENSWEAR

Chapter 11 Classic and casual overgarments

'Form' cutting is used for both classic and casual garments. They reflect the figure shape of a man. Casual garments cut from these 'form' blocks are usually more expensive because the pattern shapes, size grading and manufacture are more complex.

Note that the 'flat' blocks offered in Part two are used for garments that are often flat packed, easy fitting or are manufactured in jersey.

Classic and casual overgarment blocks

The basic jacket block

This block creates a shape for close fitting jackets.

Measurements required to draft the block
The sample illustrated is for the athletic figure (100cm chest). Refer to the size chart (page 12) for standard measurements, or the size chart (page 15) for SMALL, MEDIUM, LARGE, XLARGE sizing.

Chest	100cm
Scye depth	24.4cm
Natural waist length	44.2cm
Neck size	40cm
Half back	20cm
Jacket length	varies with style

A 1cm seam allowance is included in the block except where stated **no seam allowance**.
There is no hem allowance.
There is 0.7cm ease on the back shoulder.

Square both ways from 0.
0–1 scye depth plus 3cm; square across.
0–2 natural waist length plus 1cm; square across.
0–3 jacket length plus 1cm; square across.
2–4 21cm; square across.
0–5 ½ scye depth plus 1cm; square out.
0–6 ½ measurement 0–5; square out.
0–7 ¼ neck size minus 1.5cm; square up.

7–8 2cm; draw in neck curve.
1–9 half back plus 2cm; square up to 10 and 11.
11–12 2cm; square out.
12–13 2cm; join 8–13 with a curved line.
10–14 1.5cm.
9–15 ½ measurement 9–10 minus 1.5cm.
15–16 0.5cm.
9–17 2.5cm; square down to 18 with a dotted line.
1–19 ½ chest plus 7.5cm; square up to 20, down to 21 on waistline, 22 on hem line.
22–23 2cm (23 can be joined to any back style seam).
1–24 ⅓ chest plus 0.5cm.
24–25 ½ measurement 9–24 minus 1cm; square down to 26.
24–27 square up 2.5cm from 24; mark front pitch FP.
20–28 ¼ neck size minus 2cm; join 28 to 11.
20–29 ⅕ neck size plus 1cm; draw in neck curve.
28–30 the measurement 8–13 minus 0.7cm; join 30–27 with a dotted line.
30–31 1.75cm; join 28 to 31.
31–32 ⅔ measurement 31–27.
Draw in armhole shape through points 13, 14, 16, 25, 27, 31 curve inwards 2cm at 32.

A one-piece sleeve or two-piece sleeve can be drafted for this block (ref. pages 138 and 140).

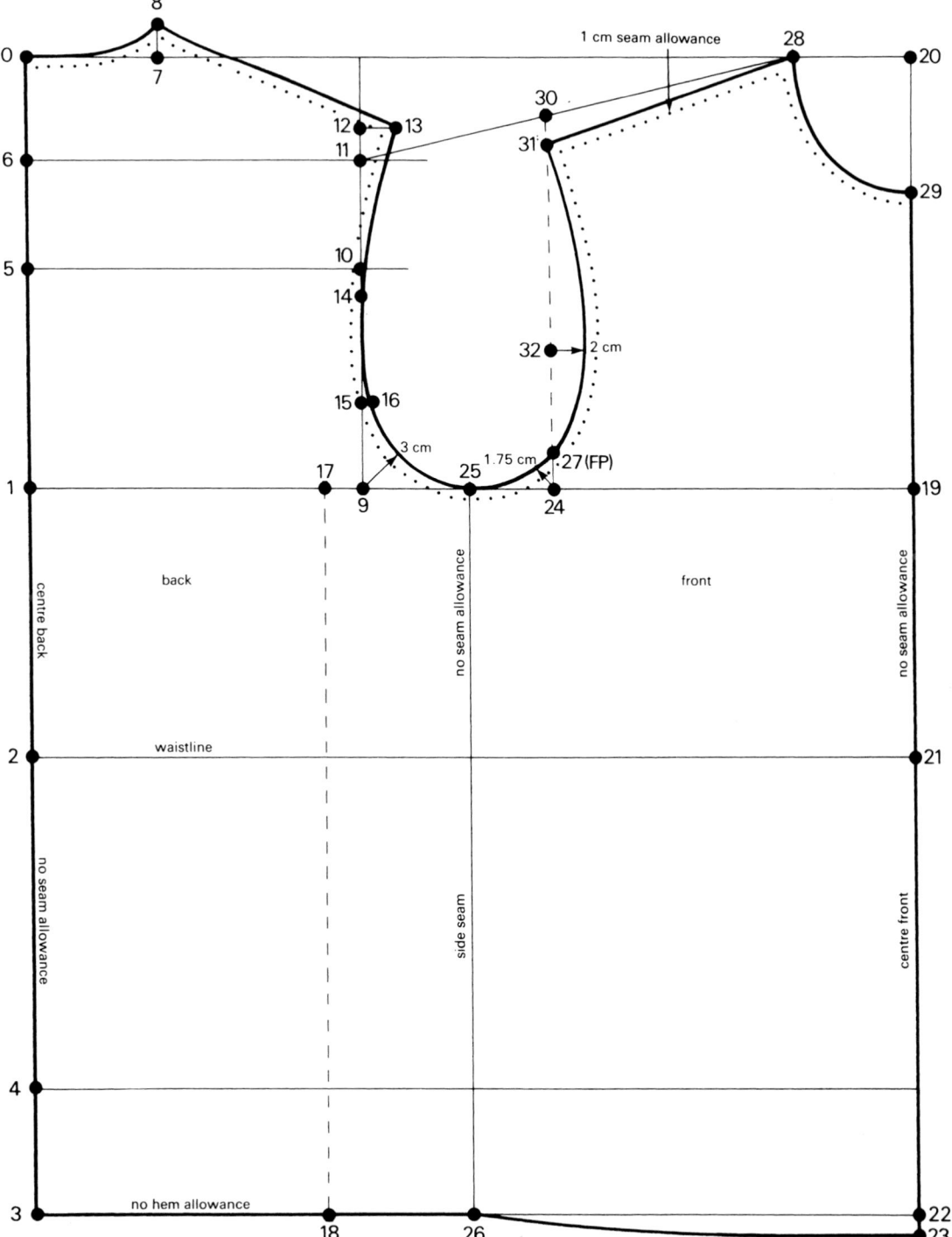

8

0

7

1 cm seam allowance

28

20

30

12 13

31

6

11

29

5

10

14

32 → 2 cm

15 16

3 cm

1.75 cm

27 (FP)

17

25

1

9

24

19

centre back

back

front

no seam allowance

no seam allowance

2

waistline

21

no seam allowance

side seam

centre front

4

3

no hem allowance

22

18

26

23

The easy fitting casual jacket block

This block creates an easier fitting jacket with a widened shoulder. For very easy fitting jackets use the easy fitting overgarment block (ref. page 136).

Measurements required to draft the block
The sample illustrated is for the athletic figure (100cm chest). Refer to the size chart (page 15) for standard measurements, or the size chart (page 15) for SMALL, MEDIUM, LARGE, XLARGE sizing.

Chest	100cm
Scye depth	24.4cm
Natural waist length	44.2cm
Neck size	40cm
Half back	20cm
Jacket length	varies with style

A 1cm seam allowance is included in the block except where stated **no seam allowance**.
There is no hem allowance.
There is 0.7cm ease on the back shoulder.

Square both ways from 0.
0–1 scye depth plus 4.5cm; square across.
0–2 natural waist length plus 1cm; square across.
0–3 jacket length plus 1cm; square across.
2–4 21cm; square across.
0–5 ½ scye depth plus 1cm; square out.
0–6 ½ measurement 0–5; square out.
0–7 ¼ neck size minus 1.5cm; square up.
7–8 2cm; draw in neck curve.
1–9 half back plus 3cm; square up to 10 and 11.
11–12 3cm; square out.
11–13 1cm.
10–14 3cm.
12–15 3.5cm; square down.

15–16 1.75cm; join 8–16, through 12, with a curved line as shown.
9–17 ½ measurement 9–10 minus 2cm.
17–18 0.5cm.
9–19 2.5cm; square down to 20 with a dotted line.
1–21 ½ chest plus 10cm; square up to 22, down to 23 on waistline, 24 on hem line.
24–25 2cm (25 can be joined to any back style seam).
1–26 ⅓ chest plus 2.5cm.
26–27 ½ measurement 9–26 minus 1cm; square down to 28.
26–29 square up 2.5cm from 26; mark front pitch FP.
22–30 ¼ neck size minus 2cm; join 30 to 13.
22–31 ⅕ neck size plus 1cm; draw in neck curve.
30–32 the measurement 8–12 minus 0.4cm; square down 1.75cm to 33. Square out.
33–34 3.5cm; square down.
34–35 2cm; join 30-35 through 33 with a curved line as shown.
35–36 ⅔ measurement 29–35.
Draw in armhole shape through points 16, 14, 18, 27, 29, 35 curve inwards 2cm at 36.

Side seam shaping for slimmer hipline.
Mark point 37 at the side seam waist point.
37–38 1cm; square down to 39 on hemline.
37–40 1cm; square down to 41 on hemline.
Draw in side seam shaping from points 27–38 and 27–40.

A one-piece sleeve or two-piece sleeve can be drafted for this block (ref. pages 138 and 140).

Note A larger but not deeper shoulder pad will be required to produce a smooth shoulder line.

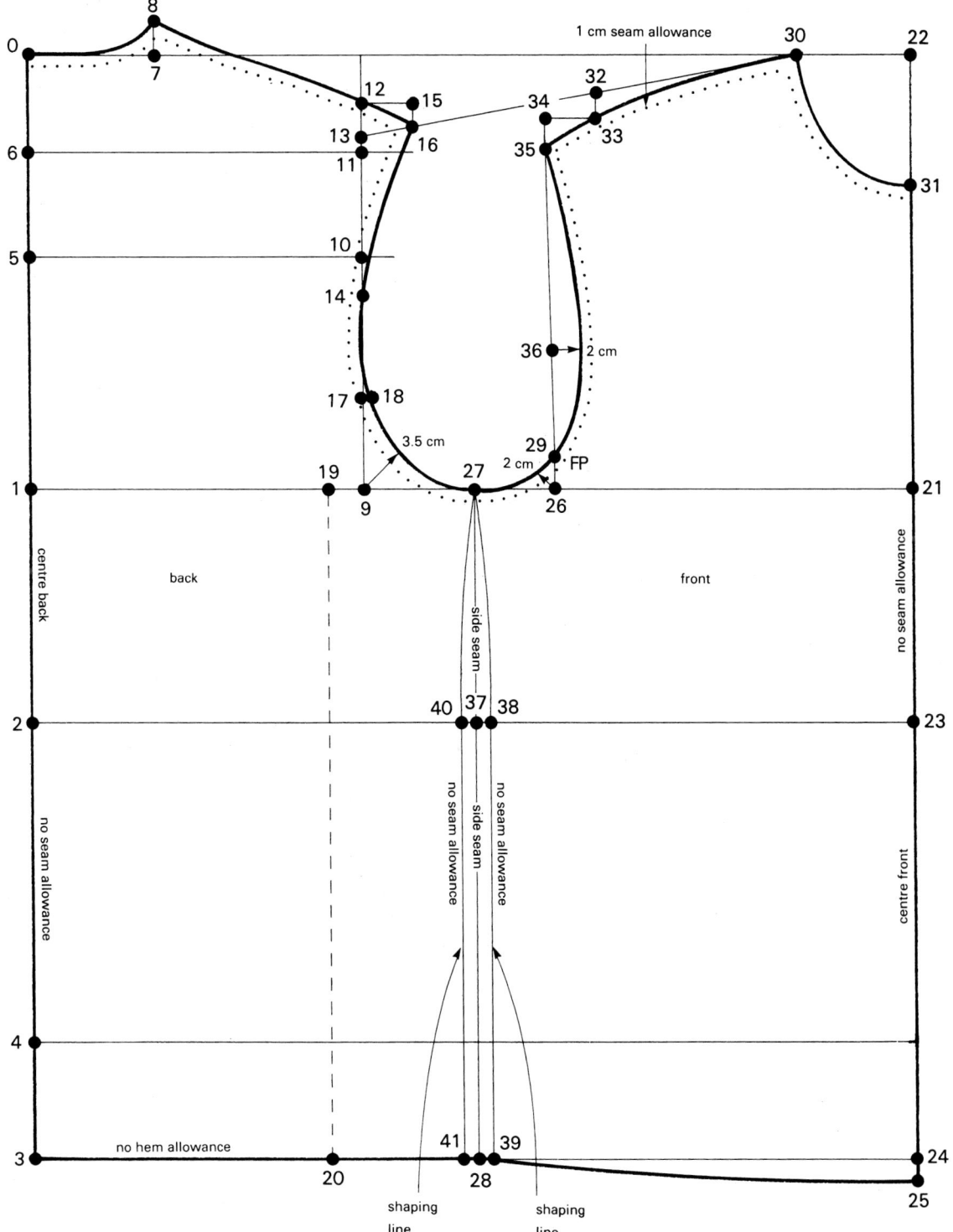

The basic overgarment block

A block developed to create classic coats.

Measurements required to draft the block
The sample illustrated is for the athletic figure
(100cm chest). Refer to the size chart (page 12) for
standard measurements, or the size chart (page 15)
for SMALL, MEDIUM, LARGE, XLARGE sizing.

Chest	100cm
Scye depth	24.4cm
Natural waist length	44.2cm
Neck size	40cm
Half back	20cm
Jacket length	varies with style

A 1cm seam allowance is included in the block
except where stated **no seam allowance**.
There is no hem allowance.
There is 0.7cm ease on the back shoulder.

Square both ways from 0.
0–1 scye depth plus 4.5cm; square across.
0–2 natural waist length plus 1.5cm; square across.
0–3 coat length plus 1cm; square across.
2–4 21cm; square across.
0–5 ½ scye depth plus 1cm; square out.
0–6 ½ measurement 0–5; square out.
0–7 ¼ neck size minus 1cm; square up.
7–8 2cm; draw in neck curve.
1–9 half back plus 3cm; square up to 10 and 11.
11–12 2cm; square out.
12–13 2cm; join 8–13 with a curved line.
10–14 2cm.
9–15 ½ measurement 9–10 minus 1.5cm.

15–16 0.5cm.
1–17 ½ chest plus 10cm; square up to 18,
down to 19 on hem line.
19–20 2cm (20 can be joined to any back style
seam).
1–21 ⅓ chest plus 2.25cm.
17–22 ½ measurement 17–21.
21–23 ½ measurement 9–21 minus 1cm; square
down to 24.
25 square up 2.5cm from 21; mark front pitch FP.
18–26 ¼ neck size minus 0.5cm; join 26 to 11.
18–27 ⅕ neck size plus 1cm.
Join 18–22 with a dotted line.
Draw in neck curve.
Construct a dart on the dotted line; width = 1cm,
length = 8cm.
26–28 the measurement 8–13 minus 0.7cm; join
28–25 with a dotted line.
28–29 1.5cm; join 29–26.
29–30 ⅔ measurement 29–25.
Draw in armhole shape through points 13, 14, 16, 23,
25, 29. Curve inwards 1.75cm at 30.
9–31 2.5cm; square down to hemline.

A one-piece sleeve or two-piece sleeve can be drafted
for this block (ref. pages 138 and 140).

Note An overgarment block fits better if the dart
shaping at the neck is retained. The dart can be
transferred into a style line if required.
If it is necessary to eliminate the dart: draw lines
from neck points of the dart to front pitch point;
close dart.
Trace round new outline.

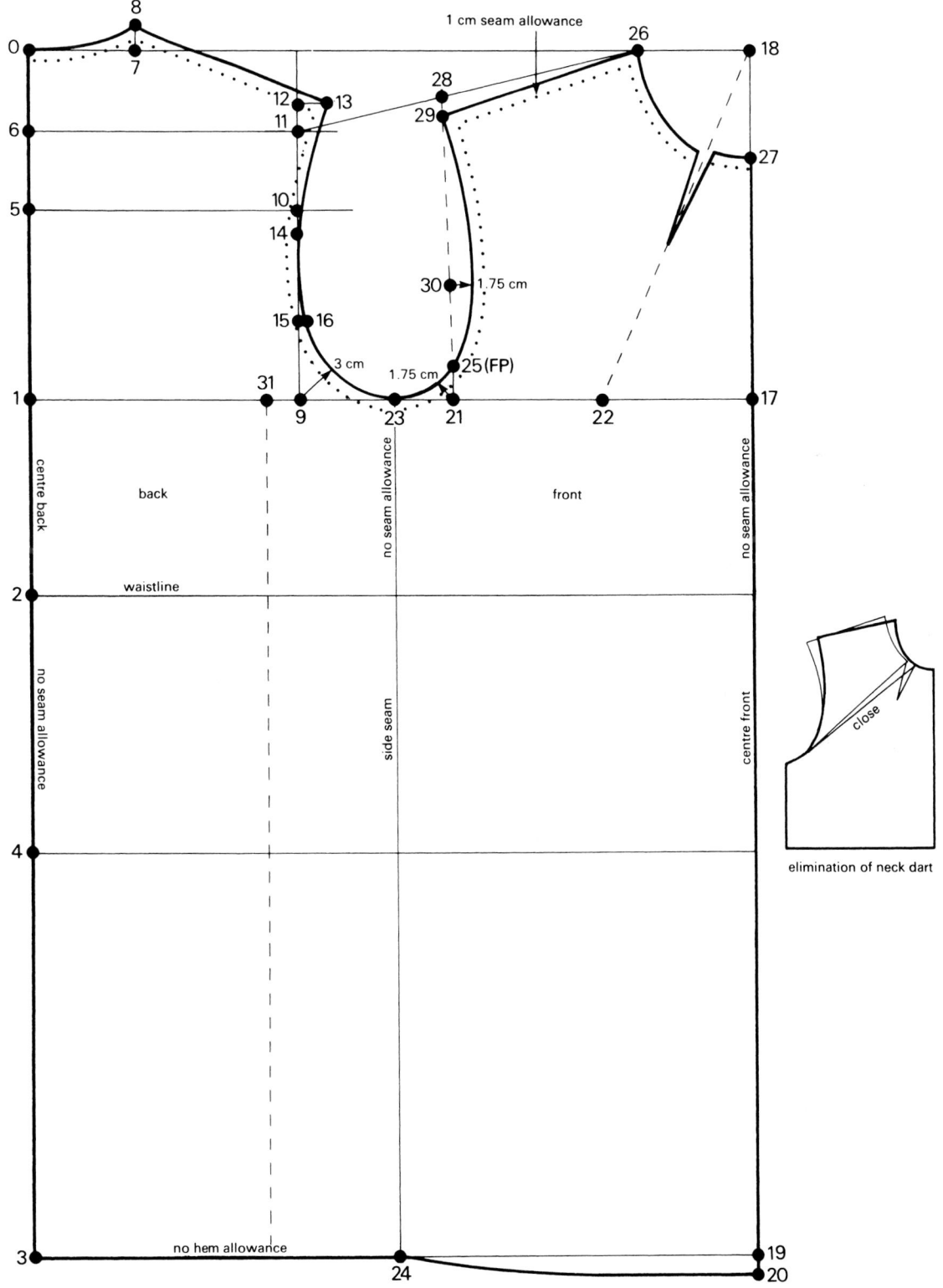

1 cm seam allowance

elimination of neck dart

The easy fitting overgarment block

A block for creating many kinds of easy fitting garments with widened shoulders.

Measurements required to draft the block
The sample illustrated is for the athletic figure (102cm chest). Refer to the size chart (page 12) for standard measurements, or the size chart (page 15) for SMALL. MEDIUM, LARGE, XLARGE sizing.

Chest	100cm
Scye depth	24.4cm
Natural waist length	44.2cm
Neck size	40cm
Half back	20cm
Jacket length	varies with style

A 1cm seam allowance is included in the block except where stated **no seam allowance**.
There is no hem allowance.
There is 0.7cm ease on the back shoulder.

Square both ways from 0.
0–1 scye depth plus 7cm; square across.
0–2 natural waist length plus 1.5cm; square across.
0–3 overgarment length plus 1cm; square across.
2–4 21cm; square across.
0–5 ½ scye depth plus 1cm; square out.
0–6 ½ measurement 0–5; square out.
0–7 ¼ neck size minus 1cm; square up.
7–8 2cm; draw in neck curve.
1–9 half back plus 4.5cm; square up to 10 and 11.
11–12 3cm; square out.
11–13 1cm.
10–14 3.5cm.
12–15 3.5cm; square down.
15–16 1.75cm; join 8–16, through 12, with a curved line as shown.
9–17 ½ measurement 9–10 minus 2cm.

17–18 0.5cm.
1–19 ½ chest plus 15cm. square up to 20, down to 21 on hem line.
21–22 2cm (22 can be joined to any back style seam).
1–23 ⅓ chest plus 4.75cm.
23–24 ½ measurement 23–19.
23–25 ½ measurement 23–9 minus 1cm; square down to 26.
23–27 square up 3cm from 23; mark front pitch FP.
20–28 ¼ neck size minus 0.5cm; join 28 to 13.
20–29 ⅕ neck size plus 1cm.
Join 20–24 with a line. Draw in neck curve; construct a dart on this line; width = 1cm, length = 8cm.
28–30 the measurement 8–12 minus 0.4cm; square down 1.75cm to 30a; square out.
30a–31 3.5cm.
31–32 2cm; join 28–32 through 30a with a curved line as shown.
32–33 ⅔ measurement 27–32.
Draw in armhole shape through points 16, 14, 18, 25, 27, 32; curve inwards 1.5cm at 33.
9–34 2.5cm; square down to 35 with a dotted line.

Side seam shaping for slimmer hipline
Mark point 36 at the side seam waist point.
36–37 1cm; square down to 38 on hemline.
36–39 1cm; square down to 40 on hemline.
Draw in side seam shaping from points 25–37 and 25–39.

A one-piece sleeve or two-piece sleeve can be drafted for this block (ref. pages 138 and 140).

Note 1 A larger but not deeper shoulder pad will be required to produce a smooth shoulder line.
Note 2 For yet further ease in the body shape see the body and sleeve adaptation (ref. 8, page 70).

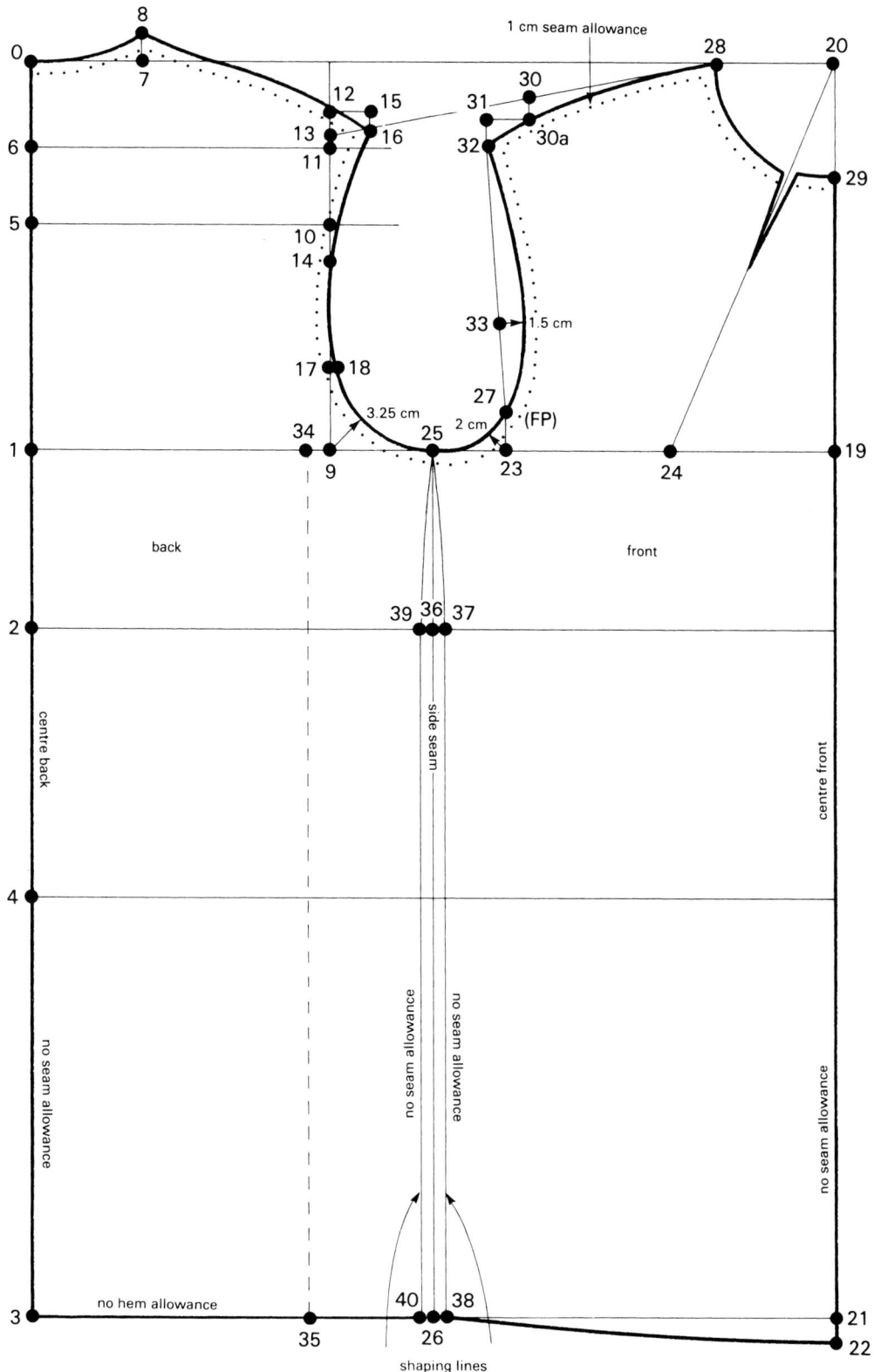

The one-piece sleeve block

A block to be used for the body blocks in this chapter.

Measurements required to draft the block
The sample illustrated is for the athletic figure (100cm chest). Refer to the size chart (page 12) for standard measurements, or the size chart (page 15) for SMALL, MEDIUM, LARGE, XLARGE sizing.

Sleeve length – one-piece sleeve   64.8cm
(For overgarments add 1.5cm to sleeve length measurement.)

A 1cm seam allowance is included in the block. There is no hem allowance.

Trace off top section of the body block above the waistline.
Extend the scye depth line beyond centre back line.
Mark front pitch point FP.
Mark underarm point 0.
Square up from 1 on scye depth line through FP.
1–2   ⅓ scye measurement; square across.
Measure outer edge of body block (see diagram opposite, measuring a curve).
1–3   ½ measurement 1–2; square across.
Where the line crosses the back scye line of the body block, mark back pitch point BP.
Mark shoulder points 4 and 5.

FP–6   the measurement 4–FP, which is measured in a *straight* line, plus 2cm; join FP–6.
6–7   the measurement 5–BP, which is measured in a *straight* line, plus 1.5cm; join 6–7.
FP–8   the measurement FP–0 measured in a *curve* plus 0.75cm; square down.
7–9   the measurement BP–0 measured in a *curve* plus 1.25cm; square down.
Square down from 6.
6–10   sleeve length–one-piece sleeve plus 1cm; square across to 11 and 12.
11–13   5cm; join 8–13.
12–14   5cm; join 9–14.
10–15   ½ measurement 10–14.
15–16   1cm; join 10–14 with a curve.
Square up 10cm from 16.
6–17   is one third the distance 6–18.
FP–18   is 4cm.
Draw in outline of the sleeve head.
9–7   hollow the curve 0.75cm.
7–6   raise the curve 1.5cm.
6–FP   raise the curve 2cm at 17, touch the line at 18.
FP–8   hollow the curve 0.75cm.
11–19   ½ measurement 8–11 plus 2.5cm; square across.

Note   It is important that all the *curved measurements* are measured accurately with the tape upright.

Sleeve modifications for the easy fitting jacket and overgarment blocks

Alterations to the sleeve block
1–2   ⅓ scye measurement minus 1cm (see the diagram, measuring a curve, on the opposite page; square across.

FP–6   the measurement 4–FP which is measured in a *straight* line, plus 1.75cm; join FP–6.
6–7   the measurement 5–BP which is measured in a *straight* line plus 1.25cm; join 6–7.

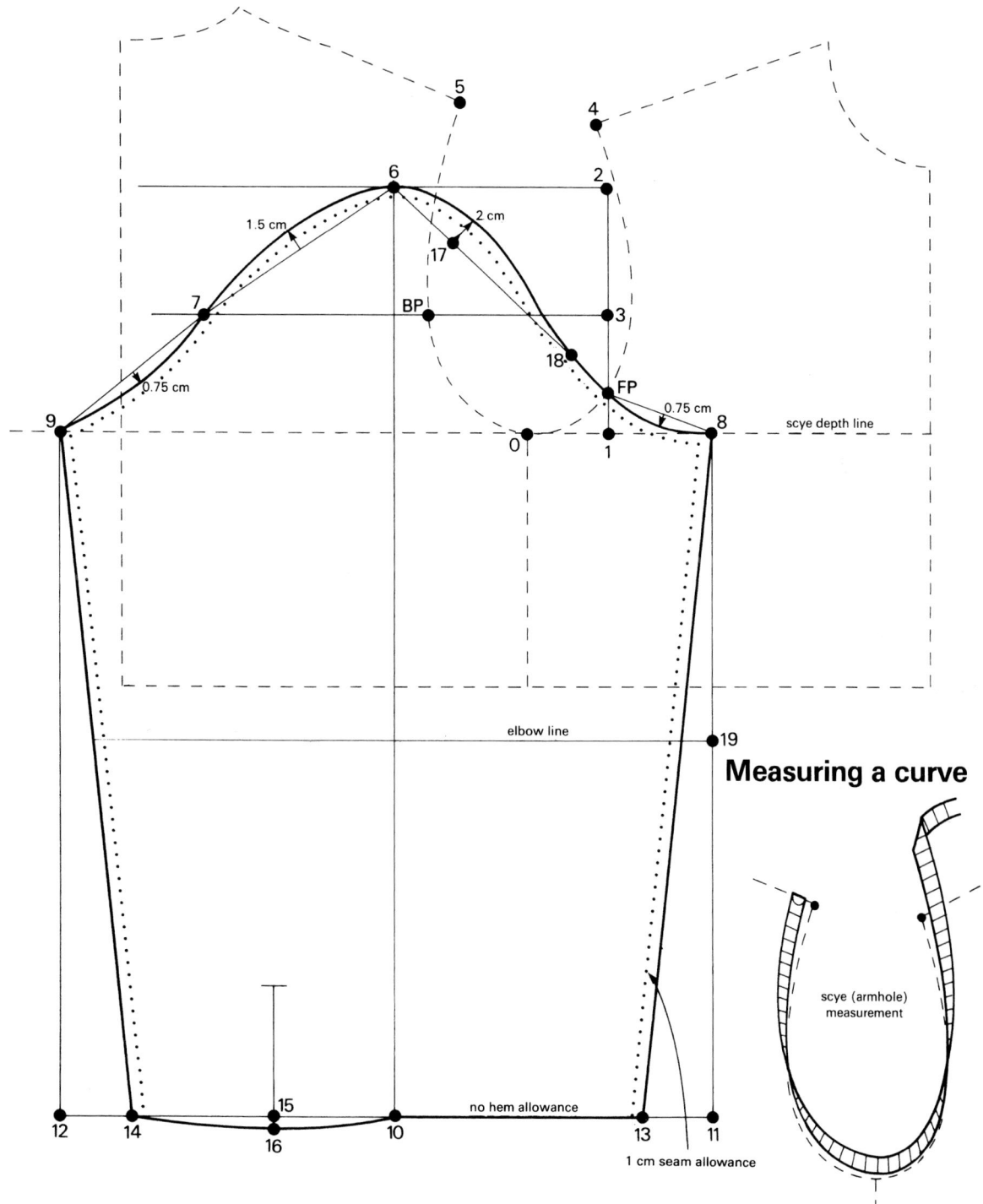

1.5 cm

2 cm

5

4

6

2

17

7

BP

3

18

FP

0.75 cm

0.75 cm

9

0

1

8

scye depth line

elbow line

19

Measuring a curve

scye (armhole)
measurement

15

no hem allowance

12

14

10

13

11

16

1 cm seam allowance

The two-piece sleeve block

A sleeve block to be used with all the body blocks in this chapter.

Measurements required to draft the block
The sample illustrated is for the athletic figure (100cm chest). Refer to the size chart (page 12) for standard measurements, or the size chart (page 15) for SMALL, MEDIUM, LARGE, XLARGE sizing.

Sleeve length – two-piece sleeve   82cm
(For overgarments add 1.5cm to sleeve length measurement.)
Cuff size   29.2cm
(For overgarments add 4cm to cuff size measurement.)

A 1cm seam allowance is included in the block. There is no hem allowance.

On body block
Mark A and B at shoulder points on body section.
Mark C at underarm point.
Mark front pitch point FP; mark D at the base of the line from FP.
Mark points 9 and 14; mark 14 at back pitch BP.

Top sleeve
Mark point 0; square across, up and down.
0–1 the measurement D–FP on body block.
0–2 the measurement 9–BP on body block; square across.
0–3 ⅓ scye measurement plus 0.75cm; measure outer edge of body block (see diagram, measuring a curve, on page 139); square across.
1–4 the measurement A–FP on body block, which is measured in a *straight* line, plus 2cm. Join 1–4.
4–5 the measurement B–BP on body block, which is measured in a *straight* line, plus 1.25cm. Join 4–5.

0–6 2cm; square down with a dotted line.
7 midway between 5 and 4.
4–8 ⅓ measurement 4–1.
Draw in sleeve head through points 5, 4, 1, 6 as shown in diagram.
5–9 1.5cm.
9–10 sleeve length two-piece sleeve minus half back plus 1cm.
10–11 ½ measurement 1–10; square across.
10–12 3.5cm; square across.
12–13 ½ cuff size plus 2cm.
10–14 2cm; join 13–10 and 10–14.
Join 6–14; curve line inwards 1cm at elbow line. Join 5–13 with a dotted line; mark 15 on elbow line.
15–16 3cm.
Join 5–13 curving the line through point 16.

Undersleeve
0–17 2cm.
17–18 0.5cm; square down with a dotted line.
10–19 2cm; join 18–19; curve line inwards 1cm at elbow line.
0–20 the measurement C–D on body block plus 2.3cm.
20–21 0.5cm.
21–22 The measurement BP–C measured in a *curve* plus 0.5cm. (21–22 is measured straight to touch the line from 2–5).
23 midway between 21 and 22.
23–24 1.75cm; draw a curved line through the points 22, 24, 21, 18.
22–25 1.5cm; join 25–13. Mark point 26 on elbow line.
26–27 ½ measurement 16–26 plus 0.8cm.
Join 25–13 curving the line through point 27.
Extend back seam line 0.5cm above 25 to 28.
Extend underarm seam line 1cm above 22 to 29.
Join 28–29.

Sleeve modifications for the easy fitting jacket and overgarment blocks

Alterations to the sleeve block
0–3 ⅓ scye measurement (see diagram, measuring a curve, on page 139; square across.
1–4 the measurement A–FP, which measured in a *straight* line, plus 1.75cm; join 1–4.

4–5 the measurement B–BP, which is measured in a *straight* line, plus 1cm; join 4–5.
12–13 ½ cuff size plus 3cm.

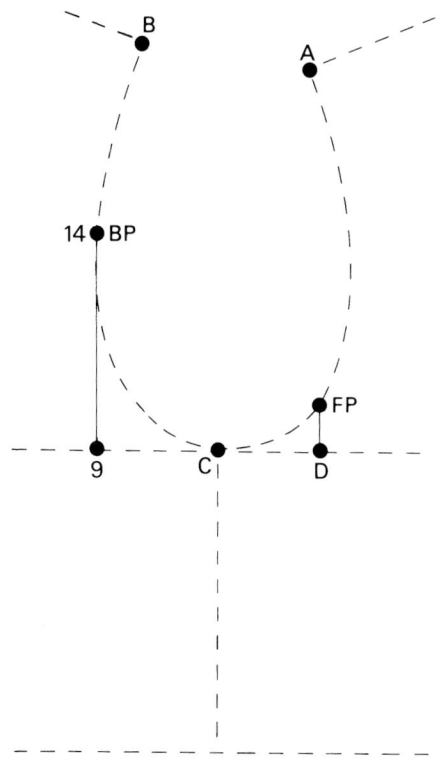

Body block

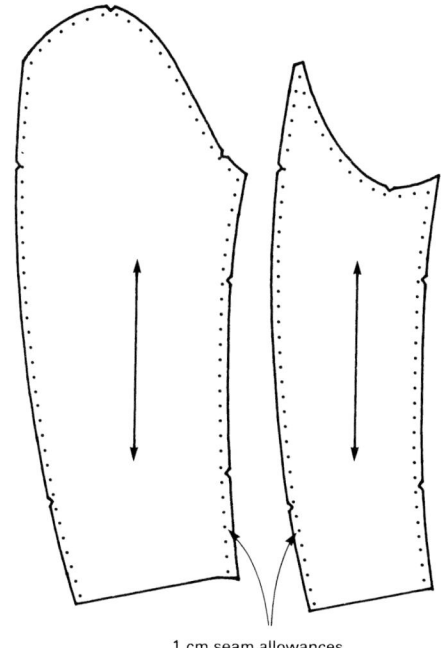

1 cm seam allowances

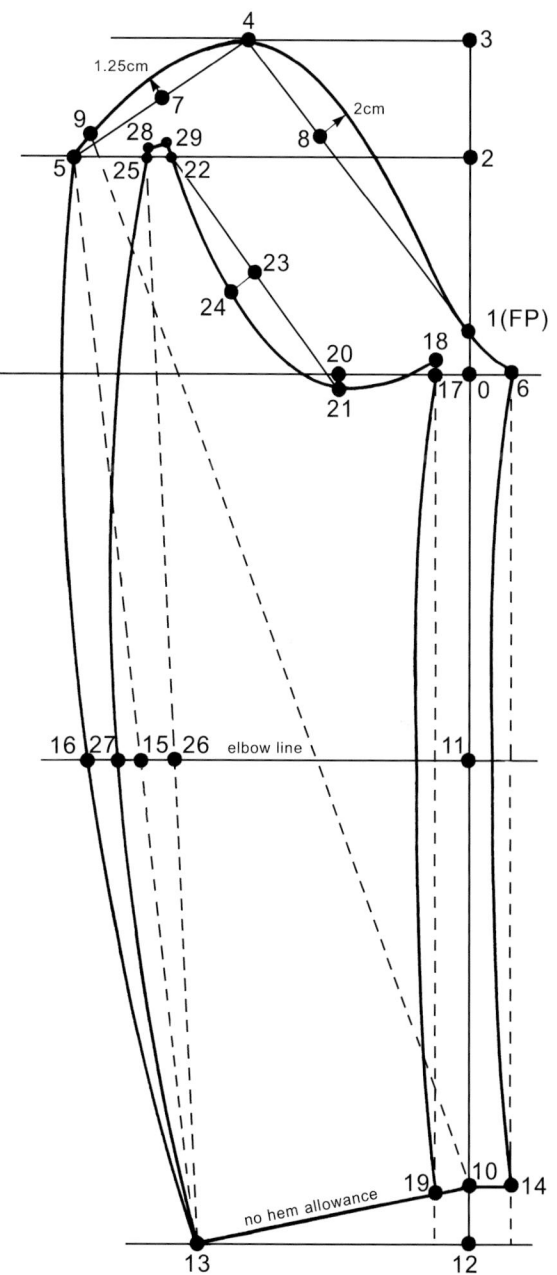

Shaping the blocks

1 Basic jacket shaping

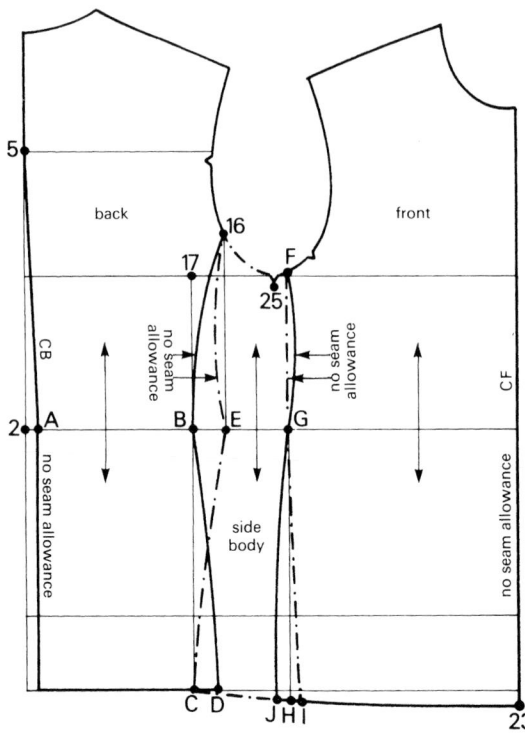

The block can be shaped on any design line. If classic waist shaping is required it is useful to follow a basic guide. Two examples are illustrated.

1 Basic jacket shaping

Trace casual jacket block, mark 2, 5, 16, 17, 23, 25.

Back   2–A is 1.5cm; square down; join A–5.
On line from 17 mark B on waistline; mark C on hem line. Join 23 to C.
C–D is 3cm; draw seam line 16, B, D.

Side body   Square down from 16 to E on waistline. Draw seam line 16, E, C, curve 16–E out 0.5cm; 25–F is 1.5cm; square down to G on waistline, H on hem line. H–I is 0.75cm; draw seam line F, G, I.

Front   H–J is 1cm; draw seam line F, G, J; curve F–G in 1cm.

2 Basic panel shaping

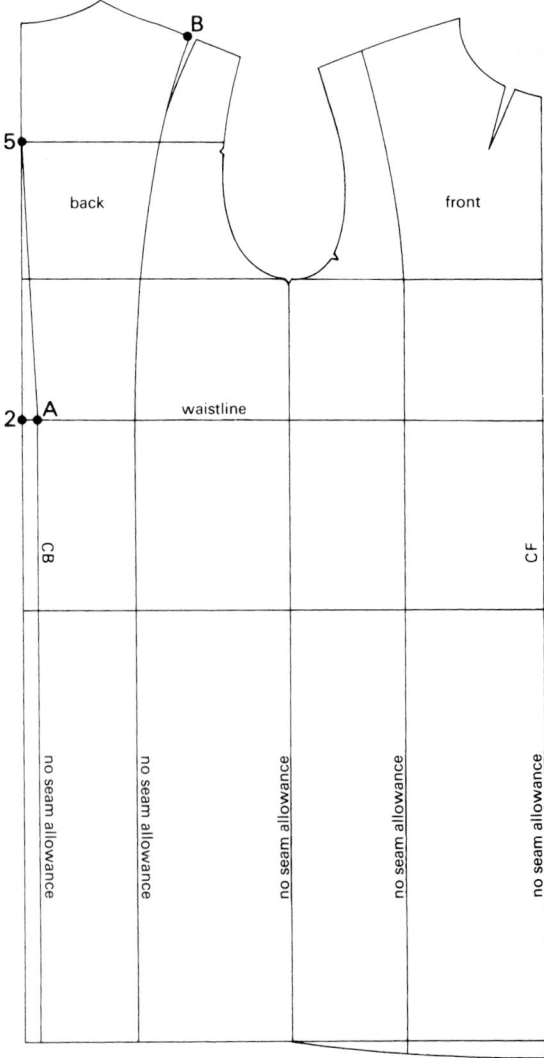

Easy fitting jacket shaping

Ignore the waist and hip shaping lines on the easy fitting block, then complete the instructions above. Trace off the sections. Take 0.5cm off the seam lines at B, C, D, E, G, I, J. Re-shape the seam lines.

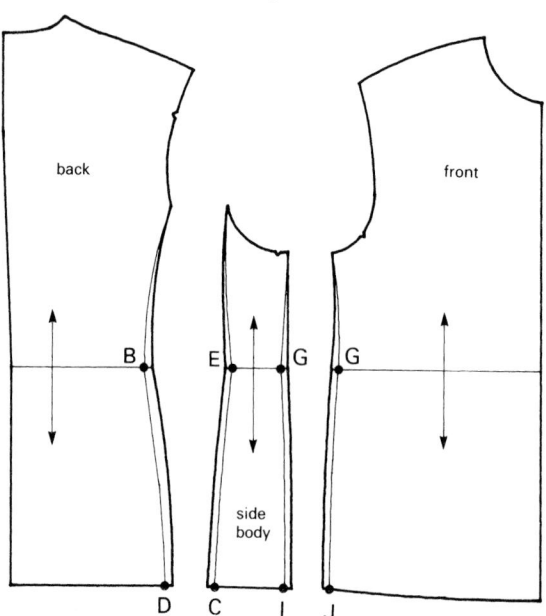

2 Basic panel shaping

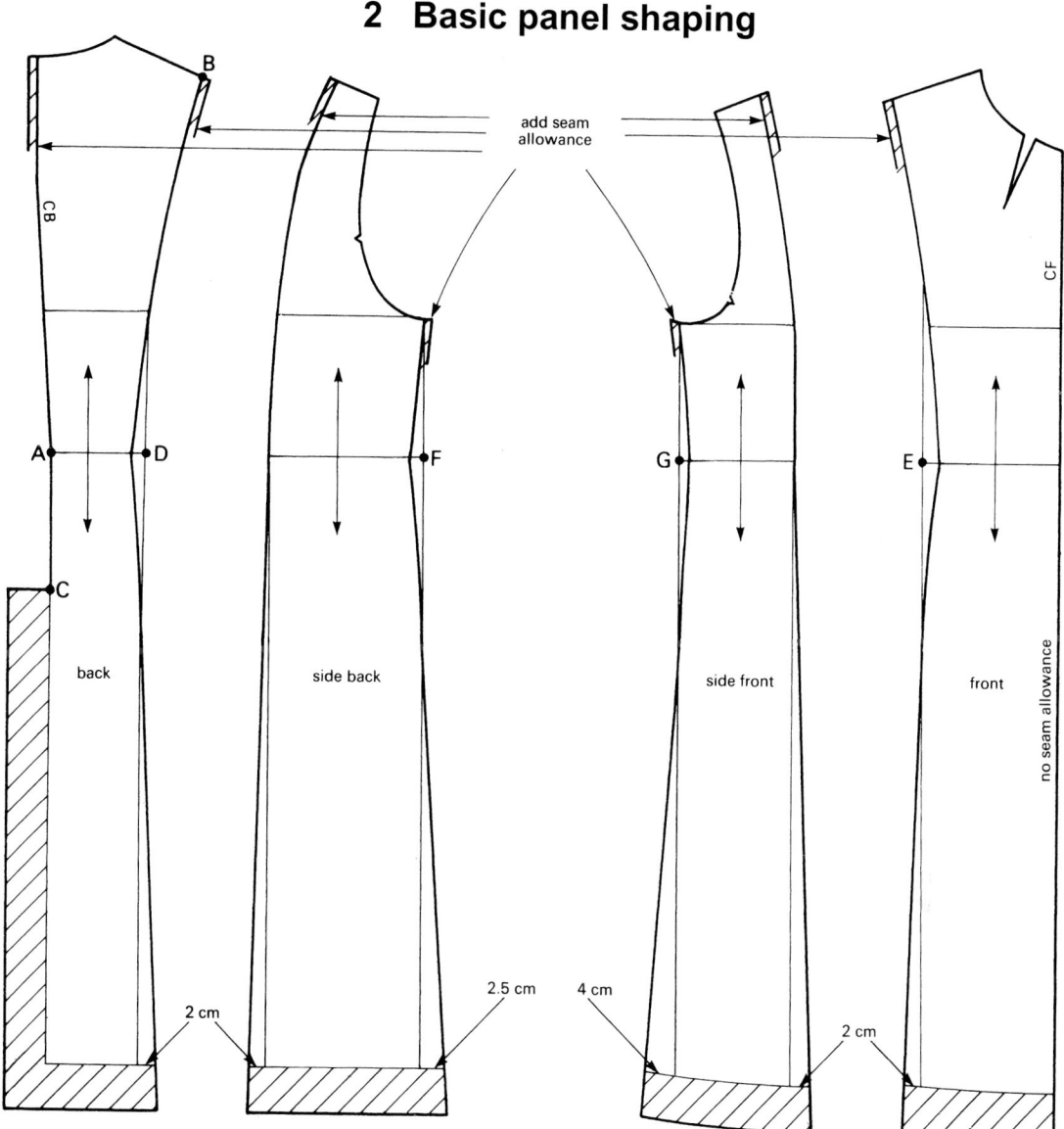

2 Basic panel shaping for belted coats

Trace basic overgarment block, mark points 5, 2.
2–A is 1.5cm; square down to hem line; join 5–A.
Draw in front and back panel lines where required;
take out 1cm shoulder ease on back panel line at B,
cut up panel lines, trace round panels.

Back A–C is 15cm; from C add back vent 5cm
wide; square down.
Shape in waist 1.5cm at D, add 2cm flare at hem.
Front Shape in waist 2cm at E, add 2cm flare at hem.

Side panels Side seams, shape in waist 1.5cm at F,
add 2.5cm flare at hem; shape in waist 1cm at G, add
4cm flare at hem.
Panel seams, add 2cm flare at hem.

Seam and hem allowances

Seam allowance is required on the back seam, panel
seams and side seams of the jacket and coat.
A 5cm hem allowance is also required. Their
addition is illustrated above.

Adaptations of the blocks

Jackets can be adapted from the basic or easy fitting casual jacket blocks. The two-piece sleeve draft gives a formal look to the designs.

The design illustrated can have a fitted or semi-fitted shape at the back. Different pockets or other design features can be used.

1a Jackets – fitted

Trace off casual jacket block two-piece sleeve.
Use the straight hemline.
Back and front body sections   Draw in finished length.
Draw in dotted line from point 17.
Mark X on centre front line 2cm below hem line.
Draw basic jacket shaping on centre back and back style line: mark points A, B, C, D, E, F, G (ref. 1, page 142).
Join X to base of the line from 17.
Add 3cm button stand: curve front edge to hem.
Mark buttonholes. Mark facing line.
Draw line from F–G. G–H is 8cm. Square across.
Construct a 1.5cm dart at I, 5cm above the waistline.
J is midway between F and centre front line.
J–K is 2cm; square down to L, 12cm below waistline.
Construct a 1cm dart on this line.
J is centre of the breast pocket; draw in pocket (on more formal jackets slant top of breast pocket 1cm). M is 5cm from the line K–L, M is the centre point of a lower pocket design. Draw in pocket (on formal jackets pockets run parallel to hem line of jacket).
Flaps are set 2.5cm above top of pocket line and extend any flaps 0.5cm–1cm on each side of pocket.
Trace off front and back body sections.
Add seam allowance to centre back seam, back style seam and front edge of jacket.
Add 4cm to lower edge of front and back hem line.
Facing   Trace off facing; add seam allowance to front edge and facing line.
Collar   Construct shaped convertible collar with hidden stand (ref. 2b, page 88).
Pockets   Trace off pockets; add 4cm facing to top edge; add seam allowance around remainder of edges.
Any flaps require seam allowances on all edges.
Sleeve   Trace off both sections of two-piece sleeve; add 6cm hem allowance.

1b Jackets – semi-fitted

Body sections   Trace off block required.
Front   Use front body section for fitted jacket but draw a straight line from point N to point C.
Back   Trace back body section using the centre back line without shaping and standard style line.
Add 2cm seam allowance to centre back seam, 1cm seam allowance to style line.
Belt   Construct belt: width required plus 2cm; length = measurement 2–G less 3cm.
Shoulder strap   Construct strap: width required plus 2cm; length is shoulder measurement plus 2cm.

1a Jacket – fitted

1b Jacket – semi-fitted

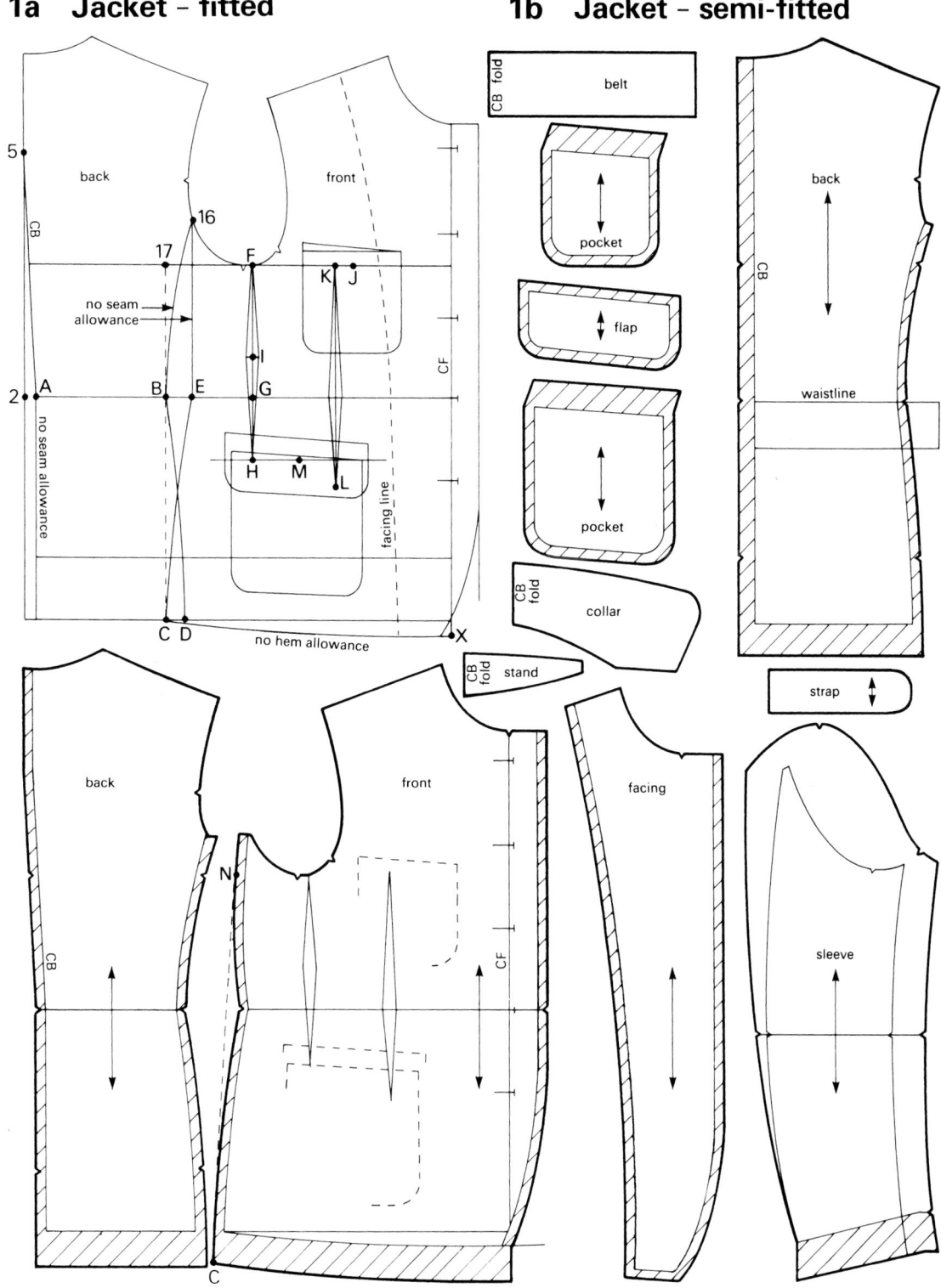

Classic easy fitting jackets are usually cut from the range of classic casual blocks in order to retain the men's longer back balance and the high shaped head of the one-piece and two-piece sleeves. These sleeves are particularly necessary if any sort of padded shoulder is required. 'Flat' overgarment shapes can be cut from the 'flat' blocks (see pages 22 and 26).

2 Easy fitting jacket

Trace off an easy fitting jacket or the easy fitting overgarment blocks and the two-piece sleeve block. Use the straight hemline.

Body sections If the overgarment block is used, temporarily swing the dart to an armhole position. Extend to the length required.

Move the side seam line 4cm towards the back. Shape in at the hem if required.

A–B is 2cm; draw a curved line from point B to the new side seam line.

Draw in button lines and button positions for a double breasted front. (Example is 5cm each side of centre line.) Add 2cm button stand.

Draw in front and back yoke lines.

Draw in pocket positions and a pocket bag shape.

Draw in facing line.

Remove seam allowance from the front neck and construct the draft for an engineered standard collar and rever (ref. 10b, page 94).

Collar Trace off collar and facing. Complete collars (see page 86).

Facing Trace off facing. Add seam allowances where shown; an extra 0.5cm will be required around the facing edge.

Front Trace off front section. Add seam allowance to front and side seam; extra seam allowance will be required on top edge for stitching.

Add 4cm hem allowance.

Front yoke Trace off front yoke.

If a darted block is used, swing dart back to the neckline. Add seam allowance to bottom edge, front edge and neckline.

Back Trace off back section.

Add seam allowance to side seam, extra seam allowance will be required on top edge for stitching. Add 4cm hem allowance.

Back yoke Trace off back yoke.

Add seam allowance to bottom edge.

Pocket Trace off pocket welt. Add seam allowance. Trace off pocket bag.

Sleeves Add 4cm hem allowance to sleeve hem.

2 Easy-fitting jacket

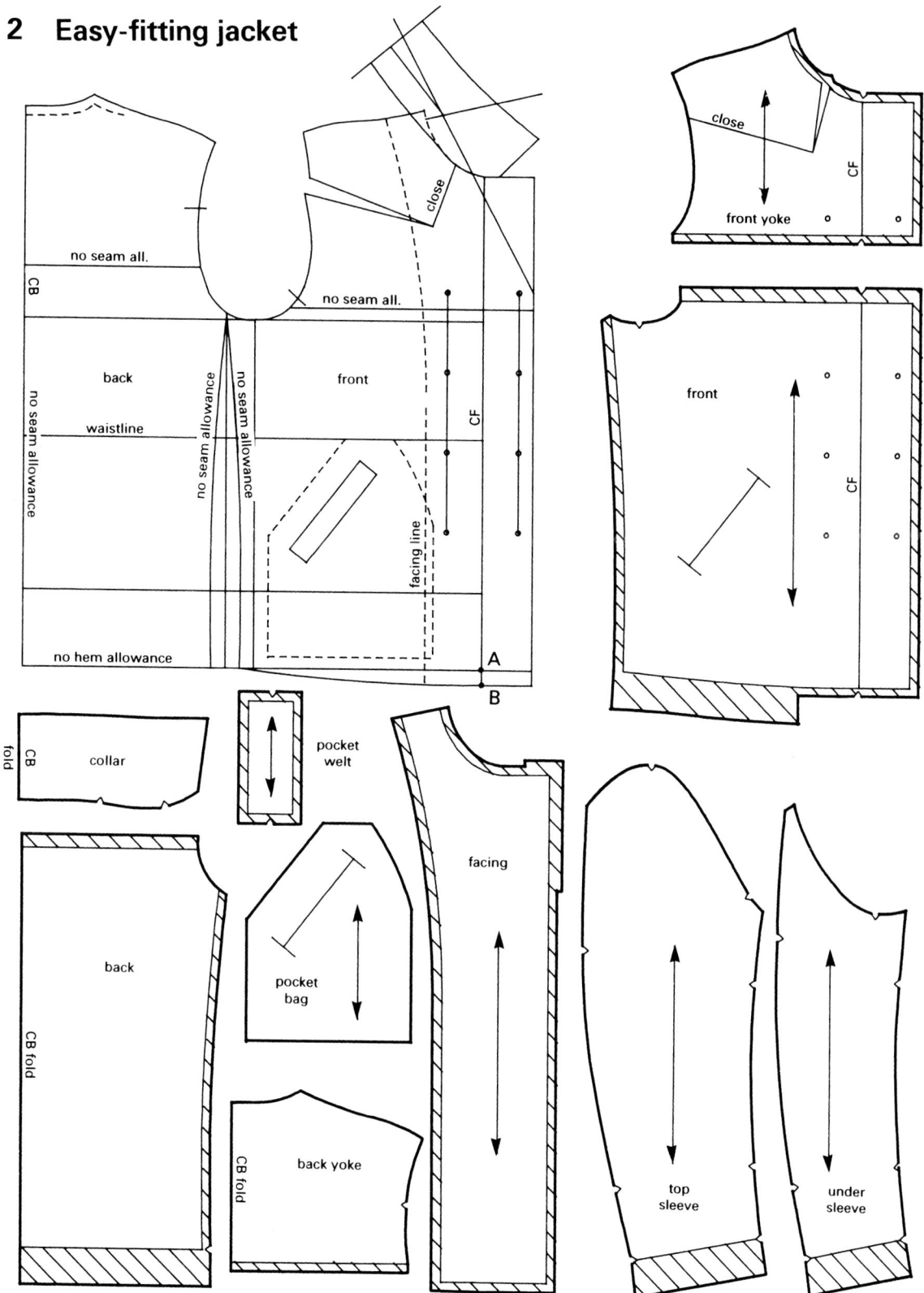

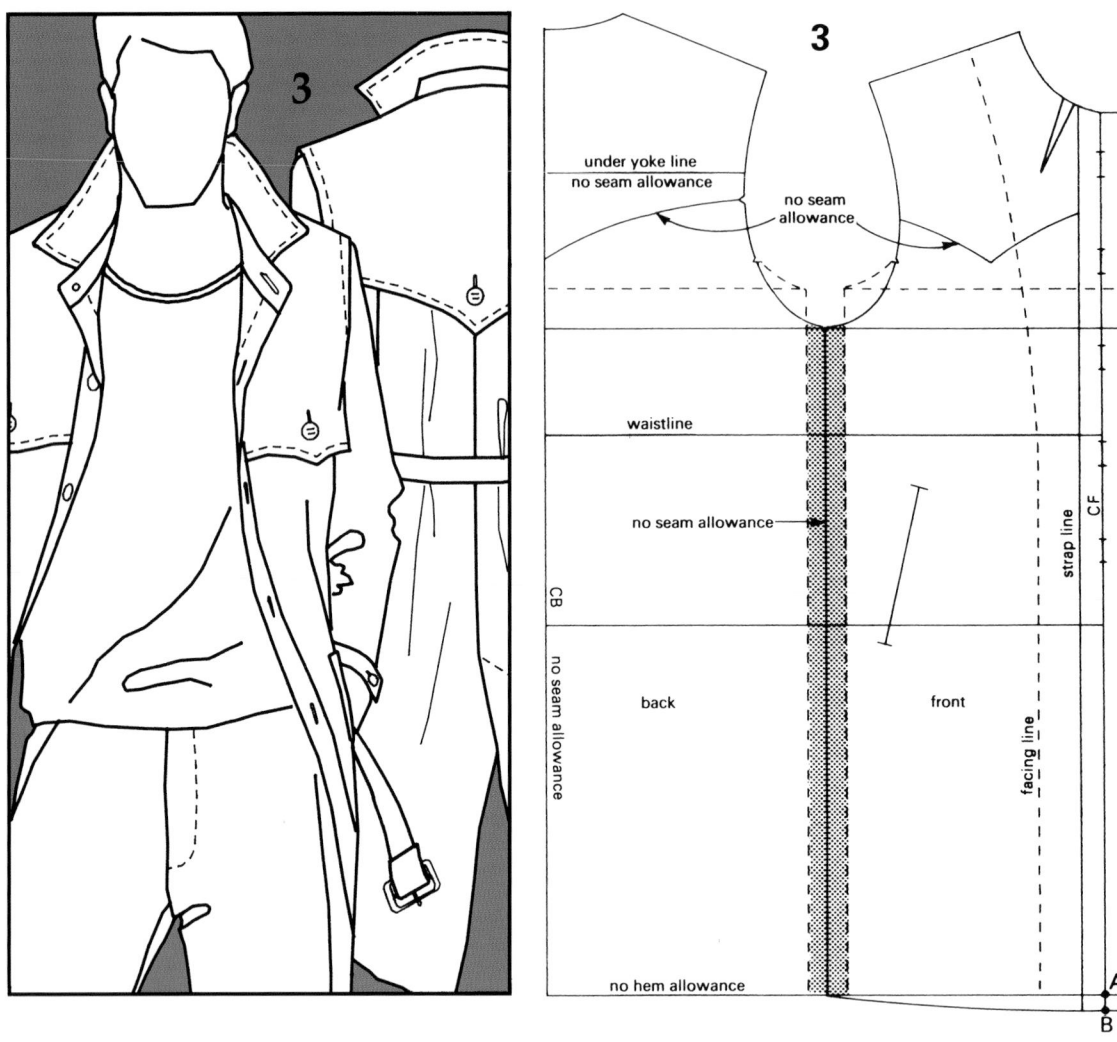

3

under yoke line
no seam allowance

no seam allowance

waistline

no seam allowance →

CB

no seam allowance

back

front

strap line

CF

facing line

no hem allowance

A

B

3   Trench coat

Trace easy fitting overgarment block and one-piece sleeve. Use the straight hemline. For extra ease, see Lowered armhole (ref. 8, page 70).

Body section   Draw in finished length.

Mark A at base of centre front line.

A–B is 2cm; join B to side seam with a curve.

Draw strap lines 2.5cm each side of centre front; mark buttonholes on centre front line.

Draw in facing line. Draw in lines of front and back over yokes. Draw in line of back under yoke.

Draw 18cm pocket opening 6cm below waistline.

Back sections   Trace lower back body section.

Add 10cm to centre back line plus 5cm for vent; add 4cm flare to side seam. Add seam allowance to side, centre back and yoke seams.

Trace back under yoke. Add seam allowance to yoke line.

Front   Trace off front on strap line; add 4cm flare to side seam.

Add seam allowance to side seam and front edge.

Add 5cm hem allowance to front and back sections.

Over yokes   Trace over yokes. Extend the neck dart to edge of front over yoke; close dart.

Add 0.5cm to shoulder lines; 2cm to armhole edges.

Add seam allowance to lower edges and front edge.

Strap-facing   Trace front strap; add extended facing to front edge; close dart in facing.

Add seam allowance to strap, hem and facing lines.

Collar   Construct shaped shirt collar (ref. 3c, page 88).

Belt   Construct tie belt, required length and twice the width plus seam allowances.

Sleeve strap   Draw in sleeve strap. Trace off sleeve strap; add seam allowances to all edges except at C.

Add 5cm hem allowance to sleeve.

3 Trench coat

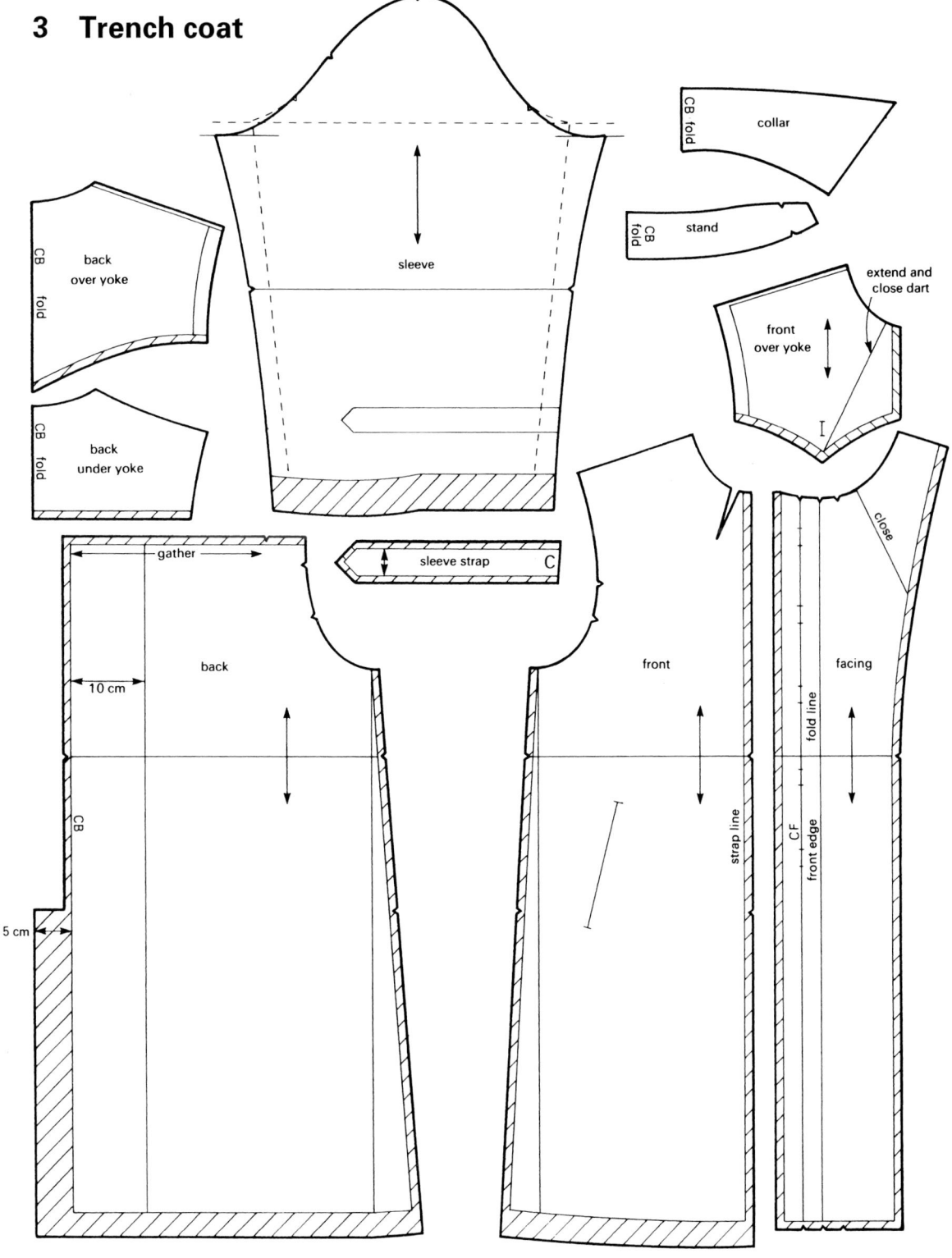

back
over yoke

CB fold

back
under yoke

CB fold

sleeve

CB fold collar

CB fold stand

front
over yoke

extend and
close dart

close

gather

10 cm

back

CB

5 cm

sleeve strap C

front

strap line

facing

fold line

CF

front edge

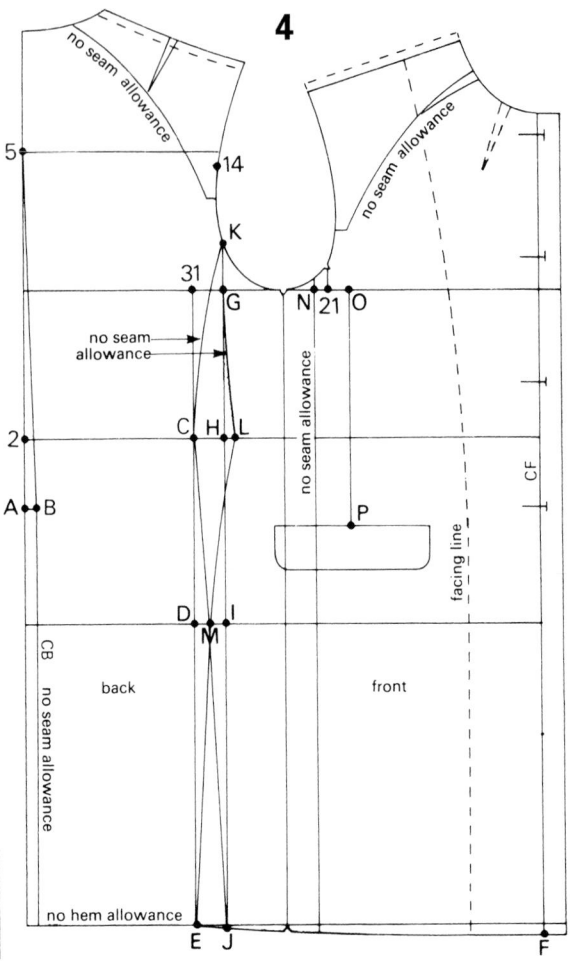

4 Coats – straight style

Trace required overgarment block and two-piece
sleeve. Use straight hemline.

Body section   Mark in points 5, 2, 14, 21, 31.
Draw in finished length. 2–A is 8cm, A–B is 1.5cm.
Join 5 to B, square down to hem.
Square down from 31 to C, D, E.
Mark F on centre front line 2cm below hem line.
Join F–E. Add 3cm button stand, mark buttonholes,
mark facing line.
31–G is 3cm; square down to H, I, J; square up to K.
H–L is 1cm. M is midway between D and I.
Shape back style seam K, C, M, J. Shape side body
seam K, L, M, E.
21–N is 2cm; square down to hem line. 21–O is 2cm;
square down to P, 10cm below waistline.
Square across for pocket line.
Draw in flap pocket approximately 18cm.
Adapt shoulders, draw raglan shaping for two-piece
sleeve (ref. 15, page 76).
Transfer front dart to raglan line.

Back   Trace off back. Add 5cm for vent from M.
Add seam allowance to centre back. raglan seam
and style line. Add 5cm hem allowance.
Side body   Trace off side body.
Add 1cm flare to hem of front style seam; add 5cm
allowance for vent from M. Add seam allowance to
both style seams. Add 5cm hem allowance.
Front   Trace off front; add 3cm flare to hem of style
seam. Add seam allowance to raglan seam, style
seam and front edge. Add 4cm hem allowance.
Facing   Trace off facing; close dart. Add seam
allowance to facing line, front edge and hem line.
Sleeve   Construct raglan two-piece sleeve (ref. 15,
page 76). Add 6cm hem allowance to sleeve sections.
Collar   Construct shaped convertible collar with
hidden stand (ref. 2b, page 88).
Shoulder strap   Construct strap: twice width
required plus 2cm; length required plus 2cm.
Pocket   Trace pocket flap. Add seam allowance.
Pocket bag   Construct a rectangle: width = pocket
flap width + 2cm; depth to a fold approx. 18cm.

4   Coats – straight style

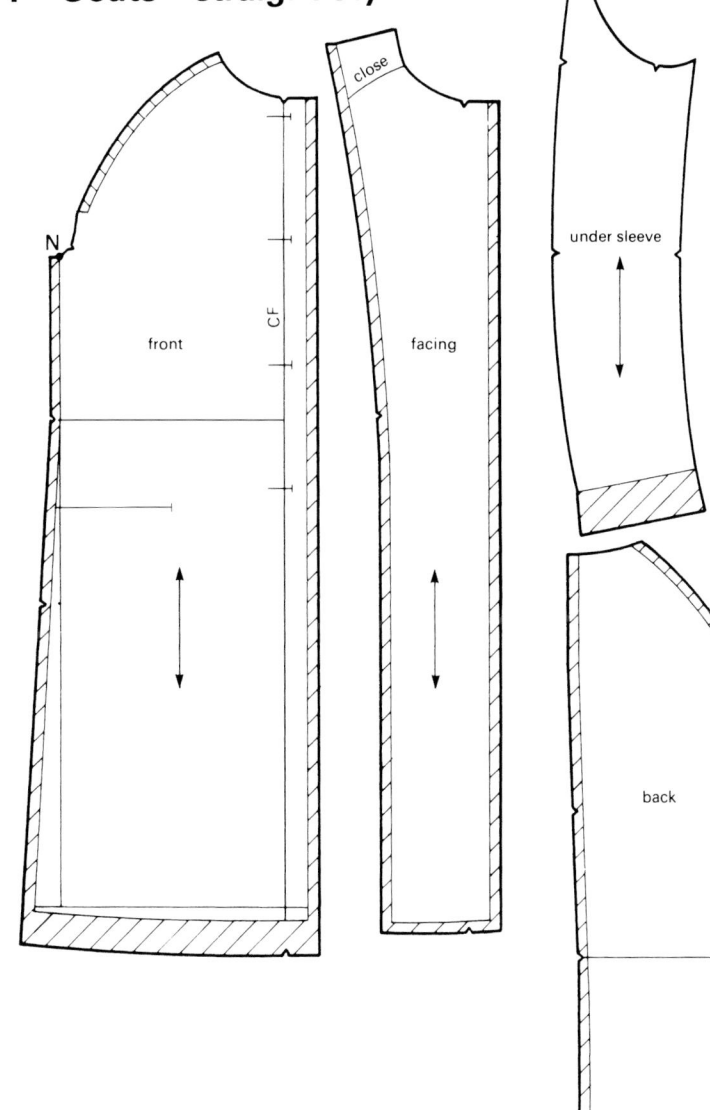
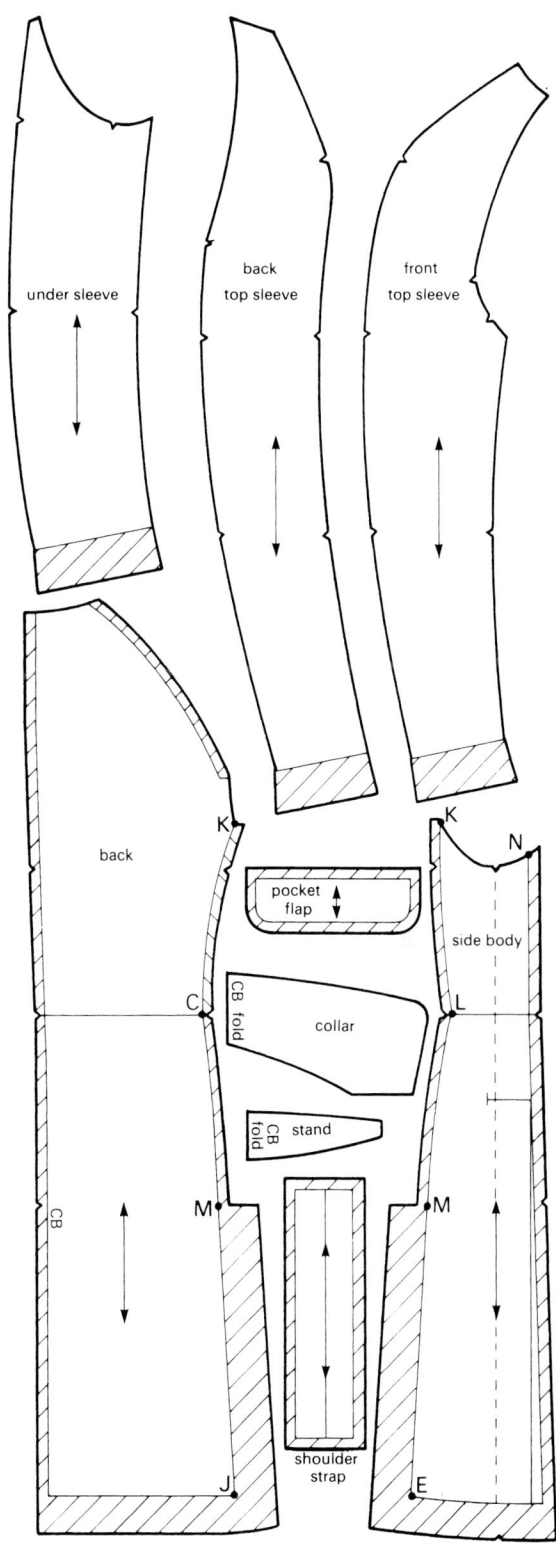

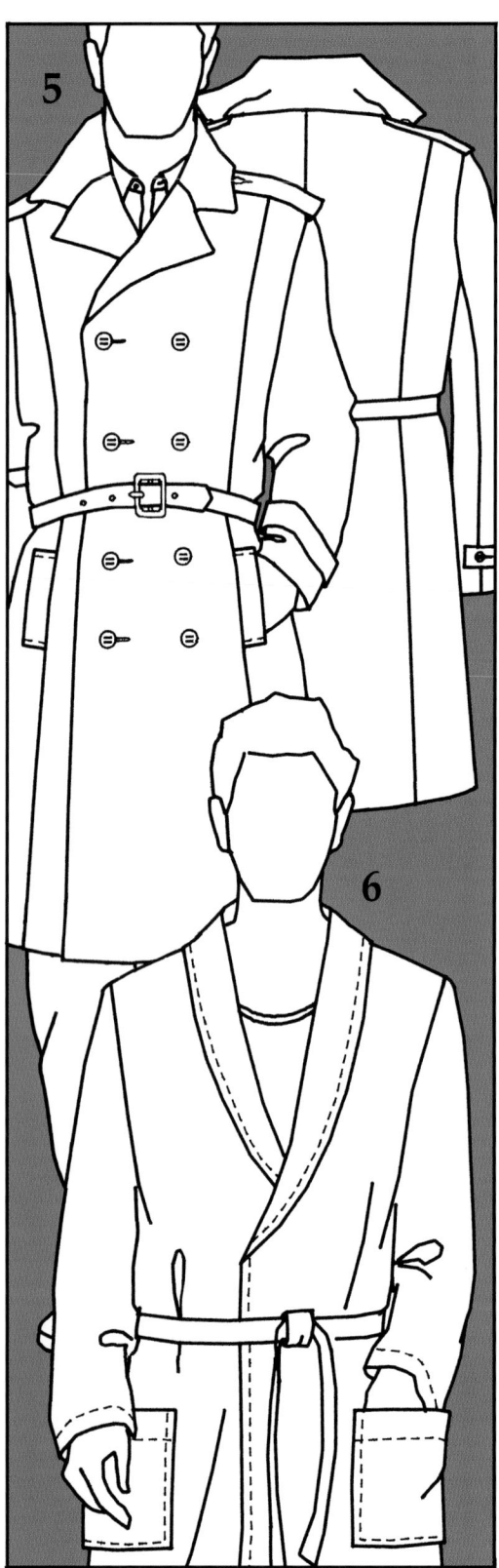

5 Coats – fitted style

Trace required overgarment block and two-piece sleeve.
Draw in length required.
Eliminate neck dart (ref. page 135).
Body sections For basic panel shaping and hem shaping
see (ref. 2, page 143).
Add seam allowance and 5cm hem allowance to all panels.
Note If a waist seam is required, lower front waist by
1.5cm.
Mark in pocket opening 5cm below waistline 16cm length;
as shown.
Front Draw in button lines and button stand for a double
breasted front; mark break point; mark buttonholes.
Add seam allowance to break point of front edge. Draw in
facing line.
Collar and facing Construct a basic collar and rever (ref.
10b, page 94). Construct facing.
Pocket welts Construct welt: length required plus 2cm;
twice the width required plus 2cm.
Shoulder strap Construct as for welt.
Belt Construct belt: length is waist measurement plus
30cm: width is twice belt width plus 2cm.
Sleeve Add 6cm hem allowance.
Sleeve strap Construct strap: length is measurement of
lower edge of top sleeve plus 8cm; twice width of strap
required plus 2cm.

6 Formal dressing gown

Trace off overgarment block and two-piece sleeve.
Body section Draw in length required.
Use the straight hemline.
To eliminate neck dart redraw dart to armhole edge,
close dart.
Draw style line on back section 3.5cm from side seam line.
Mark A on CF line. A–B is 2cm; join B to style line.
Back Trace off back section along style line.
Add 2.5cm flare at hem line.
Add seam allowance to style line.
Add 5cm hem allowance.
Front, facing, collar Trace front body section along
style line.
Add 6cm button stand; mark break point 1.
Construct a standard roll collar and facing (ref. 4, page 90).
Add required seam allowances for that adaptation.
Draw in required pocket shape 6cm below waistline.
Add 4cm flare at hem line.
Add seam allowance to style line.
Add 5cm hem allowance.
Pocket Trace off pocket shape, add 4cm to top edge for
facing.
Add seam allowance to remainder of the edges.
Belt Construct belt, length 200cm and twice width
required plus 2cm.
Sleeve Add 5cm hem allowance.

5 Coats – fitted style

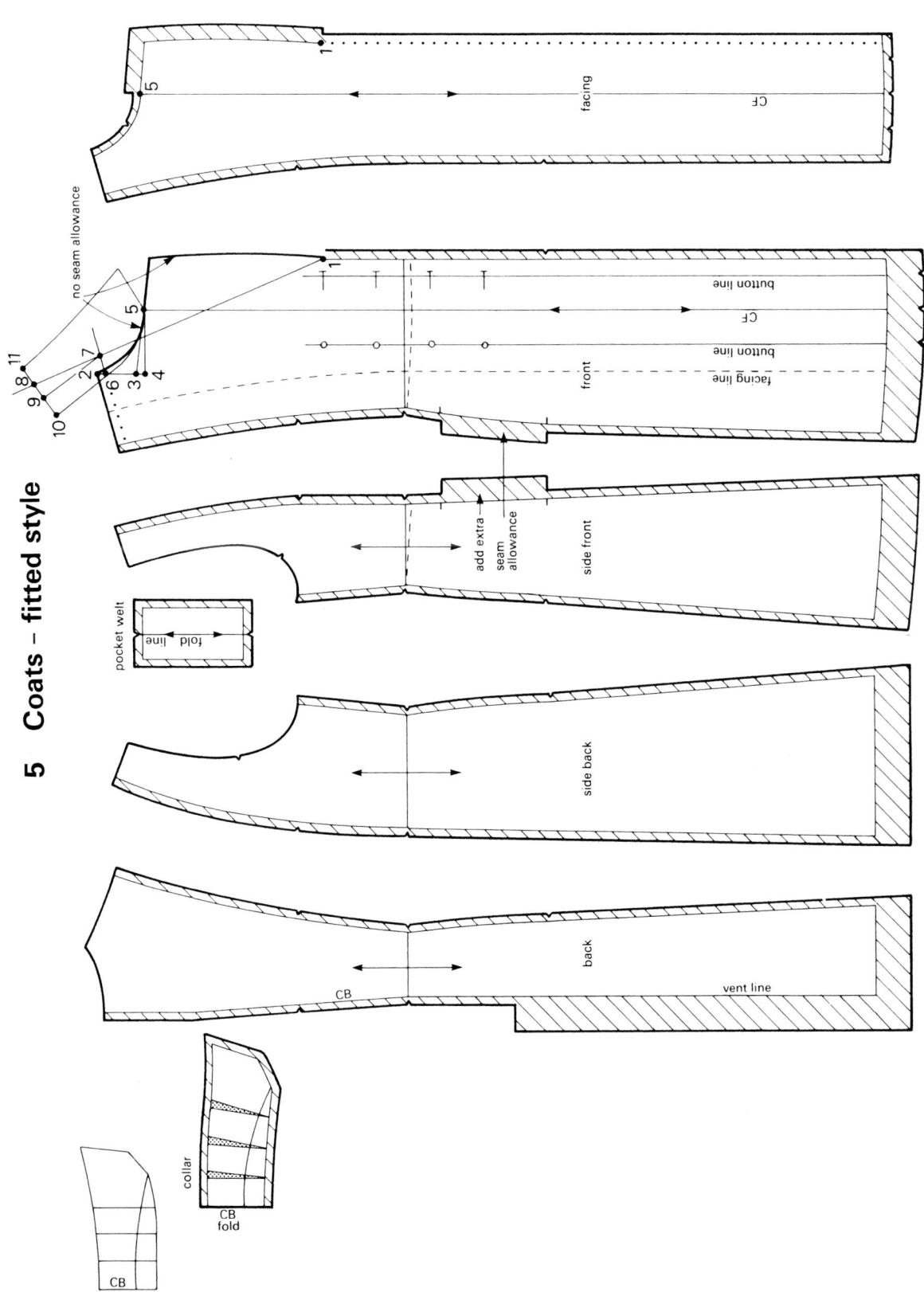

facing

CF

no seam allowance

5

11
8
9
7
2
6
10
3
4
1

button line

CF

button line

front

facing line

add extra
seam
allowance

side front

pocket welt

fold line

side back

back

CB

vent line

collar

CB
fold

CB

6 Formal dressing gown

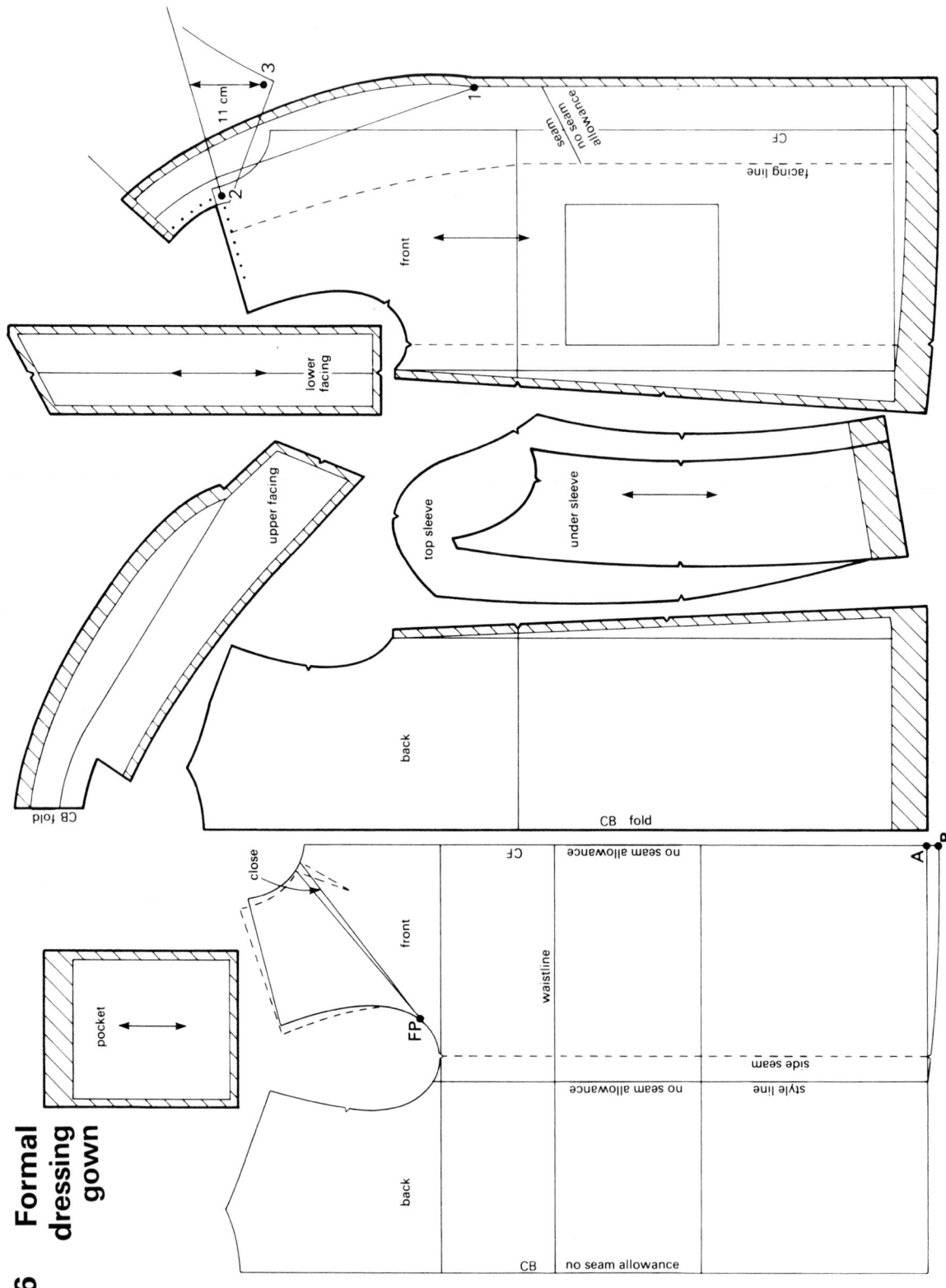

PART FOUR: SIZING AND FIT
Chapter 12 Basic grading techniques

Pattern grading

Pattern grading

Pattern grading is a technique used to reproduce a pattern in other sizes. An accurate method is to draft the smallest size and the largest size, (within a size group), then stop off the sizes between on lines drawn through the basic points, see diagram below. Although the majority of large companies use computers to grade patterns, it is necessary to understand the basic principles in order to give the correct data to the computer.

Grading patterns one size up

The method of finding a grade point by measuring horizontally and then vertically is shown in the diagram below.
From base point 1; square across.
Measure horizontally the required measurement.
Mark point 2; square up.
Measure vertically the required measurement to point 3.
Draw a line through points 1 and 3 to create a grading line.
Points for further grading can be made along this line.

Note 1 The measurement, made horizontally and vertically, is the grade rule instruction required for computer grading.

Grading examples

The examples shown on the following pages demonstrate the method of grading block patterns one size up for young men – athletic figures.

The 'form' blocks
Sizes: 88cm–104cm (size chart page 12)
The classic suit jacket block (pages 98 and 102)
The classic trouser block (page 110)
The classic shirt block; the classic and casual overgarment blocks (page 124 and pages 130–140)

The 'flat' blocks
Sizes: SML, MED, LGE, XLGE (size chart page 15)
The 'flat' shirt and overgarment blocks (pages 22–25)
The 'flat' kimono block (page 26)
The 'flat' trouser blocks (page 20)

Grading patterns one size up

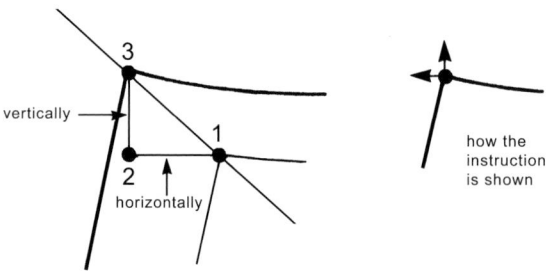

Grading four sizes up

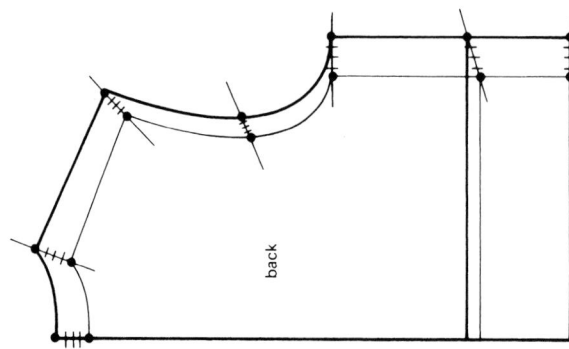

Grading the 'form' blocks

Grading one size up – *'form' cutting* (4cm intervals)
Young men – athletic figures of regular height: 104–108 chest sizes

The classic suit jacket block
Back

1 Measure 8mm hor.
2 Measure 8mm hor. 2.5mm vert.
3 Measure 6mm hor. 5mm vert.
4 Measure 4mm hor. 5mm vert.
5 Measure 2mm hor. 5mm vert
6 Measure 4mm hor. 5mm vert.
7 Measure 5mm hor.

Side body

8 Measure 3.5mm hor.
9 Measure 2mm hor. 7mm vert.
10 Measure 4mm hor. 7mm vert.
11 Measure 7mm vert.

Front

12 Measure 4mm hor. 4mm vert.
13 Measure 7mm hor.
14 Measure 8mm hor.
15 Measure 7mm hor. 2.5mm vert.
16 Measure 4mm vert.
17 Measure 4mm vert.
18 Measure 4mm hor. 4mm vert.
19 Measure 4mm vert.
CF Measure 4mm hor. 4mm vert.

Top Sleeve

1 Measure 6mm hor. 3mm vert.
2 Measure 4mm hor. 5mm vert.
3 Measure 1mm hor. 5mm vert.
4 Measure 1mm hor.

Under sleeve

5 Measure 3mm vert.
6 Measure 4mm hor. 5mm vert.
7 Measure 1mm hor. 5mm vert.
8 Measure 1mm hor.

Classic suit jacket block

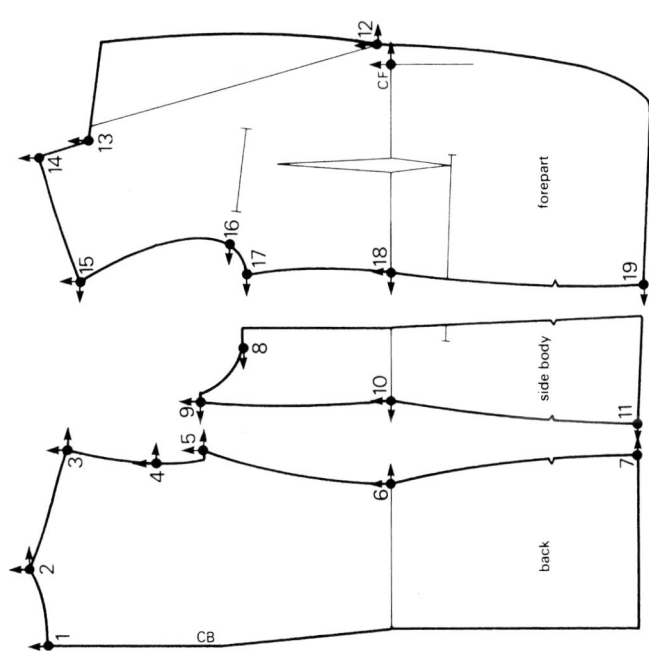

Two-piece sleeve

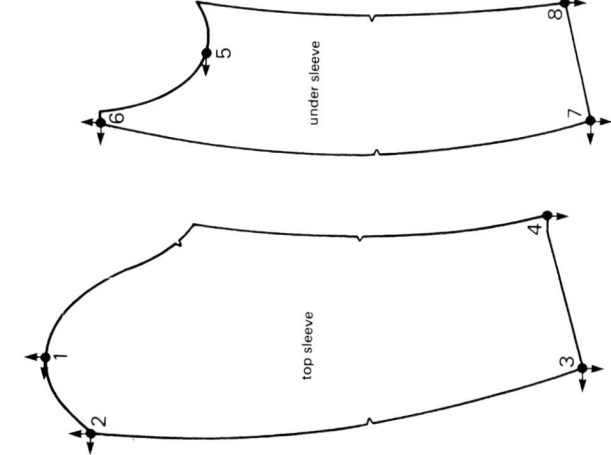

Grading one size up – *'form' cutting* (4cm intervals)
Young men – athletic figures of regular height: 104–108 chest sizes

The classic shirt block; the classic and casual overgarment blocks
Back
1 Measure 8mm hor.
2 Measure 8mm hor. 2.5mm vert.
3 Measure 6mm hor. 5mm vert.
4 Measure 3mm hor. 5mm vert.
5 Measure 9mm vert.
6 Measure 4mm hor. 9mm vert.
7 Measure 9mm vert.

Front
8 Measure 6mm hor.
9 Measure 8mm hor. 2.5mm vert.
10 Measure 7mm hor. 5mm vert.
11 Measure 7mm vert.
12 Measure 11mm vert.
13 Measure 4mm hor. 11mm vert.
14 Measure 11mm vert.

One-piece sleeve
1, 2 Measure 6mm vert.
3, 4 Measure 8mm vert.
5 Measure 4mm vert.
6 Measure 6mm hor.
4 Measure 3mm hor. 2mm vert.

Casual jacket block

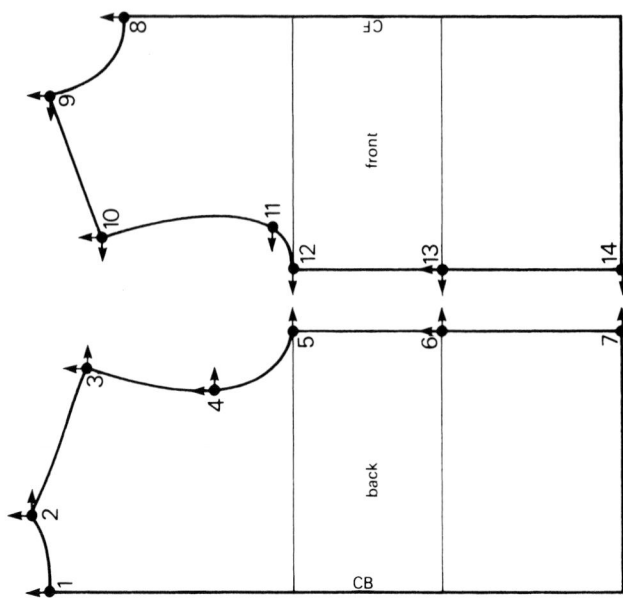

One-piece sleeve

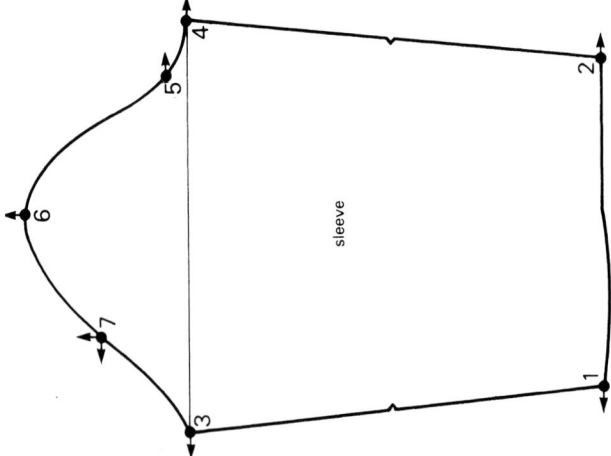

Grading one size up – *'form' cutting* (4cm intervals)
Young men – athletic figures of regular height: 104–108 chest sizes

The classic trouser block

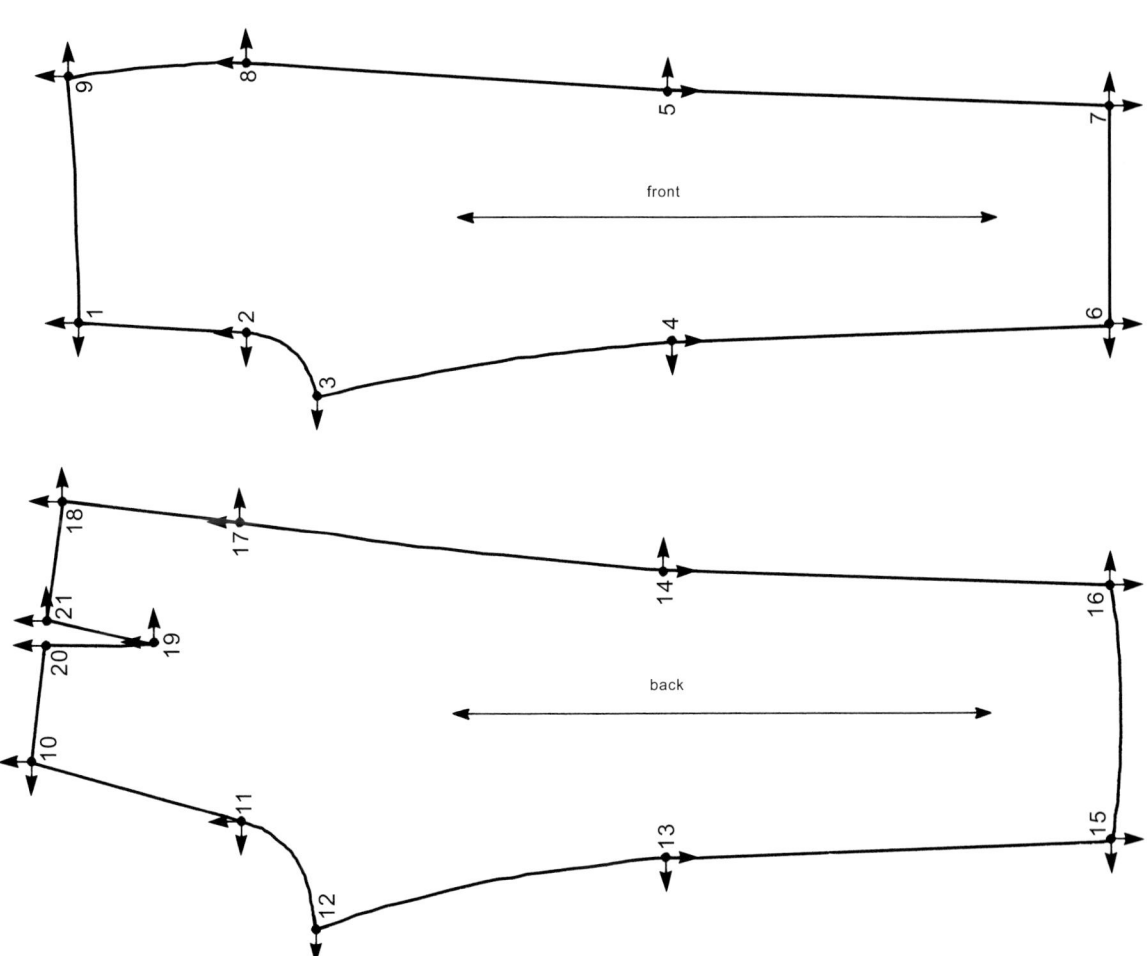

The classic trouser block

Front

1   Measure 3mm hor. 5mm vert
2   Measure 1mm hor. 5mm vert.
3   Measure 7.5mm vert.
4, 5   Measure 5mm hor. 2mm vert.
6, 7   Measure 10mm hor. 2mm vert.
8   Measure 1mm hor. 5mm vert.
9   Measure 3mm hor 5mm vert.

Back

10   Measure 3mm hor. 4.5mm vert
11   Measure 1mm hor. 5mm vert.
12   Measure 8.7mm vert.
13, 14   Measure 5mm hor 2mm vert.
15, 16   Measure 10mm hor. 2mm vert.
17   Measure 1mm hor. 5.5mm vert.
18   Measure 3mm hor 5mm vert.
19, 20, 21   Measure 3mm hor. 0.5mm vert.

Grading the 'flat' blocks

Grading one size up – *'flat' cutting* (8cm intervals)
Young men – athletic figures of regular height: sizes SML MED LGE XLGE

This size grading is used for garments of 'flat' simple construction.
For example: sportswear, weatherwear and workwear.

The 'flat' shirt and overgarment blocks
Back

1	Measure 16mm hor.
2	Measure 16mm hor. 5mm vert.
3	Measure 14mm hor. 10mm vert.
4	Measure 8mm hor. 10mm vert.
5	Measure 20mm vert.
6	Measure 8mm hor. 20mm vert.
7	Measure 4mm hor. 20mm vert.
8	Measure 4mm hor.

Front

9	Measure 12mm hor.
10	Measure 16mm hor. 5mm vert.
11	Measure 12mm hor. 10mm vert.
12	Measure 8mm hor. 10mm vert.
13	Measure 20mm vert.
14	Measure 8mm hor. 20mm vert.
15	Measure 4mm hor. 20mm vert.
16	Measure 4mm hor.

Sleeve – basic shape

1	Measure 5mm hor.
2	Measure 5mm hor.
3	Measure 5mm hor. 4mm vert.
4	Measure 14mm vert.
5	Measure 7mm hor. 1mm vert.

Sleeve – raised sleeve head

1	Measure 8mm hor.
2	Measure 2mm hor.
3	Measure 2mm hor. 4mm vert.
4	Measure 14mm vert.
5	Measure 7mm hor. 1mm vert.

The casual flat Jacket block

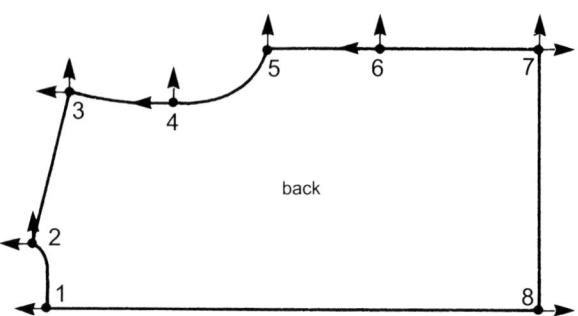

back

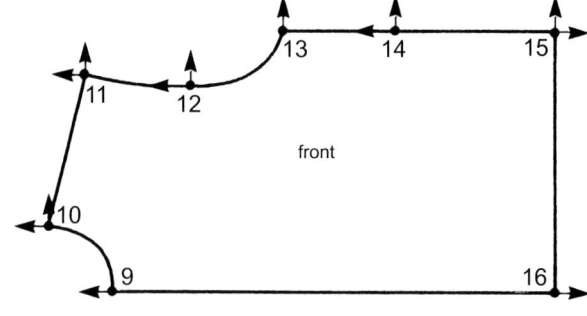

front

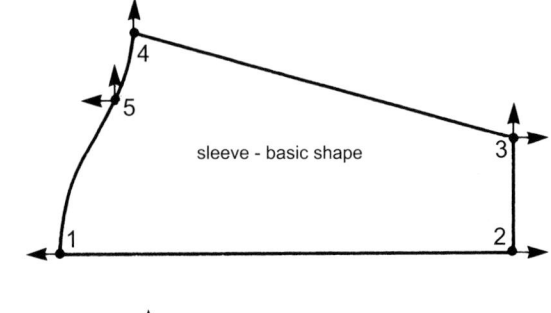

sleeve - basic shape

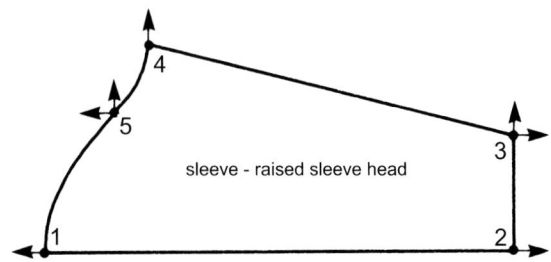

sleeve - raised sleeve head

Grading one size up – *'flat' cutting* (8cm intervals)

Young men – athletic figures of regular height: sizes SML MED LGE XLGE

The kimono block

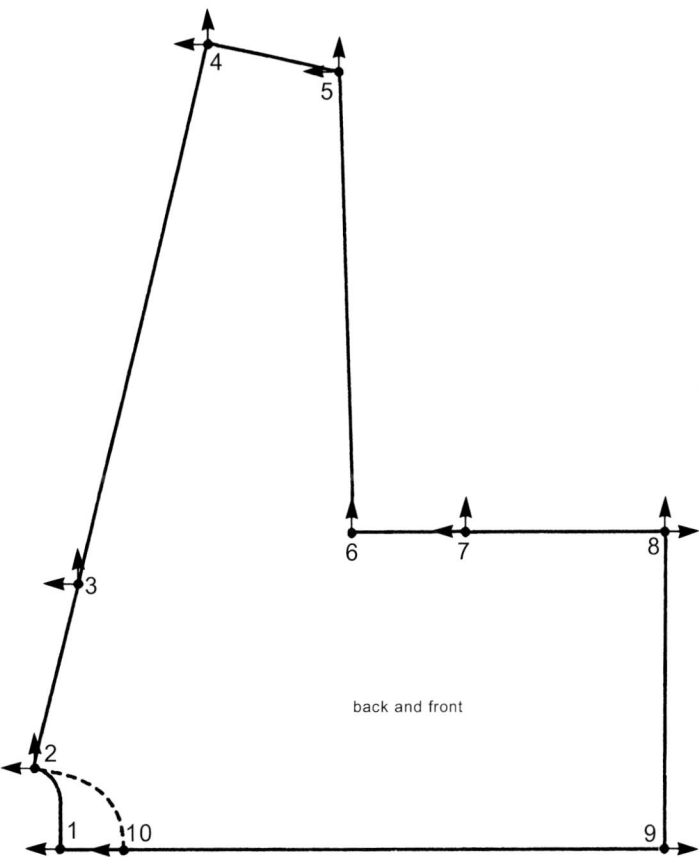

back and front

This size grading is used for garments of 'flat' simple construction.
For example: sportswear, weatherwear and workwear.

The 'flat' kimono block
Back and front
1 Measure 16mm hor.
2 Measure 16mm hor. 5mm vert.

3 Measure 14mm hor. 10mm vert.
4 Measure 12mm hor. 21mm vert.
5 Measure 9mm hor. 24mm vert.
6 Measure 20mm vert.
7 Measure 8mm hor. 20mm vert.
8 Measure 4mm hor. 20mm vert
9 Measure 4mm hor.
10 Measure 12mm hor.

Grading one size up – *'flat' cutting* (8cm intervals)
Young men – athletic figures of regular height: sizes SML MED LGE XLGE

The flat trouser block

This size grading is used for garments of 'flat' simple construction.
For example: sportswear, weatherwear and workwear.

The 'flat' trouser blocks
Front
1   Measure 6mm hor. 10mm vert.
2   Measure 1.5mm hor. 10mm vert.
3   Measure 12.5mm vert.
4, 5   Measure 10mm hor. 7.5mm vert.
6, 7   Measure 20mm hor. 5mm vert.
8   Measure 10mm vert.
9   Measure 6mm hor. 10mm vert.

Back
10   Measure 6mm hor. 10mm vert.
11   Measure 3mm hor. 10mm vert.
12   Measure 15mm vert.
13, 14   Measure 10mm hor. 7.5mm vert.
15, 16   Measure 20mm hor. 5mm vert.
17   Measure 10mm vert.
18   Measure 6mm hor. 10mm vert.

PART FOUR: SIZING AND FIT

Chapter 13 Drafting and adapting the blocks for individual figures

Drafting and adapting the blocks for individual figures

The blocks can be drafted for individual figures by substituting the personal measurements of the figure for standard ones. It is vitally important that personal measurements are taken accurately and in the correct place on the body if personal blocks are to be successful.

Blocks can also be adapted to provide a correct fit for special figure problems (pages 166–172).

Taking body measurements

The body should be relaxed.

The measurements are usually taken when the man is wearing a shirt and trousers.

Tie a string or elastic around the waist indent on the body to establish the natural waistline.

Guide for taking measurements

A–B: Back neck to waist   Measure from the bone at the nape of the neck to waistline.

A–C: Length of garment   Measure from the bone at the nape of the neck to length required.

D–E: Half across the back   Measure from centre back (15cm down from nape) to position of sleeve seam at back scye (armhole).

For a very accurate measurement, measure the full back width then halve the measurement.

F: Chest   This is the most important measurement and the most difficult. Place the tape under the arms round the body at chest level. Make sure that the tape passes over the shoulder blades or a much reduced chest measurement will be obtained. (This would be fatal to the production of the block.) It is useful for an assistant to hold the tape in position at the back.

G: Natural waist   Measure in the position of the string at the waist indent. The body should be relaxed.

H: Trouser waist position   Measure approx. 5cm below the natural waist. This is a low waist measurement, it is the position where the trousers will be worn. The body should be relaxed.

I: Seat   Measure around the fullest part of the seat, usually 21cm down from waistline.

J: Neck   Measure easily round base of neck; take the measurement on the *lower edge* of tape.

K–L: Shoulder   Measure from base of neck to the shoulder bone. This measurement is used only if the shoulders are wider than the standard figure (ref 8, page 170).

L–M: Sleeve length for one-piece sleeve   Measure from shoulder bone to just below the wrist bone.

D–N: Sleeve length for two-piece sleeve   The arm should be raised and bent. Measure from centre back (15cm below neck bone) across back, continue through O at elbow point, down sleeve to wrist bone. D–O is elbow length taken when arm is very long or short. A–L–N: Sleeve length for shirt. The arm should be raised and bent. Measure from neck bone across shoulder to L, through O to N at just below the wrist bone.

P–Q: Side seam length for trousers   Measure from the waist to the heel seam of the shoe.

R–S: Body rise   Seat the man on a stool; measure the depth from trouser waist position to top of stool.

T–U: Inside leg   Measure from high in the crutch to heel seam of shoe.

Note: The width required for the bottom of the trousers should be noted.

V: Wrist circumference   Measure wrist in the position of just above the wrist bone.

Extra measurements

W: Arm circumference   Measure the top arm which must be bent. This measurement is used when the arm is very well developed.

A–X: Scye depth   The standard measurement from the size chart should be used in most cases.

If the arm and shoulder are well developed, check that the scye depth is deep enough.

Place tape across back under arms, measure down from neck bone to centre of tape.

For tall or short men see the table on page 12.

Standard measurements

The following measurements are usually taken from the standard measurement chart using the chest measurement for reference.

Scye depth.

Cuff size of two-piece sleeve for jacket or coat.

Cuff size for shirt.

If a man is of average shape, he should conform closely to the standard measurements for his chest size. It is important to compare personal measurements against the standard measurements to ensure that the personal ones are correct.

Fitting problems

If measurements are taken carefully, the blocks will provide an excellent fit. There are, however, certain figure problems that will require adjustments to the block. It is impossible in this book to cover in depth the problems of fitting difficult figures. However, some guidance is given for correcting common figure faults on the following pages.

Personal measurements

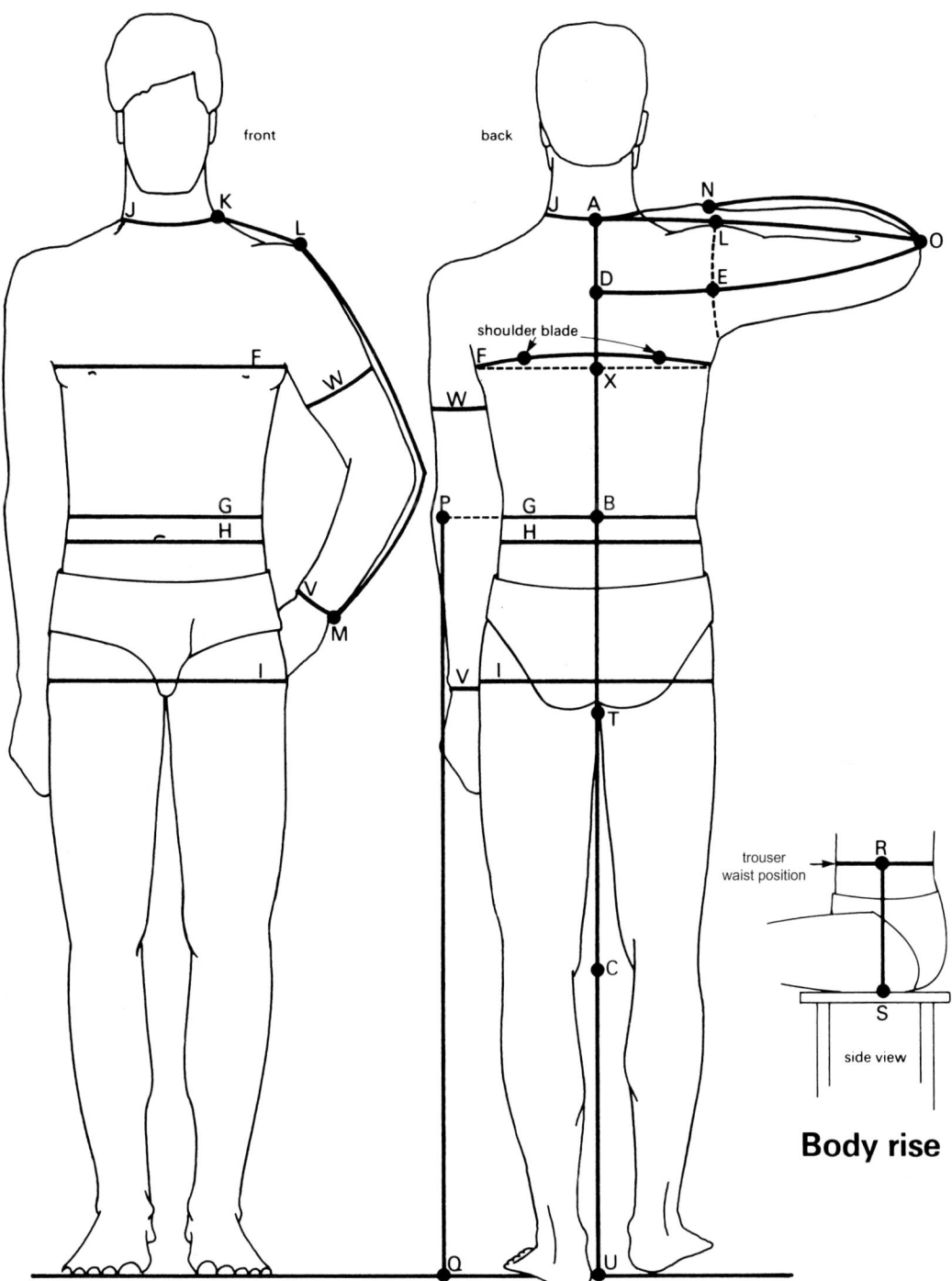

front

back

K
J
L

A
J
N
L
O

D
E

F
W

shoulder blade

F
X

W

G
H

P
G
H
B

V
M

I

V
I
T

Q
U

C

trouser
waist position

R

S

side view

Body rise

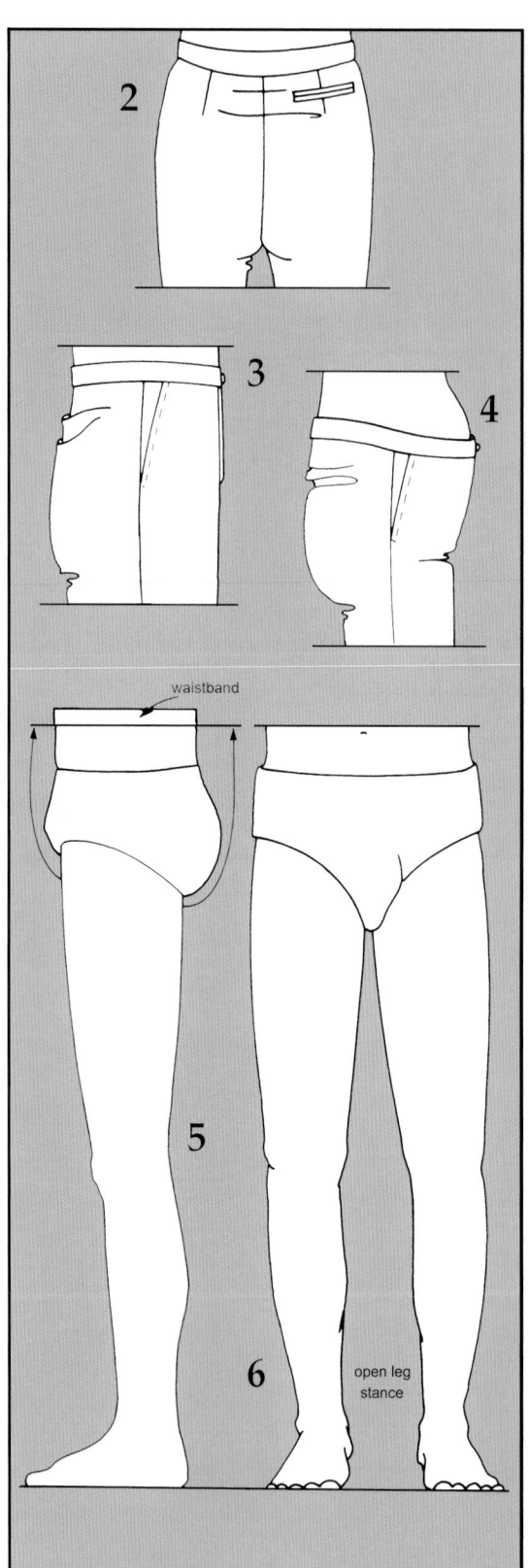

Fitting problems – trousers

1 Hip shapes
The line of side seam often has to be adjusted as the shape of the hip can vary.

2 Long back
The trouser waistband dips at back and there may be strain lines across the back.
Mark points A and B on seat line; cut along line, open a wedge at A the amount the back requires to be raised.
Trace round new outline.

3 Short back
The trousers sag at the back creating folds.
Mark point A on the waistline. A–B is the amount required to be taken out.
Join B–C on the side seam.

4 Large abdomen
The trousers dip at the front and strain lines appear across trousers.
Draw a line 15cm down from crutch line.
Mark A and B on the grain line.
Cut down the grain line from A–B; open a wedge at A and raise front waistline the amount required.
Trace round new outline.

5 Large seat
The trousers pull across seat line and create strain lines at fork. Therefore the trousers require more width across seat and more length on the fork line.
Measure through the crutch (see diagram) from base of waistband.
Calculate the amount the fork must be increased.
Mark A and B on seat line, cut along line to open a wedge at A.
Fill in seat line approx. 1.5cm.
Extend crutch line at C.
Measure the new *fitting line* to check correct amount has been inserted.
B–D is 1cm. Join C and D to knee line.

6 Leg stance
If a man stands with an open-leg stance or closed-leg stance this will affect the hang of the trousers.
Open-leg stance   Mark A and B on hem line of trousers, A–C is approx. 1.5cm. B–D is approx. 1.5cm.
Join C to crutch line, D to seat line.
The grain line is moved out 1.5cm.
Repeat adaptation on underside.
Closed-leg stance   The adaptation is the same as for open-leg stance, but in this case the leg is moved inwards e.g. A–E is 1.5cm and B–F is 1.5cm.

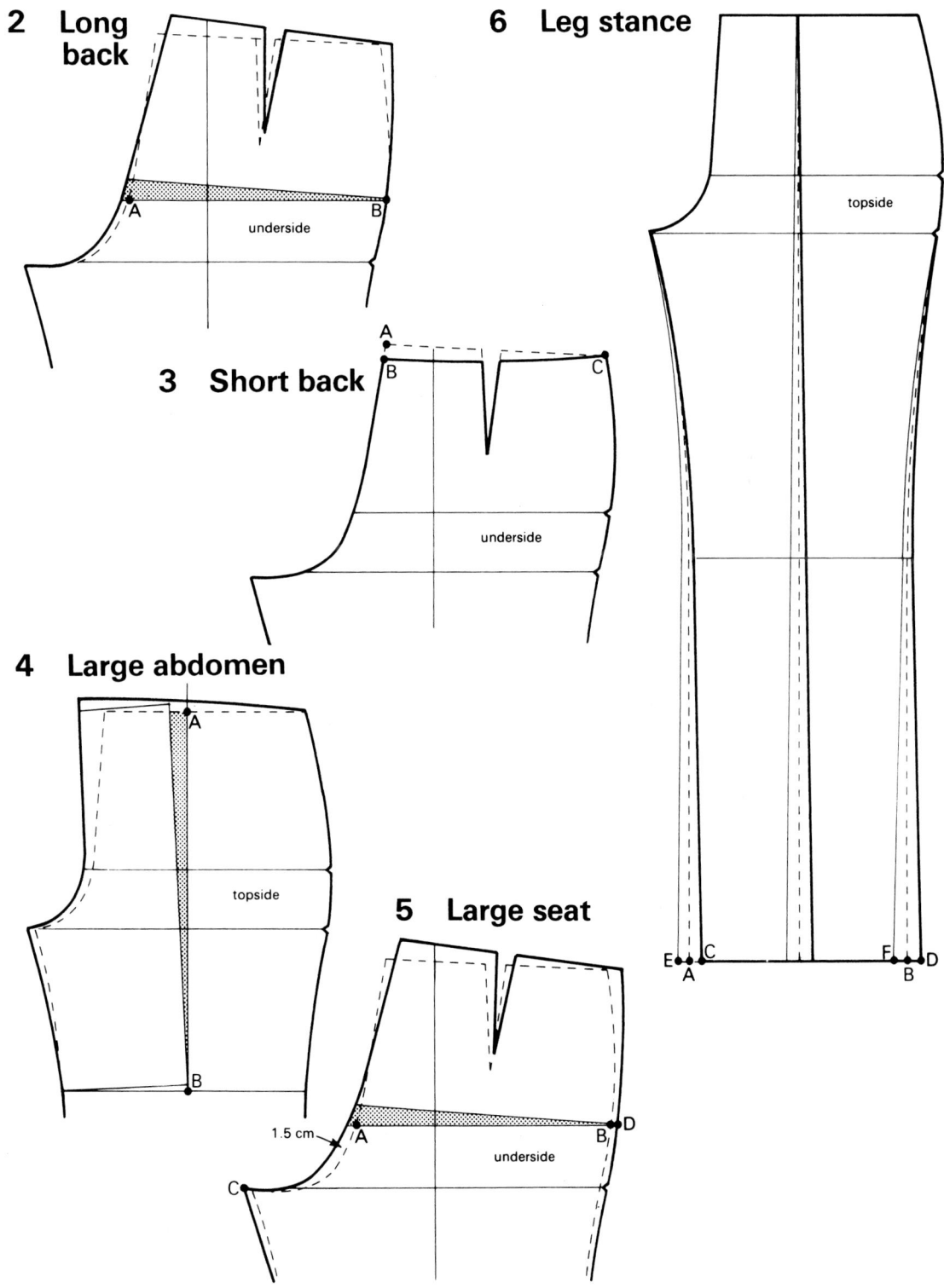

2 Long back

underside

A   B

3 Short back

A
B   C

underside

4 Large abdomen

A

topside

B

5 Large seat

1.5 cm   A   B   D

underside

C

6 Leg stance

topside

E C   F D
A   B

Fitting problems – coats, jackets and shirts

Balance-stance

If the jacket fits well but the jacket rises at front or back it is usually because the body stance is leaning forwards or backwards as shown in the diagram. The following adaptations can be made to the block.

1 Forward stance

Draw a line A–B at back pitch point; cut across this line, open a wedge at A. (Make sure neck point stays on vertical back line.)
Trace round new outline as shown.

2 Backward stance

Draw a line C–D at back pitch point; cut across this line, open a wedge at D. (Make sure neck point stays on vertical back line.)
Trace round new outline as shown.

Note   If the body is very stooped and the back requires to be raised more than 1.5cm, cut across the *whole block* on the waistline; raise the already adapted block a further amount at back waistline.
Trace round new outline as shown.

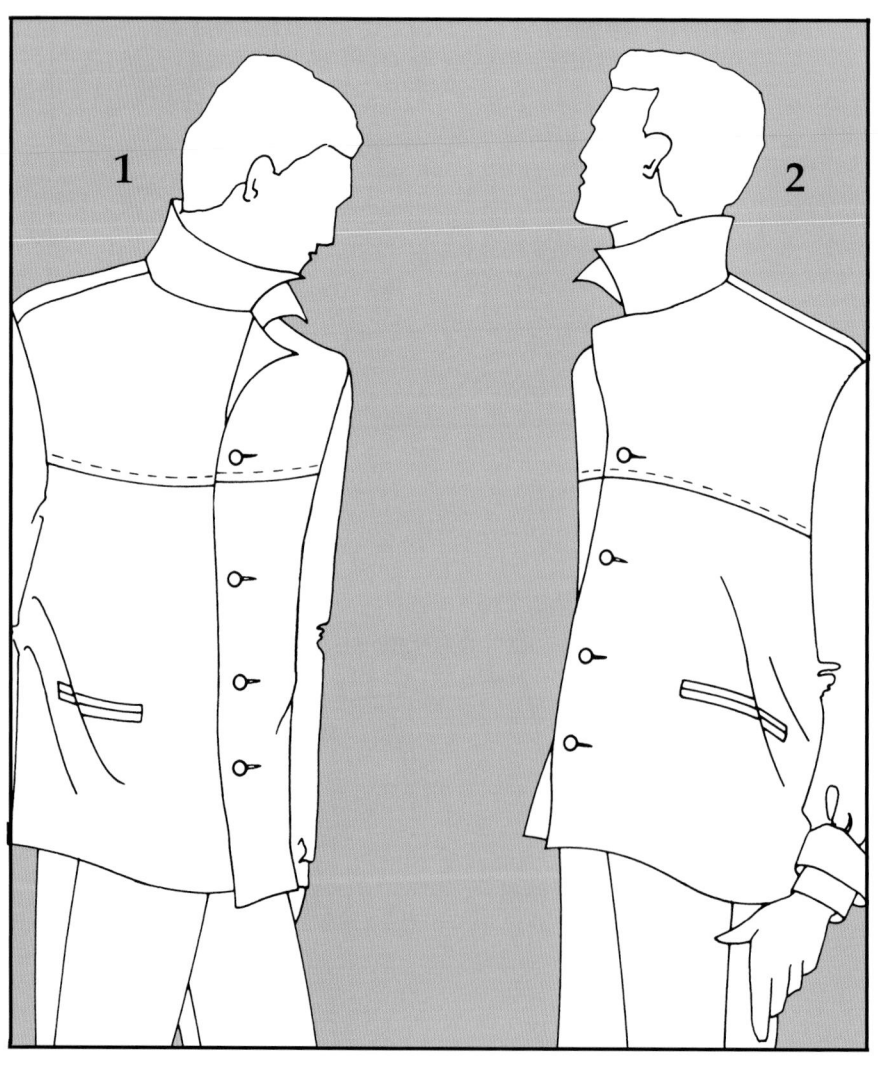

1 Forward stance

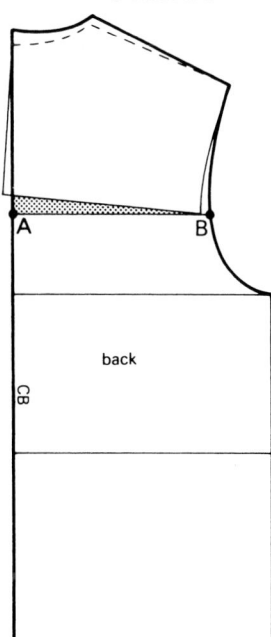

2 Backward stance

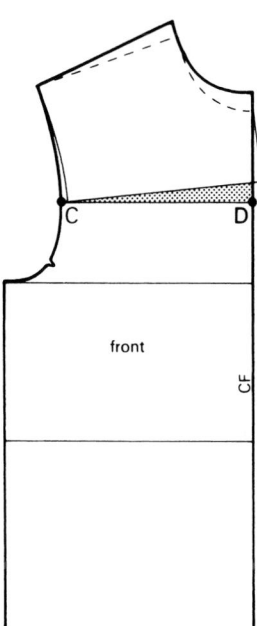

Extra stoop

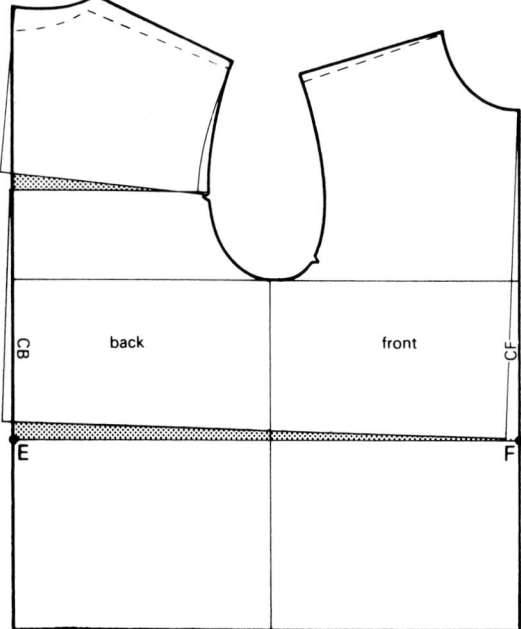

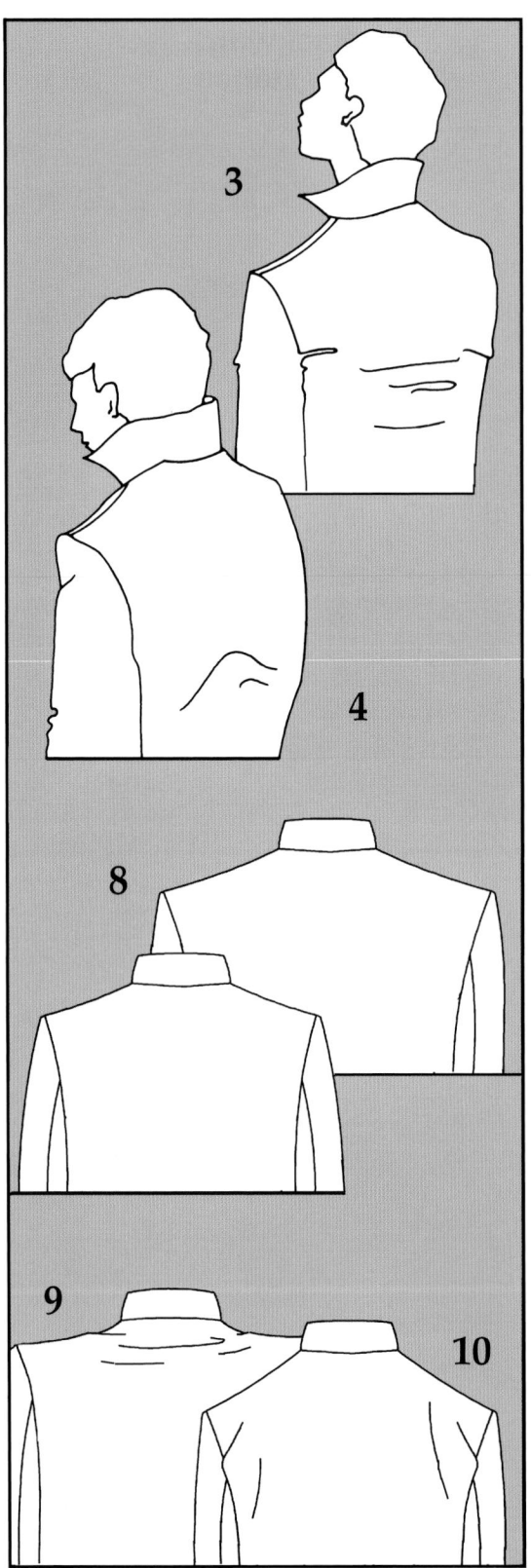

Note   The sleeve head will have to be re-drafted to fit the length between B and C on adaptations 3, 4, 5, 6.

3   Short back
Extra fullness appears across the centre back.
Draw a line A–B at back pitch point, mark C at shoulder.
Cut across line, overlap the required amount.

4   Long back
Jacket rises up because of an obvious rounded back.
Draw a line A–B at back pitch point, cut across line and open the required amount.

5 and 6   Long chest: short chest
The same adaptations described above can be made 6cm above front pitch point.

7   Short chest (at centre front only)
Cut across the line A–B, overlap top section at A (make sure that the neck point touches centre front vertical line).
Trace round new outline.

8   Wide or narrow shoulders
If the shoulder measurement differs from the standard measurement for chest size, work out the difference.
Mark A and B at shoulder points; draw horizontal lines through points A and B.
Wide shoulders   A–C and B–D = shoulder difference; join C and D to neck points and armhole.
Narrow shoulders   A–E and B–F = shoulder difference; join E and F to neck points and armhole.

9   Square shoulders
Horizontal strain lines appear below back neck.
Cut across back shoulder from A–B.
Open a wedge at B the required amount.
Raise armhole at C so that armhole measurement remains the same.
Repeat this operation on front shoulder.
Note: Many figures with square shoulders have well developed arms; in this case *do not raise armhole* but re-draft sleeve head to fit larger armhole.

10   Sloping shoulders
Diagonal lines drape at armhole.
Cut across back shoulder from D–E, overlap sections the required amount.
Lower armhole at F so that armhole measurement remains the same.
Repeat this operation on front shoulder.

3 Short back

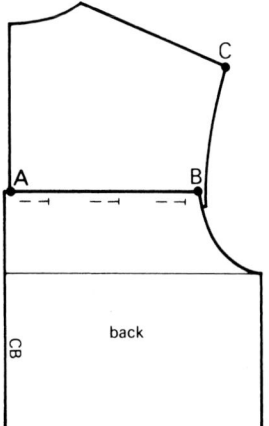

4 Long back

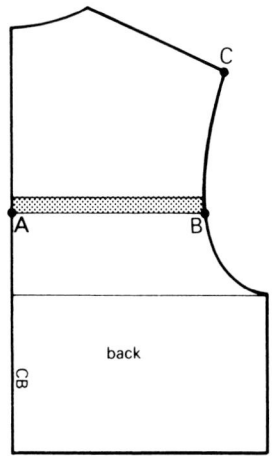

5 Long chest

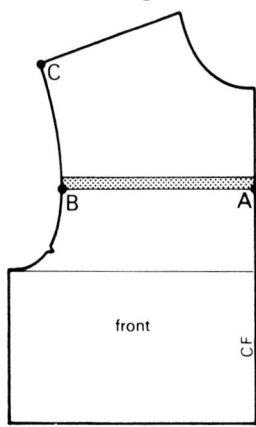

6 Short chest   ## 7 Short chest (centre front)

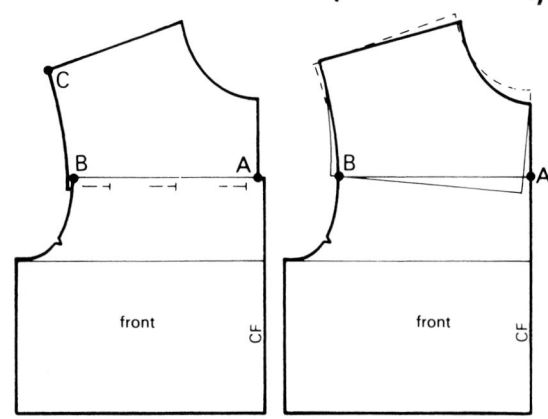

8 Wide or narrow shoulders

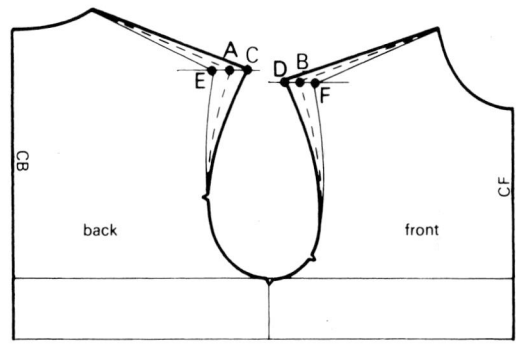

9 Square shoulders   ## 10 Sloping shoulders

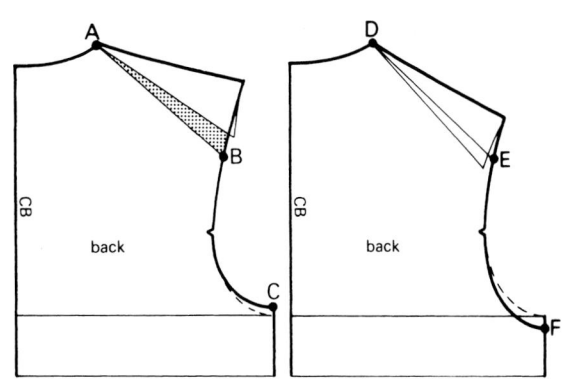

11 Sleeve pitch

The sleeve drags to the left or to the right.
Remove the sleeve from the garment and pin at the
shoulder point so that the sleeve hangs correctly.
Re-mark the balance points on the sleeve; this means
that the underarm seams of the sleeve and the body
section will move out of line.

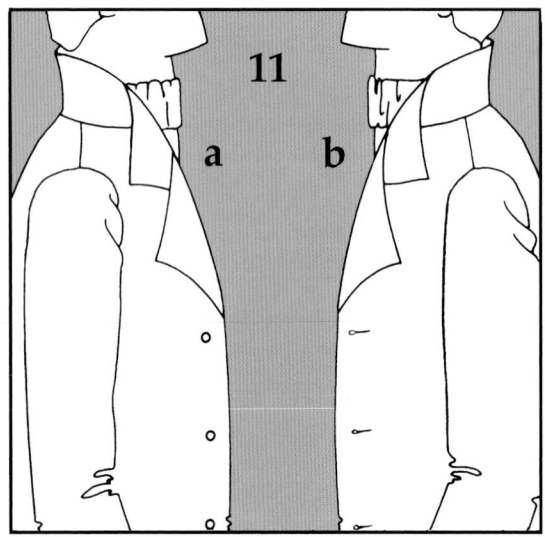

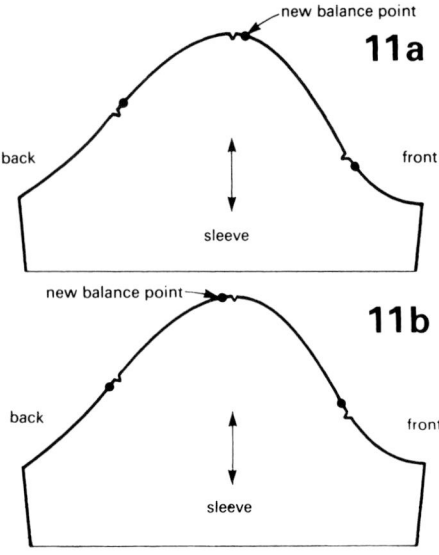

PART FIVE: COMPUTER AIDED DESIGN (CAD)

Chapter 14 Computer generated design and pattern making

Connectivity and marketing

Connectivity

The way computer aided design (CAD) is used is expanding as globalisation has made connectivity essential for clothing producers and retailers. Manufacturing locations are constantly changing and the industry seeks flexibility and productivity during the product's lifecycle from its conception to distribution. The Internet provides connections across the world and they are now a vital part of most companies' operations. It connects designers, buyers and manufacturers with text and images. Whilst large investments in systems will be made by the large suppliers, elements of CAD and production management software also benefit smaller companies. Most companies use the Windows platform, which enables the integration of different types of product management and CAD software programs.

Raster programs These use screen pixels to display and manipulate images. Illustrations or photographs can be scanned into the system and then manipulated.

Vector programs These manipulate data in the form of mathematical co-ordinates. They are used for the construction of accurate technical drawings, pattern cutting, grading and marker-making. Vector lines can be converted into raster format and many software programs can integrate the two forms.

Product Data Management (PDM) software and Product Lifecycle Management (PLM) software are the major means of connection; these programs are able to integrate visual and text information (from either format) and connect with other production and financial systems. PLM programs provide the link throughout the product's lifecycle.

Marketing

PDM systems connect many areas of the two major means of graphic imagery and integrate them with other production and financial functions. PDM systems are the engines which manage and organise information from marketers and retailers.

Connectivity in areas of design is being driven by the marketing sectors of companies. Direct links between the manufacturer and retailer are crucial in responding to changes in fashion coming back directly from the 'high street'.

Design for the major retail outlets requires that the garment designs create a total concept that relates to the retailer's image. 3D software can create virtual stores that allow merchandisers to visualize product lines in a 3D retail environment early in the collection development process. This allows them to make final changes to garment styles and colourways, and to assess quantities.

There is an increasing demand for Internet shopping; on-line catalogues can provide both retailers and customers with choice. As well as available merchandise, virtual 'draped' garments can be shown with alternative fabrics and colourways. Some catalogue retailers are showing basic garments on virtual models that customers can re-shape to their own size.

Visual merchandising in *Mockshop*, which creates an interactive virtual store with display stands and fittings. *Photograph by permission of Visualretailing ©*

A draped 'fabric simulated suit' which can be seen in alternative fabrics and colours. *Image by permission of Lectra ©*

The use of a drape program to produce a virtual image of a patterned shirt. *Personal collection.*

Design creation and illustration

Graphic software is now an integral part of design departments. The improvement in speed, memory and capacity now offers high quality imagery that is used at all stages of the design process. The Internet provides a link for many stages of design selection. Software programs that work at a very high resolution are now available. They produce high quality line output and photographic imagery. the technology allows designers to translate creative ideas at the inception stage and communicate them to buyers.

Design for menswear has changed extensively over the last two decades. Seasonal fashions for younger men are now as important as many women's wear ranges. The design development of a men's range phase now follows a similar pattern. At the start of the season, story boards are presented to buyers, they display design concepts and 'stories' for the coming season. The imagery is gathered from all kinds of sources and will often include textile and colour forecasts. Photographs, graphic images and fabrics can be scanned into the systems and collaged; new drawings and text can be added. Ideas can then be translated into visuals of garments and textile ranges at a pre-sampling stage. This is a great saving of time and costs.

The mimicking of textures, weaves, knitting, lace, logos and embroideries can now be produced on high quality paper print-outs or printed directly onto fabric to be made up into garment samples.

Line images of garments can be drawn on the digitising pad or scanned into the system. The drawing can then be modified quickly if style or colour changes are required. Prepared textile images (scanned, cleaned, scaled and placed into repeat) can be flat propagated (wallpapered) into the drawing (see male figure 1 in the illustration opposite). Different colourways can then be printed. Simulated drape programs can be used on sketches (see male figure 3 in the illustration opposite). The use of a simulated drape program on photographs gives a realistic but virtual images of garments (see page 183). Some textile programs can match colours both on the screen and on the printed output, making the technology viable for direct early choices of fabrics. All the images can be modified quickly and re-submitted.

The technology also provides companies, manufacturing basic garments such as suits, shirts or sportswear, with libraries of styles with their associated information that can be referred to and that can be modified in following seasons.

A design system developed to create textile and fashion images. *Photograph by permission of Lectra ©*

A design visual created in *Kaledo* illustrating a fashion range. *Illustration by permission of Lectra* ©

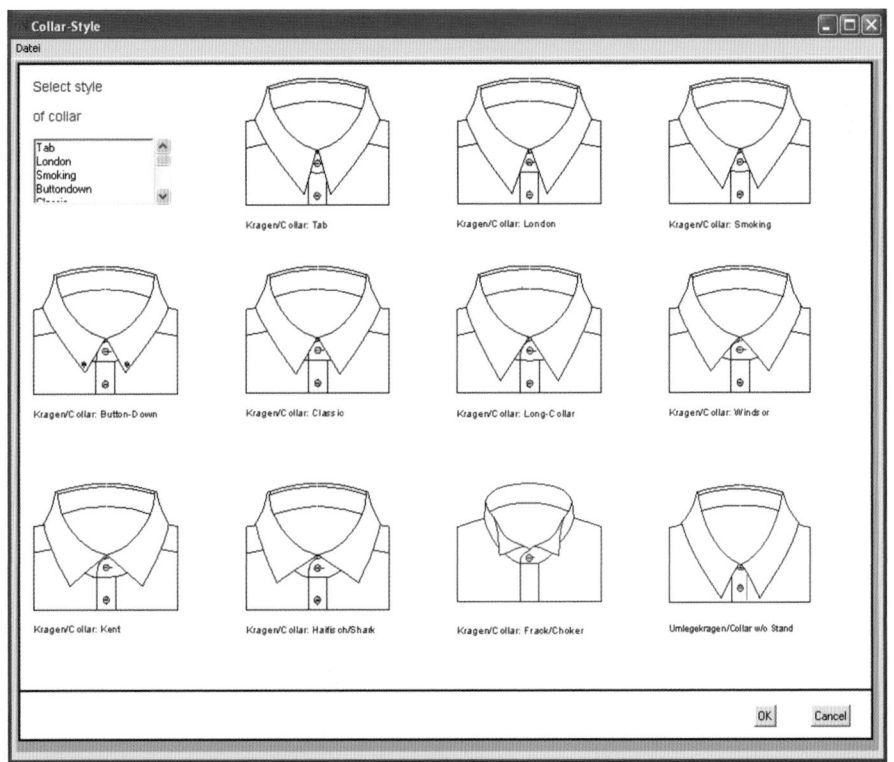

A library of men's basic collar styles. *Illustration by permission of assyst bullmer Ltd* ©

Product Data Management (PDM)

Designers, when they begin to work in a large design department, are often astonished at the amount of information and documentation that is attached to each style. This used to be an arduous manual task as styles were modified through sampling and sizing stages. Product Data Management (PDM) systems manage and organise the style information and images from design rooms. They also store information on materials and capacity and access historical data of previous production. This allows the sales departments to give accurate costings and delivery dates. A PDM system is a vital tool once a style is accepted and moves into production.

Collection planning modules are now an essential part of the design process. Style and fabric libraries can be set up, and lists of trimming suppliers. The facility to search for particular information or product data is crucial in keeping to planning schedules. As a collection becomes finalised, a folder will be set up for each style; this usually includes a cover sheet with a technical drawing of the style, the size range, fabric colourways, and trimmings. Other forms display sizes and measurement tables, fitting reports, pattern information and costing markers. PDM systems support the designer during the initial stages of design and also through the product development cycle. For example, pattern or trimming changes by the technical staff are automatically sent back to the designer and forwarded to costing and marketing.

PDM systems connect the many departments of a company, integrating both graphic and text style data with other production and financial functions. They are often integrated into Product Lifecycle Management (PLM) systems (see page 192). Organised information from the design rooms is vital for sourcing materials and manufacturing capacity, and meeting delivery dates.

Costing

Accurate costing is a major consideration for designers. Costing data includes the trimmings used and the fabric amount. A cost lay plan can be made in a marker-making program; pattern modifications can be made to give better fabric utilisation. Although grading usually takes place when orders have been placed, a reliable costing can usually be based on a sample size. For general sewing data timings, historical data of previous styles can be used. If garments are to be made up by other manufacturers, competing prices and deliveries can be accessed.

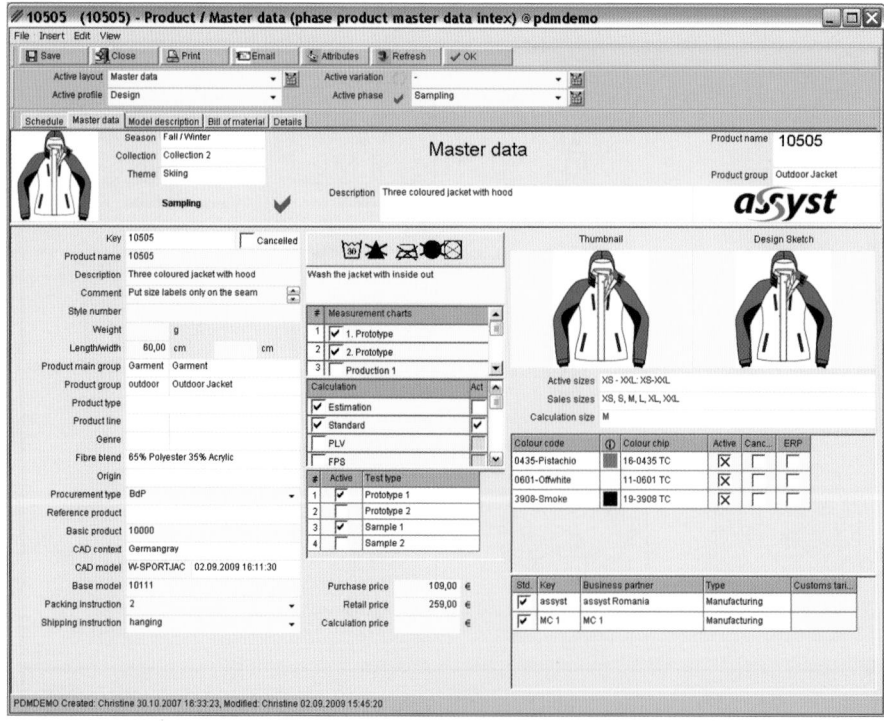

PDM: a master data form listing all the basic information for the style. *Illustration by permission of assyst bullmer Ltd* ©

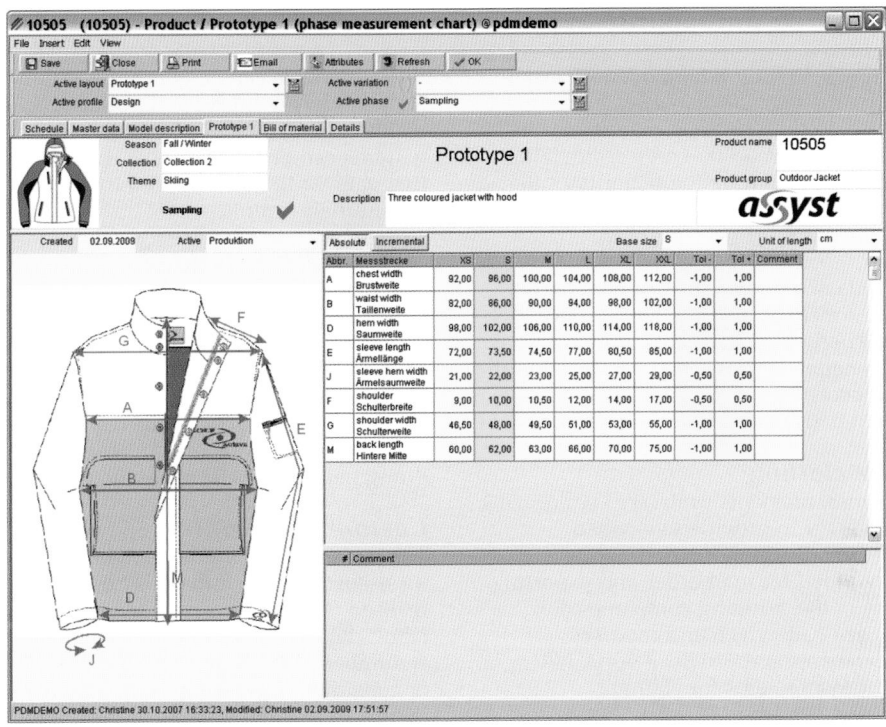

PDM: a prototype sheet listing garment measurements. *Illustration by permission of assyst bullmer Ltd* ©

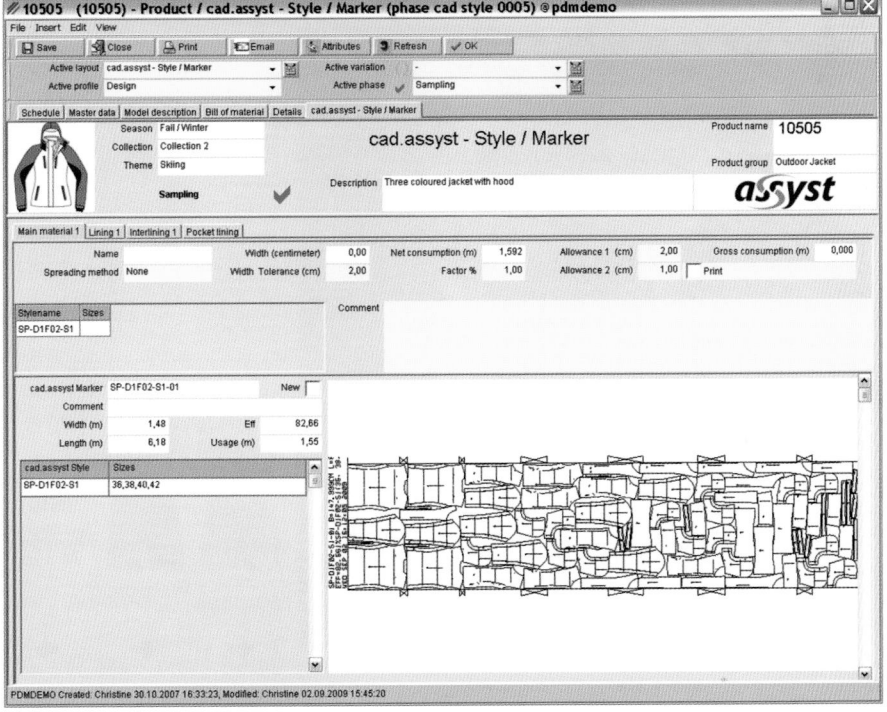

PDM: a form displaying the costing marker for the jacket. *Illustration by permission of assyst bullmer Ltd* ©

3D body scanning and sizing

3D body scanning is rapidly taking over the task of taking body measurements for large scale sizing surveys. It is also used by clothing manufacturers in particular sectors of the market. Large scale sizing surveys are essential for fitting the majority of the population.

The process
The subject stands in a body scanner booth and is measured three dimensionally in a few seconds. More than a 100 body measurements are automatically generated. These can be reduced with reference to the company's product. Calculations take into account body proportions and posture data.

Standard size clothing
Standard body measurements from large scale sizing surveys are necessary to provide size-coded garments for the retail sector. International data on sizing is now required for mail order and exporting companies. One of the scanning companies now offers clothing size data which encompasses international databases and provides up to 140 different body measurements for clothing manufacturers and retailers.

Virtual models can be generated from the 3D scans in the form of an avatar or a 3D virtual mannequin of a company's house model. 2D patterns can be realised as garments on the models (see page 183). This allows the designer to approve and fit their samples.

Size selective clothing
Companies or organisations such as the army, which holds large warehouse stocks to clothe their personnel, can use 3D body scanning selected data to employ a just-in-time outfitting process from their warehouse stocks.

A large retailer has installed a 3D body scanner in a store to scan customers who wish to select the perfect fitting pair of jeans from the huge range available.

Customised clothing
The potential of 3D body scanning to provide mass-customised clothing is now beginning to be realised. The personal measurements, plus style and fabric choice can be fed directly to the manufacturer. A number of software providers use this data to adapt or construct individually sized patterns and single-ply lay plans for cutting (see pages 187 and 191).

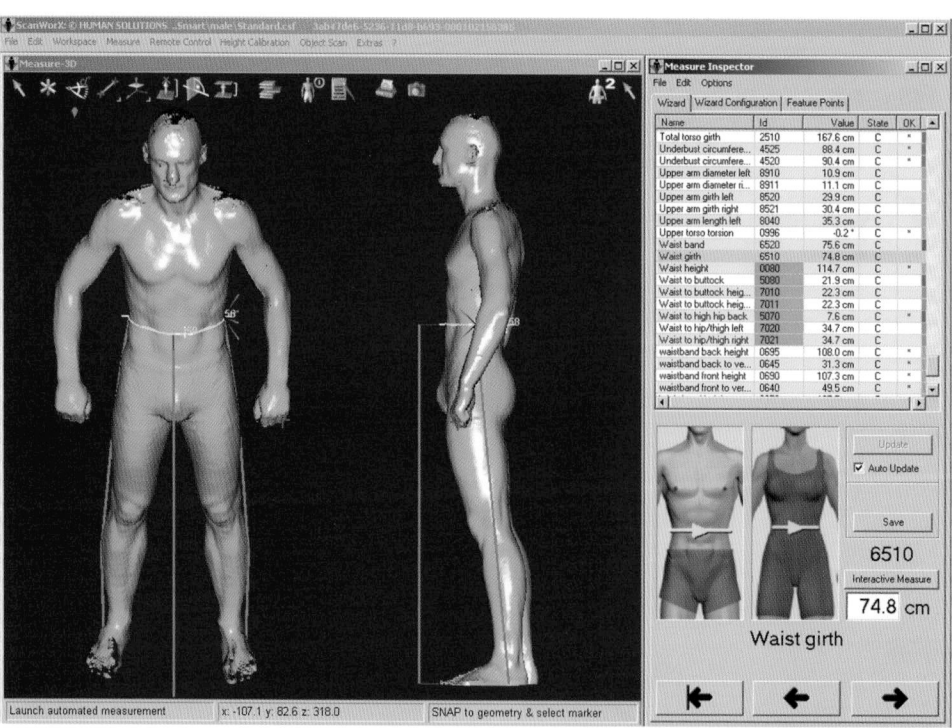

Anthroscan software automatically recording the exact dimensions and posture of a person. *Image by permission of Human Solutions GmbH* ©

Pattern design and modification

Many more companies with CADCAM technology are now pattern cutting on their systems. It could be argued that they are only modifying existing patterns; however, a great deal of basic clothing in menswear has only minor style changes each season. CAD technology is ideal for this purpose. The original pattern now has a great deal of existing data stored with it, particularly the grade rules. As in manual pattern cutting, blocks or basic patterns can be used as templates from which complex adaptations can be performed in similar interactive ways to manual cutting. Blocks can be constructed directly in the system. Alternatively, existing hard copy blocks, patterns to be adapted, or patterns in development, can be digitised into the program (see photograph below).

The basic operations that take place in 'flat' pattern cutting are not many; some examples are: drawing straight lines, curves, free sketching; deleting lines or sections, extending lines; changing lines freely or to specific lengths; measuring lines or sections; changing whole pattern shapes or sections; cutting patterns into sections; reproducing whole pattern shapes or sections; moving whole patterns or sections freely around; rotating, mirroring and joining sections or pieces; swinging pattern sections (dart movement); inserting flare into patterns; completing patterns – adding seam allowances, grain lines, notches, drill holes, text.

It is important to understand that it is how one uses these operations that makes the construction of every pattern a different procedure. A pattern cutter needs imagination, tacit knowledge, and experience of fabric characteristics. On some systems the garment designs are treated as independent styles which can be brought to the screen as a group and worked on as if on a worktable. Icons at the side or top of the screen offer simple-to-learn directions for using the pattern cutting options.

CAD can do 90% of basic 'flat' pattern cutting operations quicker than by manual methods. The speed of the pattern cutting comes from its ability to add seam allowances and associate pieces for automatic changes. Macro functions can be set that will undertake a series of operations automatically and will also generate linings and interfacings. Patterns that have been sent for grading and marker making, can still be automatically changed in these stages. As production is mainly based overseas, CAD technology is now essential for transmitting design and development changes to the sites of production.

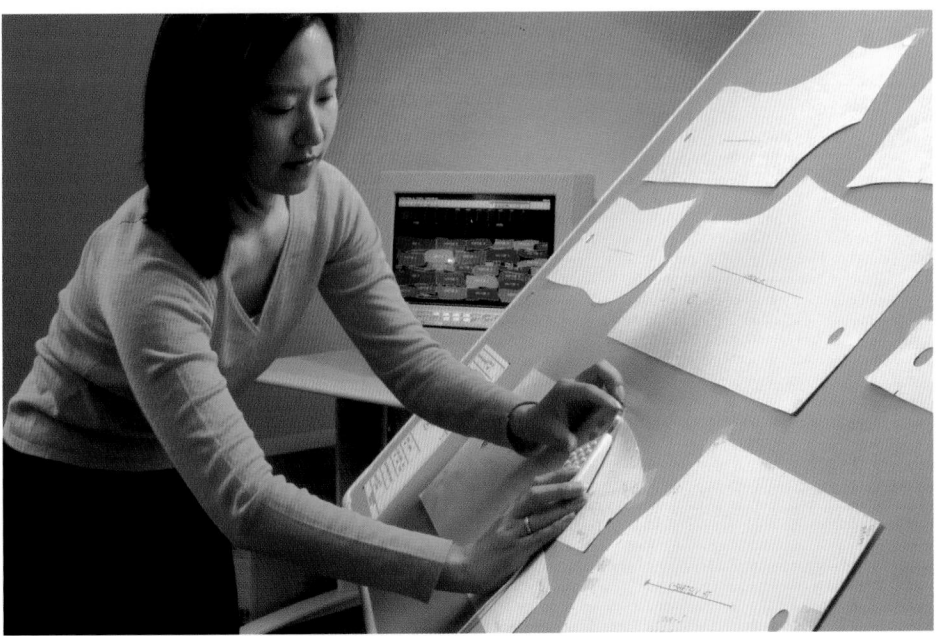

Digitising a pattern. The pieces are placed on a board, an electronic cursor records the curve and line points of the pattern. *Photograph by permission of Gerber Technology* ©

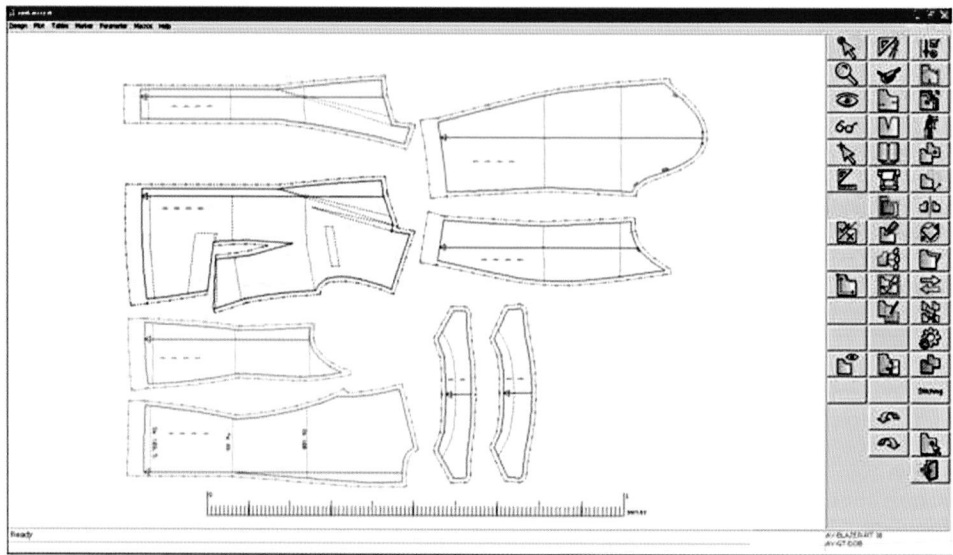

The pattern pieces for a suit displayed on screen. *Illustration by permission of assyst bullmer Ltd* ©

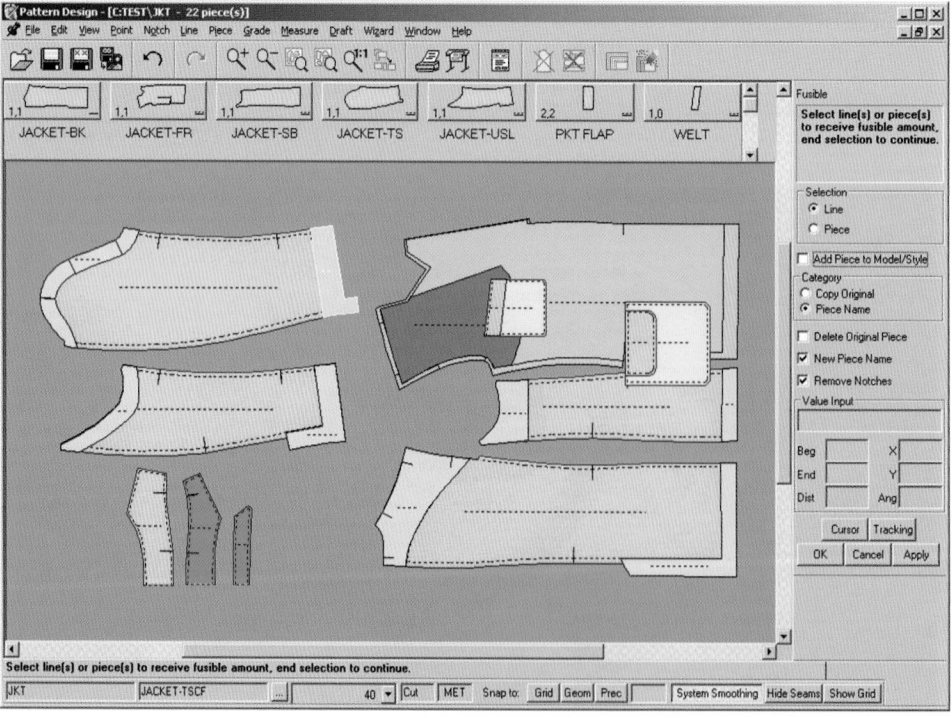

Pattern development showing fabric and trimming pattern pieces. *Illustration by permission of Gerber Technology* ©

Garment sampling – 3D software programs

At least four companies are offering CAD software programs that simulate a 3D garment sample using 2D patterns. The patterns can be 'virtually stitched' to create a sample on a virtual model or the company's dress form. This enables the designer to assess the style and fit of the garment at an early stage in the pattern cutting process.

The programs take into account fabric characteristics to create realistic draping effects. Patterned fabrics or placement prints can be scanned into the software, placed within the pattern pieces, then draped on the model. The images can then be sent to buyers for their responses before sampling.

Pattern pieces 'virtually stitched' together on a virtual model.
Illustration by permission of Browzwear International Ltd ©

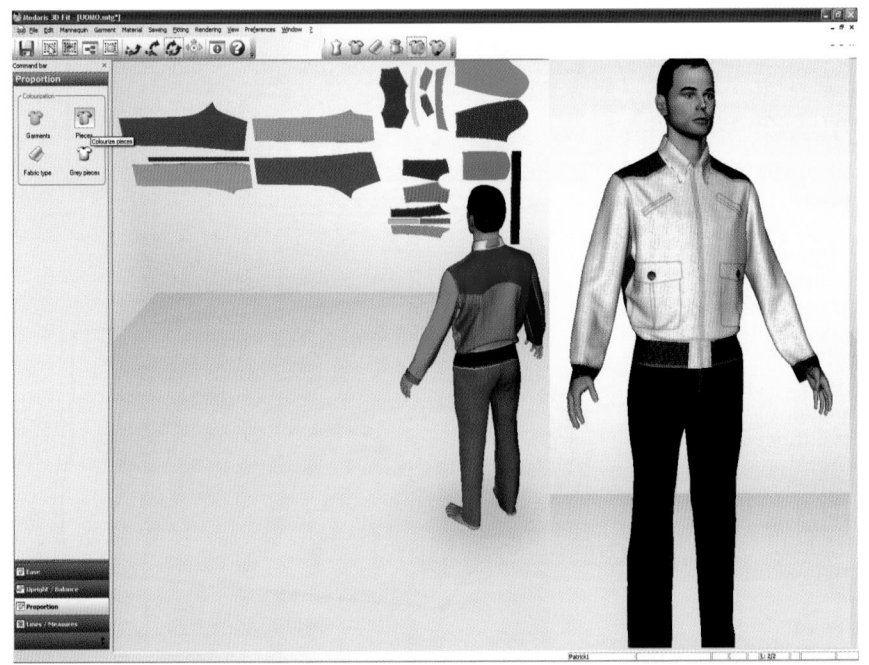

The 3D prototyping of garment pattern pieces on a virtual model.
Illustration by permission of Lectra ©

Pattern grading – 1

Grading

Pattern grading is used to reproduce a pattern in other sizes. This is usually done once a design sample is accepted and a customer places an order in a range of sizes. CADCAM grading software is faster than manual grading and is also more consistent and accurate. However, the results still rely on the skill of the grading technician and the input of the data. Records are kept of the grade rule numbers and positions for each style by means of simple diagrams as shown. Any pattern adapted from the block can also be graded by the same method. However, few patterns are as simple as the block shape. This means that new grade rules have to be calculated by the grader and these rules added to the grade rule library (see the additional grade rules required for the shirt pattern on page 186).

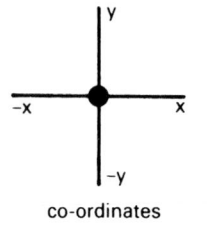

co-ordinates

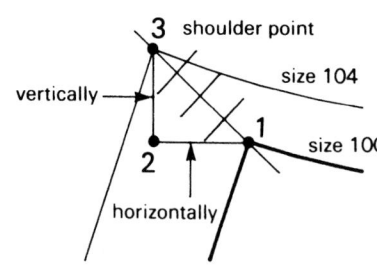

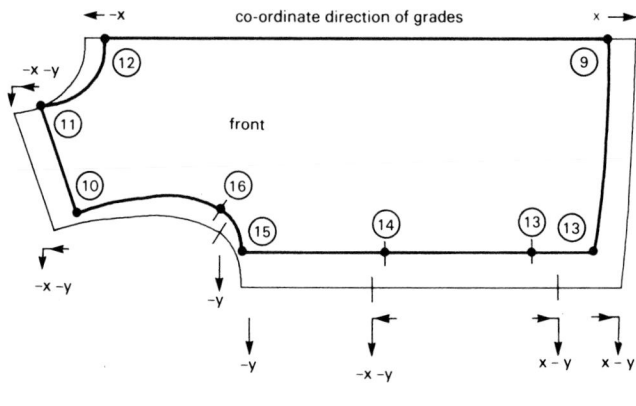

Grade rules

The grading of patterns by most computer systems is based on identifying where specific points on the pattern have to be extended or reduced to create a new size. These points are moved by means of X and Y co-ordinates which tell the computer the direction of movement. Measurements are also given to identify the position of the new point. Grade rules are usually calculated to 1/10th of a millimetre. The amount of movement in the X direction is written first, followed by the Y direction. For example, the movement of the shoulder point between sizes in 6mm horizontally and 5mm vertically.

The GRADE RULE could be written as $\frac{1}{10}$th mm; (1) −60 50 or (2) −0.60 0.50cm.

A GRADE RULE is this instruction across a range of sizes.

Inconsistent grades between sizes can be entered in the library (see grade rule 8).

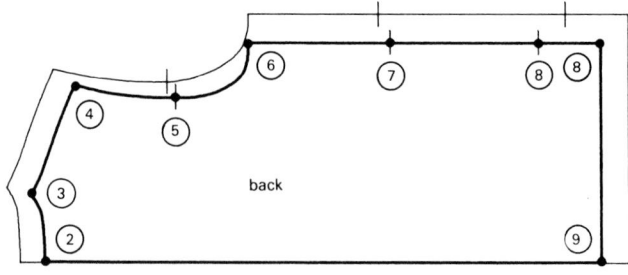

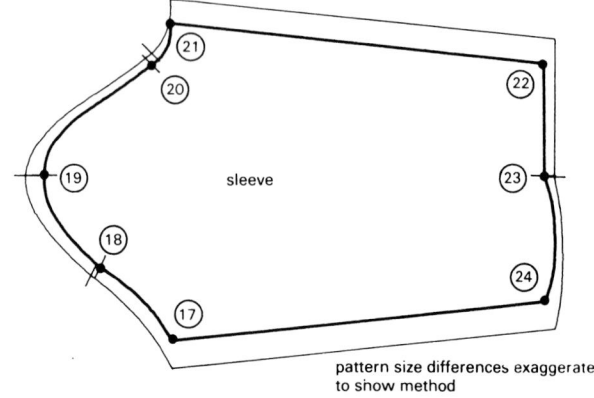

pattern size differences exaggerated to show method

Pattern grading – 2

Grade rule libraries

The company uses its graded 'nests' of blocks that have been produced manually. Each graded point on the nest is measured as shown (these points are beginnings and ends of lines and specific points, i.e. special control points or notches).

The measurements are checked with the grading increments on the size charts. It is possible to calculate many points directly from size charts or garment specifications.

The X Y measurement between each size is the grade rule. The same grade rule can be used at any point which requires the same grade.

Grade rule 1 is often written as a 0 because grade rule 1 can be used where no grade is required. The grade rule library is compiled of numbered grade rules used at the grade points.

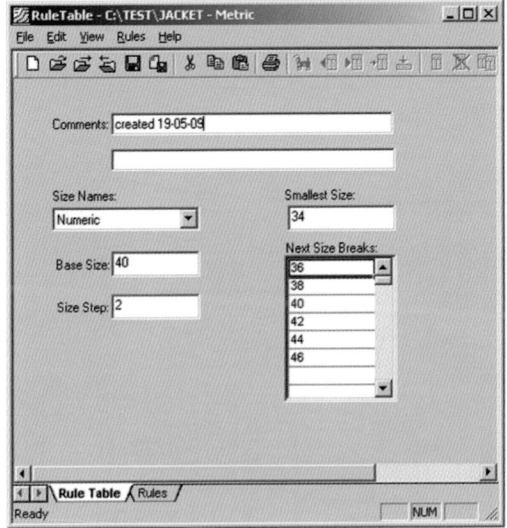
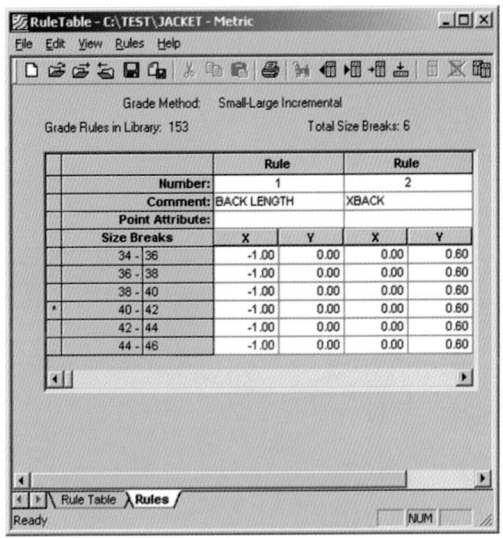

Screen displays showing the input of sizes and grade rules. *Illustration by permission of Gerber Technology ©*

Adding grade points when digitising

Patterns that have been constructed manually can still be input into the computer by tracing round the contour of the pattern on a digitiser (see page 181) and then adding the grade rules. However, the grade points and the grade rule numbers can be input as the pattern is digitised.

The pattern is placed on the digitiser and the pattern profile is entered into the computer by use of a cursor. The centre of the cross hairs of the cursor is placed on the points to be recorded. These points are grade points and other points which define the curves or corners. When a cursor button is pressed, signals are sent to the computer which are translated into a numerical record of the shape and information for the piece. Grade points can be identified with a screen cursor and the grade rule number can be entered.

Working without grade rule libraries

Some systems do not use grade rule libraries but attach the rules to individual pattern pieces and copy rules from one pattern piece to another. If a pattern is adapted from a block, or a previous pattern has been modified, then new points will be generated and extra grade rules will be required. If rules have been copied from another pattern of a previous garment, again, extra rules for the new style may be required.

Pattern grading – 3

The pattern pieces that have been stored or constructed within the software program can be brought to the screen in sequence; each grade point is then identified with a screen cursor and the grade rule can be entered. Note the extra grade rules that are required when the pattern is adapted from a block. These extra rules have to be added to the library.

When all the grade points have been added to the patterns, an instruction to grade the piece is given. This order will automatically generate a nest of grades over the range of sizes, using the grade rules attached to the piece, or from rules stored in the grade rule library. The patterns can be drawn out on a plotter for checking, or sent directly through the system for lay planning and cutting.

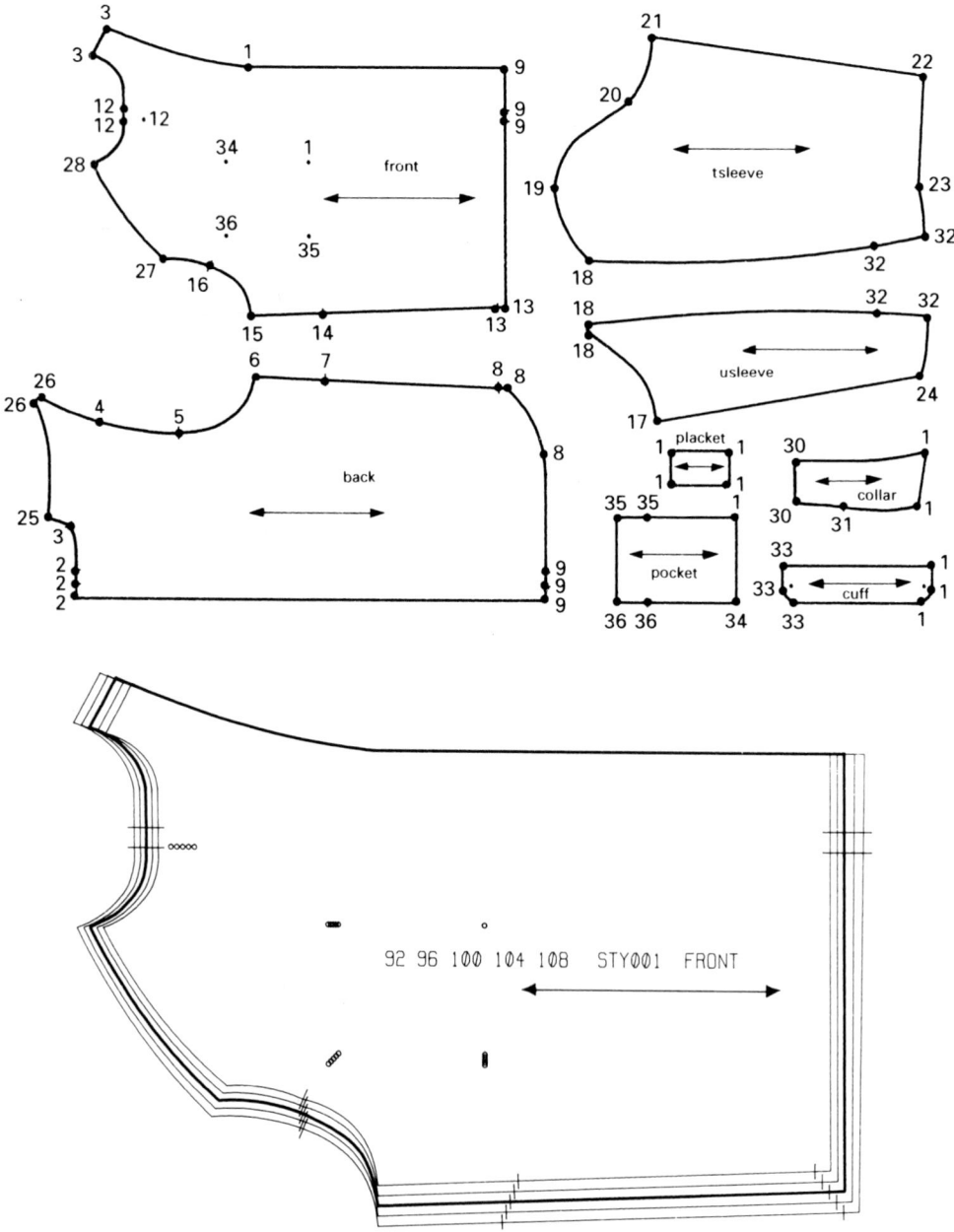

Pattern grading – 4

Other methods of grading

A manually graded nest of patterns can be digitised (see the photograph, page 181), and stored in the system without the creation of a grade rule library. Each grading point of every size is digitised into the system. The system will then reproduce the nest and automatically record grade rules for the pattern pieces.

Some small clothing companies do not have pattern cutting or grading expertise, so some software companies offer a range of patterns of basic garments (with alternative sleeves and collars) already graded. Instead of copying individual grade points from other patterns, the pattern can be laid over a similar graded shape in the system to copy all the grades. This method is only useful to companies manufacturing a very narrow restricted product range.

Grading techniques

Sophisticated grading techniques are now included in many programs. Perpendicular grading calculates the grades with reference to the angle of another line; tangental grading techniques control points along a line or the length of the line itself. If a pattern is split, the system will grade the new seam lines proportionally. If a line is altered on a pattern, it can be modified automatically through all the grades. 'Walking' graded pieces allow seams to be checked for fit along the making up lines.

A number of companies are developing systems based on parametrics. Any sizes are based on the measurements made to construct the pattern. Any new sizes are generated, not through point movements, but through measurement changes. This also means patterns can be constructed directly from measurement charts.

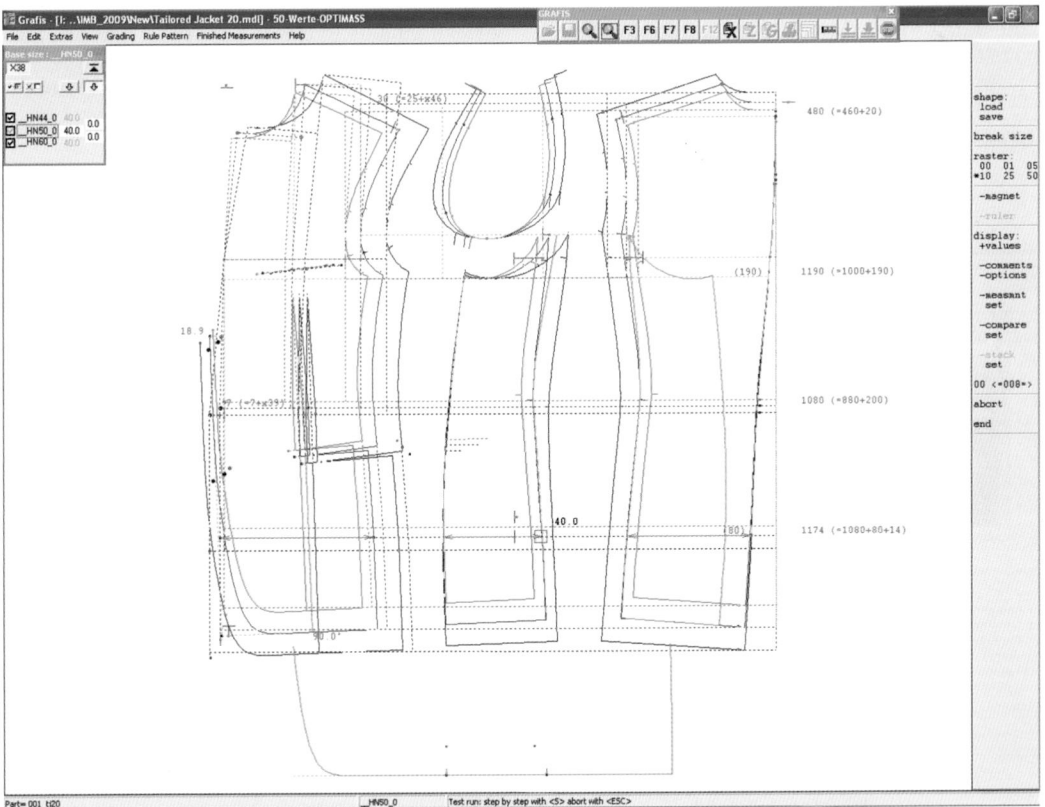

Alternative grading method, graded pieces constructed by direct measurement input. *Illustration by permission of GRAPHIS-software ©*

Made-to-measure

Up to the middle of the last century, most men had their suits made-to-measure. Bespoke tailoring declined as the retail outlets sold mass-produced suits and factory 'made-to-measure' suits at lower prices. These were based on size intervals, and catered for other figures by altering basic patterns. Today, an increasing number of ready-to-wear companies are showing an interest in mass-customisation. They argue that a fast made-to-measure service, providing a better fit, and also offering a wide choice of fabric, style, and trimmings, would appeal to many customers.

The process

The customer selects a style on screen in the store or via the Internet. They can select modifications to it, by changing the pockets, the lapels, the fabric and the trimmings. The customer's measurements are taken manually, or by one of a number of 3D scanning systems, a process that now takes less than ten seconds. This provides a 3D model of his body volume, from which body measurements and posture can be calculated. CADCAM companies access the data provided by 3D scanning companies, but also use measurement data from other sources.

The nearest appropriate standard size pattern of the style is selected from the CAD pattern grading data storage. A layer of grade rules is then programmed to cover most standard horizontal and vertical measurement alterations, and also variations in body posture. The pattern is also modified to the customer's styling options. All the associated lining and interlining pieces are automatically adjusted. Companies engaged on large contracts for military uniforms or corporate wear can have standard garment pieces such as collars or pockets pre-cut and prepared.

A lay plan is constructed for the modified pattern; this is sent directly to a single-ply cutter that cuts individual garments. The pieces are then sent to the making-up departments. The success of mass-customisation depends on the speed of the delivery of the garment to the customer.

Alternative method of pattern creation

The demand for made-to-measure software programs has led to new ways of developing the mathematics of pattern construction. Some companies are generating patterns by parametrics. The blocks and patterns are fully defined by a set of dimensions that can then be modified by typing in new measurements to create a bespoke pattern. This different method of pattern construction is particularly effective in creating an individual bespoke suit pattern for a customer based on individual measurements.

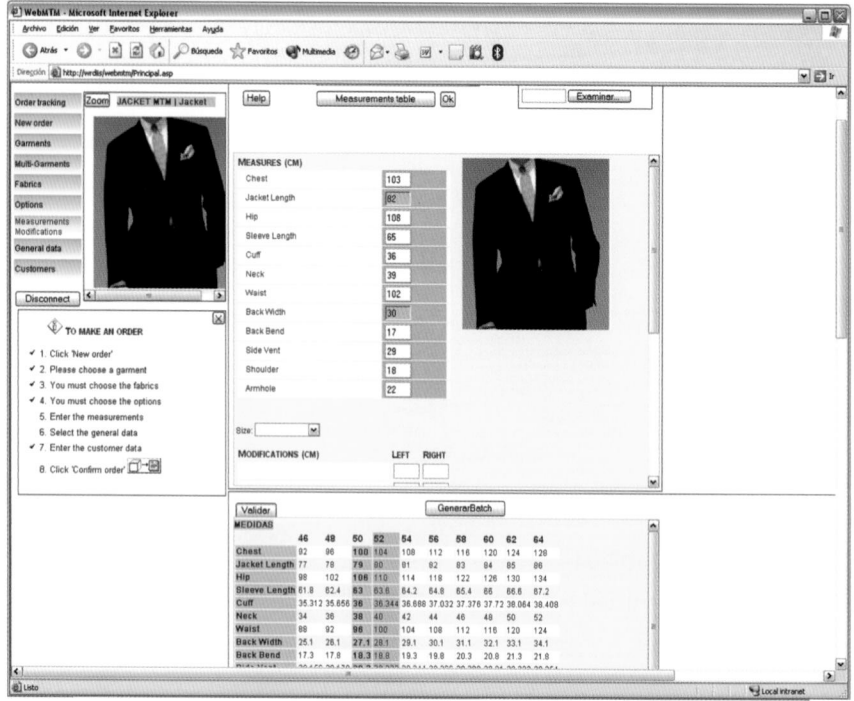

WebMTM, made-to-measure software that automatically generates patterns to a customer's individual measurements. *Illustration by permission of Lectra ©*

Production lay planning and marker-making – 1

Creating a model

CADCAM clothing systems store graded pattern shapes. These are accessed to create the models for production lay planning. More than one lay plan is usually required for each style. This depends on the number of fabrics used in a design (contrasting fabrics, interlinings and linings). Styles may require as many as five lay plans.

A MODEL for each fabric lay has to be constructed. A MODEL is the grouping of pattern pieces (collected in the correct number) to be cut in a particular fabric. The model also records if a pattern piece is single, mirrored or paired. This information is accessed from design profile sheets or from production data. A wide variety of data can be accessed directly on multi-tasking systems which allow the operator to access or work in different programs on the same screen.

Lay planning

The system is set up to recognise codes which give the constraints and requirements for the lay. These are:

1. annotation (piece name, size etc.)
2. placement and number of pieces (i.e. rotation)
3. fabric constraints (single ply, face to face, nap)
4. any areas to be 'blocked' for later manual cutting
5. buffering requirement around pieces
6. matching for stripes, checks or patterns.

The marker-making software will then display all the pattern pieces for the lay on the screen in the correct number and rotation, or in a matrix, ready for interactive marker-making (pieces are placed in the lay with an electronic mouse). As the marker (lay plan) is being constructed, the length and fabric utilisation of the marker is given. Fabric utilisation is the percentage of the cloth area used by the pattern pieces. Manufacturers expect this to be higher than 80%. The higher the figure, the less the wastage.

There are special features within most of the software programs, such as: grouping functions that will automatically associate pieces; markers can be merged; pieces can be split and seam allowances added; stripe and plaid matching capabilities; and additional styles can be retrieved and added to the marker.

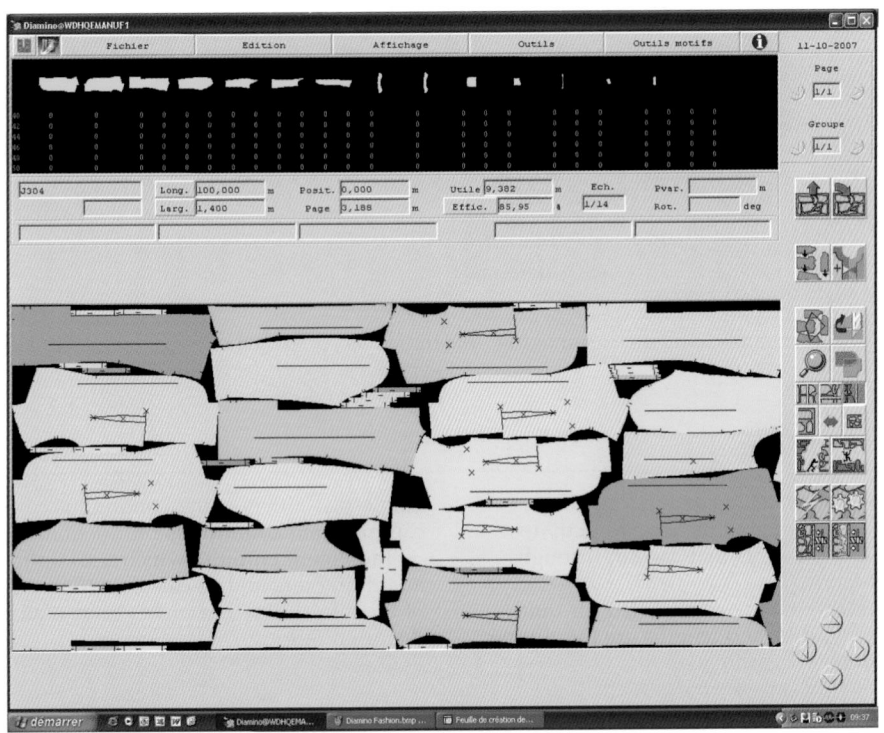

A marker-making screen display. *Illustration by permission of Lectra* ©

Production lay planning and marker-making – 2

Cut-planning

The lay plan length is determined by the number of garments in the order, and the length of the cutting tables. One order may require several lays. The distribution of the number of garments and sizes in each lay is crucial to the utilisation figures. Cut-planning programs claim to calculate the best cut-plan for the order.

Automatic marker-making

Some CADCAM clothing systems will make markers automatically. The system will try, with reference to a set of parameters, different ways of placing the pieces in the lay. It will then show the lay plan that has the highest utilisation figure. The systems used to be left overnight to complete a number of lays for examination the following morning, but the power of the latest computers means results are now fast and this is important when customers are awaiting costings. New developments claim high efficiency

and the suppliers argue that the current software now matches the skills of the expert manual marker makers.

E-commerce marker-making

Direct Web-based marker-making is now available from assyst bullmer Ltd., which offers the service to clothing manufacturers. Its advantage is the power of the main computer, which offers quality markers twenty-four hours per day, every day. It works at a very fast speed regardless of whether or not a customer has broadband connections. The service is aimed at manufacturers who are short of staff, have peak workloads, want to expand their production, or those who have production spread around the world. It is important for manufacturers to realize that compatibility between systems is no longer a problem, that data can be transferred between different CAD systems.

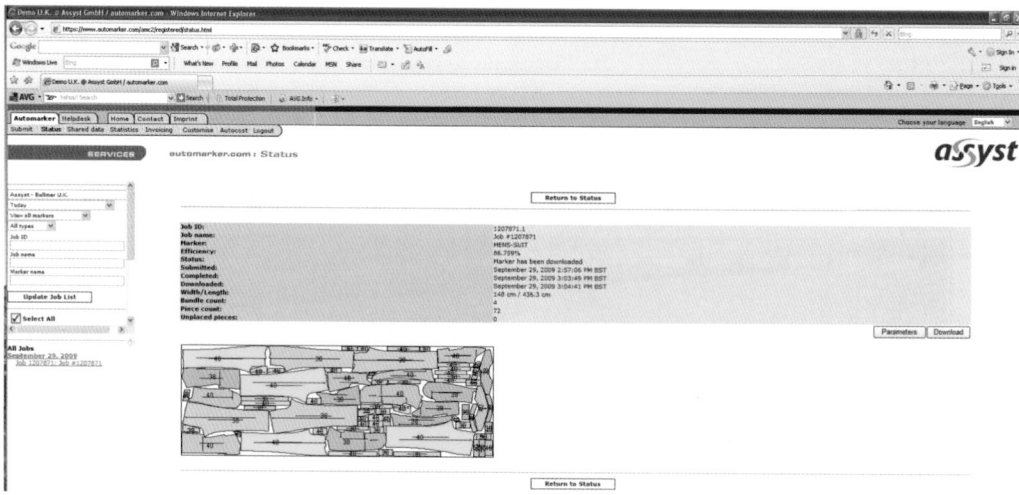

E-commerce automatic marker-making. *Illustration by permission of assyst bullmer Ltd ©*

Plotting and cutting

Markers can be plotted out for manual cutting. However, most systems send the data directly to high speed deep-ply cutters that can cut through many layers of fabric.

Single-ply cutters that are constructed for quick changes in fabric widths and lengths are for cutting samples or customised garments.

Single-ply cutters using continuous conveyor tables can maintain continuous production.

'Intelligent cutting', which uses optic options, can adapt markers and re-calculate the piece geometry of the fabric allowing pieces to be matched even on distorted fabric.

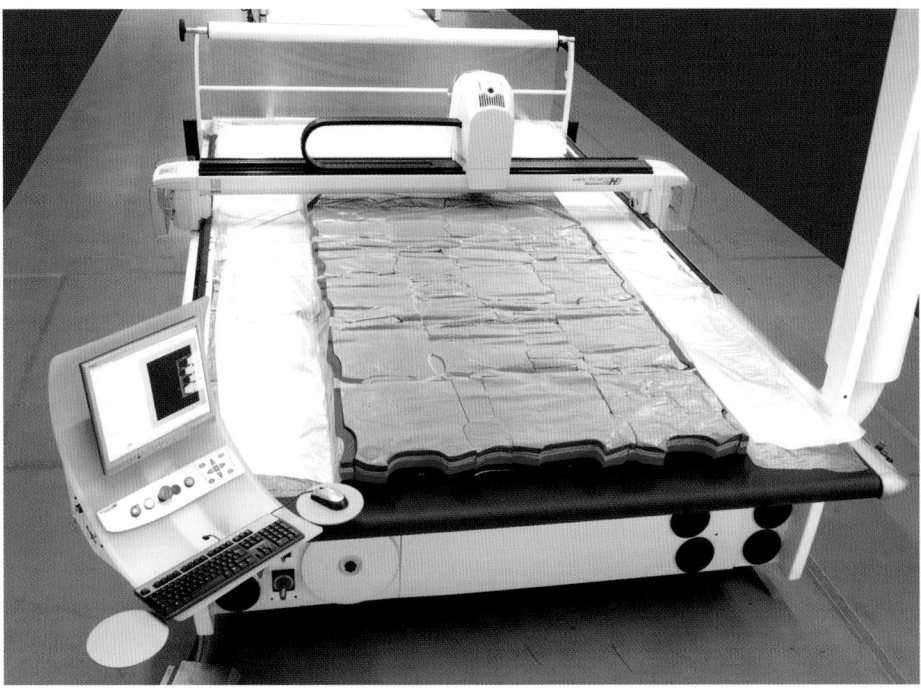

High-ply cutting of many garments from the *Vector* range of cutters. *Photograph by permission of Lectra* ©

Single-ply cutting by a *Prospin* cutter. *Photograph by permission of Lectra* ©

Product Lifecycle Management (PLM)

PLM systems have been able to develop and expand through the increasing power of the Web. Based on internet connections, the systems control the lifecycle of a clothing product from the garment's inception to it sale. The systems can integrate CAD, PDM and other management and financial software, allowing everyone who has a role in the product to participate.

The task of PLM systems is to take a style through the design development and approval stages, and once accepted, the next aim is to take it through the production process to sale, on budget and on time. The crucial steps are the following stages.

Range planning and budgeting   These initial stages often take up 40% of the time in the product's lifecycle. Because complex amounts of sketch data and style information and costings are constantly

changing, it is vital that all the people involved in the project are kept informed.

Critical path tracking   The setting up of stages in the production process with date requirements. This enables a company to track a garment's progress and identify any problems that may delay its completion.

Planning capabilities   The ability to see where there is capacity to produce the garments. This is particularly important, the majority of companies are having their garments manufactured overseas and they need the ability to switch production if problems arise.

The demand for new and varied styles has meant that there has to be collaboration between the participants in the product's lifecycle. PLM allows access to product-related real time information from anywhere in the world where there is an Internet connection.

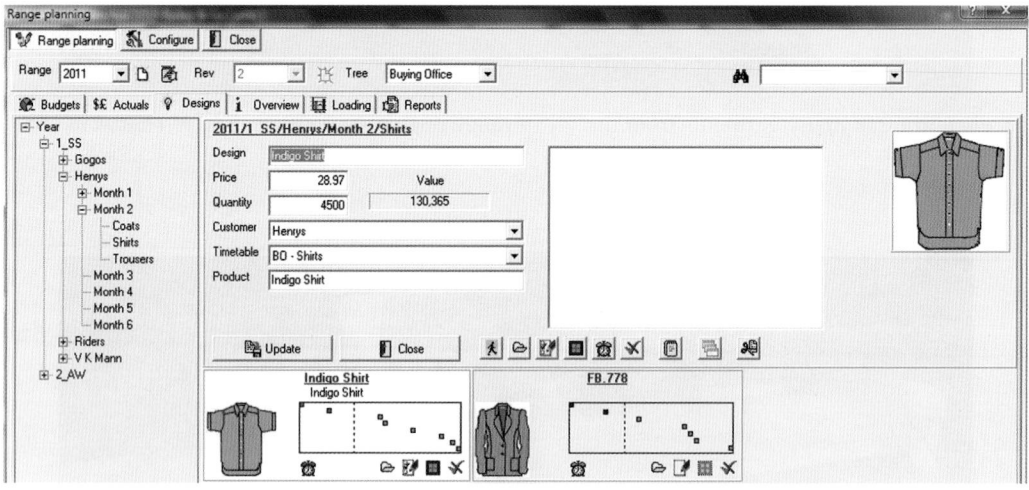

A category storyboard with initial data. *Illustration by permission of FastReact Systems Ltd ©*

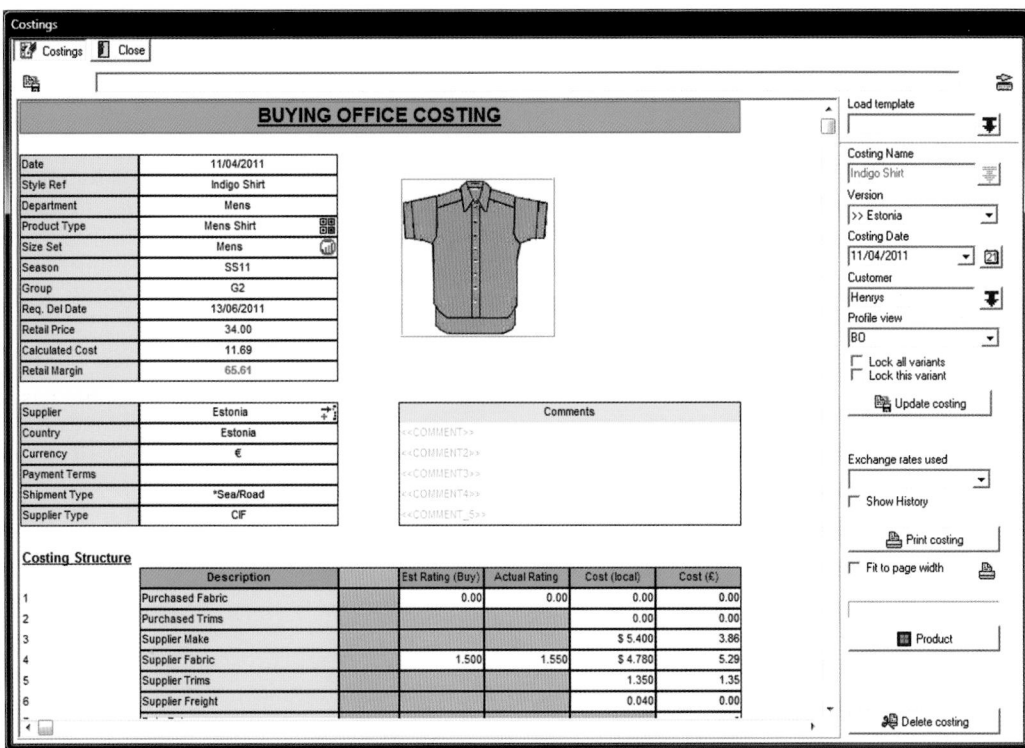

A costing sheet set up to mimic a spreadsheet. *Illustration by permission of FastReact Systems Ltd ©*

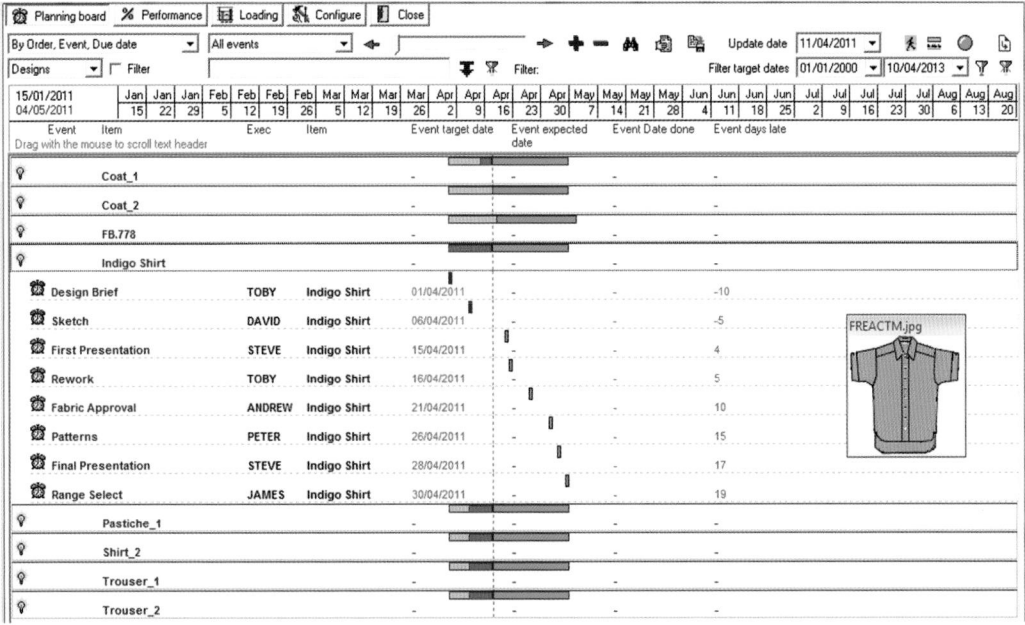

A critical path planning board. *Illustration by permission of FastReact Systems Ltd ©*

Chapter index

PART ONE: 'FLAT' CUTTING

PART TWO: STANDARD PATTERN CUTTING PROCESSES

PART THREE: 'FORM' CUTTING – CLASSIC AND CASUAL MENSWEAR

PART FOUR: SIZING AND FIT

PART FIVE: COMPUTER AIDED DESIGN (CAD)